Social Housing Law and Policy

SLC

Other works by David Hughes

Public Sector Housing Law 1st Edition 1981, 2nd Edition 1987, published by Butterworths.

Environmental Law 1st Edition 1986, 2nd Edition 1992, published by Butterworths.

Constitutional and Administrative Law 1st Edition 1990, jointly with D W Pollard, published by Butterworths.

Public Law and the Retail Sector 1988, jointly with A R Everton, published by Longman.

Housing and Relationship Breakdown 2nd (Revised) Edition 1993, jointly with T G Buck and C A Stacey, published by The National Housing and Town Planning Council.

Neighbourhood Disputes 1993, jointly with V A Karn, R Lickiss, J Crawley, published by the Institute of Housing.

A New Century of Social Housing 1991, edited jointly with S G Lowe, published by Leicester University Press.

Forthcoming

Planning Statutes jointly with V W E Moore, to be published by Blackstone Press.

Other works by Stuart Lowe

Urban Social Movements: The City After Castells 1986, published by Macmillan.

Housing in Social Policy Today series, 1984, published by Longman Educational.

'Capital accumulation in home ownership and family welfare' in *Social Policy Review 1989-90* 1990, published by Longman.

'Home ownership, wealth and welfare: new connections' in *Meeting Needs in an Affluent Society* 1992, published by Avebury.

'The social and economic consequences of the growth of home ownership' in *Housing Policy in the 1990s* 1992, published by Routledge.

A New Century of Social Housing 1991, edited jointly with D Hughes, published by Leicester University Press.

Social Housing Law and Policy

David Hughes

LLB (L'pool), LLM (Cantab), FRSA.
Professor of Law in the Environmental Law Institute at De Montfort University, Leicester.
Hon Legal Consultant to the National Housing and Town Planning Council.
Occasional Adviser to the House Builders' Federation.
Co-editor of 'Environmental Law and Management'.

Stuart Lowe

BA (Hons) in Political Theory and Institutions (Sheffield), Dip. Applied Social Studies [Community Development and Organisation] (Wales), PhD (Sheffield).
Lecturer in Social Policy in the Department of Social Policy and Social Work, University of York.
Associate of David Couttie Associates (Housing Consultants).

Butterworths
London, Dublin & Edinburgh
1995

United Kingdom	Butterworths, a Division of Reed Elsevier (UK) Ltd, Halsbury House, 35 Chancery Lane, LONDON WC2A 1EL and 4 Hill Street, EDINBURGH EH2 3JZ
Australia	Butterworths, SYDNEY, MELBOURNE, BRISBANE, ADELAIDE, PERTH, CANBERRA and HOBART
Canada	Butterworths Canada Ltd, TORONTO and VANCOUVER
Ireland	Butterworth (Ireland) Ltd, DUBLIN
Malaysia	Malayan Law Journal Sdn Bhd, KUALA LUMPUR
New Zealand	Butterworths of New Zealand Ltd, WELLINGTON and AUCKLAND
Puerto Rico	Butterworth of Puerto Rico, Inc, SAN JUAN
Singapore	Butterworths Asia, SINGAPORE
South Africa	Butterworths Publishers (Pty) Ltd, DURBAN
USA	Butterworth Legal Publishers, CARLSBAD, California and SALEM, New Hampshire

Cover photograph reproduced with kind permission of Liverpool City Libraries. Taken from Liverpool City Council Housing Committee Report of 25 July 1913.

A CIP Catalogue record for this book is available from the British Library.

ISBN 0 406 02771 4

1000463116

Printed by Mackays of Chatham PLC, Chatham, Kent

Preface

This book is the result of a long and harmonious association between its authors. Introduced by a mutual friend we soon discovered many shared interests and values. Trips between Leicester and York to teach on each other's postgraduate courses led to our first collaboration, the jointly edited *A New Century of Social Housing* (Leicester University Press, 1991) and then on to planning this volume as a replacement for David Hughes's *Public Sector Housing Law*. As it stands the book is an attempt to encapsulate a number of academic briefs.

(1) Housing is an ideal subject for inter-disciplinary research and teaching. Those who write solely from a unidisciplinary point of view may run the risk of presenting a seriously partial view of the issues involved. A legal text which sets out nothing but a recital of statutory provisions and decisions of the courts, no matter how well written, is in danger of being dust dry, and will fail to make the all important point that in housing the actuality of the law will be much more what housing administrators *do* rather than the skeletal outline laid down by Parliament.

(2) The law and practice of housing can only be properly understood when placed in their wider historical, social, political and economic contexts: equally the policy and practice of housing are best understood when they are related to an analytical exposition of the legal principles which give them formal shape, and the interpretation and application of which by the courts has the most profound consequences for policy makers and practitioners. If any proof is needed of this one has only to look at that most complex of issues, homelessness.

(3) Books are still a most appropriate way of presenting the fruits of academic scholarship and research, particularly where, as here, the object is to create a synthesis of disciplines. Books enable issues to be examined at length with 'across the board' matters relating to a topic emerging more easily and thus more intelligibly. Books enable the three great tasks of scholarship – exposition, analysis and synthesis – to be most perfectly combined.

There is one further belief – one of a social nature – which we hope is clear from this book's pages. That is this nation needs some form of continued social housing. For a decade and a half a continual assault upon the position of local authorities as landlords – an assault now, it seems, poised to turn on housing associations – has deflected attention away from the central issue that the private rental sector, both historically and currently, is unable to meet (in any way that is adequate to a civil society) the housing needs of most of those who are unable or unwilling to become home owners. While it is certainly true that it is not written in tablets of stone that social housing *has* to be provided by municipal enterprise, it is equally true that home ownership is not for everyone. Many in our society need a form of housing provision by landlords whose primary motivation is not financial. To deny this is to display a profound ignorance of both the historic progression of housing provision and the current state of the nation.

At the moment the great majority of our people are better housed than they have ever been, mostly in houses they own themselves. But there is a substantial minority whose various special needs and circumstances – matters as disparate as disability, passing through lack of resources due to relationship breakdown, to homelessness – mean they must look to others for assistance with housing. History shows us the private rental sector cannot, and will not, meet all these needs; no matter how much an obsessively preoccupied government trumpets that sector's virtues. Some form of social housing provision there must be, and we shall be happy if our work furthers debate on that topic.

Additionally, there will always be a need for housing regulators to oversee the maintenance, preservation and promotion of the condition of the nation's housing stock. Once again it is not preordained that that task must be given to local authorities, but it must exist and be entrusted to some social agency. What is more, the evidence, again both historic and current, suggests frequent reluctance on the part of both landlords and owner-occupiers to maintain their property in good order – a neglect which only serves to magnify a postponed problem. As a society we need to invest in housing maintenance: at the moment in many places we are failing to do this either by private or public enterprise. Effective and properly funded agencies are needed to address the issues of maintenance and improvement.

Before concluding we wish to express our thanks for their help and encouragement to: our families (especially our long-suffering wives Christl and Sue); our colleagues at De Montfort, Leicester and York Universities, in particular the Library staff of those institutions, especially Rashid Siddiqui and Sue Smith at Leicester; our students for being sounding-boards for our theories; our publisher for giving us the opportunity to write this book; numerous officials in central and local government and in the housing association movement who have aided our researches, answered our queries and put before us instances of their practice and experience. David Hughes wishes also to thank Barbara Goodman and Sharon Mitton for typing his portions of the text and Stuart Lowe for patiently coping with all the additional material that had to be incorporated after the initial draft text was finished.

The law is stated as at the end of September 1994. Through the kind understanding of our publishers we have been able to incorporate references to legal developments down to early 1995.

January 1995

Contents

Table of statutes

References in this table to *Statutes* are to Halsbury's Statutes of England (Fourth Edition) showing the volume and page at which the annotated text of the Act may be found.

List of cases

PAGE

Chapter One

A brief history of social housing

Introduction

The principal purpose of this text is to provide students and practitioners with
a clear and comprehensive guide to current public sector housing law – by
which term we mean the law relating to housing as provided and administered
by local authorities, housing associations and one or two other agencies such
as Housing Action Trusts. After nearly 15 years of uninterrupted Conservative
government it is no exaggeration to say that the provision and management
of social housing has entered a new era. Public sector housing, perhaps above
all other services in the public domain, was the subject of the earliest and
most radical reform by the first Thatcher government with a subsequent
plethora of legal changes and developments. Even as we write (Summer 1994)
the last untouched established statute – concerning the duties of local
authorities under what was the Housing (Homeless Persons) Act 1977 (now
Part III of the Housing Act 1985) – is the subject of a major policy review
with the government apparently set on rewriting the definition of homeless,
confining duties to very limited periods of time, and withdrawing the rights
of the statutorily 'homeless' to be rehoused outside the context of the ordinary
waiting lists (*Access to Local Authority and Housing Association Tenancies*
DoE, 1994).

Before embarking on a detailed evaluation and description of the case and
statute law, this chapter provides a background and historical context to public
sector housing. It is clear to us that policy and law are no longer best understood
as separate entities and that the legal framework and the new policy terrain
are increasingly enmeshed. In truth this has always been the case but it is
particularly important now to understand housing law in the framework of
the wider policy environment. The approach of this text is, therefore, to
integrate law and policy.

We are also keenly aware that despite the changes of recent years there are
important historical continuities which need to be appreciated if the 'new

era' is to be fully understood. For example, notwithstanding the 1980's language of customers and contractors, charters and empowerment, in specifically legal terms tenants' rights and public housing management are still basically moulded by the one-to-one contractual relationships derived from the nineteenth century pattern of commercial landlordism. Indeed one of our themes is that the 'new era' can be approached not as distinctively contemporary but rather as a throw-back to earlier values and practices. There is more than a hint of 'back to basics' in recent public housing policy.

The homelessness issue is a good illustration of our approach because it shows poignantly how law, history and policy are connected. Thus the Poor Law principles of the 'undeserving poor' and 'less eligibility' figure prominently in contemporary social policy even though the Poor Law was abolished in 1948. In their modern incarnation such concepts infiltrate the debate about homelessness – who precisely are homeless persons and in what sense is their homelessness in some way avoidable or self-induced? Is, for example, a woman driven from her marital home by a violent husband and now living in a women's refuge, despite the roof over her head, homeless? Is the standard of accommodation provided adequate to consider her truly housed by normal standards? And, despite the new patterns of generally smaller household sizes of recent decades, why are single people not considered to be in 'priority need' and therefore normally excluded from the rehousing duties of local authorities (some of whom even exclude them from registration on council house waiting lists)? Policy analysts tend to argue that the statutory definition of homelessness is essentially about the rationing of scarce resources and that 'priority need' is a policy-driven concept. The case-law around such questions, needless to say, is considerable.

Thus there is an important sense in which both the legal framework and the policy context share a mutual historical and conceptual context and need to be read in conjunction with each other. This chapter aims to describe the context within which the statutory framework evolved and the extent to which it was shaped by the events and personalities of the day. We feel that it is important at the outset to root the rest of the text in a 'Brief History' of public housing so that the continuities and changing fortunes are documented in such a way that the legal complexities described later are less cluttered and the reality of the policy framework and decision-making process and *their* influence are apparent. The chapter is structured chronologically but is fashioned around a number of themes which underlie the evolution of public housing policy. These concern the origins of the very notion of a distinctive 'housing' policy, as opposed to public health policy, why it was that local authorities were identified as the providers of social housing and an associated debate about the collapse of the privately rented sector (PRS). Another closely linked theme concerns the emergence of the home owning culture which although not a mainstream issue here is important contextually. In short, the rise and decline of 'council' housing needs to be read in the wider context of the dramatic restructuring of the British housing tenure system during the course of the twentieth century. The early decades of the century were seminal to what was to follow and so we dwell on this period at some length.

Why 'council housing'?

Since 1919 Britain, unlike any other comparable European nation, has developed a large scale public sector of housing based almost exclusively on local authority provision and management. At its peak in the mid-1970s one third of all households in the country lived in council houses. Elsewhere, and with the exception of the erstwhile communist societies, state housing was provided through a plurality of agencies including non-profit cooperative societies, housing associations, trade unions, local societies, national agencies as well as local authorities. Perhaps of greatest significance is that in most West European countries private landlords have been to a greater or lesser extent subsidised from the national exchequer, a position rarely enjoyed by British private landlords, and so have survived as major contributors to the supply of housing. It is the collapse of private landlordism in Britain that more than any other factor accounts for the surge of local authority involvement in the provision of rental housing after the First World War.

The point is, however, that at the outset of this brief history we need to stand back from our familiarity with 'council housing' as the principal source of public sector housing in Britain and ask why this is the case. It has to be explained and certainly, by comparison with our European neighbours, cannot and should not be assumed. Indeed most local authorities took a lot of persuading and, above all, a guarantee of major central government subsidy before they would tackle the job.

The second vital strand to the early part of the story is the fact that, after decades of prevarication, it was finally recognised that such subsidies were a necessary component of the new concept of 'housing policy'. Moreover, despite most accounts of the origins of council housing beginning with the Addison Act of 1919, it is clear from recent research that the need for large scale subsidised local authority provision of 'working class' housing was decided before the outbreak of the 1914-18 War. As Morton argues,

> '...it was to authorities, from as early as 1914, that the Government was looking for a crash building programme to produce some 120,000 additional houses.'

(*A New Century of Social Housing* Lowe and Hughes (eds), Leicester University Press, 1991, p 30)

This realisation, however, was painfully slow to develop.

The public health origins

The nineteenth century was, of course, a period of dynamic change with very rapid urbanisation taking place in the wake of the Industrial Revolution. The population doubled between 1801 and 1851 from 9 million to 18 million and the rate of increase never fell below 10% per annum until the early 1930s. The vast majority of this expansion took place in industrialised towns and cities. The abolition in 1834 of poor relief under the Speenhamland System, which subsidised from local rates the wages of virtually destitute agricultural labourers, swelled the ranks of those families who now turned to the industrial cities in the hope of finding work and a better life.

What they in fact found in many cases was a life characterised by appallingly high morbidity and mortality, poverty and slum housing. The housing problem was caused by the already poor quality of the stock and its very scarce supply. Consequently overcrowding was rife and rents were very high in relation to average industrial earnings. At the heart of this, and really the most enduring of 'the housing questions', was a contradiction between the relatively high costs of building compared to the return available to the developers and landlords. During the nineteenth century the vast majority of housing (over 90% up to the 1914-18 War) was provided by private landlords, mainly through small investments made by the urban middle class, small businessmen or industrialists. Production of low cost working class housing entailed a difficult financial equation. Employers, for example, needed a workforce near the factories; but they dare not set rent levels too high for fear of putting pressure on wages. It was, however, further assumed that rental housing would produce a profit and for many decades the idea of state intervention to assist the urban poor was a political and philosophical anathema. Housing standards were therefore often extremely poor as Enid Gauldie describes in her seminal book *Cruel Habitations* (Gauldie, E, Allen and Unwin, 1974) and anyone who has read the novels of Dickens will get a whiff of the Victorian slum.

In an obvious sense one source of housing policy was in the attempt to deal with the public health problems which were endemic to the slums. Indeed, some historians have read into this the notion that the origins of council housing are to be found in the Victorian public health legislation (see, for example, Wohl, A S *The Eternal Slum: Housing and Social Policy in Victorian London*, Edward Arnold, 1977). A brief examination of the issue suggests this is not really the case but that the adverse impact of these measures on the profitability of private landlordism is highly significant. We are mindful also that this legislation is the foundation of the modern public health system which includes various duties which local authorities have in relation to housing standards – now often shared in joint public or environmental health and housing departments (see Chapter Seven).

Up to almost the close of the century there were basically three sets of public health powers conferred on local authorities which had a 'housing' dimension:

1) powers to close and demolish insanitary dwellings;
2) powers to clear areas of insanitary housing;
3) powers over new building and the prevention of unhealthy use of existing houses.

The powers over individual insanitary dwellings were granted initially under the Artizans' and Labourers' Dwellings Act of 1868, popularly known as the 'Torrens' Act after its parliamentary sponsor. These powers were entirely discretionary and placed no obligation on the local authority to rehouse the occupants following demolition.

The Artizans' and Labourers' Dwellings Improvement Act 1875 was rather more important because its sponsor, Cross, was the Home Secretary in Disraeli's government. His seniority is important because it enabled the accusations of 'socialist' interference in the rights of freeholders to be more effectively deflected. Local authorities were empowered, but not obliged, to clear whole areas of unfit housing and, significantly, were allowed to enable the rehousing of displaced families on the same site. Compensation was paid to the owners. The test of unfitness was whether the property could be brought up to a 'sanitary' standard, so that this is still very firmly public health and not 'housing' legislation. Rehousing under the Cross Act was undertaken mainly by 'model dwelling companies' and philanthropic trusts, the local authorities having sold the sites to the trustees of the companies. There was certainly no question of subsidies to the tenants through rents set at below cost and the assumption was for the companies to achieve at least a 5% return on the investment. Model dwelling companies were important in providing low cost, good quality housing to the relatively well-to-do working classes in the period before the 1914-18 War. Indeed by that time they had built over 50,000 dwellings, twice as many as the local authorities themselves. There were many such companies – the Peabody Trust (set up by a wealthy American), the Improved Dwellings Company, The Guinness Trust – all run by businessmen aiming not to replace the market, but to show how the market could be made to operate more effectively (Merrett, S *State Housing in Britain*, Routledge and Kegan Paul, 1979).

Even though cheap loans were available to them from the Public Works Loans Board and the sites, already cleared, were sold at below market price, these companies were never able to provide for the poorest social strata. Rents were simply too high. Furthermore, the management of these new dwellings – often tenements much criticised for being not dissimilar in appearance to workhouses – was exceedingly paternalistic and thoroughly imbued with the Poor Law morality of the 'deserving' and 'undeserving' poor. Having passed tests of eligibility for housing, tenants' behaviour was tightly controlled; for example, evening curfews were imposed. This tradition of housing management is very important in the subsequent history of public housing which was to unfold after 1919 and council housing has never entirely shed the accusation of paternalism in its organisation and management.

Although the Torrens and Cross legislation was amended at the end of the 1870s it remained largely ineffective and in fact created more problems than it solved. For low income households in particular it is clear that the situation was made considerably worse by the clearance of slum dwellings and was, indeed, the cause of further overcrowding problems. More substantial, longer-term benefits accrued from the Public Health Act 1875 which consolidated previous public health legislation and had a specific housing content through the grant to local authorities of powers to make byelaws. Byelaws regulating the width and layout of streets, the air spaces above houses, areas of windows etc had existed as an indirect consequence of the Local Government Act 1858. These derived from model powers in an accompanying Form of Byelaws. They helped in particular to control the 'back-to-backs'. This was a form of dwelling, built by speculative developers, in which a terrace of houses shared a back wall, each dwelling facing away from each other and having windows and access only at the front. Their advantage was that they were cheap to build and contained a high density of population and, although better in some ways than tenements, they frequently did not have internal water or sanitation and lacked proper ventilation. By ensuring that each dwelling had a separate area of open space, usually meaning a back yard, byelaws gradually eradicated back-to-backs, although they were still being built in Leeds well into the 1930s even though it was illegal to build them for the 'working classes' from 1905 onwards. Byelaws were not required to be in place in local authority areas in Victorian England because it was construed that they infringed the rights of freeholders. Nevertheless as Burnett suggests,

> '...(they) acted as a useful guide to the more progressive
> towns and, at the same time, created an important precedent for
> national involvement in housing matters.'
> (Burnett, J *A Social History of Housing 1815–1985*, 1978 p 158)

The 1875 Act consolidated the previous law and many local authorities did subsequently adopt model byelaws issued by the Local Government Board in 1877 which considerably extended and also clarified the 1858 powers. Local authorities were empowered to compel developers to deposit plans for inspection and amendment if necessary and could also inspect construction sites and change work which contravened their byelaws.

Although real progress was being made through this fairly mundane route the usefulness of the byelaws was limited because they were permissive only and not mandatory. Towns which already had laws in place did not need to amend them to the higher standard and, of course, the model byelaws could apply only to new dwellings, leaving untouched the vast mass of slums. Byelaw housing built between the late 1870s and 1914 was undoubtedly progressive in design and amenity standards. It was particularly appropriate for construction on green field sites which increasingly came into play with developments in public transport in the last three decades of the century. By 1905, for example, the London County Council estimated that 820,000 workmen were making extensive daily journeys from the new suburbs to work. Cheap travel by electric trams was responsible for the rapid growth of suburban areas in many towns and in progressive cities, such as Sheffield, was the basis of some of the earliest examples of local authority housing provision under the terms of the 1890 Housing of the Working Classes Act (Pollard, S *A History of Labour in Sheffield*, University of Liverpool Press, 1959).

But there is no doubt that the additional costs engendered in the construction of such housing tipped the affordability equation well beyond the pockets of low paid workers. Byelaw housing thus tended to intensify the differences between the 'better class of poor' and the desperately low paid workers. Real incomes had grown by up to 50% between 1850 and 1900 and for large sections of the working class in the later decades of the century, despite periodic economic recession, there was marked improvement in housing and consumer standards. It is also abundantly clear that the inner cities still contained a mass of poor working people whose situation was getting worse. The new building standards, the sanitary controls and the clearance powers all acted to reduce the profitability of private landlordism. The majority of private landlords in the nineteenth century were individual middle class people, and some better-off artisan workers, who were quite content to harbour their savings in housing. It had been a generally safe investment. With the clearances and stricter building standards many private landlords began to look for alternative investment opportunities. These were not difficult to find and overseas investment was becoming particularly attractive. The extension of the franchise during the 1880s also served to damage the interests of the private landlords because property taxes increased, particularly in the form of local rates. Even before the First World War profits were being squeezed because of the increasing demands placed on ratepayers.

Thus the origins of state intervention in housing do have a 'public health' dimension but it should not be read as a logical progression guided by enlightened reform. Rather, this influence helped to shape the investment crisis which contributed to the beginning of the long decline of private landlordism in Britain. A major factor in the long-term development of council housing is its role in filling the vacuum left by the historic failure of private landlords to continue to supply low rent dwellings for working class families (see Merrett, 1979).

'... the stye that made the pig'

These words, taken from the Report of the Royal Commission on the Housing of the Working Classes published in 1884, are a graphic expression of the gathering realisation, in a society dominated by utilitarian principles and habits, and a *laissez-faire* market economy, that the squalor of Victorian 'slumdom' was a *housing* problem and not the consequence of feckless and undeserving inhabitants. This shift in perception in part arose from the evidence collected for the Royal Commission itself, and was of a measurable deterioration of conditions, in inner London in particular, caused by an acute shortage of affordable housing. It is important because it recognises in a way unusual for the day the relationship between demand and supply in the housing market. Attention was particularly focused on the incomes of certain types of workers – dockers , costermongers and others – and the rents they were paying. It was found that incomes among such people were well below Charles Booth's poverty line and, moreover, they were paying a very high percentage of this income in rent. Booth's independent study of the inhabitants of the East End of London was a pioneering work of social investigation conducted between 1888 and 1901 and published in seven volumes of his *Life and Labour of the People of London* (Booth C 1902 (ed)). One of his most startling findings, published in 1889, was that 30.7% of the population of London (over one million people) lived below his scientific measure of poverty with disastrous results for health and industrial efficiency. The problem for the Royal Commissioners was not difficult to evaluate. The property boom of the 1870s ended in the early 1880s and there was a major supply and demand problem. Their analysis is summed up neatly by Morton,

> 'The inner urban poor were being driven outwards by a conver-
> sion of city centres to public and commercial uses but were be-
> ing halted in their tracks by lack of access to newer, cheaper
> housing further out ...'

(Morton, in Lowe and Hughes 1991, p 14)

Lord Salisbury's shortlived government of 1885 put through a somewhat obscure Housing Act which drew in a few of the Commission's recomm- endations and redefined the term lodging house to include individual dwellings, later to be an important change. There was no question yet of local authorities generally being involved as it was clearly thought that the market would eventually adjust. It was, however, recognised that the state did have an obligation to ease the situation in the meantime and especially for families affected by clearances arising from municipal activity and also where conditions were very poor.

It was not until Salisbury returned to power in 1886 with a programme to reform local government that the housing crisis was addressed. The Local Government Act 1888 put in place a unified system of local government by the creation of county and county borough authorities across the whole country.

The previous framework for the *ad hoc* provision of urban services was gradually incorporated into a system of local administration which lasted more or less intact until the major local government reforms of the mid 1970s. With housing supply tightening and some local authorities already experimenting with building projects the Housing of the Working Classes Act was approved by parliament in July 1890. This was key legislation because it provided the context in which local authorities could intervene positively to address the housing crisis. In this sense it can be understood as the first statement of the need for a national 'housing policy'. The Act was very largely consolidating legislation and Parts I and II brought together the Torrens and Cross Acts, but in Part I there was provision for local authorities to redevelop a site directly if no other agency came forward, and in Part III they were empowered to build and also to renovate and improve 'working class lodging houses', defined (from the 1885 Act) to mean individual dwellings. Thus after 1890 as Gauldie points out, '...it was legally possible for an enlightened local authority to pursue an enlightened housing policy' (Gauldie, 1974, p 294).

The assumption remained that housing schemes should be self-financing and at first a rate of return was even stipulated and, as before, this certainly meant that authorities were not going to cater for low income households. It was still generally assumed that the model dwelling companies were the main source of 'social' housing. Authorities had to obtain the permission of the Local Government Board, and in the case of the London County Council the Home Secretary, in order to build. Despite innovative projects, notably those by the LCC which set high design and quality standards, the rents charged were very similar to the model dwelling companies. The problem of finance had not been solved. The use of the local rate fund to support building was severely constrained by the political influence of the local ratepayers.

A new slump in the building industry took hold about 1905 and opinion, largely shaped by the experience of the more progressive local authorities, began to veer towards the need for some kind of subsidy to make rents for new housing affordable for working class people living on average incomes. It was clear that despite the growing interest of local authorities in building under Part III of the 1890 Act there was very little direct benefit for the really poor, although there was some evidence of filtering down. Nevertheless local authorities did respond to the new housing crisis and by the outbreak of the war in 1914 316 councils had built using Part III permissions and between 1910 and 1914 over 11,000 council houses were built. By the outbreak of the war the total local authority provision was about 28,000 new dwellings nationally, about 90% of which had been built since the 1890 Act. This was a much smaller contribution than that of the model dwelling companies and the charitable trusts who had a combined total of about 50,000 dwellings (Morton, in Lowe and Hughes, 1991, p 29). Despite this numerical superiority it was to the local authorities that the government turned to provide what amounted to a crash programme of building. In the context of the times it is not difficult to see why. In the first place the model dwelling companies were private companies and, with notable exception, mainly focused their activities on London. Almost always their interest was to provide for the 'better class of poor'. Becoming anything more was not a role for which they were suited and neither, as Best points out, was it one they sought (Best, R 'Housing Associations 1890-1990' Chapter 10 in Lowe and Hughes, 1991). Second, as Morton shows, '...the sheer quality of council-house building' was incomparably superior to anything that had been built in the voluntary sector. As such it provided a model for the future and, despite an element of subsidy in their developments, authorities had demonstrated what could be done using limited finances.

In addition, harking back to achievements in the public health field, it should not be underestimated that virtually every authority now contained a body of professional inspectors. Their role in the interpretation and implementation of standards in local byelaws had given the profession a prestige and authority (Holmans, A E *Housing Policy in Britain*, Croom Helm, 1986). Local authorities had shown that they were capable of building and all over the country had delivered, albeit in small quantities, 'council houses'. They had officers with development experience and a well established body of inspectors familiar with the technical standards and design principles of housing.

Here, then, is the specific answer to the question 'why council housing?' Even before the outbreak of the First World War it was widely recognised that the building slump had to be addressed by some form of temporary intervention. The government was looking to a programme of 120,000 dwellings and it was clear that they could not find a programme of this magnitude through reliance on the philanthropic trusts and model dwelling companies. Reluctant actors as they might be, authorities were waiting in the wings. The traumatic events of the 1914-18 war determined that it was not long before they would be thrust centre stage.

Subsidies and the private landlords

Thus far the explanation for the rise of state housing provision in Britain has focused on explaining why authorities came to play such a significant role. We have suggested that limited and temporary use of authorities to build rental housing was widely acknowledged before 1914. We also suggested earlier that private landlordism was under considerable pressure in the latter decades of the nineteenth century due in large measure to the new byelaws and public health controls. A number of historians have also pointed to the additional factor that housing was increasingly subject to taxation at this time, particularly through the local rates, and private landlords were adversely affected by this. Profits were squeezed and capital values eroded (Daunton, M J *Housing the Workers*, Leicester University Press, 1990, p 23). Rather than opting for council housing one possible solution to the problem might, therefore, have been to improve the tax position of the private landlords, restore their profitability, and so ameliorate the need for state housing.

Before we arrive at the point in 1919 when the mechanism for the first large scale, nationally mandated and highly subsidised council house programme was put in place, one further piece in the jigsaw needs to be fitted. Why were landlords not protected from high taxation and, eventually, from rent controls, and why did they not become the recipients of state subsidies? Was this, therefore, the beginning of the end for private landlordism in Britain being, in effect, the early stages of a permanent, structural collapse? (Merrett, 1979; Ball, M *Housing Policy and Economic Power*, Methuen, 1983). If the latter position is generally affirmed then there is a further crucial factor which underpins the rise of the municipal alternative. This argument carries forward the point made above that the main consequence of public health legislation for private landlordism was not the administrative response, although as we have seen that was important, but is found in the supply and demand pressures created by inner city clearances and by the inability of poor families to escape to the new suburbs. It helps explain the exceptionally large quantity of council housing eventually to be built in Britain over an extended period of time (1919-1979). Moreover, uniquely in the wider European context, it explains the concentration of the provision of state sponsored social housing on the local authorities. Why it was to authorities that the government looked for its crash building programme in 1919 is closely related to the specific character of British political culture.

Two very useful points are made here by Daunton. First, that compared to their European counterparts private landlords in Britain were a relatively powerless social and political force. As local ratepayers they certainly wielded influence but they were politically disorganised and certainly did not have the powerful voice enjoyed by, for example, the German private landlords. Daunton sums up the point,

> 'One factor (in the Anglo-German contrast) was the lack of political power of small property owners within the British political system, both at local and national level. There was in Britain nothing equivalent to the three-class voting system of the Prussian state and municipal government which gave more weight to property owners.'

(Daunton, 1990, p 24)

As a result municipal housing was not tolerated in Germany where, instead, non-profit co-operatives and trade union based associations organised themselves autonomously. Even these were opposed but, even more surely, so was the large scale municipal alternative. On the continent generally, and not just in Berlin – in Paris, Brussels, Vienna – the municipal route was not a preferred option and as a result there was a more diverse response to the problem of working class housing, including the subsidisation of private landlords by various means. The British lower middle class, which was the cradle of nineteenth century landlordism, was to an extent on the fringes of both main political parties. The Liberals sought to tax landowners, which in many cases meant urban landlords, out of existence and yet the Conservatives, with their roots firmly planted in rural landed interests, were not entirely at ease with small urban property investors.

Daunton's second point concerns the character of the Labour movements in the early years of the twentieth century and follows closely from his analysis of the contrasting nature of the political systems in European societies. In Germany, for example, the trade unions and Labour movement regarded the state as politically biased and treated it with a great deal of suspicion. In Britain, however, after a century of struggle and, it may be added of, defeats, the British working class movement was essentially reformist in character. The Labour Party came into existence essentially to represent the trade unions in Parliament. The state was regarded as being class-neutral both nationally and locally. Moreover, Labour made quick gains through the local political route in some cities and were able to use the powers of the Housing of the Working Classes Act to experiment with 'council' housing. In Sheffield, for example, a design competition led to one of the earliest garden suburbs being built. As a result the idea of the co-operative alternatives failed to take root and the British Labour movement looked squarely to the municipalities for solutions to their housing problems.

The 1914-18 war and 'Homes Fit for Heroes'

As in so many aspects of social and political life the traumatic events of the First World War jolted Britain out of its Edwardian complacency. The horrific military campaign was compounded by the threat seemingly posed by Bolshevism. It was a time of turmoil, and individual and social trauma. In the housing context it is indeed a seminal point in time. At the close of hostilities, large scale central Exchequer subsidies were introduced through the Housing and Town Planning etc Act of 1919. This legislation turned council housing from a small, somewhat experimental form of housing provision into a major sector. Although it was not to be, at the time Addison Act housing (named after the parliamentary sponsor) was regarded as a one-off expedient to cope with the major shortages of housing resulting from the war; it is estimated that household numbers grew by over one million during the war and the 1921 Census revealed that 1,150,000 households out of a total of just under 8,000,000 were sharing accommodation, that is to say over one-eighth of all households.

The significant legislation in the war era was the Increase of Rent and Mortgage Interest (War Restrictions) Act 1915 which controlled rents and mortgages at their 1914 levels. In the face of social unrest in some cities resulting from a crisis in landlord-tenant relations the government had no real alternative but to control the market. The focal point of civil unrest was Glasgow, an important centre of munitions production, where profiteering by landlords was intense and led to a collapse of already fragile relations between tenant and landlord. In Scotland the basis of the contract between landlord and tenant was significantly different from England. Up to 1911 most tenancies were annual with a single date of renewal agreed through an annual 'missive'. Rents were paid quarterly in arrears but in cases of late payment landlords were able to recover the whole year's payment through seizure of property to the value of the annual rent. After 1911 tenancies were put onto a monthly footing which gave tenants more flexibility but landlords were able to evict tenants who were only seven days in arrears of payment at 48 hours' notice. Relations especially at the bottom of the market were very strained and litigious. The opportunity to recoup profits, which had declined in Glasgow due to surpluses in the market prior to the war, caused an outrage because the landlords tried to force up rents, not only at the bottom end of the market, by using powers of summary eviction (Dau,nton, 1990 p 21). It is clear that in Scotland, and especially on Clydeside, landlord-tenant relations were very tense and already highly political well before the outbreak of the First World War. In the summer of 1915 the situation boiled over into a series of rent strikes and this civil unrest threatened to engulf the munitions factories.

In England the situation was less fraught because tenancies were invariably based on weekly lets which allowed flexibility for tenants although little security. Powers of summary eviction, however, were rarely used because it took at least 28 days to secure an eviction, with a probable loss of rent. The events of the summer of 1915 in Glasgow were a major contributory factor to the introduction of rent controls which in turn led to a further reduction in the profitability of private landlordism. It became increasingly clear by the middle of the war that a large programme of council housing would have to be a main part of the solution to the housing problem. As a result of rent restriction, rents were forced down in real terms so that at the close of hostilities not only were shortages very grave indeed but effective demand was much higher than it had been before the war. This problem also has a political dimension to it, as Bowley observes,

> 'Increases in rents staved off in deference to public opinion dur-
> ing the war could scarcely be regarded as an appropriate form of
> peace celebration.'

(Bowley, M *Housing and the State 1919–1944*, Allen and Unwin, 1945)

As we have argued above a subsidy to encourage the return of private landlords was not a likely strategy in Britain given the weak political position of landlordism, and the behaviour of the landlords during the war did nothing to suggest that they could become the focus of a popular and sustained building programme. The shortages were too great and politically sensitive to be left to them. In any case, they had virtually abandoned building working class housing before the war and seemed unlikely to return under the prevailing conditions. Apart from anything else building costs and interest rates after the war were high. The rent freeze further limited the profitability of the private landlords.

Thus the First World War transformed the nature of the housing question in Britain, and faced with massive shortages of rental housing, social unrest, a system of private landlordism that was failing and discredited, the government had no real alternative than to intervene. The decision to engage local authorities to provide the crash building programme, as we have seen, pre-dates the events of the war so that what happened during the war made the outcome almost inevitable.

The election of November 1919 resulted in a reduced coalition of Liberals and Conservatives led by Lloyd George. They won the campaign principally on the famous slogan of 'Homes Fit for Heroes'. In order to appease the ratepayers and to persuade reluctant local authorities to build, the subsidy under the 1919 Act was very generous. The finance was variable to take account of local conditions, particularly variations in building costs which were high at this time. Authorities for their part were in a strong bargaining position because it was certain that only they could see such a large scheme through. Their co-operation was obtained by limiting their liability to the product of an annual penny rate with the whole of the balance made up from the Exchequer. The scale of this programme was in a completely different league to pre-war council housing. When the Addison Act programme was aborted by the government in July 1921 there were 170,000 houses built or contracted. The programme ended because the Conservative section of the coalition opposed the escalating costs and because at the outset the programme was conceived as a temporary measure arising from the special post-war circumstances.

Apart from marking the beginning of mass council housing, the Addison legislation is important because it established a basic administrative, legal and financial framework for the production of a large scale national programme of municipal housing. Council housing was to be paid for out of rents, central subsidy and rate fund contributions with the local authority as the developer/ landlord. They would borrow money at market cost and rates of interest (later on the payment of interest charges on loans became a major problem). More or less all the council house programmes from 1919 to the end of the 1960s were built under this basic system, the only differences being the variations in the levels of subsidy, for what purpose they were granted (typically general needs or slum clearance housing) and the length of time over which the subsidy would be paid. The question of local authority housing finance is considered in more detail in Chapter Four. But we should not miss at this point the importance of the 1919 Act in setting the agenda for what was, unknown at the time, to be the conventional pattern for the financing, production and management of British council housing.

The premature withdrawal of the subsidy is argued by some historians to demonstrate that the local authority building programme was initiated mainly to quell the threat of civil unrest. Once the threat had receded there was no need to continue the programme. As Swenarton, for example, argues money spent on housing was as much '... an insurance against Bolshevism and revolution' as it was a programme to provide 'homes fit for heroes' (Swenarton, M *Homes Fit For Heroes: the Politics and Architecture of Early State Housing in Britain*, Heinemann 1981, p 71). There is some truth in this but it does not do justice to the case outlined above that the need for a large scale programme of state rental housing was widely supported even before the war and neither, as Kemp points out, does it explain why the Conservative Government reintroduced subsidies for private and local authority building through their Housing Act of 1923 (Kemp, P 'From solution to problem? Council housing and the development of national housing policy' Chapter 4 in Lowe and Hughes, 1991, p 46). The fact of the matter was that 'normal' housing market conditions were not returning and that the underlying logic of private landlordism was in abeyance. When the circumstances improved for housing investment, as they did in the 1930s, there *was* a temporary return to investment in private renting. Some 900,000 houses were built for letting in the inter-war period, mostly in the 1932-37 period when building costs were very low and house prices were declining. The proportion of houses built for rent as opposed to purchase by owner occupiers grew from 11% to 30% at that time (Merrett, 1982, p 13). Through the 1920s and early 1930s economic conditions were, however, generally unfavourable even though rent controls did not apply to new houses.

It should not, by the same token, be assumed that council housing was widely or enthusiastically embraced. It was accepted out of necessity due to the continuing and persistent shortages of housing which is the backdrop to most of the inter-war period. This position would certainly seem to explain the Housing Act of 1923 introduced by the Conservative Minister of Health, Chamberlain. It also helps account for why the rate of council house building through the inter-war period fluctuated very considerably, and was never positively embraced except by the short-lived Labour Government of 1924. Merrett shows how the council house programme was persistently subject to cuts in subsidy rates and cost cutting reductions in building standards (Merrett, 1979). Even before the Addison Act subsidy was axed the average floor space of the model three-bedroomed dwellings had fallen.

The equivocal position of council housing through the inter-war period can also be explained by the important role played by the private house-building for sale industry which enjoyed a period of unprecedented growth from the mid-1920s to the outbreak of the Second World War. Output rose from a 100,000 per annum to peak at over 250,000 in the five years before the war. Private construction thus overshadows the municipal building programme in scale of production. The growth of 'home ownership' was encouraged by several factors at work in the wider economy of the 1920s and 1930s. First of all despite mass unemployment during the Depression years the number of people in secure, mainly white collar salaried posts increased very sharply – jobs in banking, insurance. At the same time an increase in marriages led to a rapid growth in new household formations and there was a strong trend for households generally to be smaller because of a declining birth rate and more single person households resulting from the ability of people such as widows and widowers to live alone. Holmans argues that house prices were also at an historically low point in relation to other prices influenced by low building costs, cheap land on suburban greenfield sites and very weak planning controls allowing 'urban sprawl'. There was in addition a readily available source of finance through the rapidly expanding building societies.

That having been said the build and design standards of 1920s council housing were mainly very good and superior to most private sector speculative housing. The influence of the seminal design standards and ideas of Raymond Unwin, the architect of the Rowntree garden suburb village at New Earswick in York, Letchworth New Town, and Hampstead Garden suburb is particularly noteworthy. Significantly, Unwin was a member of the Tudor Walters Committee which was set up during the 1914-18 war by the Local Government Board to '… consider questions of building construction…of dwellings for the working classes.' Their Report was published in November 1918 and as Burnett suggests,

> '…the Tudor Walters Report on the standards of post-war local authority housing were revolutionary, constituting a major innovation in social policy and in the future character of working-class life.'
> (Burnett, 1978, p 222)

The Design Manual for local authorities which accompanied the report was largely drawn by Unwin himself and became a blue print for the now familiar styles of council housing built during the 1920s and 1930s. Gone were the Victorian tenements and the monotonous byelaw terraces and in came the working class cottage style epitomised by Unwin's New Earswick designs, a development built very early on in the century in the first flush of the garden suburb movement.

Under the Conservative's legislation council housing indeed played an entirely subordinate role to the private builders. The 'Chamberlain' Housing Act of 1923 provided building subsidies to both the public and the private sectors. The Treasury offered local authorities only £6 per dwelling over 20 years with no requirement for rate fund contributions. The aim was to limit the scope and scale of local authority housing programmes and encourage private builders to supply housing for sale to the working classes. Central controls were more stringent than under the Addison legislation and to begin with local authorities had to demonstrate to the Ministry that the private sector was not supplying the housing needs of the area before they were given permission to build. The 1923 Act was not repealed until 1929 but only 75,900 council houses had been built compared with 362,000 subsidised private sector dwellings.

The equivocal position of council housing at this time is further demonstrated in the vigorous programme of rehabilitation and reconditioning of properties in the privately rented sector. This was regarded as an alternative to new building and also slum clearance in the public sector; between 1919 and 1930 about 300,000 per annum houses were made fit for habitation by statutory improvement orders made against private landlords.

The first Labour Government

There was no equivocation in the attitude of John Wheatley the Minister of Health in the first Labour Government which came to power for only nine months in 1924. Wheatley was a 'Red-Clydesider', a Glaswegian, Catholic socialist hardened by years of campaigning in Clydeside local politics who by some astute manoevering found himself responsible for the housing programme in the Labour Cabinet. His ideal was to use municipal construction to replace the privately rented sector but he stopped short of outright nationalisation because he was a pragmatist. Instead he opted to build on the existing system using a much improved level of subsidy. Wheatley's intention, through the Housing Act 1924, was to establish a long-term investment programme in high quality council houses. His vision was that council housing would be a socially and geographically ubiquitous housing tenure. Authorities no longer had to demonstrate 'housing need' to get building permission. The private rental sector showed few signs of reviving and so, according to Wheatley, could not be relied on to build working class housing. The subsidy was significantly increased and was to be payable over 40 years, instead of 20 years under the 1923 legislation, and the rate fund contribution to council house building was restored. The private sector was also able to benefit from this subsidy so long as it could be shown they were building for working class households.

Wheatley used the terms of this legislation and his Labour Movement credentials to negotiate a deal with the trade unions in the building industry which removed many of the trade's restrictive practices. This facilitated the housing drive in the public sector but also spilled over into the private sector where de-skilling in the construction industry accompanied by large scale unemployment helped to create the conditions for the boom in house building in the 1930s. Wheatley also forced up the rate of construction by setting production targets for authorities and withheld subsidy unless they met their quotas.

Wheatley's was a long-term, strategic view of council housing and very different, therefore, to the housing legislation of his Coalition and Conservative predecessors. The 1924 Act restored the general needs role for this sector of housing which had been abandoned to a residual role in the 1923 legislation and also re-established the debate about housing standards, arguing very strongly in favour of high quality. Although the Labour Government was quickly replaced by a new Conservative administration the Wheatley Act subsidies continued in place until 1933 by which time over 500,000 houses had been built under its terms. Thus for several years both the Chamberlain and the Wheatley subsidies operated in tandem. The Conservatives very reluctantly retained the Wheatley subsidy because investment in the privately rented sector had ground to a halt and there was no other source of large scale building for rent. The subsidy needed to be generous to persuade some of the more reluctant authorities, of whom there were many, to build. Although the central government was able to give direction to the public housing programme, for example, the impending switch to slum clearance, authorities were fairly autonomous bodies at this time and this led to a considerable variation in provision of council houses across the country. Conservative controlled authorities were quick to utilise both subsidies to channel central government finance into the private building industry (Finnigan, R 'Council houses in Leeds, 1919-39 : social policy and urban change' in Daunton (ed) *Councillors and Tenants: Local Authority Housing in English Cities, 1919-39*, Leicester University Press, 1984, p 109).

Housing for the poor?

Council housing built in the 1920s under the terms of the Addison, Chamberlain and Wheatley subsidies varied very considerably in size and standard. The output figures fluctuated from year to year in response to the cuts in subsidies, building costs, labour shortages and also uncertainties about the relationship between subsidy levels and rents. There was no smooth progressive growth in council housing and with the exception of the few months of the Labour Administration support from central government for the progress of council housing was unstable and extremely hesitant. The growing number of Labour controlled local authorities after the mid-1920s ensured more progress than would otherwise have been the case. And, in the main, the standards of building were far superior to any previous working class housing, and the best Addison and Wheatley dwellings were better than any comparable housing in the private sector. For millions of people this was the beginning of a new life on 'council estates' built very broadly in the cottage garden vernacular style based on Unwin's Design Manual. What was happening, as Burnett describes it, was '...a minor revolution in the standards of working-class housing and living' (Burnett, 1978, p 234).

There need, however, be no hesitancy about one crucial point. This housing was not the solution to the problems of poor working class families. Even with the high level of subsidy under the 1919 Act rents were well out of range of the poor. Rents were meant to be set in line with controlled rents in the PRS but authorities tended to set higher rents than those in the private sector. Rents under the Chamberlain Act were higher still because the level of subsidy was considerably reduced. Wheatley housing was supported by rate fund contributions and was specifically designed to reduce rent levels. But at this time council housing was occupied as Bowley suggests by, '...better-off families, the small clerks, the artisans, the better-off semi-skilled workers with small families and fairly safe jobs' (Bowley, 1945, p 129). Studies of tenants in London and Liverpool both revealed a similar pattern in the social composition of council housing. Burnett cites research in Liverpool which showed that 20% of the occupants were non-manual workers.

There were, of course, variations in this situation. Once subsidy contributions became fixed amounts (they were variable under the Addison finances) central government was generally uninterested in local authority rent setting policies, so some authorities tried to allocate to poorer households but at the cost of reducing building standards. There is no question, however, that it was not until the slum clearance programme of the 1930s that poor working class households accessed council housing in large numbers. The affordability problem for the mass of poor and, increasingly unemployed, working classes was not solved by council housing in the 1920s.

Slum clearance

The absence of any sustained support for council housing is clearly apparent in the abandonment of general needs building in the 1930s. Against a background of economic crisis and mass unemployment (3 million by 1931) the second Labour Government was increasingly limited in its ability and will to continue the provision of general needs council housing. As we have suggested standards were already falling and at the very least were variable across the country well before the shift in policy made by Labour to tackle the slum problem, which was now urgent. The new government defended the Wheatley subsidies from the threatened termination and through the Housing Act 1930 introduced a new subsidy to encourage local authorities to clear slums and rebuild. The clear intention was to upgrade the conditions of the millions of slum dwellers so far untouched by 'general needs' council housing. Local authorities were required to submit plans for their slum clearance programme to be achieved in five years. The subsidies were related to the number of people being displaced, and this was useful in helping larger families to be rehoused. Budgetary constraints and the low incomes of these households meant that such a programme was going to be of limited scope and was achieved only at the expense of further reducing the design and building standards, which included the more widespread use of flats – a significant departure from the Tudor Walters Manual.

The 1930 Act also required local authorities to set 'reasonable' rents with powers to set up rent rebate schemes. The aim here was to enable authorities to charge lower rents to poor families at the expense of the better off. Subsidies would thus be more focused on the less well-off. Rent rebates were not popular with the tenants who saw them as divisive and degrading (they were means-tested by the Public Assistance Boards). Indeed, a large and successful rent strike was mounted by tenants in Birmingham against such a scheme. Local authorities were not, in any case, particularly motivated to let to poor tenants. As Malpass and Murie suggest, '…from the point of view of a landlord, better-off tenants are an easier proposition' (Malpass, P and Murie, A *Housing Policy and Practice*, 2nd edn, Macmillan 1987, p 64). The introduction of housing revenue accounts through the Housing Act 1935 sought to compel local authorities to use rebate schemes – subsidies under the different Acts were pooled into a single account and rents were related to the use-value of different types of dwellings – thus, in theory, enabling councils to charge differential rents irrespective of the origins of the subsidy for particular houses. But very few authorities had schemes running by the outbreak of war in 1939.

The commitment to generally subsidised council housing continued for a while through the reduced Wheatley Act subsidies, but the Labour Prime Minister, Ramsey MacDonald, sabotaged his own party over the issue of expenditure cuts, and joined a Conservative dominated 'National' Government – which held office from 1931 until the end of the war in 1945. This government abolished the Wheatley subsidies in 1933 so that the only subsidy for council housing between 1933 and 1939 was for slum clearance. The long-standing trend to reduced standards was confirmed in what in effect was a 'residual' role for council housing not dissimilar to its pre-1919 position. Housing policy for most of the 1930s thus abandoned the notion of general responsibility for supporting working class housing beyond the commitment to slum clearance. Between 1932 and 1935 council housing fell from about one third of new building to only one eighth. It was argued that, in addition to the public expenditure crisis, the boom in private housing construction, mostly for sale to owner occupiers, was such that government no longer needed to provide for general housing. As the new middle classes moved out to the private suburbs so their vacated byelaw terraces would filter down. The slum clearance subsidy would provide for the needs of those in the very worst housing and unable to move in the market. In practice the Greenwood subsidies (Greenwood was Labour's Minister of Health and responsible for the Housing Act 1930) provided nowhere near enough new dwellings to meet the need of the millions of families living in the squalid inner cities of Britain, trapped by the grip of economic depression. By 1939 a total of only 265,000 new council houses had been built under the slum clearance programme. The limited achievement is revealed by the fact that during the same period (1933-9) the number of houses built in the privately rented sector was more than the total council house programme (Kemp, in Lowe and Hughes, 1991, p 50). Investors took advantage of the very favourable conditions for building, stimulating a temporary but significant revival in private renting. Between 1934-35 and 1938-39 about 66,000 houses per annum were built for new private renting (Merrett, S *Owner Occupation in Britain*, Routledge and Kegan Paul 1982, p 14). This revival further supports our view that the collapse of the PRS was not principally a function of rent controls, although the economic position of private landlords was impaired by controls. New houses to rent were not subject to rent controls. It is the decline in the long-term investment potential of this sector of housing that is the root of the problem.

The situation in 1939

The overall picture of change in the inter-war years is dramatic. By 1939 very nearly one third of the housing stock was new. The local authority contribution to this was substantial and since 1919 councils had built 1,112,000 houses and flats, representing one quarter of new construction and accommodating one in ten households. But this achievement is highly qualified as we have seen by the prevarication about the role of council building, its financing, its standards and above all by the fact that until well into the 1930s very few poor working class families benefited, and even then by lower quality dwellings. The Poor Law principle of 'less eligibility' is close to the surface of housing policy at this time. Malpass and Murie argue that these lower standards were part of the drive to establish home ownership as the normal housing tenure for all but the poorest left as an 'undeserving' class of people in a residual public sector (Malpass and Murie, 1987, p 62).

Indeed, in the 20 years before 1939 the private builders had put in place very nearly three million dwellings, 430,000 of which were built with state-aid. Moreover, so poor was the investment return that over one million privately rented dwellings were sold by landlords, commonly to sitting tenants (Merrett, 1982, p 16). The net effect, including losses through slum clearance, was that the PRS lost about half a million dwellings. Owner occupation grew by 2.9 million dwellings by the combination of new building (60%) and sales from private renting (40%) and was clearly in the ascendent. By 1939 the owner occupied housing stock accounted for 32% of total dwellings. Although private renting remained the majority tenure (58% of dwellings) it was being eclipsed by home ownership and by council housing, a pattern of tenure restructuring that was to accelerate after 1945. Indeed, the polarisation between public housing for rent and private housing for sale was to become a feature of the post-1945 era. For the working class poor, however, very little had changed through the 1920s and 1930s and those that had not escaped to the suburbs continued to live in adequate but comfortless 'byelaw houses' and many millions more in the downwardly spiralling sub-standard conditions of the inner city. There was still much to be done.

After World War Two

It was, indeed, some time before the needs of low income households living in the Victorian slums were seriously addressed and for more than a decade following the end of the war the main emphasis in housing policy was to address the chronic problem of shortages of supply. The solutions adopted were not significantly different from those of the inter-war period and the role of public sector housing continued to be, in essence, to fill the gap left by the continued decline of the PRS. Housing output contracted rapidly after 1939 as the nation went onto a war footing. Any new works had to be licensed by Ministerial Order and the number of workers in the building industry fell dramatically. Very little new construction took place for the duration and normal repair and maintenance was severely constrained. Repair of war damaged property was, however, quite considerable and was aided by a system of war damage compensation. The Blitz in 1940 and the 'doodle bug' attacks in 1944 destroyed or rendered uninhabitable 475,000 dwellings and damaged a further 3.5 million.

More important than this was the dramatic increase in the number of new household formations arising from early marriages (two million during the six war years) and also from an increase in family dissolutions. Holmans estimates that there was a shortfall of two million dwellings by 1945 including a large number of concealed households, people living with families and friends (Holmans, A E, 1987, p 92). In addition the condition of the slums remained untouched and deteriorating. At the time even the Ministry of Reconstruction estimated a figure of half a million new dwellings to cater for replacing slums and overcrowding. During the war years the birth rate grew very sharply and by 1946 the population of Britain, despite the war casualties, had grown by over a million. There was, thus, a severe shortage of housing supply caused mainly by a massive increase in demand and this problem was the context for the housing policies of the next two decades.

The Labour Government

The Labour Party won the July 1945 election on a tide of popular belief that the sacrifices of the war years should lead to a renewal in Britain's social and economic life. The disparity in supply and demand, the shortages of manpower and materials in the construction industry and the dangers of an inflationary explosion were formidable. The immediate response was to continue building controls and the private sector was controlled through a system of licensing. The Minister in charge of the emergency situation was Aneurin Bevan, Minister of Health. Bevan was vociferously opposed to the role of the private sector saying that he refused to let the private developers, '…suck at the teats of the state' and that they were essentially an '…unplannable instrument' (quoted in Foot, M *Aneurin Bevan, Volume 2*, Granada, 1975, p 71). The programme of reconstruction was to focus on the needs of working class families and would operate through authorities. His vision was similar to that of John Wheatley, arguing forcefully for a housing policy that was not socially divisive. In essence Bevan argued that local authority housing should provide for all social classes and that the speculative building industry should supply under a system of licences to complement the wider policy objectives. Unlike Wheatley, Bevan was not concerned to nationalise the PRS but war-time rent controls were retained in order to allow control of that sector in the overall strategy. The control of land and speculative gain was additionally limited through the Town and Country Planning Act 1947 which, while stopping short of the election manifesto commitment to, '…work towards land nationalisation' introduced a 100% betterment levy on the changed value of land arising from the granting of planning permission.

In the event the Labour Government oversaw the building of 1,017,000 dwellings before it was defeated in the election of 1951. 146,000 of these were 'pre-fabs' built in 1946-47, but nevertheless this scale of programme was impressive and was the first large scale positive investment in public housing since the Wheatley legislation. 80% of dwellings completed during Labour's terms of office were built in the authority sector. It should be noted that the high quality of both 'Wheatley' and 'Bevan' housing reflects the vision of two socialist politicians who both held Ministerial office at a time of national political crisis following wars. It is this, as Malpass and Murie suggest, that answers the question '…of why governments should choose to build the best houses at the most difficult times, and to reduce standards later on.' (Malpass and Murie, 1982, p 73).

Nevertheless the 1945 Labour Government fell considerably short of what might have been achieved and what, indeed, was needed. This was largely to do with the inability of the government to exert sufficient control over its development programme due to reliance on private companies to undertake most of the construction. The problem was that authorities had to rely on the response of the companies for the fulfilment of their projects. Labour and materials shortages compounded this problem and the very severe winter of 1946-47 also held up the building programme. These difficulties led to restrictions being imposed on tender approvals in 1947 and a further round of constraints were implemented following the economic crisis of 1948. Local authorities achieved a level of 100,000 dwellings in 1948 but the government fell very far short of its target – by as much as 240,000 units per annum – and one of the main causes of Labour's defeat in the 1951 election was dissatisfaction with its record on housing. Despite the high quality of the 'Bevan' houses the quantity of production was seriously lagging given the massive scale of demand.

The Conservative Party's pledge to build 300,000 houses by a combination of public and private provision was a major plank of their election victory. Moreover, in the 13 years of Conservative government public sector housing completions never fell below 100,000. Harold Macmillan, the Minister for Housing and Local Government, outlined a strategy which favoured the expansion of owner occupation but accepted the need for authorities to make up any deficits in production targets. Initially this meant that the council house programme was in the ascendant and council starts increased sharply from 171,000 in 1951 to 231,000 in 1953 during which year the Conservative's pledge to build 300,000 houses was redeemed. This, however, was achieved by decimating the building and design standards insisted on by Bevan and, although numerically dominant for a few years, the slashing of standards shows the essentially residualist policy for the public housing sector that was the intention of national housing policy throughout the period of Conservative government to 1964. In the private sector licensing was gradually phased out and abolished in November 1954. The Town and Country Planning Act 1953 abolished the betterment levy and the combination of the ending of controls on building and land supply created the conditions for the second twentieth century boom in construction for owner occupation. Building starts in the private sector broke the 100,000 barrier in 1954 and accelerated year on year to peak at 247,000 in 1964 and was never far short of 200,000 up to the mid-1970s. Advances by building societies grew in conjunction with this boom era in home ownership. Personal disposable income grew from £377 per annum in 1948 to £581 in 1965. Inflation was modest and unemployment by the standards of the 1930s, 1980s and 1990s was very low. Macmillan was not far short of the truth when he told the nation that 'they had never had it so good'. It was by no means the whole truth as the evidence of the growth of homelessness in the early 1960s was to demonstrate.

Once the private sector boom took hold, during 1954, the basic function allotted to the public sector became clear. As private building accelerated so the programme of council house building declined. Thus by 1961 local authorities built the relatively modest total of 105,000 dwellings, less than half their 1954 output. At this time the surging output of the private sector convinced the government that the problem of the slums could now be tackled once again, having been held in abeyance since 1939. This development further served to underpin the essentially residual role of public housing. The policy was stated unequivocally by Macmillan, 'Local authorities and local authorities alone can clear and rehouse the slums, while the general housing need can be met, as it was to a great extent before the war, by private enterprise' (quoted in Samuel et al 'But nothing happens', in *New Left Review*, 1962). The Housing Repairs and Rents Act 1954 restarted the slum clearance programme and encouraged private sector improvement. It was made increasingly clear that authorities had no general needs function and it was no surprise that in the 1956 Housing Subsidies Act the general needs subsidy was all but abolished. Subsidy was retained only for slum clearance and for the construction of one-bedroomed flats for the elderly.

Two other elements in the reorientation of policy in the mid-1950s were important. First, rent policy from 1955 began to compel local authorities to increase their rents towards market levels, called 'realistic rents', and to protect low income households by the increased use of rent rebate schemes. This policy intensified over the years and gradually lead to the ending of 'bricks and mortar' subsidies in favour of targeted means-tested benefits for low income families. Housing subsidies in other words became more closely attached to, and for a while paid by, the social security system.

The high-rise era

The second innovation was contained in the 1956 Act and concerns the encouragement given through the subsidy system to local authorities to build high rise flats. The era of mass council house building was about to take on a very literal form. Experiments with prefabricated technologies by a number of the major construction companies made it appear that high rise building, particularly in inner city slum clearance areas where space was limited and land relatively expensive, would solve the problem of high output combined with low cost. Le Corbusier's vision of 'machines for living in' suddenly found support, particularly in Labour controlled local authorities in London and some north of England cities, as the answer to mass housing. It is clear that this 'solution' played into the hands of a resurgent building industry dominated by relatively few giant companies and that a high proportion of high-rise blocks were built by only half a dozen companies (Dunleavy, P *The Politics of Mass Housing in Britain 1945-75*, Clarendon Press, 1981). The grandiose vision of architects and politicians incurred great cost to working class social and community life and further damaged the already fragile legitimacy of public housing. This housing was out of touch with the shape and pattern of working class life which it replaced and architects and politicians rarely lived in it. To an extent the new mass housing did offer a home and haven for millions of people away from the Victorian slums but the social cost was very great and many of the worst and most gargantuan schemes were out of date and spiralling downwards into housing estates typified by social deprivation almost before they were complete. At the peak of the high-rise boom in 1966 blocks of flats over five storeys high accounted for over a quarter of public sector building approved for construction by central government and in some places a much higher share. For example, in the GLC area 91% of completions in 1967 were flats and two-thirds of these were high-rise blocks (Power, A *Property Before People*, Allen and Unwin, 1987, p 45).

Financial packages were offered which tied local authorities into huge debt repayment costs and undermined rent systems as tenants were called on to pay a higher and higher share of their rent in effect as interest payments to the financial institutions. This was not after all a cheap solution, and in the wake of the Ronan Point disaster in 1967 – when a tower block in the London Borough of Newham partially collapsed following a gas explosion, killing 13 people – and arriving at a point in time when the worst of the post-war shortages appeared to have been dealt with, the era of high rise construction terminated abruptly. The construction of prefabricated maisonettes and lower rise blocks of flats persisted into the 1970s, accounting for nearly 40% of approvals in 1970.

The Rent Act 1957

Earlier in the chapter we argued that the structural decline of the privately rented sector was a key to understanding the need for and the expansion of public housing. The revival of private renting was an additional feature of Conservative housing policy in the 1950s and continued to follow the logic of Chamberlain in the 1920s, that private landlordism was really in temporary abeyance until 'normal' circumstances returned. The Rent Act 1957 was the new incarnation of this belief and was the third strand in the web of Conservative housing policy. The principal emphasis was on private sector solutions to general needs housing supported by a residual role for public housing. The latter was focused on slum clearance and housing for the elderly, neither of which could be achieved at the minimum acceptable standard within the profit margins of the private construction industry. The significance in an account of public sector housing of the 1957 Act relates, as we shall see, to its failure to revive the PRS. This failure compelled the Conservatives to re-think their strategy towards council housing in the early 1960s leading to the reintroduction of general needs housing subsidies for local authorities. A new housing crisis emerged at this time with increasing evidence of the growth of homelessness, discussed below and in Chapter Six.

As we argue above, it was the poor economic return available to private landlords that led over the long-term to the demise of the PRS. Within this general situation one of the contributory factors to its decline was rent control and the associated guarantees of security of tenure for tenants. Various modifications to the blanket controls introduced in 1915 were enacted in the 1920s particularly an element of decontrol introduced in the Housing Act

1923. Some tightening followed in 1933 but newly built private rental housing was not subject to control at any time. This patchwork of controls over rents in the private sector was put on ice in 1939 when all rents were frozen at their September levels for the duration of the conflict, and, in fact, this level of control remained virtually untouched until the Rent Act of 1957. The aim of the 1957 Act was to allow landlords greater freedom in rent setting by the decontrol of tenancies of certain rateable values and new tenancies. The intention here was to establish a creeping decontrol of the sector and so bring about the expected revival of private landlordism. In fact there is no evidence that this happened and on the contrary, in so far as tenants had to pay higher rents, they were induced into owner occupation, and as house prices began to accelerate landlords were encouraged to sell into the market, preferably on vacant possession. The spectre of Rachmanism (so named after a large-scale private landlord in London who induced tenants through unscrupulous harassment into new agreements or sometimes to vacate property) haunted the 1957 Act: the image of private landlordism was tarnished further by Rachman and the seedier elements in the sector. Private landlordism did not 'revive' as had been forecast by the government and, as Kemp suggests, 'Decontrol thus proved to be a necessary, but not a sufficient, condition for the return of the private investor in rented housing' (Kemp, in Lowe and Hughes, 1991, p 53).

The new housing crisis

By the early 1960s the government was forced to reconsider its *laissez-faire* strategy in the face of the evidence on homelessness (see Chapter Six for details) and the further decline in private renting following the 1957 Act. The Housing Acts of 1961 and 1964 gave authorities considerably enhanced powers to compel landlords of multiply-occupied houses to undertake repair and improvement of the property. Renewal policy was no more successful than attempted deregulation and from about this time it was recognised that housing renewal in the private sector was not going to be achieved through reliance on landlords. Grants to owner occupiers were, by contrast, up to 70,000 per annum in the early 1960s and in order to avoid the further degeneration of the housing stock it became apparent that the promotion of home ownership and renewal were inter-dependent. More important here is the point that the continuing failure of private landlords to supply general needs rented housing and evidence of an increase in homelessness forced the government to reconsider the role of authorities. They published a White Paper (*Housing in England and Wales*, HMSO, 1961) and in the following legislation, Housing Act, 1961, general needs subsidies were reintroduced, although at two rates and in a complex system of local calculations. In order to demonstrate that private renting could be made to work and in the absence of any significant return on investment the 1961 Act made loans available for establishing cost-rent housing societies, now called 'Associations' (Cullingworth, 1979). With the election approaching the Conservatives pushed further in this direction and in the Housing Act 1964 set up the Housing Corporation aimed at encouraging housing associations to build for letting at cost rents and with powers to borrow up to £100 million a year from the Treasury. The encouragement of a so called 'third arm' of provision through the revival of housing associations was held in check, however, as a result of the 1964 election which returned a Labour Government under Harold Wilson.

'The party of council housing'?

Housing was a key issue in the 1964 General Election and Labour under Harold Wilson won on a manifesto which included a commitment to build 500,000 houses. This period of Labour government, however, was not to be a return to the visionary years of Wheatley or Bevan. In the 13 years since 1951 the Conservatives had sustained the role of the local authorities albeit reluctantly. Indeed far more council houses had been built under Conservative or Conservative dominated coalition governments than under Labour. Labour nevertheless were known as the 'party of council housing' but during the 1960s they began to distance themselves from this image and at some considerable pace. When they returned to power in 1964 their policy stance, compared to the 1945 government, was radically different. Merrett probably overstates the position when he says that, 'The main shift was to accept the residualist principle of Toryism' (Merrett, 1982, p 42). The evidence needs to be evaluated with care. In the 1965 housing White Paper council housing is pigeon-holed into a number of defined roles,

> 'The Expansion of the public programme now proposed is to
> meet exceptional circumstances; it is born partly out of short-
> term necessity, partly out of the conditions inherent in modern
> urban life. The expansion of building for owner occupation *on
> the other hand is normal.*' (emphasis added)

It seems most probable that this statement reflects several somewhat contradictory processes which were inherent in the circumstances of the mid-1960s. Principal among these was that the nation was reaching the period which marked the end of the post-war shortages and, as Holmans points out, there was a significant weakening in the demand for council housing, illustrated, for example, in the emergence of so called 'difficult to let' estates (Holmans, 1987).

Initially, however, the expansion referred to above took place under Labour's 'National Housing Plan' and the rate of council house building accelerated for several years reaching a post-war peak of 180,000 in 1967. This programme was reined back following the devaluation of the pound in

November 1967 and never really recovered its former pre-eminence at any subsequent stage. The planned 500,000 dwellings was dropped quietly from the policy statements as the economic crisis bit very deeply into Labour's social programme.

An indication of Labour's approach can be seen in the improved building standards which were made mandatory in 1969 with the adoption of the 1961 Parker Morris Report – which recommended an optional standards yardstick. The report argued for increased space standards so that modern families could experience greater privacy, have more storage room and, noting changing social habits, advocated larger kitchens where families could sit to eat meals and a generally more flexible use of living space which at the time was quite radical and certainly anticipated and encouraged new perceptions of the 'home'. Technical issues were also highlighted in the report, particularly the need for better heating standards. In fact a high proportion of local authority dwellings built in the mid-1960s already met these standards. The mandatory adoption of Parker Morris standards is, however, illustrative of Labour's pragmatically supportive approach to council housing.

Nevertheless, the use of this standard became tangled into the need to reduce the building programme due to economic crisis. The Parker Morris standard caused a significant increase in building costs (Burnett suggests evidence of up to 15%; Burnett, 1986, p 309) and so itself became a cause of the reduced building programme. More important, a Cost Yardstick was introduced in 1963 by the Ministry of Housing. It involved a sliding scale of subsidies which compared house size with number of occupants – higher densities attracted more subsidy – and was controlled, within Parker Morris minimum standards, by central government. In effect the Yardstick operated as a mechanism for regulating tender approvals and so the rate of building output. Labour was thus still supportive of council housing and good quality production but increasingly was enmeshed in financial problems. Good intentions tempered by financial realities seems to sum up their position and it is clearly not the case that they saw no future role for council housing or that their attitude was 'residualist'; seeing council housing as a last resort for people unable to access the market.

From redevelopment to rehabilitation

Community action was also a feature of the major change in the direction of housing policy this time announced in a White Paper 'Old Houses into New Homes' (Cmnd 3602, HMSO, 1968) signalling the switch away from slum clearance and general rehousing towards the private rehabilitation of the housing stock through the voluntary take-up of improvement grants. Resistance had built up to the most excessive mass slum clearance 'rolling programmes' now threatening to engulf areas which by no stretch of the imagination could be considered to be slums. Residents' associations and community action groups sprang up nationwide to resist the onslaught of the bulldozer (Lowe, S G *Urban Social Movements: the city after Castells*, Macmillan, 1986). Because slum clearance was specifically an authority role the era of local authority housing as the agency for this task was drawing to a close. As Kemp observes, 'The switch to rehabilitation removed a significant part of the demand for new local authority housing' (Kemp, 1991, p 55).

As we pointed out earlier in the chapter this is also the period which coincided with the growing dissatisfaction and disillusionment with high rise housing. Families with children and elderly people found this form of living difficult and even dangerous. Costs were much higher than initially forecast by the construction companies and were causing authorities severe problems with their housing revenue accounts because debt charges were consuming an increasingly large share of their resources. Some city councils with large building programmes found that the whole of their rental income was spent on interest repayments. This issue underlay a gathering tide of resentment among the tenants themselves and the period was marked by a series of rent strikes culminating in the overthrow of Labour councils in several cities, notably Sheffield which fell to the Conservatives in 1968-69 for the first time since Labour took control of the city council in 1926 (Lowe, 1986, p 89).

So it was that the disillusionment with high rise housing, community action of various sorts, the severe economic crisis facing the mid-term Wilson government and declining demand saw public sector housing, now responsible for housing nearly a third of the population, reach a significant turning point. Labour's National Housing Plan was in tatters and private rehabilitation of the existing housing stock gradually supplanted public redevelopment as the principal plank of housing policy and marked the end of the high out-put era.

The Housing Act 1969 accordingly introduced General Improvement Areas and the Housing Act 1974 added Housing Action Areas in which grants for house improvement were supplemented by environmental improvements. This policy, pursued by the second Wilson and then the Callaghan Government (1974-79), in fact conceals a significant withdrawal of state expenditure on housing. By 1977 public sector completions had fallen to a post-war low of only 88,000. The withdrawal of investment in the development programme, often associated with the Thatcher governments after 1979, was in fact a well established trend under Wilson and Callaghan. These cuts were closely connected to the worsening economic situation in the country and were a direct consequence of restrictions on state expenditure imposed by the International Monetary Fund in December 1976. This changed environment for housing finance led to a stricter system of cash limited controls on local authority capital expenditure, administered through an annual Housing Investment Programme.

Thus the dominant theme during this period was the problem of housing finance. It was a confusing picture and the general thrust of housing finance was unclear with controls on rent increases, interest rates rising sharply and the scale of tax reliefs to owner occupiers generating an increasingly regressive system of housing finance, by which high income owner occupiers gained compared to standard rate tax payers because relief was obtained at the highest tax threshold of the mortgagor. Subsidy was also being clawed back from the public sector and so financial gain accrued to better-off households both within the home ownership sector and between home owners and council tenants. A major review of housing finance was accordingly established, but events moved quickly and when the Housing Policy Review Green Paper appeared in 1977 a general pattern of all party consensus had emerged and spending controls on local authorities were already well established. For historians of housing policy this document is of more than passing significance for it encapsulates Labour's thinking on housing policy at this time and is generally regarded as a conservative paper, particularly regarding their advocacy of home ownership (*Housing Policy: A Consultative Document*, Cmnd 6851, HMSO, 1977).

Let it be clear, however, that the 1977 Housing Policy Review argued quite strongly for the continuation of the public sector as a major supplier of housing, albeit at lower levels of output than in the past and more targeted at locally identified needs rather than large scale national plans. The Green Paper emphasised the need for a more pluralistic approach to these smaller scale needs incorporating housing associations and the private sector as main providers in such circumstances. There can be no doubt that Labour sought to narrow the scope and role of public housing, and sustain the existing trends in the tenure structure focused on the expansion of owner occupation. But, as we have suggested at several points in our account, the document needs to be read carefully and within the context of the longer term trends. Forrest and Murie's characterisation of the 1977 Green Paper as, '...Labour's capitulation to owner occupation and acceptance of a limited, residual role for council housing...' (Forrest, R and Murie, A *Selling the Welfare State: The Privatisation of Public Housing*, 1988, p 32) is an exaggerated position. The Green Paper described the historic role local authorities across the country had in ameliorating the squalor of the Victorian slums and demonstrated the impact council housing had had in raising housing standards. Labour still regarded authorities as bastions of this long campaign and that they still had an important future role to play, albeit in new circumstances and in a more pluralistic housing system.

Labour and owner occupation

Before turning to discuss the approach of the Conservative governments (Heath, Thatcher and Major) in this new era of reduced shortages there remains the as yet unanswered question of Labour's attitude to home ownership.

Labour's advocacy of owner occupation was, by the late-1970s, well established. In that sense the 1977 Green Paper is a statement of a long-standing position and not a 'capitulation'. As Kemp points out even after the war it was never supposed that council housing would be the only form of provision and that under normal circumstances owner occupation would be the principal form of supply (Kemp, 1991). Indeed, in the 1965 White Paper, Labour described home ownership as 'a long-term social advance' and contrasted the public housing programme (which it was argued should focus on short-term necessity and on exceptional needs) with the more normal 'expansion of building for owner-occupation'. Richard Crossman, the Labour Housing Minister at this time was keenly aware of the need to limit his party's identification as the party of council housing, partly out of sheer electoral necessity. Owner occupiers were by the mid-1960s nearly a majority of voters. In his famous Diaries, Crossman wrote that, '...we only build council houses where it is clear they are needed' and he went on to say that the main aim of Labour's housing policy should be to encourage owner occupation. Labour was thus firmly committed to reforms in all the main housing tenures, but by the mid-1960s had a clear vision of home ownership as a symbol of social advance.

During the period of the first Harold Wilson government the fiscal advantages of owner occupation were further enhanced, following the abolition of Schedule 'A' taxation on the imputed rental income of the home owner in 1963 by the Conservatives. Home owners were exempted from paying capital gains tax on the sale of their principal dwelling, tax relief was retained for home improvements, and mortgage interest tax relief was retained when most other forms of tax reliefs were abolished. In the light of the abolition of Schedule 'A' taxation this meant that owner occupiers with mortgages were in effect being subsidised for the purchase of the dwelling as consumers and because they paid no capital gains tax reaped a considerable financial gain as investors. In order to widen the social base of home ownership a system of 'Option Mortgages' was introduced in the 1967 Housing Subsidies Act and allowed both local authorities and building societies to offer mortgages at 2% lower than the standard rate for households on low incomes. Option mortgages thus enabled lenders to increase the amounts they loaned or reduce monthly payments of people of 'modest incomes'. The main form of subsidy to owner occupiers, through tax relief on their mortgage payments, was not available to non-taxpayers who by default were excluded from fiscal subsidy. This series of measures considerably enhanced the position of owner occupiers but caused, as we have shown, imbalances in housing subsidies which now favoured home owners against public tenants and was generally regressive.

There was, in short, no doubting Labour's commitment to owner occupation. Neither should it be doubted that their view of council housing was quite distinctive from that of the Conservatives. They saw it as a necessary contribution to meeting the housing needs of the nation and this was as much the case in 1979 as it was in 1945. However, in a period which was no longer dominated by the shortages issue and where the worst slums had been demolished there was a considerable degree of agreement between the two parties in the mid-1970s about the general drift of housing policy with home ownership and provision through the market as its cornerstone. The idea that there was a major reversal in Labour's position at this time is not a wholly justifiable case because home ownership had always been recognised by them as a central feature of British housing. Where the two major parties most sharply diverged was over the treatment of the PRS, with Labour at this time looking to housing associations as an alternative to the PRS.

The last important housing measure taken before the advent of the Thatcher governments was the Housing (Homeless Persons) Act of 1977. It may be thought ironical that at a time when council building had reached a post-war low this measure was enacted. In it local authorities were given duties to house very specifically defined groups of 'deserving' homeless people – households with dependent children, 'vulnerable' people such as the elderly, and people made homeless due to an emergency such as a flood or fire. As we saw earlier in the chapter there had been mounting evidence of a growing problem of homelessness through the 1960s and 1970s but this was not seen as a 'housing' problem, rather one arising from the isolated difficulties of individual families in local housing markets. The main housing related issue was regarded as the continued decline of the PRS. The attempted decontrol of the PRS under the Conservative administrations was halted by Labour through the 1965 Rent Act, which gave security of tenure in unfurnished accommodation and introduced a 'fair rents' system, through which rents were set by Rent Officers according to the type and quality of the property but excluding consideration of local market conditions. This allowed for a controlled increase in rent levels in the private sector.

Housing subsidies under the Conservatives

One of the consequences of this new system of rent setting was that very soon private sector rents were accelerating away from those in the public sector and as a result there was some concern about this disparity and the role of subsidies in the public sector. With the return to power of the Conservatives under Edward Heath in 1970 this issue became a major focal point of policy in which the aim was to reduce the distorting effect of subsidies to the public sector. Rents and house prices were to be set through the open market and council house rents were to become part of this market-orientated system. This programme is a reassertion of the standard Conservative view which in the era of declining shortages was re-focused on strategies for the incorporation of state rental housing into the logic if not the actual housing tenures in the private sector. In a similar vein the government removed restrictions on the sale of council houses to sitting tenants which had been in force since 1968. Converting council housing to owner occupation and drawing the rents in the public sector closer to the market were different strands of a common policy stance. The aim was both to reduce public expenditure on subsidies to council housing and to make council housing more expensive, with protection for worse off tenants through a mandatory rent rebate system.

The legislative instrument for dealing with public sector rents was the Housing Finance Act 1972. Local authority discretion in rent setting was largely removed and council rents were linked to the 'fair rent' system operating in the PRS since the Rent Act 1965. To protect poorer tenants from the consequences of increasing rents a mandatory rent rebate system was also introduced. The significance of this was that it foreshadowed the system of housing finance which was to become a feature of Thatcherite housing policy; an emphasis on means-tested targeted subsidies to individuals – operated through the social security system – rather than 'bricks and mortar' subsides for housing construction. This had been inherent in the housing finance system since the adoption of rent pooling in the mid-1950s, but the 1972 Act, although shortlived, signalled the direction of future policy and is an important juncture in the history of public housing because it established a clear break from the 'historic cost' system of public housing finance which had operated since 1923. As Malpass points out the 1972 Act breached at least three long established conventions by providing that: existing subsidies should be phased out; rents should be set in relation to current incomes and house prices, and general subsidy should now be set on a deficit basis. Notional rents were to be calculated in advance, based on market principles, with the (lower) subsidy then paid in relation to the total of higher rental income and management and maintenance costs. When subsidies became fixed it was rent levels that were the flexible element in the calculation, and this led to considerable variations round the country depending on the quantity and age of the housing stock. Accordingly the 1972 Act introduced, for a while, a new logic which, as Malpass suggests, established a new way of thinking about rent setting and subsidy.

> 'The 1972 Act was too controversial and too flawed to survive,
> but it stands as a major landmark in the development of public
> sector housing finance.'
> (Malpass, 1991, p 70)

In practice the economic climate was unfavourable to this change because interest rates were increasing sharply, construction costs and land prices were also accelerating and house prices rose. These conditions actually led to a slump in the private sector building industry and to many potential purchasers being unable to enter the market. Council house waiting lists grew. Thus although the purpose of the 1972 Act was to make public sector tenants pay higher, more market determined, rents and so reduce central subsidies, the outcome once again was completely different from the intention. Subsidies grew by nearly 100% between 1972 and 1974 and although some Labour controlled authorities mounted a (largely unsuccessful) political campaign against the 'Fair Rent Act' – mostly focused on the rebate system and the centralisation of rent setting – many authorities were helped through a difficult financial period due to the protection afforded to low income tenants by the rebate system. Almost the first action of the incoming Labour government following the 1974 General Election was to abandon fair rents for council housing and the market orientation of the now curiously distorted subsidy system. A rent freeze was announced, with a return in law to the concept of 'reasonable rents', and Labour's National Housing Plan reinstated the general needs building programme via the '500,000' target.

The rise of housing associations

Although overshadowed by the political turmoil caused by the 1972 Act the fair rent system also applied to the tenants of housing associations and the Housing Corporation was given wider powers and increased resources to lend to associations. The Housing Corporation thus widened the scope of their activity away from the co-ownership projects and the so-called 'third arm' of provision of rental housing was set to emerge. Housing associations enjoyed all-party support at the national level, although continuing to be opposed by some mainly Labour local councillors who saw their growing role and funding as competition to the democratically mandated role of authorities. In principle, however, Labour's stance was to support the associations as an alternative to the PRS while the Conservatives saw them as an alternative to the local authorities.

The introduction of Housing Association Grant (HAG) in the Housing Act 1974 gave the associations a completely different financial regime from the historic cost approach which had typified council house finance. Since the Housing Act 1923 authorities had been paid a subsidy per dwelling over a set number of years. This amount was predictable and, once paid, the burden of any expenditure increases or inefficiencies were the liability of the local authority. We describe this system of finance in more detail and discuss its implications for the development of public housing in Chapter Four. Under the HAG system associations were enabled to build schemes or renovate property and enjoy an almost complete write-off of the development costs at the beginning of the life of the project. Through the Housing Corporation and its accountancy controls central government was able to exert a considerable influence over what housing associations did and, as Best suggests, '…an important linkage had been created between the state and the voluntary sector' (Best, R 'Housing Associations: 1890-1990' in Lowe and Hughes 1991, p 153). They were certainly more open to control than were authorities and it is largely for this reason that they grew in importance during the 1980s. Indeed the Housing Act 1980 further tightened the auditing and performance monitoring of associations. Thus, for example, in the period from the 1974 Act to the early 1980s their role was strongly redirected to rehabilitation, so that by 1979-80 nearly 40% of their completed schemes were of this type compared to only 6% in 1974-75 (Malpass, P and Murie, A *Housing Policy and Practice*, Macmillan, 1987, p 170). The speed with which associations were able to move was also a factor in their new status and from a base of only 170,000 properties in 1970 they had grown by 1990 to over 600,000 homes, including 50,000 hostel places and shared housing schemes.

The Thatcher years

The Conservatives returned to their themes on housing subsidies with a vengeance after the election of the Thatcher government in 1979, although their agenda on housing ran much deeper than merely reforming the subsidy system. An important strand of Thatcherism was premised upon the belief that council housing was an inherently inferior form of housing provision compared to owner occupation and represented a stumbling block to the creation of a nation of home owners. It was council housing above all else that was the anathema of modern British society. This belief led to the rapid drawing to a close of the tradition of council housing established in 1919. It was not a sudden change as some commentators have argued – we saw earlier that the Labour governments under Wilson and Callaghan had both re-focused the emphasis of housing policy towards owner occupation – but it is undoubtedly a 'new era', because with almost unprecedented reforming zeal, the aim of Conservative housing policy has been to destroy council housing as a mainstream housing tenure. Thus since 1979, their approach to council housing has been radically different from their previous position. As we have seen far more council houses were built under Conservative administrations than under Labour and generally they had accepted that council housing had a distinctive purpose and role in meeting certain types of housing need. Since 1980, however, the number of council houses has fallen year by year as a result of the right to buy policy enacted in the Housing Act 1980. This gave secure tenants a statutory right to purchase their dwelling after three years occupancy, with a sliding scale discount on the market value of the property according to the length of time they had been council tenants. The Housing and Building Control Act 1984 reduced the qualifying period for 'the right to buy' to two years and enhanced the size of the discounts; tenants of flats, for example, were allowed up to a 70% discount. Within the decade well over a million houses had been sold and the share of council housing in the overall stock of dwellings had fallen from 31.5% to 23.6%. The social consequences of this dramatic change are described in Chapter Two when we consider in detail the disposal of council housing.

The second strand of Conservative policy was to reduce spending on the capital programme, in line with the general strategy of public expenditure cuts. However, the axe fell with particular severity on the housing programme, initially through restraining the Housing Investment Programme (HIP) system. The housing programme was cut by over 75% between 1979-80 and 1986-87. At this time the policy instrument used for implementing this reduction (HIPs) became less effective because councils were accruing large amounts of receipts from the sale of their council houses and so HIP allocations declined in significance as a lever over the authorities. Capital spending was strictly controlled after 1980 but to some extent authorities were able to circumvent the system by creative use of the proportion of capital receipts available to them. However, the 'new financial regime' introduced through the Local Government and Housing Act 1989 re-asserted the influence of central government. We discuss in more detail the policy process and the consequences of the battle over housing finance at this time in Chapter Four. The fundamental point is that the role of local authorities as developers of large quantities of public housing came to an end, and councils looked to others, mainly housing associations but also private developers, to join with them in 'partnerships'. Whether the Conservatives had tapped a deep seated vein of public opinion, which favoured the political agenda of privatisation, or were able to impose their will sustained by a powerful electoral mandate is debatable. It is clear, however, that they encountered very little resistance from a fragment of society which was isolated from the mainstream of owner occupied 'middle England'.

The 'enabling role' and beyond

Towards the mid-1980s the government intensified its attack on local authorities as inefficient and bureaucratic managers. William Waldegrave, one of several Housing Ministers during this phase said that he saw no future role for council housing and that '…the next big push should be to get rid of the state as a big landlord and bring housing back to the community' (quoted in Malpass, P 'Housing Policy and the Housing System Since 1979' in *Implementing Housing Policy*, (eds) Malpass, M and Means, R, Open University Press, 1993, p 30). Two reports by the Audit Commission severely criticised the performance of housing management and local authorities' record on housing maintenance. This seemed to signal a new stage in the development of policy which was positively hostile to the very existence of council housing. This new phase, while continuing the promotion of owner occupation as the core policy, also included a growing recognition that the housing system needed a revived PRS if nothing else in order to facilitate labour mobility during a period of considerable and growing disparities in regional house prices. This new phase was formalised after the 1987 General Election in a White Paper *Housing: the Government's Proposals* (DoE, 1987) and put on the statute book via the Housing Act 1988 and the Local Government and Housing Act 1989.

Key developments here concerned the role of authorities as 'enablers' and the determination of the government to 'demunicipalise' council housing by dispersing it in large chunks to other landlords in the private sector and to quasi-private housing associations. This package of legislation also enacted a 'new financial regime' for all providers of housing in the public sector and is the next stage in the enduringly complex web of local finance. Important changes to the basis of the calculation of subsidy were made in Part VI of the 1989 Act. In essence the system here has been simplified so that the three main sources of subsidy payment – general subsidy, rent rebate subsidy and local rate fund contributions – have been amalgamated into one subsidy. The net effect is to bring most authorities back into subsidy and to re-establish a considerable degree of influence over local rents. A more detailed discussion of the 'new financial regime' as it affects local authorities and housing associations is provided in Chapter Four. Here we wish to note the point in terms of the policy process that the 1989 legislation marks the government's attempt to re-assert the control at the centre with the aim of pushing rents towards fully market-related levels. However, because the calculation of rent is now related to local capital values in the private housing market there have been considerable implementation difficulties. For example, guideline rents have been much higher in the south of the country than in the north where some authorities would have reduced rents. In fact a complex system of 'dampening' has smoothed out the peaks and troughs with the implication that tenants in low house price areas (generally in the north) are forced to pay higher rents than forecast by the model. We return to this later in the book as there is an important debate here about the historical-legal definition of rent and the policy process itself.

At the heart of the 1988 Act was an intention to re-define authorities as enablers, giving them a more strategic and co-ordinating role and at the same time reviving the private rental sector – by then reduced to a fragmented shell accounting for only about 7% of households – and considerably strengthening the role of associations as the main direct providers of social housing. At the time it was planned that the remaining council housing, still numbering well in excess of four million households, despite the right to buy, would be sold or transferred to alternative landlords. The government itself would facilitate some transfers through the establishment of Housing Action Trusts (HATs) and so would by-pass the authorities and in theory demunicipalise some council stock by taking that out of local authority control. Estates were to be specially designated by the Secretary of State as HAT areas and it was hoped that the promise of additional public funds and an injection of private finance would 'turn round' the fortunes of downwardly spiralling communities. Central to these plans, therefore, was the vision of market forces and private finance in conjunction reviving the private and quasi-private rental sectors of housing while 'council' housing would wither on the vine of commercial enterprise.

None of these measures accomplished its specific aim, although the consequences of the attempt to implement them have been considerable, particularly for the tenants of housing associations and the character of the housing association movement itself. It is difficult to separate out the general developments here from the specific implications for the rents of tenants of housing associations and the detailed discussion of this issue is left for Chapter Four. As we have persistently sought to show in the chapter, the outcome of a policy is often at variance with its intention.

Briefly on each of the key issues in the 1988 Act, the 'revival' of the PRS through the traditional mechanism of deregulation of the rent system has largely failed. The 'assured' tenancy and the 'assured shorthold' tenancy, which allow landlords to set market level rents on a change of tenancy, have been unable to induce substantial new investment into the PRS. At a time when house prices fell sharply, after the peak of the boom in the summer of 1988, households able to afford assured rents for the small quantities of reasonable quality private rental housing available could generally afford a mortgage for properties at the lower end of the market. It seems probable that the limited evidence there is of a revival in renting further reflected the slump in house prices between 1989 and 1994 as developers were forced to rent out newly built dwellings as a temporary measure until profitability and turnover in the property market improved. At the same time young (often single) adults, who were the mainstay of the active section of the PRS, were unable to afford rents much beyond Housing Benefit levels and so the 'market' to a very large extent was constrained by the low income of the customers. The programme of tax reliefs announced for investors in the Business Expansion Scheme (BES) in the 1988 Budget (not part of the 1988 Act), also failed to produce general affordable rental housing but did have a limited impact in the south of the country providing good quality rental accommodation for more affluent, younger and upwardly socially mobile tenants (Crook, A D H, et al *Tax Incentives and the Revival of Private Renting*, York, Cloister Press, 1991). Some housing associations and universities saw the BES as a way of securing new loans at relatively low cost and universities in particular have made extensive use of BES to build student accommodation.

The measure in the 1988 Act to introduce Housing Action Trusts (HATs) was rejected in every area where a HAT was initially proposed. As announced in the White Paper *Housing: The Government's Proposals* (Cm 214) September 1987, there was to be no participation by tenants themselves in the arrangements for setting up a HAT or its ultimate transfer to another landlord – which specifically would not be the local authority. But a vociferous campaign by tenants' associations around the country against these procedures forced the government to revise this proposal. It has been suggested that Lord Caithness, the Minster of Housing at the time, was cornered by David Dimbleby in a BBC television interview and '...blurted out that tenants in HAT estates would get a ballot' (cited in Karn, V 'Remodelling a HAT', in Malpass and Means, 1993, p 78). Ironically this concession to tenants' demands made the first wave of HATs impossible to implement. The ballots were unsuccessful and none of the original six targeted estates went forward. By early 1994 only four HATs were operating (Waltham Forest, Liverpool, Castle Point and Hull), and in each case with the support of massive injections of public subsidy and the co-operation of authorities. As a vehicle for dismantling council housing by the wholesale declaration of HAT estates the policy has failed and more recently it has been superseded by somewhat more subtle incentives via the regeneration of inner city and peripheral housing estates through schemes such as City Challenge. For a detailed discussion of the legal framework of this policy see Chapter Two.

The new world for housing associations

The 1988 Act intended to draw the housing association movement firmly in the direction of a private and 'independent' rental forms of provision. It was supposed that greater exposure to the disciplines of market forces would lead to greater cost efficiencies and thereby increase housing output relative to a given public subsidy. Allocation of funding was to be based on associations' ability to meet unit cost targets. The key change introduced in the legislation was to abandon the old 1974 HAG system and replace it with a funding mechanism based on a *fixed* level of grant: previously grant had written off most of the capital cost of a scheme at the beginning of the life of the dwellings but under the new regime a high proportion of funding is derived from private finance and a much greater share of the financial risk is borne by the associations. We describe the new system and its consequences in more detail in Chapter Four.

Here we note that the Housing Act 1988 has changed the face of the traditional housing association movement from a diverse set of mainly small scale providers specialising in people with special housing needs and with a strong record of inner-city housing renovation, towards a larger scale, more homogeneous style of development mounted mainly by a few very large national associations. The significantly higher financial risks and liabilities have undermined the voluntary movement and produced a commercial ethos which has changed the services they offer, the type of people catered for and the kind of housing being built. Serious problems on some of the new large estates have opened up a new seam of criticism which is not far removed from those levelled at local authorities in the past – their administrative inefficiencies, the over-large scale of estates, the poor record of management, and a potent sense of being a residual housing tenure. The future of associations at the time of writing is by no means clear and at this point in time the government has developed a distinctly critical policy stance towards housing associations because they no longer appear to be a substitute for the PRS but rather a re-emergent, albeit miniature, form of municipal housing.

The Major Government

The Conservatives came to power for a fourth consecutive term in May 1992 under the leadership of John Major who had succeeded Margaret Thatcher as Prime Minister in 1991. Space here does not permit a detailed account of events over the last few years and we are only able to signal some of the key developments. Indeed at the time of writing a major review of the homelessness legislation is being conducted. A previous review conducted in 1989 concluded that homelessness procedures were working effectively. But in a recent consultation paper (*Access to Local Authority and Housing Association Tenancies*, DoE, 1994) the Government has brought forward proposals for a series of changes which will fundamentally alter the rights of statutorily homeless households to gain access to housing quickly and permanently. The essence of the case presented in the consultation paper is that because the applicants on council house waiting lists and households accepted as homeless by local authorities are broadly similar types of people the latter have an unfair advantage over the former in gaining access to housing. In short there is a 'fast-track' route to public housing which operates to the detriment of those households on the waiting list. The Government thinks that the homelessness legislation is being abused and many undeserving households are 'playing the system' to get housed ahead of equally or more deserving families on the waiting lists. The proposed solutions to this problem involve abandoning the present duty to provide for people in priority need in favour of a new duty to *assist* applicants in emergency need for a limited period of time to find suitable accommodation. There would no longer be a duty to provide permanent accommodation and the sole route to such provision would be through the waiting list. The current procedural and legal position regarding local authority duties towards homeless households as well as a more detailed description of the proposed changes are in Chapter Six.

There are many reasons for questioning the validity of the new proposals and the DoE has been inundated with critical responses. A common criticism is that changing the administrative procedures for allocating scarce housing does nothing to increase the supply of affordable social housing and may well lead to families with children and other high priority cases having to remain in wholly unsuitable surroundings for much longer. The emphasis in the proposals on the length of time people have been on the waiting list as a main criteria for allocation to housing is potentially a source of significant injustice and social problems. After all households presenting and accepted as homeless by local authorities are by definition in immediate need and the statute and Code of Guidance issued under it at the very least screen out genuine cases of need – albeit of certain categories of need and somewhat unevenly interpreted according to the local authority's policy stance and administrative procedures. Increasing the priority given to waiting list applicants in general over vulnerable homeless households has the effect of weighting the system against those in greatest need and in effect seeks to define a problem out of existence. Restricting the duties of authorities to homeless households and limiting their discretion to operate their own waiting lists is a significant change to a long established system which began life with all-party support and has been a stable part of public housing administration and law for almost two decades.

Although it is not clear what the outcome of these proposals will be it is nevertheless important to recognise the type of policy stance being adopted by the Major Government with regard to this central feature of public housing. Two other features of this period are of particular significance because they both have potentially significant consequences for the future direction of public housing: large scale voluntary stock transfers (LSVT), which dates from the end of the 1980s, and the introduction of compulsory competitive tendering for council house management. Each has its own legal framework and policy ramifications and these are discussed in detail in Chapters Two (LSVT) and Three (CCT).

Large scale voluntary stock transfers emerged in the late 1980s when some authorities explored the possibilities of transferring their entire stock to an existing or a newly created housing association. This was not a central government policy although there was a legislative framework for it in the Housing Act 1985 which gave authorities powers to dispose of housing and land. The initiative often arose from officers of authorities anxious about the future of their housing stocks in the 'new financial era'. Between 1988 and 1994 31 local authorities, mainly rural authorities in the south of England, did divest themselves of their housing. More recently a system of 'trickle down' transfer – whereby individual houses are transferred when a tenancy terminates – has been adopted by larger, urban authorities. There are problems with the funding of LSVTs, which we discuss in Chapter Two, and the potential impact of LSVT and 'trickle down' transfers as they are currently constituted is limited in scale. It should be noted, however, that recently interest has been expressed by some *urban* authorities in this form of disposal largely because the proceeds derived from the transfer of large quantities of housing stock might enable them to pay off historic debts and then be in a position to build new housing, albeit in small numbers. It may well be that LSVT in one form or another becomes the way in which the remaining historic core of authority housing is substantially and finally disposed of in bulk. By December 1994 the number of approved transfers was 35, involving 157,000 homes and gross receipts of £2.2 bn.

Of equal significance for authority tenants is the policy of subjecting council house management to compulsory competitive tendering (CCT), introduced in Part III of the Local Government Planning and Land Act 1980 and further extended by the Local Government Acts of 1988 and 1992. Under this legislation authorities will have to invite bids for running estates or other housing functions, such as rent collecting. The precise activities which have to be put out to tender have been listed recently in a statutory instrument (SI 1994/1671) under powers exercised by the Secretary of State. In effect CCT takes housing management into a 'post-Right To Buy' era because it recognises that after nearly one and a half decades of sales and disposals some four million council tenancies still remain and that there is unlikely to be any major reduction in this figure through RTB sales. Unable to extend full property ownership to these households the government now seek to expose council housing to the rigours and supposed benefits of the market via the quasi-privatisation of the management functions. Government research indicated that annual efficiency savings of between 6% and 15% had been achieved in services exposed to CCT, such as school catering and refuse collection. It is supposed that housing management can become equally efficient.

These 'benefits of the market' are to be imposed compulsorily on the tenants whose rights of veto over changes in housing management structures and control, established in section 105 of the Housing Act 1985, have been amended so that there is no veto over management changes arising from the CCT procedure. Tenants' organisations will, however, be consulted over the choice of contractors and there is provision for tenants to take over the management of their own estates subject to tests of competence and ability to do so 'efficiently and effectively'. CCT is limited to specific functions and there is no provision for this process to lead to the wholesale privatisation of authority housing management functions. We describe in detail the rights of tenants to participate in housing management, details of the procedures, and the prescribed functions which have to be put out to competetive tendering in Chapter Three.

Although this process is at a relatively early stage it is already clear that there is considerable, if patchy, interest both geographically and in particular services. As might be expected better-off estates are likely to be of more interest than difficult to let estates in the inner cities. Associations have shown some interest as the scope of their own work has been threatened by recent restrictions on their development plans and CCT might well provide scope for the expansion of their traditional role. They have the particular advantage of having a proven track record of competence and a range of specialist housing management skills. Concern has been expressed about the possible *increase* in costs and *loss* of efficiency as services are duplicated across estates but the new language of customer and consumer has been powerfully evoked and there is no doubt that CCT is leading the large remaining core of council tenants into a new era and, for better or worse, council house management is unlikely to return to its former incarnation.

The current state of play

Public sector housing has reached a point in its 100 year history from which it is not likely to recover. The proportion of dwellings accounted for by 'council' housing is shrinking daily and local authorities have been unable to use the capital receipts from the sale of their own stock to regenerate or re-build. Capital receipts are now being used to pay off historic debts and permission to borrow is almost non-existent. Instead authorities are engaging in partnership arrangements with associations and private developers to scrape together handfuls of new social housing often using the very limited opportunities offered by the planning legislation to encourage developers on certain sites to incorporate a small element of 'affordable' housing into the scheme (see Chapter Six). It is a complex negotiating procedure and is very dependent on good co-operation and the availability of 'cheap' land which can inject an element of subsidy into the financial package.

The housing association movement has changed almost beyond recognition since 1988, as we described above. Its future also seems very tenuous and bound up in deals and partnerships, and in a diversification of their traditional role into the management of former council houses via the CCT process, partnership arrangements with the private sector, involvement in specially targeted funding projects such as the homelessness hostels or the Living Over the Shops initiative (mechanism for the conversion and regeneration of empty rooms above shops for use as accommodation) and even in community development.

The tenants of authorities in their current position stand in a somewhat ambiguous position in this new world. On the one hand those tenants who have been unwilling or unable to buy their homes have been left as a residual core of public sector householders. Their average incomes have dropped considerably in the 1980s and their characteristics have become more homogeneous – a high proportion of unemployed, single parents and the elderly. Housing management has been severely criticised but many authorities have responded with programmes of devolution and renegotiated relationships with their 'customers'. Undoubtedly the threat of sweeping change has radicalised and reinvigorated traditional housing management practice in many places. These managers will be in a good position to compete in the tendering process under the CCT system. Tenants continue to be bound, whatever else changes, by the fact that they are marginal to the decision making process

about their future and even when they are able to generate changes they are powerless to see these implemented. As Stewart shows in the case of the HATs none of the originally declared project estates went ahead because the contractual link was between the Trust and the local authority and '... ultimately there was no way that tenants could enforce the bargains they had so vigorously negotiated by incorporating them into their tenancy agreements...' (Stewart, A 'Rethinking Housing Law: A Contribution to the Debate on Tenure *Housing Studies* Vol 9, No 2, 1994, p 276).

The government for its part appears uneasy that such a large amount of traditional council housing still remains intact and seeks not to empower these tenants through direct control of services but by the compulsory introduction of private management. There remains, therefore, an ambiguity at the heart of public housing whereby tenants are extended the benefits of the status of customers but are held at a very considerable arms-length from direct consumer choice by a government which continues to exert stringent financial control from the centre. The possible extension of LSVTs to larger urban authorities also raises a new set of options and it may be that the next phase in the reformation of public housing will be its disposal to associations and consortia of associations. Finally, it is already clear that authorities' duties towards the homeless are being considerably narrowed with a supposedly reinvigorated PRS taking a greater part in the short term, the centre exerting more control over waiting list procedures and a generally far less secure provision for those for whom even the basic comfort of a home is an increasingly distant dream. The 1994 Budget further reduced public support for social housing provision, and required associations to look to the private sector for up to 42% of capital investment in 1995.

Having outlined the historical and policy context of public housing the rest of this chapter is devoted to an introduction to the current legal framework within which social housing is provided.

What is housing and who provides it?

A number of provisions in the Housing Act 1985 define 'house', 'flat', and 'dwelling' for a variety of purposes, but there is no one unified definition, and the approach of the courts seems to be to take a common sense view in deciding whether as a matter of fact any given set of premises can be reasonably called, for example, a 'house' and then to decide further, as a matter of law, if it falls within the particular provision of the legislation in question; see *Reed v Hastings Corpn* (1964) 62 LGR 588 and *Okereke v Brent London Borough Council* [1967] 1 QB 42, [1966] 1 All ER 150. In *Gravesham Borough Council v Secretary of State for the Environment* (1982) 47 P & CR 142 McCullough J pointed out, in a case under planning law that an important factor to consider is whether any given set of premises provides facilities

required for daily private domestic existence. See also *Lake v Bennett* [1970] 1 QB 663, [1970] 1 All ER 457. As a general rule premises constructed as a house will continue to be treated as such unless they are drastically reconstructed, as for example, where premises are reconstructed as a block of self-contained flats, see *R v Kerrier District Council, ex p Guppys (Bridport) Ltd* (1985) 274 Estates Gazette 924, though whether the process of reconstruction goes far enough in any given case to warrant holding that the character of the original house has been lost must be a question of fact; see *Pollway Nominees Ltd v Croydon London Borough Council* [1987] AC 79, [1986] 2 All ER 849.

So far as flats are concerned, in many cases they are treated as the equivalents of houses, but in particular instances there are distinctions made, for example with regard to the Right to Buy, see Chapter Two below. The most important point to remember is that it is not the 'label' a particular owner or occupier puts on a building which determines what might pass in everyday language as a definition of 'house' or 'flat'. The task of definition is for the law.

The housing authorities

Outside Greater London in the English shires the principal local housing authorities are the district councils, see section 1 of the Housing Act 1985. County councils have only limited powers such as to provide homes for persons employed or paid by them, for example school caretakers – under section 29 of the Housing Act 1985. In the Metropolitan areas Metropolitan District Councils are the housing authorities. In the Greater London area the Common Council is the housing authority for the City of London. In the rest of the metropolis the London Boroughs are, under section 1 of the Housing Act 1985, the principal housing authorities within their areas. In Wales the position from 1 April 1996 will be governed by the Local Government (Wales) Act 1994 under which local government functions are entrusted to 'principal areas', ie counties (largely corresponding to the old historic counties of Wales before the changes made by the Local Government Act 1972) together with a number of large urban areas given county borough status, see Section 1 and schedule 1 of the 1994 Act, though note that Cardiff will rank as a county in its own right. Section 17 and schedule 8 of the 1994 Act transfer housing functions to the new Welsh counties and county boroughs.

Part XVI of the Local Government, Planning and Land Act 1980 provides for the creation of special corporations to regenerate urban areas, for example, London's docklands. Under section 153 of the Act the Secretary of State may provide by order that such a corporation may assume total and exclusive or shared housing powers under the Housing Acts within its area or in any part thereof.

Housing Action Trusts may also take over housing functions within designated areas under the Housing Act 1988. Their powers and constitution are considered in Chapter Two. Other statutory bodies may also provide housing such as the Development Board for Rural Wales. The Urban Regeneration Agency established under Part III of the Leasehold Reform, Housing and Urban Development Act 1993 has certain powers over land which is derelict, neglected or unsightly, or which is likely to become derelict etc as a result of subsidence. The agency has no power to provide housing otherwise than by acquiring existing housing and making it available on a temporary basis for purposes incidental to its principal objects, see section 160 (2). It would thus appear that the housing function of the agency is primarily that of an enabler. It has extensive powers to acquire land and buildings, but it is not to provide new housing itself. Its task is rather to ensure that appropriate land is made suitable and available for housing provision by others.

The local authority duty to provide housing

This duty is contained in Part II of the Housing Act 1985. (All references hereafter are to this Statute unless otherwise stated.)

Section 8 provides that it shall be the duty of every local housing authority to consider the housing conditions in their district and the needs of their district with respect to the provision of further housing accommodation.

Authorities must review from time to time the housing information with which they have been presented about their district, whether that has been provided by their own officers or otherwise, and the consideration of housing conditions in their district under section 605.

Under section 9 accommodation may be provided by erecting houses or by converting buildings into houses, on land acquired by the authority, or by the acquisition of existing houses. These powers may also be used where the houses to be provided are subsequently to be disposed of, and housing land may also be disposed of to persons intending to provide housing on it, see section 9(3).

Supplementary powers to fit out and furnish section 9 accommodation are granted by section 10, and powers to provide meals, refreshments, including the sale of alcoholic liquors for consumption with meals, laundry facilities and services are granted by section 11. However, under section 9(5), as inserted in 1989, authorities are *not* required to hold any housing land or stock, and a number of semi-urban and rural districts have in fact divested themselves of their stock, see Chapter Two below. They remain, of course, housing authorities for a variety of purposes, for example with regard to homelessness, and have to make appropriate arrangements for this purpose.

Section 12 provides that the local authority may, with ministerial consent, provide alongside housing accommodation, shops, recreation grounds and

other land or buildings which the minister considers would benefit the occupants of the housing provided, a power wide enough, according to the opinion of Peterson J in *Conron v LCC* [1922] 2 Ch 283 at 297, to cover the provision of public houses so long as they are 'conducted on the most improved lines'.

Section 23 permits the making of byelaws with respect to the use of any land held under section 12, and *not* covered by buildings or within the curtilage of a building or forming part of a highway, and for the management and regulation of local authority housing. Little use appears to have been made of this power in the past. Greater use may result in the future as authorities begin to use this power to regulate activities such as the repairing and purchasing of cars on their estates – matters which can frequently lead to inter-neighbour disputes. The process of making such byelaws is, however, slow consequent on the need for ministerial approval.

The London Boroughs also have powers to provide and maintain commercial premises along with housing accommodation, under section 15(1). Section 13 grants powers to lay out public streets, roads and open spaces on land acquired for housing purposes. In *Meravale Builders Ltd v Secretary of State for the Environment* (1978) 36 P & CR 87 it was held that this power only empowers a local authority to build such roads as fairly and reasonably relate to the provision of housing accommodation, and not to create new major roads, interchanges and extensions which have a purpose independent of housing. Section 607 requires local authorities to have regard to 'the beauty of the landscape or countryside, the other amenities of the locality, and the desirability of preserving existing works of architectural, historic or artistic interest' when proposing to provide housing. As a matter of strict law authorities enjoy considerable powers to acquire land for housing purposes under section 17, either by agreement, or, subject to ministerial approval, by compulsion. In practice these powers are now very little used because of the move in housing policy away from authorities as *providers* of housing and towards their being overall strategic enablers of others, such as associations, to undertake this task.

Provision of housing by associations

Associations, as will be discussed in detail below, are voluntary bodies having a number of legal forms, but all with the purpose of providing housing of one sort or another either generally or for those with particular needs. They have their own representative organisations in the form of the National Federation of Housing Associations (NATFED) which does much by the promotion of training and the circulation of 'best practice' guidance to ensure that the association movement is highly self regulating. However, because associations are generally in receipt of public funds central statutory agencies are required to ensure, inter alia, accountability.

The Housing Corporation

This exists under Part III of the Housing Associations Act (HAA) 1985, and its tasks, under section 75, are to promote the development of associations, and their proper functioning; to maintain a register of associations (which must be open to the public, see section 3) and to supervise those that are registered; to act as agent for the Secretary of State with regard to the making of grants to registered associations, and to undertake the provision of dwellings and hostels, their management, and sale, as the case may be. The Corporation must, under section 76 of the HAA 1985, act in accordance with directions given by the Secretary of State, and may, under section 77, offer legal, architectural and other technical advice to associations, or those contemplating forming an association. Section 78 imposes a duty on the Corporation to make an annual report.

The Corporation (the detailed organisation of which is contained in Schedule 6 of the HAA 1985) has power to lend to registered housing associations under section 79 of the HAA 1985, and may lend to individuals for the purpose of assisting them to acquire dwellings for their occupation from the Corporation or an association. Section 83 gives a power to guarantee, with the Secretary of State's consent, the repayment of the principal and interest on sums borrowed by registered housing associations. The aggregate amount of loans guaranteed must not exceed £300 million, though the Secretary of State may increase this up to £500 million. Section 92 of the HAA 1985 empowers the Corporation to borrow from the Secretary of State, and from other sources including the European Investment Bank or the Commission of the European Communities, or on the open money market, but these powers are subject to an aggregate limit under section 93 of £2,000m, which may be increased to up to £3,000m with Treasury consent. The Treasury may, under section 94, guarantee in such manner or on such conditions as they think fit, the repayment of the principal of interest on any sums borrowed by the Corporation from any source other than the Secretary of State. The Corporation may invest portions of its funds, see section 96 of the HAA 1985, and may, under section 98, acquire stocks and shares etc in companies. Proper accounts and audits are required by section 97, and grants in aid of administrative expenses may be paid to the Corporation by the Secretary of State under section 95. Despite the range of its powers, the Corporation is not, as its annual reports make clear, a trading body seeking to make a return on its capital. Its policy is that the money it advances to associations as loans is charged at a rate of interest sufficient to meet that on its own borrowings.

Section 88 of the HAA 1985 empowers the Corporation to acquire land by agreement, or compulsorily if so authorised by the Secretary of State, for the purpose of selling or leasing it to registered housing associations, or to provide hostels or dwellings for rent or sale itself. The procedure for compulsory acquisition is that under the Acquisition of Land Act 1981. Section 89 further empowers the Corporation to provide or improve dwellings or hostels on its land. They may insure and repair their buildings and manage them, doing all such things as are conducive to facilitating the provision or improvement of dwellings or hostels on the land, including the provision of ancillary developments for commercial, recreational or other non-domestic purposes. Section 90 authorises the disposal of land on which no dwellings have been provided to a limited range of bodies, principally registered associations or subsidiaries of the Corporation. Where dwellings have been provided, they may be disposed of to, inter alia, registered associations. The Corporation may sell or lease individual dwellings to persons for their occupation. Certain disposals require the consent of the Secretary of State, see section 90(3) to (6) of the HAA 1985. In the context of the HAA 1985 generally 'hostel' is defined by section 106(1) as a building in which is provided for persons generally, or for classes of persons, residential accommodation *not* in separate and self-contained sets, *and* either board, *or* facilities for the preparation of food adequate to the needs of those persons, or both.

Under section 46 of the Housing Act 1988 the functions of the Housing Corporation in Wales were transferred to Housing for Wales (Tai Cymru), while under section 47(1) associations with registered offices in Wales, or which are registered charities in Wales, are registered with Housing for Wales. The structure of legal regulation is, however, parallel in both England and Wales. (The equivalent body in Scotland is Scottish Homes, but the law of housing in Scotland is outside the scope of this work.) The Corporation has considerable powers of oversight over registered associations, including the power to monitor associations by requiring production of their books, accounts, and documents and to demand explanations of them, see section 27A of the HAA 1985 inserted in 1989. For the further supervisory functions of the Corporation see Chapter Three below.

The types and structures of housing associations

As associations are voluntary bodies, they are not generally subject to the rules of judicial review, so that even where they receive public funds which they are obliged to apply in particular ways, that does not turn *their normal and essential functions as landlords* into the exercise of a reviewable statutory power, see *Peabody Housing Association Ltd v Green* (1978) 38 P & CR 644, though the Corporation as a statutory regulatory agency is open to judicial review. The position *may* be different where an association has been formed to take over all the authority provided housing in an area, see *R v West Kent Housing Association, ex p Sevenoaks District Council* (1994) 'Inside Housing' 28 October, p 3.

Housing associations are further defined by section 1 of the HAA 1985 (section 5 of the Housing Act 1985). They are societies, bodies of trustees or companies established for the purpose of providing, constructing, improving, managing, facilitating or encouraging construction or improvement of housing accommodation, *and* which do not trade for profit, or whose constitution or rules prohibit the issue of capital with interest of dividend exceeding such a rate as may be prescribed by the Treasury. This covers a multiplicity of forms.

Associations which are 'societies' will in general exist under the terms of the Industrial and Provident Societies Act 1965. They will be run by a Committee of Management and may have charitable status, depending on their constitution, or they may be self-help bodies such as co-operative or self-build organisations. Charitable status applies to those associations who act to relieve 'aged, impotent and poor people'. These words must be read disjunctively, for the aged need not be necessarily also impotent or poor, nor the poor aged etc. What is required is that the body alleviates need attributable to the aged, impotent, or poor condition of the recipient of relief, and that that need is one which those persons could not alleviate, or would find it hard to alleviate, from their own resources, see *Joseph Rowntree Memorial Trust Housing Association Ltd v A-G* [1983] Ch 159, [1983] 1 All ER 288. The rules of a '1965 Act' society determine its legal entity, its powers, and the internal relationships of its members. Such societies may only do what their rules permit them to do.

Associations which are charitable trusts derive their powers from their trust deeds and will come under the jurisdiction of the Charity Commissioners under the Charities Act 1960. '1965 Act' societies are outside this jurisdiction, whether or not 'charitable', as they are supervised generally by the Registrar of Friendly Societies and the Housing Corporation. An association which is a company will derive its powers and functions from its memorandum and articles of association under the terms of the Companies Acts.

Associations which are 'fully mutual' are those with rules that restrict membership to persons who are tenants or prospective tenants of their association and which preclude granting or assigning tenancies to persons other then members. Co-operative housing associations are those that are both fully mutual and societies registered under the 1965 Act.

The next point is that an association may be registered or unregistered with the Housing Corporation under section 3 of the HAA 1985. Registered associations are eligible for loans and grant aid, but, of course, are supervised by the Corporation. An association may be registered under section 4 of the HAA 1985, as amended in 1988, if it is a registered charity, that is a charity registered under section 4 of the Charities Act 1960 (and that will apply to companies wishing to register with the Corporation), or if it is a '1965 Act' society fulfilling certain conditions. These are that it must not trade for profit, ie it does not make profit extractable by its members, and must be established for the purpose of, or have among its objects or powers, the provision, construction, improvement or management of houses to be kept available for letting, or houses for occupation by members of the association where it is fully mutual, or hostels. Where an association has additional purposes etc. they must fall within the following:

1) providing land or services or constructing, repairing or improving buildings for the benefit of an association's residents;
2) acquiring, repairing or improving houses, or creating houses by conversion to be disposed of by sale or lease;
3) building homes to be disposed of on a shared ownership basis;
4) managing residential property;
5) encouraging and giving advice on the formation of other associations;
6) providing services for, or giving advice on the running of associations;
7) providing services of any description for owners or occupiers of houses in arranging or carrying out works of maintenance, repair or improvement. See generally *Goodman v Dolphin Square Trust Ltd* (1979) 38 P & CR 257.

An association is not ineligible for registration simply because its powers include powers: to acquire commercial premises as an incidental part of a housing project; repair, improve or convert commercial premises so acquired; repair or improve houses after a tenant has exercised the Right to Buy; acquire houses to be disposed of to tenants of charitable associations. This extension to association powers in 1988 was designed to enable them to pursue certain commercial and socially useful objects ancillary to housing provision, eg to renovate shops in run down urban areas where an association is involved in housing renewal. Such activities should, however, be self financing.

Registration is at the discretion of the Housing Corporation under section 5. They consider the financial soundness of the association, its management and development abilities and what part it has to play within its proposed area of operation. Deregistration may take place under section 6(1) where the Corporation concludes that a registered body has ceased to exist or does not operate. The Corporation must give the body at least 14 days notice before removing it from the register. Registered bodies may request deregistration under section 6(4) where they have not at any time received certain specified grants. A body aggrieved by a decision to deregister may appeal under section 7 to the High Court. The Corporation also has powers under section 16 to remove members of a registered association's committee of management if they are bankrupt, or incapable of acting because of mental disorder, of have not acted, or cannot be found or do not act and absence or failure to act impede proper management. Due notice must be given of action. New members may be appointed in place of those removed, or where there are no committee members, or where it is necessary for the proper functioning of an association, by the Corporation under section 17. The powers under sections 16 and 17 may only be exercised in respect of an association which is a registered charity where the association has been granted aid under specified provisions. See section 18 of the HAA 1985. Where a registered association is a company incorporated under the Companies Act, or is a '1965 Act' society to which the winding-up provisions of the Companies Act apply under section 55(a) of the Industrial and Provident Societies Act 1965, the Housing Corporation may petition for it to be wound up on the ground that it is failing to carry out its purposes or objects properly.

Section 8 of the HAA 1985 grants a general power to registered associations to dispose of land, but this is subject to the consent of the Corporation under section 9. Such consent may be given generally or to particular associations, or in relation to particular land and may be subject to conditions.

Current or past members of registered associations, members of their families, companies of which they, or members of their families, are directors may not, under section 13 of the HAA 1985, be made gifts or paid sums by way of dividend or bonus by a registered association. Payment of interest on capital lent to an association in accordance with its rules is allowed. Sums paid in contravention may be recovered, and the Corporation has powers to direct the taking of proceedings to make such recovery. The Corporation also has powers to specify under section 14, the sums which a registered association which is also a '1965 Act' Society may give by way of fees or remuneration of expenses to its officers and employees, and the reimbursement of committee member's expenses. Committee members are not allowed to profit from their membership. Section 15 prohibits registered associations which are '1965 Act' societies from making payments or granting benefits to, committee members, officers and employees, their close relatives and concerns trading for profit of which any such person is a principal proprietor or manager save as allowed, for example as wages.

Certain other actions by registered associations which are also '1965 Act' societies are also subject to control by the Corporation, these are changes of rules, see section 19, and proposals to amalgamate with another society, or to dissolve, see section 21. Where a '1965 Act' society is dissolved under the 1965 Act, section 23 of the HAA 1985 directs that so much of its property as remains after its liabilities have been met is transferred to the Corporation, or to such other registered associations as the Corporation specifies. The accounting requirements for associations are laid down in section 24 to 27 of the HAA 1985.

Local authorities and housing associations

Section 58 of the HAA 1985 empowers authorities to promote the formation or extension of associations, and to assist them. A number of authorities have done this as part of a programme of voluntary divestment of housing stock. They may make grants or loans to associations, subscribe for share or loan capital in an association, guarantee sums borrowed by associations on such terms as they think fit, save that they may not limit the aggregate of rents payable in respect of relevant dwellings, nor specify a limit which the rent of a dwelling is not to exceed. Thus authorities may not impose any restrictions concerning rent on associations aided. Giving such grants, loans and guarantees is generally restricted to registered associations under section 60. The consent of the Secretary of State under sections 24 and 25 of the Local Government Act 1988 may also be needed where financial assistance is given in connection with the acquisition, construction, conversion, rehabilitation, improvement, maintenance or management of housing to be let by, inter alia, associations. Authorities may make use of these powers to promote the work of associations within their areas, and may seek rights to nominate tenants to association developments, sometimes up to 50% of the lettings.

Housing trusts

A housing trust under section 2 of the HAA 1985 (section 6 of the Housing Act 1985) is a corporation or body of persons which is required by its constitutive instrument to use all its funds, including surpluses arising from its operations, to provide housing accommodation *or* is required to devote all, or substantially all, its funds to charitable purposes and *in fact* uses all, or substantially all, such funds to provide housing. Such a trust may be a registered charity, and registered also under section 4 of the HAA 1985. Housing trusts may, under section 35, sell or lease to the local authority houses provided by the trust, or make over the management thereof to the authority; this power does not apply to registered associations, though in other respects such trusts qualify as associations. A housing trust which is a charity may grant secure tenancies. Housing trusts may be initiated and partly funded by central government bringing together local authorities with run down estates and sources of private finance so that non profit-making trusts are set up to take over estates.

Conclusion

In this chapter we have attempted to provide readers with an insight into the main policy developments and issues that surround and inform an understanding of public housing and, towards that end, have included an introduction to the current legal framework. This mix of a 'long view' followed by current practice is, we believe, necessary partly because there are many continuities over the decades and the present day legacy of public housing, and public housing law is deeply embedded in the past. In particular we are anxious to make clear that a purely 'legal' approach to public sector housing law or, by the same token, an exclusively administrative or policy centred focus provides a very one-dimensional view of what is a complex reality.

Because this is a textbook and to some extent a work of reference we do not compromise in detailing the current state of the case law or statutory duties. Where appropriate we weave into the text explanations of the wider policy context and administrative practice because it is our firm belief that at the implementation stage factors relating to both law and policy coalesce and shape the evolution of public sector housing.

Further reading

History of Housing

Burnett, J *A Social History of Housing 1815-1985* (Methuen, 1986)
Holmans, A *Housing Policy in Britain: a History* (Croom Helm, 1987)
Lowe, S and Hughes, D (eds) *A New Century of Social Housing* (Leicester University Press, 1991)
Merrett, S *State Housing in Britain* (Routledge and Kegan Paul, 1979)
Swenarton, M *Homes Fit For Heroes* (Heinemann, 1981)

Housing Policy

Birchall, J (ed) *Housing Policy in the 1990s* (Routledge, 1992)
Clapham D, Kemp, P and Smith, S *Housing and Social Policy* (Macmillan, 1990)
Malpass, P and Means, R (eds) *Implementing Housing Policy* (Open University Press, 1993)
Malpass, P and Murie, A *Housing Policy and Practice* (Macmillan, 1993)

Chapter Two

The disposal of social housing

Introduction

Sale of *council* housing has been an issue ever since municipalities first began to provide housing. Central and local policies have varied greatly from time to time and place to place. It has been the subject of fierce and often bitter controversy. This chapter is concerned with individual disposals under the 'right-to-buy' (RTB) (a central plank of government policy on housing since 1980) and block disposal under the Housing Acts 1985 and 1988. When speaking of disposal of social housing one is referring to disposal of council houses. The law is principally concerned with reducing the role of authorities as active landlords while boosting that of associations. Before that law is examined, however, some examination of the development and impact of disposal policies must take place.

The sale of council houses

Before 1980 the sale of council houses was a significant if subsidiary issue in the century-long history of public housing. Because the emphasis until the 1970s was on high output of dwellings to meet burgeoning housing demand selling council houses made very little impact on the rapidly expanding public housing sector. As we argued in Chapter One the legitimacy of council housing has always been somewhat fragile in the face of private sector competition and, since the 1930s, the drive to become a nation of home owners. Indeed, the origins of council housing in the modern period, in the shape of the Housing of the Working Classes Act 1890 incorporated the requirement that council houses should be sold into the private sector within ten years of their completion. As we saw this legislation pre-dated the historic decision on housing subsidies leading to the beginning of the era of mass council house building after the First World War and very few council dwellings were actually sold under the terms of the 1890 legislation.

During the inter-war period power existed for the sale of council houses but required Ministerial consent. It was not widely used because the notion of rental housing as a desirable, indeed, competitive form of housing provision was widely accepted. Moreover, according to the conditions of consent sales had to be made to obtain the highest possible price for the dwelling (for a detailed account see Forrest, R and Murie, A *Selling the Welfare State: the Privatisation of Public Housing*, Routledge, 1988). During the Second World War and throughout the period of post-war Labour government consent for the sale of publicly rented housing was withdrawn. The return of the Conservatives to power in 1952 changed the thrust of housing policy; building licenses in the private sector were revoked and along with this change a general consent to encourage the sale of council houses was issued in 1952. This enabled local authorities to sell with notification to the Minister following the completion of the sale. The Housing Act 1952 also removed the requirement that the authority should obtain the highest possible price. Authorities were empowered to pre-empt resale of dwellings if any attempt was made to sell or lease them within five years. Guidance was further given in the general consent regarding the sale price which was generally to be not less than twenty times the net rent for pre-1949 dwellings and the whole cost (land and construction) for newer property (Forrest and Murie, 1988).

The impact of this policy was very limited and by 1956 only 5,800 council houses had been sold under the terms of the general consent, involving about one-third of authorities. In the period up to the election of the Labour Government in 1964 sales continued to be limited despite the issuing of a new general consent in 1960 which sought to ensure authorities recovered, as a minimum, the construction costs of post-war dwellings. Effective demand continued to be very muted and between 1957 and 1964 only 16,000 council houses were sold, a small fraction of the hundreds of thousands of new dwellings built at the time (see Chapter One). According to Forrest and Murie, Labour did not reverse the general consent because they supported sales but rather because the government did not wish to damage the delicate state of central-local relations by appearing to exert excessive control from the centre. A number of Conservative councils flew in the face of Labour's reticence particularly in areas of high housing stress and positively promoted sales. Birmingham was a particularly vociferous proponent of council house sales and provoked the government to issue a Circular which defined the terms and conditions of sales more fully. It required that sale prices should be based on the vacant possession market value of the property with a discount of up to 20% to take account of the restrictions on resale and valuation costs. Considerable pressure grew within the Labour Party against sales on the grounds that it was unjustifiable to sell public assets for private gain. The government refused to withdraw the general consent but issued a new Circular (42/68) which imposed limits on the sale of council houses in the main conurbations.

Circular 42/68 was withdrawn immediately the Conservative Party took office again in 1970, under Edward Heath, and sales were again permitted on the same terms as the 1967 general consent. The Conservatives espoused home ownership as a core doctrine and this commitment overrode every other consideration. Support for sales strengthened particularly in the Party's ascendent right-wing which was opposed in principle to council housing and there were moves to increase the discount for what became increasingly known as 'right to buy' sales from 20% to 30%. Sales peaked during the Heath government in 1972 when over 46,000 council houses were sold (*Housing and Construction Statistics*, London, HMSO). Pressure to increase this level of sales intensified with some politicians arguing for the adoption of a policy of compulsory sales because many authorities refused to sell 'their' stock. But the boom in house prices which took place in 1971-72 blunted the edge of the sales policy because, without considerably extending the level of discount, prices were becoming unaffordable. During the Conservative's period of office (1970-1974) about 100,000 council dwellings were sold.

The Conservative Party's 1974 General Election Manifesto included a commitment for tenants of three years standing to buy their house with a one third discount from its market value. The Labour Party had made no such pledges and on resuming government in 1974 simply continued the general consent from 1967 for authorities to sell if they so wished with a 20% discount. Due to considerable gains made by the Conservatives in the local elections during the Wilson/Callaghan governments sales in some areas increased rapidly. In 1975 only 2,700 houses were sold but by 1978 this had risen to over 30,000. By now the Conservatives had adopted a housing policy which was overtly centred on the right of tenants to buy their dwelling and the Manifesto committment for the 1979 election was clear and unequivocal in this regard, with no mention of housing need, homelessness or new house building.

On assuming office a new Circular restored the 1970 position and increased the permissable level of discount on the market price. This was, however, merely a holding operation while major housing legislation on the issue of the right to buy, a new subsidy system, and other issues was drafted. In the Housing Act 1980 all the previous limitations arising from local discretion and general housing needs were replaced by a system of centrally directed, compulsory sales with a much more generous level of discount. Tenants of three years standing were entitled to an immediate 33% discount and for every additional year of tenancy a further 1% discount was added, up to a maximum of 50% of the property valuation.

These terms were further extended in the Housing and Building Control Act 1984, including extension of the RTB *inter alia* to secure tenants in public sector leasehold property, tenants of housing for the disabled, and qualification for children succeeding to secure tenancies (previously discretionary). The residence qualification was reduced to two years and the maximum discount was increased from 50% to 60%. The Housing Act 1985, which is described in detail below, consolidated all the legislation to that time on individual RTB sales.

Effects of the right to buy

Following the 1980 legislation RTB sales accelerated rapidly. Even though the section of the Act permitting sales to secure tenants of three years standing did not come into force until early October 1980 over 81,000 council dwellings were sold, mostly under previous schemes. In 1981 the figure exceeded 100,000 and sales peaked at 201,880 in 1982 with over 90% of these sales being under the RTB. As we noted in Chapter One this was a period of sweeping and radical change in the definition and role of public sector housing and was accompanied by a dramatic reduction in public spending on housing, falling by more than 50% beween 1979 and 1987 (although somewhat mitigated by increases in spending on housing benefit). The point to be made here is that council house building declined very rapidly. Indeed as early as 1980 itself the output of new council houses was less than the number of sales of council dwellings representing a net reduction to authority stock for the first time since 1919.

It is important to note that the pattern of these sales was very uneven geographically and socially. A high proportion of sales were in the south of England where owner occupation was already high. The vast majority of RTB tenants were midle-aged, skilled manual workers with adolescent or grown-up children. Very few high-rise flats were sold compared to the rapid purchase of houses on the more suburban estates, and so these sales created a much less diverse housing stock causing considerable housing management problems. The 1984 Greater London Council Survey, *The implications of council house sales for local authority housing in London*, indicated that 94% of sales had been of houses, while three-quarters of sales had taken place in the outer London Boroughs. The major effect of the RTB policy has been, therefore, to create a residual housing sector increasingly occupied by the poorest sections of society and disproportionately representing the long-term unemployed, elderly people and single-parent households living in less desirable housing types such as high rise flats, and less favoured housing locations in inner city areas or on socially stigmatised 'hard-to-let' estates. (See further *Roof* November/December 1982, p 19 and January/February 1984, p 7). As we saw in Chapter One this residualisation has also come about because of the low level of re-lets available in a shrinking housing sector and the statutory duties of the authorities towards homeless households. The average income of council tenants fell from 73% of the national average in 1981 to only 48% by 1990 (Page, D *Building for Communities: a study of new housing association estates*, Joseph Rowntree Foundation, 1993).

Problems for tenants arising from RTB

It should not be assumed that for purchasers an automatic housing utopia has followed the exercise of RTB. Sudden changes in financial circumstances, consequent for example on short time working and redundancy, have led to some purchasers being unable to meet mortgage commitments. This has been so particularly in the recession of the late 1980s and early 1990s. Owner occupation may be desirable for many, but there are some who should be seriously counselled not to exercise RTB. This is especially so where tenants are allured by prospects of generous discounts: house purchase is an expensive business involving not just mortgage repayments, but also the payment of council tax and maintenance costs.

The 1991 DoE survey, *The Right to Buy: A national follow-up survey of tenants of council houses in England,* found that 18% of purchasers had experienced problems in keeping up with mortgage payments in the context of also having to meet repair and maintenance costs and other household bills. 5% had found difficulty in changing to budgeting on a monthly mortgage payment basis as opposed to weekly payment of rent. Particular problems have been encountered by those who have taken long leases of flats subsequently found to be unsaleable because of high repair costs in respect of the blocks in which they are situated; while some mortgage lenders are unhappy about lending on flats with particular modes of construction, or above particular levels. In other cases the housing of homeless persons in flat blocks makes flats there unmortgageable: *The Times* on 26 January 1994 estimated there were 120,000 'former council tenants ... trapped in homes they cannot sell and facing bills they cannot pay'. Partly to meet this problem the government announced on 29 June 1994 a 'buy-back' plan whereby unsaleable flats may be sold back to local authorites in *part exchange* for a more desirable dwelling. Authorities already have a discretionary power to repurchase, and this may be supplemented by delegated legislation and circular guidance.

Financial consequences of RTB

By 1987, at the end of the second term of Conservative government under Margaret Thatcher, over one million houses and flats had been sold by authorities and New Towns under the terms of the 1980 legislation and their subsequent amendments. This scale of depletion was quite unprecedented and for a total original stock of just under six millon dwellings was a massive transfer into owner occupation. In total between 1979 and 1990, over 1.5 million council dwellings were sold representing consideably in excess of 20% of the whole stock (Forrest R and Murie, A *Selling the Welfare State* 2nd edn, Routledge, 1990). Forrest calculated that the value of the discounts given to facilitate these purchases was in excess of £2,700 million (Forrest, R et al

Home Ownership:Differentiation and Fragmentation, Hyman, 1990). The RTB has been one of the most successfully implemented social policies in the post-war era but the financial cost of achieving it has been staggering and as we observed above the social cost has been equally dramatic. Council housing accounted for nearly 32% of households when the Conservatives took office under Mrs Thatcher in 1979 and at the end of her term of government had declined to only 22% and currently accounts for about 20% of households. Nearly £23 billion has been generated by council house sales since 1979 making it by far the largest privatisation of public assets during the Thatcher era. But very little of this went back into new building and under the 'new financial regime' most of the accumulated recepts have to be used to pay off historic debts (see Chapter Four for detail).

1987-1990: Large scale disposals

After 1987, as we saw in Chapter One, a new phase of policy developed partly around the growing awareness of the need for a rental sector of housing. The RTB was concerned to move better off council tenants individually into home ownership. The approach after 1987 was to continue the RTB policy but to consider strategies for the wholesale transfer of council stock to new landlords either in the form of the 'independent' private sector or housing associations. One form of this policy took shape in the form of Housing Action Trusts (HATs) announced in the Housing White Paper of 1987, followed by a Consultation Document and subsequent legislation contained in the Housing Act 1988 (see Chapter One for more detail).

HATS were not the principal form of wholesale disposals and it was through the process known as Large Scale Voluntary Stock (LSVT) transfer, from the late 1980s, that a very large quantity of council housing was sold to a variety of types of housing association, some existing and some specially created.

Voluntary transfer of stock to housing associations

Between 1988 and 1994, 31 local authorities, predominantly in rural areas in the south of England, and nearly all controlled by Conservative councils, have divested themselves of their housing, involving 140,000 tenancies. The motivation for this form of disposal was quite varied but mainly concerned anxieties about central government policy changes such as the threat of Tenants' Choice transfers to predatory landlords under the Housing Act 1988 and the consequences of the introduction of the 'new financial regime' under the Local Government and Housing Act 1989 (for example, the threat of sharp increases in rents due to the incorporation of Housing Benefit subsidy into the Housing Revenue Account). One very clear motive behind LSVTs was the possibility of generating very large proceeds from the sale of housing stock. The London Borough of Bromley, for example, raised £117 million from the sale of their stock to Broomleigh Housing Association and were able to wipe out the authority's capital debts with one fell swoop (*Independent* 1 August, 1994).

In its first phase LSVT disposals typically have been stimulated at the local level, by officers and councillors rather than tenants, and it is clear that while LSVTs were not initially inspired by central government, they are now controlled by them and are potentially a radical option for the disposal of very large quantities of urban as well as rural housing stocks.

Powers for local authorities to dispose of land and dwellings, subject to the consent of the Secretary of State, were incorporated in the Housing Act 1985 and further extended in regard to consultation procedures with tenants in the Housing Act 1988. Subsequently the DoE and the Housing Corporation have clarified the terms and conditions on which such transfers can be made, notably to ensure the independence of the new association from the local authority. Although essentially a local initiative LSVTs have been controlled by central government because of the implications any mass exodus from local authority control would have on the available supply of private finance for the housing associations' development programme (ADP). At the heart of the LSVT process is the willingness of private financiers to sponsor the purchase of the authority's housing stock. Private finance is very scarce due to the limitations on this class of lending imposed by the banking regulators. Its use in sponsoring LSVTs has jeopardised the Government's desire to increase the privately funded element in development finance for ordinary housing associations funded through the so called HAG system (Housing Association Grant). LSVTs absorb large amounts of private finance because they are a much easier and more secure investment vehicle than HAG sponsored schemes. It was estimated in 1991 that an additional 20 LSVTs per annum would require £1.1 billion of private finance which is double the amount needed by housing associations to complete their HAG funded schemes (cited in Mullins, D, Niner, P and Riseborough, R 'Large-scale voluntary transfers' in *Implementing Housing Policy*, Open Univeresity Press, 1993).

Interest has been shown in so called 'trickle down' transfers whereby council housing is gradually transferred to a housing association at a change of an individual tenancy. This scheme is already being used in a diverse group of authorities because it has the potential to avoid large outlays of capital inherent in the LSVT route. This scheme is also being scrutinised by the DoE as an alternative to large scale disposal.

As we write, in the summer of 1994, Labour local authorities are beginning to co-operate with the notion of large scale transfer because there is a considerable potential for the use of the capital receipts which would be generated in the construction of new public housing, which it is generally recognised is needed to meet housing demand. Tenants in Labour controlled urban areas are likely to support such schemes because of guarantees that rent increases will be limited. It should be noted, however, that figures released by the Audit Commission in 1993 (*Who Wins? Voluntary Housing Transfers*) showed that though stock transfer leads to increased expenditure on housing repairs and new development, it also resulted in rent increases of, on average, £14.30 per week. A number of studies of the implications and practicality of large scale disposal of council housing in urban authorities are due to report in the autumn of 1994 but it seems certain that the government will press forward with such schemes fairly rapidly and probably in advance of the findings of the research (*Independent*, August, 1994).

The 'right to buy' under the Housing Act 1985 (as amended)

RTB is enshrined in Part V of the 1985 Act, and unless otherwise stated all subsequent references are to that legislation.

Section 118 grants secure tenants (see Chapter Three for the definition of 'secure tenant') the right to acquire the freehold of their dwellings where they are houses, and the landlord owns the freehold, or, where the dwelling is a flat, or where the landlord does not own the freehold, to take a long lease of it. Dwelling-houses and flats are defined by section 183 so that:

(a)   where a building is divided horizontally the units into which it is divided are *not* houses;

(b)   where a building is not structurally detached from its neighbours it is *not* a house if a material part of it lies above or below the remainder of the structure (this covers maisonettes and flats built over shop developments);

(c)   where a building is divided vertically the units may be houses so a dwelling in a terrace is a house, provided it is otherwise a structure reasonably so called.

Any dwelling which is not a house must be treated as a flat for sale purposes. Any land used for the purposes of the dwelling may be included in the disposal by agreement between the parties (section 184(2)) and land let with a dwelling is to be treated as part of the dwelling unless it is agricultural land exceeding two acres (section 184(1)).

RTB only arises after the *secure tenant* has enjoyed the status of a *public sector tenant* for a period of not less than two years, or for a number of shorter periods amounting together to two years. During that period neither the landlord nor the dwelling-house need have been the same throughout so a secure tenant can build up entitlement to buy, for example, during a time in which he/she moves from one secure tenancy with one authority to another, see section 119 and Schedule 4.

A 'public sector tenancy' is one where the landlord is, inter alia, a local authority, a new town corporation, a housing action trust, an urban development corporation, or a registered housing association which is not a co-operative association, or such other landlord as is specified by the Secretary of State, see SI 1992/1703 which brings government departments and ministers, amongst a host of other bodies, into the list of relevant landlords.

A period qualifies towards exercise of RTB, under Schedule 4 paras 2-5A, where the secure tenant, or his/her spouse (provided they are living together at the relevant time) or a deceased spouse of his/hers (provided they were living together at the time of death) was a public sector tenant, or was the spouse of such a person and occupied the house of which that person was the tenant as his/her only or principal home. Joint tenants are deemed to fulfil these requirements provided they occupied the dwelling as their only or principal home. Likewise where the public sector tenant of a dwelling has died, or has otherwise ceased to be a public sector tenant of the relevant dwelling, and thereupon a child of that tenant who before occupied the dwelling as his/her only or principal home becomes the new public sector tenant of the dwelling, a period during which that new tenant, since reaching the age of 16, occupied as his/her only or principal home a dwelling-house of which a parent was sole or joint public sector tenant, counts towards qualifying to exercise RTB, *provided* that that period was the portion of time at the end of which the new tenant became the public sector tenant or it was a portion of time ending not *more* than two years before that date. Time spent by the secure tenant, or his/her living or deceased spouse, in accommodation provided for regular armed forces also counts towards qualification. Similar provisions apply in respect of periods during which the tenant enjoyed the Preserved Right to Buy, see further below. The periods may be aggregated together where applicable and necessary. The essential point is that though RTB attaches to the dwelling of which a qualifying person is the tenant, it is those periods spent as a public sector tenant in the circumstances outlined above that qualify the tenant to exercise the right.

Where a secure tenancy is a joint tenancy, irrespective of whether each of the joint tenants occupies the dwelling as his/her 'only or principal home' RTB belongs jointly to all of them, or to such one as they may agree. Such an agreement is only valid if the person who is to exercise RTB occupies the dwelling as his/her 'only or principal home', see section 118(2). In any case a secure tenant may, under section 123, join up to three members of his/her family in RTB even if they are not joint tenants provided those members occupy the dwelling as their only or principal home, and:
(a)   they are either the tenant's spouse, or
(b)   they have been residing with the tenant throughout the period of 12 months preceding the notice claiming RTB, or
(c)   the landlord consents.

The claim to join members of a family in the purchase must be made in the notice claiming to exercise RTB.

By virtue of section 186 a person is a member of a tenant's family if he/ she is his/her spouse, parent, grandparent, child, grandchild, brother, sister, uncle, aunt, nephew or niece: relationships by marriage count as relationships by blood; half-blood counts as whole blood, and step-children count as ordinary children, with illegitimate children being treated as legitimate, and also treating persons living together as man and wife as being members of a family. Once a section 123 notice is effective RTB belongs to the tenant and the 'joined' persons and they are to be treated as joint tenants. Such a deemed joint tenant has sufficient security to be able to press a sale to completion even where otherwise not qualified to be a successor tenant under section 87 (see Chapter Five below), see *Harrow London Borough Council v Tonge* (1992) 25 HLR 99. Contrast, however, *Bradford Metropolitan City Council v McMahon* [1993] 4 All ER 237, [1994] 1 WLR 52 where a tenant began the process of purchase and died without completing it, but did *not* join any family member in the transaction.

Section 120 and Schedule 5 (as amended) lay down certain exceptions where RTB does not apply. These are:

(a)   Where the landlord is a housing trust or is a housing association *and* a charity.

(b)   Where the landlord is a co-operative housing association.

(c)   Where the landlord is a housing association which at no time received public funding under certain specified statutes.

(d)   Where the landlord does not own the freehold or some other interest sufficient to grant a lease, in the case of a house, for a term exceeding 21 years, or, in the case of a flat, for a term of not less than 50 years.

(e)   Where the dwelling-house is comprised in a building held by the landlord mainly for non-housing purposes *and* consisting mainly of non-housing accommodation, or is situated in a cemetery, *and* the dwelling was let to the tenant or a predecessor in consequence of the tenant's or that predecessor's, employment by the landlord or the local authority, etc.

(f)   Where the dwelling has features substantially different from ordinary dwellings designed to make it suitable for occupation by physically disabled persons, *and* it is part of a group which it is the landlord's practice to let for occupation by such persons, *and* social services or special facilities are provided in close proximity to assist those persons.

In this context note that in *Freeman v Wansbeck District Council* [1984] 2 All ER 746 the Court of Appeal held that the special features referred to above comprise matters such as ramps instead of staircases, special doors, cooking surfaces at special heights, etc, and *not* facilities such as additional downstairs lavatories. The special features will be 'designed' to make a dwelling suitable for occupation by a disabled person where the building is designed and built with those features;

merely to add special features to an ordinary dwelling with the *intention* of having a disabled person reside there is not enough.

(g)   Where the dwelling is one of a group of houses which it is the landlord's practice to let for occupation by persons who are suffering, or have suffered, from mental disorder, *and* social services or special facilities, are provided to assist those persons.

(h)   Where the dwelling is one of a group particularly suitable, having regard to location, size, design, heating systems and other features for occupation to elderly persons, and which it is the landlord's practice to let for occupation by persons aged 60 or more or for occupation by such persons *and* physically disabled persons, *and* special facilities consisting of, or including, warden alarm and common room facilities are provided for such persons in close proximity.

(i)   Where the dwelling is particularly suited having regard to its location, size, design, heating system and other features for occupation by elderly persons, *and* it was let to the tenant (or his/her predecessor in title) for occupation by a person aged 60 or more. But in determining suitability no regard is to be had to features provided by the tenant. Matters of dispute arising under this exception are to be determined by the Secretary of State provided they are raised by the tenant. The exception only applies to dwellings first let before 1 January 1990, see further DoE Circular 13/93 Part II and Annex B which *inter alia* lists the matters making a dwelling suitable for occupation by elderly persons.

(j)   Where the dwelling is held by the landlord on a Crown tenancy, subject to certain exceptions.

A sale in contravention of an exception though technically void may still pass the property to a purchaser *provided* the sale has been registered. The title will be protected by the Land Registration Act 1925, and the court may decline to rectify the register, see *Hounslow London Borough Council v Hare* (1990) 24 HLR 9.

Under section 121 RTB cannot be exercised where either:

(a)   the tenant is, or will be, obliged to give up possession of the house in pursuance of a court order, or

(b)   where a bankruptcy petition is pending against the person to whom RTB belongs, or where he/she is an undischarged bankrupt, or has made a composition with creditors. Where a possession order in respect of a council house or flat is obtained by the landlord *after* the tenant has served notice claiming to exercise RTB, the tenant is precluded from continuing with the purchase, because exercising RTB is a continuing process until the sale is completed, and so the tenant can be prevented from exercising the right at any time before completion if any of the circumstances mentioned above occur, see *Enfield London Borough Council v McKeon* [1986] 2 All ER 730, [1986] 1 WLR 1007.

The position is similar where a secure tenant loses that status before a purchase is completed, for example by quitting the property, see *Sutton London Borough Council v Swann* (1985) 18 HLR 140, or by moving out to take up a residential job and sub-letting the house in breach of tenancy condition, see *Muir Group Housing Association Ltd v Thornley* (1992) 91 LGR 1 or by dying before completion, see *Bradford Metropolitan City Council v McMahon*, supra. However, once all matters concerning transfer to the would-be purchaser have been finalised so that an injunction could be obtained to force completion, possession proceedings cannot prevent the exercise of RTB, see *Dance v Welwyn Hatfield District Council* (1990) 22 HLR 339.

But as was explained in the *Bradford* case, there are five stages in exercising RTB: (i) claim to exercise the right; (ii) admission of the claim; (iii) statement of the purchase price and the terms of sale; (iv) agreement on the terms; and (v) transfer, which can be enforced by injunction, under section 138. It appears implicit in the legislation that the would-be purchaser must remain a secure tenant until the fifth event: RTB ceases if there is no longer a secure tenant immediately after or within a reasonable time of the fourth event, eg because of death.

The price to be paid for the house or flat

By section 126(1)(a) the price is the 'value at the relevant time' which, under section 127, is the price the dwelling would fetch on the open market at that time, that is the date, under section 122(2), on which the tenant's notice claiming to exercise RTB was served, on a willing vendor basis but subject to certain assumptions:

(a)   the vendor was selling for an estate in fee simple, or was granting a lease, for the appropriate term defined in Schedule 6 paragraph 12, *generally* 125 years, at a ground rent of not more than £10 per annum *with vacant possession*;

(b)   neither the tenant nor a member of his/her family residing with him wished to acquire the property;

(c)   any improvements made by the tenant or his/her predecessors in title together with any failure by them to keep the property in good internal repair are to be disregarded;

(d)   that the conveyance, or grant of the lease, is on the terms laid down in Part V of the Housing Act 1985;

(e)   that any service charges or improvement contributions payable will not be less than the amounts to be expected in accordance with notices served under section 125 (see below).

This price must be discounted according to section 126(1)(b). The discount is, under section 129 as amended, in the case of a house, 32% plus 1% for each complete year by which the qualifying period of entitlement exceeds two years up to a maximum of 60%, and, in the case of a flat, 44% plus 2% for each complete year by which the qualifying period exceeds two years, up to a maximum of 70%. Under section 129(2A) the Secretary of State may order maximum and minimum discounts and the amount of percentage increase per annum to be *increased*, and, under section 129(2B) such orders may make different provision with respect to different cases or types of case. The qualifying period for discount entitlement is calculated, as is the period for determining qualification to exercise RTB, by reference to Schedule 4 (see above). Thus discount entitlement is built up where the secure tenant, or his/her spouse (provided they are living together at the relevant time, see section 122(2) supra), or a deceased spouse of his/hers (provided they were living together at the time of death) was a public sector tenant (see above) or was the spouse of a public sector tenant and occupied as his/her only or principal home the dwelling of which spouse was such a tenant. A person who, as a joint tenant under a public sector tenancy, occupied a dwelling house as his/her only principal home, is treated as having been the public sector tenant under that tenancy. Likewise entitlement will be built up by the child of a public sector tenant of a dwelling where that tenant has died or otherwise ceased to be such a tenant, and thereupon the child, having occupied the dwelling as his/her only or principal home becomes the new public sector tenant. A period during which that new tenant, since reaching the age of 16, occupied as his/her only or principal home a dwelling house of which a parent of his/hers was the public sector tenant, provided that period was the period at the end of which the child became the new public sector tenant *or* it was an earlier period ending *two years or less* before that period, is to be treated as a period during which the child was a public sector tenant.

The legislation is retrospective so that time spent, for example, as an authority or association etc, tenant before 1980 counts towards discount entitlement and qualifying to exercise RTB.

Where two joint tenants exercise RTB, Schedule 4 is applied so that for the secure tenant is substituted that one of the joint tenants whose discount entitlement is greatest.

There is to be deducted, under section 130, from the discount an amount equal to any previous discount qualifying because it was given before the relevant time on a conveyance or lease by a public sector landlord, *and* was given to the person, or one of the persons exercising RTB, *or* to the spouse of that person (provided they are living together at the relevant time) or to a deceased spouse of that person (provided they were living together at the time of death). Furthermore, under section 131 as amended, except where the Secretary of State so determines, the amount of discount may not reduce the purchase price below the amount which, in accordance with his determination, represents so much of the costs incurred in respect of the dwelling in the period of eight years before the tenant claimed to exercise RTB. If the price before discount is below that amount there is no discount. Furthermore discount may not reduce the price by more than such a sum as is prescribed from time to time by the Secretary of State.

Where the price is discounted section 155 requires the purchaser to covenant to repay *on demand* a specified amount of discount, if within a period of three years he/she further conveys, leases, or assigns, as the case may be, the dwelling acquired. The amount of discount repayable is the discount reduced by one-third for each complete year elapsing after the date of transfer to the purchaser. Liability to repay discount is, under section 156, a charge on the premises.

Liability to repay arises in respect of 'relevant disposals' as outlined above, see further section 159 and later material on restrictions on the resale of dwellings in rural areas. However, liability to repay does not arise if the disposal is 'exempted' under section 160. This will be considered in greater detail below, but note that it exempts disposals under wills and intestacies, under the terms of the family provision and inheritance legislation, certain disposals within families and disposals of dwelling houses under section 24 of the Matrimonial Causes Act 1973 (property adjustment orders in connection with matrimonial proceedings). In *R v Rushmoor Borough Council, ex p Barrett* (1988) 20 HLR 366, a married couple had purchased their council house at a discount. The conveyance required repayment of discount should they dispose of the property within the period specified by law. One year later the marriage was dissolved and within three months the court made an order requiring the home to be sold and the proceeds divided equally. This order was made under *section 24A* of the 1973 Act. It was held an 'exempted disposal' under section 24 of the 1973 Act is not one where a dwelling is sold and the proceeds divided, but one for example, where a house is transferred between former spouses so that one of them continues to live in the house after transfer, gaining no liquid cash advantage thereby. The sale in the present case was *not* an exempted disposal and there was liability to repay discount.

Exercising RTB

Under section 122(1) the tenant must serve on the landlord written notice claiming to exercise RTB. If this notice is not withdrawn the landlord must, under section 124, serve written counter notice *generally* within four weeks either admitting the right, or denying it, stating the reasons why, in the landlord's opinion, it does not exist. Disputes as to RTB are determined by the county court, see section 181. Once RTB has been established the landlord must serve, under section 125, as amended, within eight weeks where the right is to acquire the freehold, or within twelve weeks where it is to acquire a leasehold interest, a further notice on the tenant. This will describe the dwelling-house and state:

(a)   the price at which the tenant is entitled to purchase, and further stating the value of the dwelling at the relevant time, and any improvements disregarded under section 127 in determining value;

(b)   the appropriate discount, and the discount period taken into account under section 129;

(c)   the provisions which should be included in the conveyance/lease;

(d)   where the notice states provisions which would enable the landlord to recover service charges or improvement contributions, it must also contain estimates and other information required by sections 125A (service charges) and 125B (improvement contributions);

(e)   a description of any structural defect known to the landlord affecting the dwelling or the building in which it is situated;

(f)   rights to have the value of the dwelling fixed by the district valuer, and rights under sections 125D and 125E (see further below).

Under section 125A the landlord's section 125 notice must state as regards service charges the estimate of average annual amounts (at current prices) which would be payable in respect of each head of charge in the 'reference period' and the aggregate of those estimated amounts, and shall also contain a statement of the reference period adopted for estimate purposes. For the purposes of sections 125A and 125B (see below) the 'reference period' is effectively five years beginning on a date specified reasonably by the landlord as a date by which the conveyance/lease etc will be completed, such date not to be more than six months after the section 125 notice is given. With regard to *flats* certain charges must be separately itemised under section 125A(2), which provides that the notice must, as regards service charges in respect of repairs (including works to make good structural defects) contain:

 (i)   in respect of works itemised in the notice, estimates of the amount (at current prices) of the likely cost of, and of the tenant's likely contribution in respect of, each item, and the aggregates of those costs and contributions;

 (ii)   for non-itemised works, an estimate of average annual costs (at current prices) which the landlord considers likely to be payable by the tenant;

(iii)   a statement of the reference period adopted for the purpose of the estimates;

(iv)   a statement of the effect of paragraph 16B of Schedule 6 (see below) and

 (v)   a statement of the effect of section 450A (see below).

Paragraph 16B of Schedule 6 provides that where the lease of a flat requires the tenant to pay service charges in respect of repairs (including works to make good structural defects) liability to pay in respect of costs incurred in the 'initial period' (see later) is restricted, so that the tenant is not required to pay in respect of works itemised in the estimates contained in the section 125 notice any more than the amount shown as the tenant's estimated contribution in respect of that item, together with an allowance for inflation. In respect of works not itemised the tenant is not required to pay at a rate exceeding:

(a)   as regards parts of the 'initial period' falling within the reference period (see above) for estimates contained in the section 125 notice the estimated average amount shown in the estimates;

(b)   as regards parts of the initial period falling outside the reference period, the average rate produced by averaging over the reference period all works for which estimates are contained in the notice, together with, in each case, an allowance for inflation. Such inflation allowances are to be calculated according to methods prescribed by the Secretary of State under paragraph 16D of Schedule 6. The 'initial period' of a lease is effectively five years from the date of its grant.

Section 450A provides that the Secretary of State may provide by regulations that where the lease of a flat has been granted in pursuance of RTB and the landlord is the *housing authority (which includes a registered housing association) who granted the lease, or another housing authority*, the tenant shall have the 'right to a loan', to be charged on the security of the flat, see section 450C, in respect of certain service charges. These are charges in respect of repairs (including works for making good structural defects) payable in the period beginning with the grant of the lease, and ending, generally, with its tenth anniversary. The right may be specified by the regulations only to arise in respect of specified amounts of a service charge. Where the landlord *is a housing association* the right is to a loan from the Housing Corporation. In any other case it is a right to leave the whole or part of the service charge outstanding. (Section 450B creates a *power* to grant loans etc in circumstances falling outside the right to a loan.) See further SI 1992/1708 and DoE Circular 21/92.

'Service charges' are defined by section 621A to be amounts payable by purchasers or lessees of premises which are payable directly or indirectly for services, repairs, maintenance or insurance or the vendor/lessor's costs of management, and the whole or part of which may vary according to 'relevant costs'. These latter are the costs or estimated costs incurred, or to be incurred, in connection with the matters for which the charge is payable, including overheads.

Under section 125B the landlord's notice in respect of a flat will also, as respects 'improvement contributions', contain a statement of the effect of paragraph 16C of Schedule 6 (see below) and estimates for works in respect of which the landlord considers that costs may be incurred in the reference period (see above). The works must be itemised, and estimates must show the amount (at current prices) of the likely cost of, and the tenant's likely contribution in respect of, each item, and the aggregate of costs and contributions. Section 187 (as amended) provides that 'improvement' means any alteration in or addition to a dwelling, including additions or alterations to a landlord's fixtures and fittings or to ancillary services, the erection of wireless or television aerials and carrying out external decoration. 'Improvement contribution' means a sum payable by a tenant of a flat in respect of improvements carried out to the flat, the building in which it is situated, or any other building or land, other than works carried out in discharge of obligations under paragraph 16A of Schedule 6 (see below) to repair or reinstate property etc.

Paragraph 16C of Schedule 6 provides that where the tenant of a flat is required to pay such contributions, liability in respect of costs incurred in the initial period (see above) of the lease is restricted so that he/she is not required to make any payment in respect of works for which no estimate was given in the landlord's section 125 notice, and he/she is not to pay in respect of works for which an estimate was given in that notice any more than the amount of the estimated contribution in respect of that items with an allowance for inflation (see above).

The section 125 notice (as amended) must further inform the tenant of the right under section 128 to have the value of the dwelling determined by the district valuer. The tenant must follow the procedure laid down in section 128 and serve written notice within three months of having received the section 125 notice, requiring the district valuer to determine the value of the property at the 'relevant time', that is the date on which notice claiming to exercise RTB was served. The three month period is extended if there are proceedings pending on the determination of any other question arising under Part V of the 1985 Act. In such a case the notice may be served at any time within three months of the final determination of those proceedings. Where such proceedings are commenced *after* a determination made by the district valuer, a redetermination may be required under section 128(3) of the Act by either of the parties within four weeks of the conclusion of the proceedings. The district valuer must consider any representations made to him by either landlord or tenant within four weeks from the service of a notice under section 128. It is the duty of the authority under section 128(5) to inform the tenant of the outcome of any determination or redetermination made by the district valuer. The jurisdiction of the district valuer is exclusive.

In addition the section 125 notice, under changes introduced by the Leasehold Reform, Housing and Urban Development Act 1993, must also inform the tenant of the effects of sections 125D, 125E, 136(2), 140 and 141, the effect of Part II, Chapter I of the 1993 Act (Rent into Mortgage) and 143B.

Sections 125D and 125E (which were inserted to take account of the new 'rent into mortgage' scheme – see below) provide that where a section 125 notice has been served, the tenant must, within 12 weeks of service of that notice, serve written notice of intention to proceed with RTB on the landlord, or notice of withdrawal of the claim, or notice of intention to acquire on rent to mortgage terms under section 144 (as substituted). Where the tenant neglects to do this in time the landlord may, by a further written notice, require the tenant to serve notice as to his/her intentions within 28 days, and stating the effect of section 125E(4) which is that failure to comply with the landlord's notice leads to the claim to exercise RTB being deemed withdrawn. There is, however, discretion to extend the time periods within which a response is required where it would be unreasonable to expect the tenant to comply with the notice.

Miscellaneous points

Where a former secure tenant has given notice claiming to exercise the right to buy and is superseded by a new secure tenant under the same secure tenancy (otherwise than on assignment made as an exchange under section 92), or under a periodic tenancy arising after the end of such a tenancy under section 86, the new tenant is in the same position *as if the notice had been given by him/her*; see section 136. For the purposes of entitlement to exercise RTB and also discount entitlement it is, however, the former tenant's circumstances that must be considered, see *McIntyre v Merthyr Tydfil Borough Council* (1989) 21 HLR 320.

Where there is a change of landlord, by transfer of the freehold, after the service of notice claiming to exercise RTB, section 137(1) lays down that all parties shall be in the same position as if the acquiring landlord had been landlord before the notice was given and had taken all steps which the former landlord had taken. However, if any of the circumstances after the change differ in any material respect, as where, for example, an exception to RTB becomes applicable, section 137(2) requires that all concerned must, as soon as possible, take such steps as are necessary for securing that the parties are, *as nearly as may be*, in the same position that they would have been in had those circumstances previously obtained.

Under section 140, as amended, the landlord may at any time serve written notice on the tenant requiring him/her, if all relevant matters concerning the grant and finance have been agreed or determined, to complete the transaction within a specified reasonable period of at least 56 days, *or*, if any relevant matter is outstanding, to serve on the landlord a written notice specifying the matter to be settled. This is the 'first notice to complete' and it must inform the tenant of the effect of the notice, and of the landlord's power to serve a 'second notice to complete'. Such a 'first notice' may not be served earlier than 12 months after service of the landlord's notice under section 125 (see above) *or* where a notice under section 146 has been served (see below) the service of that notice.

Under section 141 where the tenant does not comply with the first notice to complete, the landlord may serve a second notice requiring completion within a specified reasonable period of at least 56 days, and informing him/her of the effect of the notice. Where the tenant fails to comply the notice claiming to exercise RTB is deemed withdrawn at the end of the specified period.

Conversely under section 153A, as amended in 1993, where a secure tenant has claimed to exercise RTB and the landlord is guilty of delay by, for example, failing to admit/deny the existence of the right, an 'initial notice of delay' may be served which specifies the last action taken by the landlord and specifies a period of not less than one month within which the landlord may serve a counter notice to cancel the initial notice of delay – which can only be done if the landlord has taken requisite steps or does so contemporaneously with the counter notice. A failure by the landlord to serve a counter notice enables the tenant to serve under section 153B, an 'operative notice of delay' after which any payment of *rent* is to be treated additionally as a payment on account of the purchase price. These provisions were considered likely to be controversial when introduced under the Housing Act 1988, but there seems to have been no litigation on them. Similar powers exist with regard to 'Rent into Mortgage' acquisitions, see below.

Completing the transfer

Once all the above steps have been taken, the matters relating to the transfer and the arrangements as to mortgage finance, etc, have been completed, section 138(1) binds the landlord to convey or lease, as the case may be, the dwelling to the tenant. On completion the secure tenancy comes to and end; section 139(2). The landlord is not bound to complete while the tenant is found to be in arrears with the rent or other tenancy outgoings for a period of four weeks after the money due has been lawfully demanded from him (section 138(2)). If there are no impediments to the transfer the landlord must go ahead with it. The duty is enforceable by way of an injunction (section 138(3)) and the court has no discretion to refuse an injunction, for example, on the ground of hardship to third parties, see *Taylor v Newham London Borough Council* (1993) 25 HLR 290.

The actual transfer takes place according to the registered conveyancing procedure under section 123 of the Land Registration Act 1925.

Rent into mortgage

To assist purchasers of dwellings under RTB there was in the legislation from 1980 a concommittant 'right to a mortgage' (for details of which see Hughes, *Public Sector Housing Law*, 2nd edition 1987 pp 61-64). However, under the Leasehold Reform, Housing and Urban Development Act 1993, this right was abolished as from 11 October 1993, along with the right to defer completion and the right to be granted a shared ownership lease, which, it appears, had been very little used (for details see Hughes, op cit, pp 72-75, and for transitional provisions see DoE Circular 13/93). In their place was introduced the right to acquire on rent to mortgage terms ('Rent into mortgage' or RIM.) Under this a secure tenant who wishes to exercise RTB but who cannot afford to pay the full purchase price in 'one go' may transmute the rent he/she pays to the discounted purchase price of a 'share' of his/her dwelling along with a right to purchase the remainder at some future time; ie he/she may make an 'initial payment' out of money otherwise payable as rent while the rest of the purchase is financed by a mortgage to be redeemed at a future date. Whether this will dramatically increase the numbers of sales remains to be seen: many tenants will be excluded because they are 'on' housing benefit, while those entitled to a RIM purchase are probably likely to be able to raise the full purchase price from the ordinary mortgage market.

A new section 143 provides that where a claim to exercise RTB has been made, established and remains in force, RIM also applies, *save where*, under section 143A it is determined that the tenant is or was entitled to housing benefit, or an outstanding claim for housing benefit has been made by or on behalf of the tenant during the 'relevant period', ie the period beginning 12 months before the claim to acquire on RIM terms and ending on the day on which the transfer of the property to the would-be purchaser is made. Acquisition under RIM is also excluded under section 143B if the minimum initial payment (see below) in respect of the dwelling *exceeds* the maximum initial payment, which is 80% of the price the tenant would pay on exercising RTB. Minimum initial payment (MIP) varies from case to case. In a case, for instance, where the weekly rent at the time the landlord admits the RIM claim under section 146 (see below) does not exceed the relevant amount (ie a sum declared from time to time by the Secretary of State), MIP is determined as $P = R \times M$, where $P = MIP$, R = weekly rent and M is the Secretary of State's specified multiplier. The object of the equation as declared by section 143B(6) is that 'the relevant amount and the multipliers ... shall be such that ... they will produce a minimum initial payment equal to the capital sum which, in the opinion of the Secretary of State, would be raised on a 25 year repayment mortgage in the case of which the net monthly mortgage payment was equal to the rent at the relevant time calculated on a monthly basis'.

Thus where MIP is *less* than 80% of the price otherwise payable under RTB, acquisition on RIM terms is generally available. The tenant may calculate what 'share' he/she would be able to buy if the present rent level was a monthly mortgage repayment, though a larger 'share' may also be acquired. The 'share' is then acquired and financed by a mortgage.

Under section 144 (as substituted) where a tenant wishes to acquire on RIM terms, written notice to that effect must be served on the landlord, whereupon any notice served by the landlord under sections 140 or 141 (see above) are deemed withdrawn, and no further such notices may be served while the section 144 notice remains in force. Under the new section 146 of the 1985 Act the landlord must as soon as practicable serve a notice either admitting or denying the tenant's claim. Where the claim is admitted the notice must also set out the terms and consequences of a RIM acquisition. Section 146A then requires the tenant to serve a further written notice on the landlord, within 12 weeks of service of the section 146 notice, stating that the tenant intends to proceed with the RIM acquisition and stating the amount of the initial payment proposed (which must be not *less* than the minimum initial payment or *more* than the maximum), *or* that the RIM claim is withdrawn in order to pursue a 'standard' RTB purchase, *or* that the tenant is withdrawing from acquisition. Once the 12 week period has elapsed the landlord may, under section 146B, serve on a tenant who has failed to respond a written notice requiring a response and stating the consequences of failure. Where there is a failure to respond within 28 days the RIM claim is deemed withdrawn. Where, however, the tenant pursues the RIM claim the new section 147 requires the landlord to serve another written notice stating the landlord's 'share' and the initial discount available. These figures are calculated under a substituted section 148 which provides that the landlord's 'share' will be calculated by the formula:

$$S = \frac{P - IP}{P} \times 100$$

where S is the landlord's share, P is the price payable on a 'standard' RTB sale, and IP is the amount of the tenant's initial payment. The initial discount (ID) is determined by the formula:

$$ID = \frac{IP}{P} \times D$$

where IP and P have their above meanings and D is the amount of discount available on a 'standard' RTB sale.

A substituted section 149 provides that where the interest of the landlord in the dwelling passes to another body (eg on a transfer of stock from an authority to an association) *after* a secure tenant has given notice claiming the right to a RIM acquisition, all the parties shall, in general, be in the same position as if the 'other' body was the landlord *before* the tenant's notice was given and had been given that notice and had taken all the steps the landlord had taken.

Where all formalities relating to a RIM acquisition have been completed, section 150, as substituted, requires the landlord to make a transfer of the *freehold* of the dwelling (where it is a house and the landlord owns the freehold) or (where the dwelling is a flat or the landlord does not own the freehold) to grant a lease of the property. Section 151, as substituted, then provides for the terms and effect of the transfer to conform with Schedule 6 of the 1985 Act (see below), subject to certain modifications to ensure that on a leasehold transfer where a service charge is payable that charge is abated to take account of the 'shared' nature of the transaction.

After the transfer, of course, there is a somewhat strange legal 'beast'. The purchaser has acquired the freehold/leasehold, but that is subject to the landlord's 'share' and that share at some time has to be 'redeemed'. Provision for that is made by section 151A and Schedule 6A of the 1985 Act as introduced in 1993. A *right* to redeem at any time is guaranteed by Schedule 6A, para 2, while an *obligation* to do so is imposed by para 1 on the happening of particular events. These are: making a relevant disposal which is not otherwise 'excluded', and the expiry of one year beginning with a 'relevant death'. Disposals of the property thus attract the obligation *unless* they are transfers between spouses, or take effect under a will or intestacy, or under the terms of section 24 of the Matrimonial Causes Act 1973 or section 2 of the Inheritance (Provision for Family and Dependents) Act 1975. Similarly the obligation will arise within one year of the death of the acquiring tenant, or the survivor where there was a joint acquisition. Schedule 6A also makes provision for the value of the landlord's share to be determined for redemption purposes, and also for redemption to take place on a staged *or* interim payment basis at any time. Where the *obligation* to redeem arises, under section 151B, introduced in 1993, the liability is secured by mortgage on the property. For the purposes of completeness note that sections 152 and 153 of the 1985 Act, as amended, supply powers to landlords to 'hurry along' a dilatory purchaser with regard to RIM acquisitions similar to those with regard to RTB sales under sections 140 and 141 supra. For further detail see DoE Circular 13/93.

The terms of the freehold sale or long lease

Section 139(1) and Schedule 6 contain the terms on which transfers take place.

Leasehold terms: Schedule 6, Parts I and II

1)   The lease must be, *in general*, for a term of not less than 125 years at a ground rent of not more than £10 per annum. But if in a building containing two or more dwellings one has already been sold on a 125 year lease since 8 August 1980, any subsequent long lease granted under RTB provisions may be made for a term of less than 125 years so as to expire at the same time as the initial 125 year term.

2)   Following transfer the purchaser will continue to enjoy common use of any premises, facilities or services enjoyed previously as a secure tenant unless both parties agree otherwise.

3)   The landlord is made subject to quite onerous repairing covenants:

(a)   to keep in repair the structure and exterior of the dwelling, and also of the building in which it is situated (including drains, gutters and external pipes) and to make good any defect affecting that structure;

(b)   to keep in repair any other property over or in respect of which the tenant has any rights by virtue of Schedule 6, for example any common parts;

(c)   to ensure, so far as practicable, that any services which are to be provided by the landlord and to which the purchaser is entitled are maintained at a reasonable level, and also to keep in repair any installation connected with provision of such services;

(d)   to rebuild or reinstate the dwelling and the building in which it is situated in the case of destruction or damage by fire, tempest, flood or any other normally insurable risk.

It will be seen that these covenants are extensive, but liability will not be absolute. Landlords are not liable for any breach of covenant unless they are given notice of the defect, and the standard of repair required will depend on the age, character and locality of the dwelling, see *Lurcott v Wakely and Wheeler* [1911] 1 KB 905.

Under paragraph 16A of Schedule 6 a lease may require a tenant to bear a reasonable part of the landlord's costs in discharging, or insuring against, obligations to repair, make good structural defects and also to provide services mentioned above, or in insuring against the obligation to rebuild or reinstate. Where the lease requires a tenant to contribute towards insurance, the tenant is entitled to inspect the policy at reasonable times. Where the landlord does not insure against the obligations imposed by the covenant to rebuild or reinstate, the lease may require the tenant to pay a reasonable sum in place of the contribution otherwise required if there were insurance. Paragraph 16A has effect subject to paragraph16B which, as we have seen, limits certain costs payable by a tenant during the initial period of the lease.

Paragraph 18 of Schedule 6, as substituted, makes it clear that a provision in a lease, or an agreement collateral thereto, is void in so far as it purports either to authorise the recovery of contributions in respect of those repairs, etc, mentioned in paragraph 16A otherwise than in accordance with paragraphs 16A and 16B, or to authorise the recovery of any charge in respect of the landlord's costs incurred in discharging the obligation to rebuild or reinstate, or the recovery of an improvement contribution otherwise than as allowed by paragraph 16C.

Schedule 6 also makes void any term of the lease purporting to prohibit or restrict assigning or subletting the dwelling.

Those who purchase *long leasehold* interests in flats may also rely on the provisions of sections 18 to 30 of the Landlord and Tenant Act 1985 as amended. These are particularly concerned with further regulating service charges.

A 'service charge' is an amount payable by a tenant as part of, or in addition to, the rent, in respect of services, repairs, maintenance or insurance or the landlord's costs of management and which amount varies or may vary according to the costs or estimated costs incurred or to be incurred in any period by the landlord in providing the service. These costs are known as 'the relevant costs' and include overheads. See section 18 of the Landlord and Tenant Act (LTA) 1985.

Section 19 of the LTA controls the extent to which costs can be recovered as service charges by a test of reasonableness. The tenant will only have to pay where costs can be shown to have been reasonably incurred and where they are for services or works only if the services or works themselves are of reasonable standard.

Section 20 of the LTA, as substituted, places a limit on costs incurred in carrying out works on buildings which can be recovered without getting estimates and complying with other requirements. This amount is £25 multiplied by the number of flats in the building or £500 whichever is the greater. The Secretary of State may specify other figures. Any costs incurred in excess of this amount cannot be regarded as relevant costs unless these requirements are satisfied in the case of a tenant *not* represented by a recognised tenant's association:

(a)   at least two estimates for works must be obtained, one from a person wholly unconnected with the landlord;

(b)   a notice with copies of the estimates must be forwarded to the tenant concerned or displayed in the building and, if one exists, forwarded to the relevant tenants' association. The notice must describe works to be carried out and invite observations by a date not earlier than one month after the date of service or display of the notice;

(c)   the landlord must consider observations received and must not commence works before the date specified in the notice unless required urgently.

In proceedings relating to a service charge, the county court, if satisfied that the landlord acted reasonably, may dispense with all or any of the requirements set out above.

The requirements applying to tenants who *are* represented by a recognised tenants' association are similar, though here some communications may take place via the association's secretary.

The landlord must, under section 21 of the LTA, supply, on written request by a tenant or secretary of a relevant tenants' association, a written summary of costs incurred and from which service charges are determined. This information must be provided, under section 21(4) within six months of the end of the previous accounting period or within one month of the request whichever is the later.

Terms common to freehold and leasehold sales

Schedule 6, paragraph 2(1) provides, inter alia, that as regards any rights to support or access of light and air, the passage of water, or sewage or of gas or other piped fuel smoke and fumes, to the use or maintenance of pipes or other installations for such passage, or to the use or maintenance of cables or other installations for the supply of electricity, are subject to certain conditions. These are that purchasers will acquire rights of usage and maintenance equivalent to those enjoyed under secure tenancies or under any collateral agreement or arrangement on the severance of the dwelling from other property then comprised in the same tenancy, and second that dwellings will remain subject to all such rights for the benefit of other property *as are capable of existing in law* and are necessary to secure to persons interested in other properties as nearly as may be the same rights against purchasers as were available when they were secure tenants, or under any collateral agreement or arrangement made on severance.

Restrictions on resale, etc

One of the chief fears of those opposed to indiscriminate sales of social housing has been that the most attractive houses only will be purchased leaving landlords with less desirable homes. This argument has also been heard in relation to *areas* of houses. There is a danger that houses in rural areas may be purchased by their tenants and then sold to wealthy city dwellers looking for second or holiday homes, thus further eroding the already limited stock of dwellings available to people living and working in rural areas. Section 157 goes some way towards allaying such fears by placing restrictions on the resale of certain houses.

Where a transfer is made by, inter alia, a district council, a London Borough council, or a housing association, of a dwelling situated in a National Park, an area designated under section 87 of the National Parks and Access to the Countryside Act 1949 (area of outstanding natural beauty) or an area designated by order of the Secretary of State as a rural area, covenants may be imposed limiting the freedom of the purchaser and his/her successors in title to dispose of the dwelling.

The limitation is that until such time as is notified by the landlord to the tenant, there may be no 'relevant disposal' which is not an 'exempted disposal' without the landlord's written consent, though such consent may not be withheld if the disposal is to a person who has throughout the period of three years immediately preceding the application for consent had his/her place of work in a region designated by order of the Secretary of State which is wholly or partly comprised in the National Park or area, *or* has had his/her only or principal home in such a region *or* has had the one in part or parts of that period and the other in the remainder, though the region need not have been the same throughout the period. This enables rural workers and dwellers to move from one designated region to another over a short period and yet retain the ability to purchase houses otherwise subject to resale restrictions. A 'relevant disposal' is, under section 159, a conveyance of the freehold or assignment of the lease, or the grant of a lease for more than 21 years, otherwise than at a rack rent. An 'exempted disposal' is under section 160:

(a)   a disposal of the whole of the dwelling and a further conveyance or assignment to a 'qualifying person', ie a person, or one of the persons, by whom the disposal is made, or the spouse or former spouse of that person, or one of those persons, or a member of the family of that person(s) who has resided with him/her throughout the period of 12 months ending with the disposal; or

(b)   a vesting of the whole dwelling under a will or on an intestacy; or

(c)   a disposal under section 24 of the Matrimonial Causes Act 1973 or section 2 of the Inheritance (Provision for Family and Dependents) Act 1975;

(d)   a compulsory disposal, as under a compulsory purchase order;

(e)   a disposal of property consisting of land let with or used for the purposes of the dwelling house.

Disposals in breach of covenant are void. Similarly there must be no disposal by way of tenancy or licence without the landlord's written consent *unless* the new occupier satisfies the foregoing residence requirements, *or* where the tenancy or licence is granted by a person whose only or principal home is, and throughout the duration of the tenancy or licence, remains the dwelling house.

With the consent of the Secretary of State *or the Housing Corporation where the landlord is a housing association* the covenant may be that until the end of the period of ten years beginning with the initial disposal there will be no further sale or long lease, etc other than an exempted disposal, unless;

(a)   the tenant or his successor in title first offers to re-transfer the dwelling to the original landlord, and

(b)   they refuse the offer or fail to accept it within one month of its being made.

The purchase price to be paid in such cases will be, under section 158, the price agreed or determined by the district valuer, reduced to take account of any liability to repay discount.

The powers of the Secretary of State

The sale of social housing, particularly council houses, to sitting tenants is a fundamental plank of government housing policy. The government shows its determination to pursue that policy by the grant in sections 164 to 170 of extensive powers of intervention to the Secretary of State in cases where landlords attempt to resist or hinder sales policy.

Where it appears to the Secretary of State, presumably on reasonable evidence, that a tenant or tenants of a particular landlord, or landlords, are finding it difficult to exercise RTB effectively and expeditiously, he may, by giving written notice of intention to do so, intervene in the given situation, under section 164. Once such notice is in force, and it is deemed to be given 72 hours after it has been sent, he may do *all* such things as appear to him necessary or expedient to enable the exercise of RTB, etc. The Secretary of State's notice has the effect of preventing further action by a vending landlord with regard to RTB, and nullifies any previous action taken. The rights and obligations of the landlord are vested in the Secretary of State though he is not bound to follow the exact sales procedure required of a landlord in the exercise of RTB. See on this provision *R v Secretary of State, ex p Norwich City Council* [1982] QB 808, [1982] 1 All ER 737.

For the purpose of making a transfer section 165 empowers the Secretary of State to make a Vesting Order which has the effect of:
(a)   vesting the property in the tenant on the appropriate tenurial basis; and
(b)   binding landlord and tenant, and their successors in title, by the covenants it contains.

A vesting order, on presentation to the Chief Land Registrar, requires the registration of the tenant as proprietor of the title concerned.

Under section 166 where the Secretary of State receives money due to a landlord in consequence of using his powers, he may retain it, while the section 164 notice is in force, and the interest thereon. He may furthermore recover costs, with interest, as a debt from the landlord, and may do this by withholding any sums due from him to the landlord. Section 167 gives the Secretary of State power to direct landlords not to include certain covenants in conveyances or grants of dwellings where inclusion of such covenants would lead to inconformity with the requirements of Schedule 6. Such a direction can have a retrospective effect under section 168, to such extent or in such manner as the notice provides. Section 169 grants the Secretary of State extensive powers to obtain documents, and other information where that appears necessary or expedient for the purpose of determining whether powers under sections 164, 166, 167 or 168 are exercisable, or for, or in connection with, exercising those powers. This power is exercised by written notice to the landlord. Any officer of the landlord designated in the notice or having custody of documents or possessing information must, without instructions from the landlord, take all reasonable steps to ensure that the notice is complied with. Finally section 170 gives the Secretary of State powers to grant assistance to a party to proceedings in connection with RTB, etc, other than valuation proceedings, who applies to him for assistance. Assistance may be granted on grounds that the case raises issues of principle, or that it is unreasonable, having regard to the complexity of the issues, to expect the applicant to deal with the matter unaided. The assistance may take the form of giving advice, or procuring, or attempting to procure, a settlement, arranging for legal advice and/or representation, or any other form of aid considered appropriate.

General powers of disposal

RTB is not the only plank in sales policy. Not every tenant will wish to buy the house he/she occupies, and there may be individuals or organisations who wish to purchase houses offered for general sale.

Section 32 of the Housing Act 1985 empowers authorities to dispose of housing land and stock. In general disposals other than by way of a secure tenancy or under RTB require the consent of the Secretary of State. It appears, however, that it is not unlawful for an authority to have a general policy of progressive disposal of their stock, see *R v Hammersmith and Fulham London Borough Council, ex p Beddowes* (1986) 18 HLR 458, and, of course, by virtue of section 161 of the Local Government and Housing Act 1989 authorities are not bound to have a housing stock at all. Section 34 (as amended) makes provision for the giving of either general or individual consents. In giving consent the Secretary of State must consider the extent to which the proposed transferee is likely to be subject to influence from the authority. Ministerial consent may also be required for disposals *by* the transferee under section 133 of the Housing Act 1988.

Sales may also take place at a discount as provided for by section 34(4). The provisions in section 35 relating to the payment of discount on an early disposal mirror those of section 155 of the 1985 Act.

Section 33 allows authorities only limited freedom to impose such covenants or conditions as they think fit on a disposal. Certain covenants and conditions may only be imposed with ministerial consent.

Section 37 applies similar restrictions on resale of houses situated in National Parks, areas of outstanding natural beauty and other designated rural areas, to those contained in section 57.

The Secretary of State, in exercise of powers under section 34, has issued general consents that equate, in so far as possible, disposals of individual houses under the power of sale with those under RTB; see the Ministerial Letters of 2 and 4 June 1981 to English and Welsh authorities and DoE Circular 21/84.

However, the power to dispose of housing is being used by some authorities to dispose of whole estates, with or without sitting tenants. By mid 1986, 53 privatisation schemes comprising 6,000 untenanted dwellings, and two schemes with 3,000 tenanted properties had been centrally recorded, while schemes for a further 15,000 dwellings were proposed.

Voluntary stock transfers

As we described in the introduction to the chapter, by the summer of 1994 31 authorities had transferred housing on a voluntary basis. These authorities were mainly in the south of England and had disposed of their council housing to an association or a group of associations through the LSVT process. After a flurry of LSVTs at the end of the 1980s the government moved to regulate this form of disposal because of the implications for the wider housing association movement of the large amounts of private finance tied up in LSVTs.

Apart from the constraints imposed by the availability of private finance these transfers are subject to a degree of consultative control by virtue of section 106A of the 1985 Act, inserted in 1986.

Section 106A and Schedule 3A regulate the duties of authorities proposing to dispose of *dwellings subject to secure tenancies* and those of the Secretary of State in considering whether to give consent to disposals. These provisions, which replace the normal consultation requirements of section 105 of the 1985 Act in relation to questions of disposal, require regard to be had to the views of tenants likely to lose secure tenant status in consequence of the disposal. Where an authority disposes of an interest in land as a result of which a secure tenant of theirs will become the tenant of a person *other than* a body falling within section 80 of the 1985 Act, the Secretary of State must not entertain an application for consent to the disposal unless consultation requirements have been complied with. These are that the authority must have served written notice on the affected tenant giving appropriate details of the proposed disposal, including the identity of the person to whom disposal will take place, the likely consequence of the disposal *for the tenant* the preservation of RTB and the effect of the provisions of Schedule 3A. The tenant must also be informed of the right to make representations to the authority within a specified reasonable time. Any representations received must be considered, and further notice served on the tenant stating any significant changes to the proposal, and the right to object to the Secretary of State. The tenant must also be informed that consent must be withheld if it appears that a majority of relevant tenants oppose the proposal. The Secretary of State may require further consultation to take place, but must not give consent if it appears a majority of relevant tenants do not wish the disposal to proceed, though he may refuse consent for other reasons. In coming to a decision the Secretary of State may have regard to any information available to him. However, consent is not invalidated by failure by the Secretary of State or the authority to comply with the requirements of Schedule 3A, and so purchasers of affected dwellings would be protected in cases of irregularity. Presumably in circumstances where tenants believed, for example, that consultation requirements were not being fulfilled they would have to seek judicial review *before* the giving of consent or face being left without a remedy. The consultation provisions cover in effect only secure tenants in occupation. They could not apply where housing had already been *cleared* of tenants. See also DoE Circular 6/88. Further guidance was given in a DoE paper: 'Large Scale Voluntary Transfers of Local Authority Housing to Private

Bodies' (June 1988), supplemented since 1993 by the DoE's 'Large Scale Voluntary Transfers – Guidelines'. This identified suitable transferees as those which are:

(a)   independent of the authority; in this connection council membership or shareholding should be *clearly* in a minority (under 20%), and there should be a minimum of commercial agreements between the transferee and the authority; retention of nomination rights and waiting lists by the authority was not then considered acceptable, and neither would a power to specify staff from the authority to be transferred to the new landlord;

(b)   able to demonstrate stability and responsibility with long term commitment to providing rented housing, ie those who take account of housing demand and conditions in lettings policies and who normally relet property falling vacant at rent levels affordable by those in lower paid employment;

(c)   committed to providing a good service to tenants.

The Secretary of State also indicated unwillingness then to see authority monopolies of rented accommodation turned into private monopolies, and hoped that disposals would take place to a number of transferees, even in the area of small authorities. This would not seem to have been borne out in practice. Early disposals seem to have fallen within the 5,000-10,000 limits for disposal to a single purchaser.

The Secretary of State also indicated that authorities seeking to transfer should be able to demonstrate ability to discharge statutory obligations *after* transfer, particularly with regard to homelessness. This *can* be done by contractual arrangements with other landlords in their areas, including transferees of council stock.

The terms of transfers should be that sales are at market value subject to tenancies with an allowance for necessary repairs. Purchasers should seek private sector funding for sales. The 1993 guidelines repeat the 5,000 unit figure and indicate that only transfers to associations approved by the Secretary of State and the Housing Corporation are likely to be approved.

(The Ground of Possession, paragraph 10A in Schedule 2 to the Housing Act 1985 (as amended) allows for recovery of possession of dwellings subject to re-development schemes centrally approved under Part V of Schedule 2, following due tenant consultation, see Chapter Three.)

Central powers over local authority stock disposal

Controls over the rate at which LSVTs can occur are operated centrally to ensure that, inter alia, sufficient private finance is available, and as this problem is overcome it seems probable that there will be an increased flow of transfers, including larger urban authorities, as it clearly is government policy to encourage voluntary stock disposal. Section 135 of the Leasehold Reform,

Housing and Urban Development Act 1993 provides that 'qualifying disposals' may only take place within a financial year if they have have been included in a central 'programme' of disposals for that year. A qualifying disposal is one which requires the consent of the Secretary of State (see above) *and* the aggregate number of dwelling houses included in the disposal (ie the number at that point to be disposed of, *plus* the number previously disposed of *by* the authority *to* the disponee within the five years ending with the date of the disposal) exceeds 499. Authorities may apply for disposals to be included in a programme, but in drawing a programme up the Secretary of State is to take into account, inter alia, any costs to the Exchequer of the disposal (eg housing benefit costs), and whether or not a particular disposal is likely to be opposed by affected tenants. Programmes have to be made in the form of a statutory instrument, and different programmes may be drawn up for different types of authority. Section 136 further provides that where stock is disposed of under a programme a levy is to be paid by relevant authorities to the Secretary of State, the rate to be fixed by a formula whose elements will be largely centrally determined, but effectively the levy will be 20% of a net sum determined to have been received by an authority following a programme disposal. The purpose of this levy is to compensate the Treasury for the greater expenditure it has to bear on housing benefit in respect of increased rents charged by 'new' landlords following stock transfer.

Block disposals may involve the rehabilitation of existing stock, units of which are subsequently sold for owner occupation, and may be on the basis that the person/organisation acquiring housing land and stock from an authority does work on other authority housing as consideration rather than making a capital payment.

RTB will, however, continue to apply to dwellings transferred out of the public stock as Preserved Right to Buy (PRTB) by virtue of section 171A to 171H (as amended) of the Housing Act 1985. The RTB provisions continue to apply where a person ceases to be a secure tenant by reason of the disposal (a 'qualifying disposal') by the landlord of *an interest* in the dwelling to a person who is *not* an authority or other body within section 80. The provisions accordingly refer to the 'former secure tenant' and the 'former landlord'. PRTB does not apply where the former landlord was a body falling within Schedule 5, paragraphs 1,2 and 3 to the 1985 Act, that is charities and certain housing associations, against whom RTB could not be exercised, *or in any other case provided for by order of the Secretary of State*. Under section 171B former secure tenants have PRTB so long as they occupy 'relevant dwellings', see below, as their only or principal homes, but this is subject to, inter alia, the requirements of paragraph 6 of Schedule 9A whereunder PRTB is a registrable interest under the Land Registration Act 1925, and so requires registration to be protected, such registration to be effected by the Chief Land Registrar on the disposal of relevant housing stock, the disposing body to ensure that the Chief Land Registrar is informed of all necessary particulars.

PRTB is exercisable only by a 'qualifying person', that is the former secure tenant, a person to whom a tenancy of a dwelling is granted jointly with a person having PRTB in relation to that dwelling, and a 'qualifying successor', that is either:

(a)   a member of the former secure tenant's family who has acquired the dwelling under the will or intestacy of the former secure tenant, or to whom the former secure tenant has assigned the property, *provided* immediately before the death/assignment, as the case may be, the former secure tenant was an assured tenant of the dwelling in question (transfer of a dwelling from an authority to an association or private landlord will, of course, result in a tenant becoming 'assured'); or

(b)   a person who becomes the tenant of the dwelling in place of the former secure tenant by virtue of orders under the matrimonial legislation.

PRTB is also exercisable *only* in respect of a qualifying or 'relevant' dwelling. Such are:

(a)   in relation to former secure tenants, dwellings subject to the disposals under which they ceased to be secure;

(b)   in relation to qualifying successors, the dwellings of which they became the tenants; and

(c)   in relation to persons to whom tenancies of dwellings are granted jointly with persons who have PRTB in relation to them, those dwellings.

However, if a person having PRTB becomes the tenant of another dwelling, *and* the landlord is the same as the landlord of the previous dwelling, *or*, where the landlord is a company, is a connected company, the new dwelling is the relevant dwelling for PRTB. 'Connected companies' are, under section 736 of the Companies Act 1985, subsidiary or holding companies. PRTB is accordingly not lost on transfers between dwellings of the same landlord.

Section 171C empowers the Secretary of State to make regulations to modify the provisions of the 1985 Act with regard to PRTB, see currently SI 1993/2241.

The Housing Act 1988 – Part IV – PAL (Pick a landlord) Schemes

In 1987 the government proposed that secure tenants should have a new right to transfer to other landlords, especially where their current landlords gave bad service. The initiative was to be with tenants who would identify a new landlord willing to take them on, such landlords having to be centrally approved. Arrangements for putting tenants in touch with prospective new landlords were proposed. What came out in the legislation is somewhat different.

Under section 94 a 'person' approved (in England) by the Housing Corporation (in Wales, Housing for Wales) (public sector landlords, eg authorities, may *not* be approved) may, under section 93, have 'The Right to

Acquire' from a 'public sector landlord' freehold buildings comprising one or more dwellings provided they are occupied on the relevant date (ie the date of application to exercise the right) by qualifying tenants (ie generally *secure* tenants who hold directly from the landlord who is the *freeholder*, and who are not subject to a possession order, and who do *not* fall within any of the exceptions to RTB) and reasonably required ancillary freehold land. Under section 95(5) once an application is made to acquire, the relevant land is 'frozen' and no other approved person may apply to acquire until after the first application has been disposed of. Under section 96 the approved person must make the application to exercise the right to the landlord in prescribed form specifying property to be acquired. The landlord must then, under section 97, within four weeks of this 'the relevant date' furnish the approved person with a list of names and addresses of every tenant or licensee of relevant dwellings. The approved person then has *four weeks* from the date of this section 97(1) notice in which there are rights of access to information and relevant documentation. There is also a *twelve week* period running from the relevant date during which the landlord must serve on the approved person notices determining property to be included in the acquisition, see section 98, and containing the proposed terms of the conveyance. The approved person has four weeks from the date of this section 98(1) notice during which to bring to the landlord's attention matters of disagreement. If a dispute occurs it must be referred for determination by a person agreed by the parties or, in default, by the Secretary of State. Within *eight weeks* of agreeing the property and the terms, or after the final resolution of disputes, the landlord must, under section 99, specify the price. This is to be market value on a willing vendor basis, subject to existing tenancies *and* an obligation on the acquirer to do repairs necessary to fulfil the landlord's repairing obligations, and on the understanding that the only bidders for the property would be approved persons. If the cost of necessary repairs *exceeds* the value of the property there will be a shortfall – a 'disposal cost' – and that has to be borne by the vendor. The approved person has *four weeks* from the service of the section 99(1) notice in which to notify the landlord in writing of any matter in the valuation not accepted. Disputes as to valuation are determined by the District Valuer. Subsequently if dwellings are excluded from transfer because their tenants have voted to stay as tenants of their current landlord, there must be an adjustment to the selling price. Thereafter, under section 102, there is a prescribed period during which the approved person must consult with relevant tenants. Consultation with affected tenants only takes place *after* the price has been decided, and the consultees will only be those secure tenants or 'long tenancy' holders who were in residence on the date of the bid, *and* who remain so during the consultation period, *and* whose dwellings are subject to transfer. Furthermore tenants entering their homes after the date of the bid do not need to be consulted, nor can they be granted secure or assured tenancies, and any tenancy/licence they are given is, under section 101, subject to four weeks' notice to quit expiring at any time during the tenancy. Further requirements are contained in the Housing (Change of Landlord) Regulations 1989, Part V (SI 1989/367). Consultation has to be in prescribed form, and affected tenants *may* be assisted by the advice and information service which the Housing Corporation is empowered to set up under section 106. The transfer to an acquiring body can be blocked if *less* than 50% of the consultees have given notice of their wishes in prescribed manner, *or* if the number of those consultees who have given notice of their wish to continue as tenants of their current landlord *exceeds* 50% of the total number of those who have the right to be consulted, see section 103.

The Housing (Change of Landlord) Regulations 1989, Part VI, lays down consultation requirements. The basic period for consultation is 14 weeks (reg 14). The prescribed information, and the need for an independent teller, is laid down in reg 16 and Schedule 3 – the object is to ensure that tenants have described to them in unambiguous terms the nature of the proposal and its consequences for them, together with the overall policy stance of the approved body. See also DoE Circular 11/89.

Within two weeks of the end of the consultation period, the approved person may, under section 103, serve on the landlord notice of intention to proceed, provided there is no sufficient level of opposition.

Under section 100 the Secretary of State must make regulations to deal with those tenants who do not wish to be transferred. Where such a tenant occupies a *house* it must be excluded from the acquisition. Where the dwelling is a flat a lease must be granted to the current landlord so the sitting tenant can become a sub-tenant. However, tenants not wishing to be transferred must indicate their positive desire to stay as tenants of the current landlord before the end of the consultation period. When the approved person serves notice of intention to proceed under section 103, lists of tenants and properties to be excluded by virtue of the above mentioned option must be given to the landlord, who then has two weeks to signify any disagreement with the terms. Thereafter the landlord is under a duty to complete the transfer, and this is enforceable by injunction, see section 104.

Tenants transferred cease to be secure, and will be 'assured', though they will have PRTB. Under section 105 once acquisition has taken place the property may not be redisposed of by way of sale, lease, disposition of any interest, contract or option etc except with the consent of the Secretary of State, but this consent may be given generally to particular classes of disposition.

There may be tenants who are tempted to go from secure to assured status by offers of improvement, good quality repairs and better management services, and some potential approved persons may genuinely believe they can deliver such a package. However, tenants who are transferred may face rent increases.

The Housing Corporation, however, requires a 'sealed deed' as a condition of approval as an 'approved person' – this forms a contract and contains a commitment to charge only affordable (ie 'lowish') rents.

See also Chapter Three on assured tenancies and the guidance on the Tenants' Guarantee issued by the Corporation. Schemes under Part IV have not taken off to any great extent. *Roof* (May/June 1990 p 12) revealed that only 15 bodies had become 'approved' (all, save one, registered associations). The total number of dwellings involved was a mere 20,178.

Part III of the 1988 Act (HATs)

The 1987 White Paper on Housing, Cm 214 (para 6.1 et seq) addressed the problem of run-down inner urban council estates. Housing Acting Trusts (HATs) were proposed to: improve housing; provide other community needs such as shops, workshops and advice centres; encourage local enterprise, *and* to give authority tenants a greater diversity of landlords. HATs were seen as intermediate bodies to take over housing, improve it, and then to pass it on to others. A DoE consultation paper expanded this. Areas suitable for HAT treatment were identified as those containing large numbers of poor quality public sector dwellings etc in deprived environments with high vandalism rates and other social problems such as unemployment, a high proportion of residents in receipt of state benefits, poor estate design, and general decay. The task of a HAT is to reverse such decline.

Part III of the Housing Act 1988 contains the new law.

Section 60 enables the Secretary of State to designate a HAT area which *may* comprise two or more areas of land which need not even be contiguous or situated in the same district. This discretion is extremely wide, but particular regard may be had to the proportion of housing in a proposed HAT area in authority ownership, its physical state and design type, its housing management record, the living conditions of residents and their social and general environment.

The Secretary of State must consult with affected authorities, see section 61, and must also notify all secure or other classes of prescribed tenants of the proposal. He must make arrangements for a poll to be conducted, by independent persons, of notified tenants with a view to establishing their view, *or* otherwise hold a ballot or poll of those tenants to ascertain their views. He may *not* make the designation if it appears a majority of those who expressed an opinion oppose designation. Where there is majority support the designation *may* be made by order laid before, and approved by Parliament.

HATs are created under section 62 and Schedules 7 and 8 of the 1988 Act. Each HAT has a chairman and between 5 and 11 other members. The Secretary of State must have regard to the desirability of appointing local people to

HATs, and must consult the authority before making an appointment. HAT members must not have any financial or other interest that could prejudice their membership function.

HATs' primary objectives are laid down in section 63:
(a)   to secure improvement and repair of their stock;
(b)   to secure proper housing management;
(c)   to secure diversity of housing tenure and a diversity of landlords of tenanted property;
(d)   to improve social and general environmental conditions.
    To this end they may:
(a)   provide and maintain housing and shops, and other community facilities;
(b)   acquire, reclaim and dispose of land, and carry out operational development;
(c)   ensure provision of main services;
(d)   carry on businesses etc.

Under section 64 as soon as practicable after establishment a HAT is to draw up proposals for its area. It must consult with every affected housing authority, and must publicise its proposals within the affected area and give those likely to be affected an opportunity to make representations, which must be taken into account by the HAT. The Secretary of State must be kept informed of the HAT's work in this respect.

Section 65 empowers the Secretary of State to grant to a HAT extensive housing powers, those mentioned, however, do not include Part III – Homelessness.

A HAT, under section 67, may be designated as a planning authority for its area, even, in specified instances to the exclusion of other authorities.

The Secretary of State has a general power to give directions to HATs under section 72. Thus, for example, ministers have indicated HATs will be required in general to hold their meetings in public, and will also be requested to set up tenants' advisory groups.

Section 74 empowers the Secretary of State to transfer housing and ancillary land from an authority to a HAT on such terms *as he thinks fit*, including financial terms, which may include payments *from* an authority to a HAT. Transfers of housing stock to HATs do not take place on the basis that the HAT will assume responsibility for the entire debt and loan charges incurred in relation to provision of the houses. Instead the basis is that the 'price' of the housing is the *estimated market value of the houses* subject to existing tenancies. That 'price' may well be lower than the debt and loan charges figure. Before making the transfer the Secretary of State must, under section 75, consult with affected authorities and must publicise the proposal so that persons such as secure tenants may know what is proposed, there is, however, no obligation to *consult* with them.

HATs are not destined to be permanent bodies, and are intended to dispose of areas revived. Section 79 gives them wide land disposal powers, subject to ministerial direction. Houses subject to secure tenancies may (subject to section 84, which grants authorities powers of pre-emption in respect of housing disposals by HATs), be disposed of to a person or body approved by the Housing Corporation (who may not approve 'public sector' landlords, or other persons or bodies *not* independent of such institutions). Subsequent disposals by such 'approved' persons or bodies are also subject to ministerial consent under section 81. Some disposals are exempt, eg the granting of an assured tenancy. Likewise subsequent disposals are subject to consultation requirements involving relevant tenants. It should, however, be noted that RTB disposals are not caught by the various requirements outlined above, see sections 79(2), 81(8)(a), and 83 of the 1988 Act.

The rights of tenants in HAT areas

Initially the transfer of housing from authority to HAT has no immediate effect on tenants. They continue to be 'secure'. However, over time this position *could* change. Housing conditions will be improved: to pay for the improvements rents may rise. Furthermore the government's intention was that a HAT should seek to pass on improved dwellings to new owners. Much housing could be transferred to other bodies, eg associations. Section 84 imposes obligations on HATs in respect of secure tenants affected by such disposals. A HAT may only dispose of land with ministerial consent (section 79).

Section 84 of the 1988 Act (as amended in 1993) further applies where a HAT proposes to dispose of one or more dwellings let on secure tenancies where the consequence would be that a secure tenant would become the tenant of 'another person' which is not an authority. Before applying for ministerial consent, the HAT must serve written notice on the relevant local housing authority informing them of the proposed disposal and requiring them, within not less than 28 days, to serve notice on the HAT informing the HAT in respect of relevant houses of the likely consequences for each affected tenant if the authority were to acquire the houses. Thereafter, but before ministerial consent is applied for, the HAT must inform affected tenants of the proposed disposal, together with: the name of the disposee; the likely consequences of the disposal for secure tenancies; the likely effect of acquisition by the authority, if they have so indicated; the right of tenants to make representations in connection with becoming an authority tenant (see further below), and the right to make general representations about disposal. Any representations generally made must be taken into account. Where, however, tenants represent that they (or even one of them) wish to become authority tenants, that triggers action under section 84A (inserted in 1993). The Secretary of State, the authority and the tenant(s) have to be served with notice of this fact by the HAT which must also amend its disposal proposal so as to exclude property made subject to representations. The Secretary of State must then transfer the dwellings, by order, from the HAT to the authority – note that in the case of a flat block such an order is to be made if the *majority of tenants* in that block *making representations* represent that they wish to be authority tenants.

HATs in practice

Though never expected to spring up rapidly nationwide, in theory HATs could become increasingly important tools in the 'kit' central government has assembled to interfere in traditional local government issues. The Secretary of State could intervene in urban areas to take control over whole areas of housing and entrust them to a HAT with a view to the diversification of its ultimate ownership. Tenant resistance to HATs has, however, been considerable. Between July 1988 and November 1989 seven HATs were proposed (Lambeth, Leeds, Sandwell, Southwark, Sunderland, Tower Hamlets, Waltham Forest – NB all urban areas where RTB and voluntary transfers would make little impact). Apart from the Waltham Forest HAT which was actually *requested* by tenants (and where £150m over ten years in resources was promised) all were decisively rejected by ballot. Only one HAT proceeded rapidly towards fruition, that in North Hull. The North Hull HAT (which was promoted by the local authority) was put to a ballot in March 1991, £50m over ten years in resources being promised. The North Hull HAT has been very active, issuing its own newsletter to tenants detailing the very considerable progress made in renovating properties. Tenants have been involved in redesigning their houses. The HAT 'team' are principally seconded officers from Hull City Council housing department, but the DoE as 'paymaster' keeps a very tight rein on the budget and functioning of the HAT.

The Waltham Forest HAT came into operation on 9 December 1991, while there are also HATS in Liverpool, Hull, Castle Point and Tower Hamlets. The most recently designated HAT is at Stonebridge (SI 1994/1987) in the London Borough of Brent. At the time of writing these were the only operational HATs. As we argued in Chapter One HATs remain as one fairly small part of a package of measures at the disposal of the government for the regeneration of inner cities and peripheral estates – in many ways the most difficult and least subtle of these provisions. Schemes such as City Challenge have yielded more fruitful and rather less controversial results. Purely in terms of the strict focus of this chapter– the disposal of council houses – HATs have been one of the least successful policies, dogged, as is clear, by implementation problems.

Disposals under Part I of the Leasehold Reform, Housing and Urban Development Act 1993

This legislation enables certain 'qualifying' long leaseholders of flats to 'collectively enfranchise', ie to acquire the freehold of the premises in which their dwellings are found, see section 1. (A parallel right exists for such leaseholders to acquire individual lease extensions, see sections 39-62; this will not be dealt with here.) The mechanism in general operates by means of a 'nominee purchaser', appointed by the flat owners, who conducts the enfranchising application, though in many cases it is thought a company will be set up by the flat owners to receive the transfer of the freehold. The right of collective enfranchisement (RCE) also extends to the freehold of other premises owned by the freeholder of the flats to be enfranchised provided this is 'appurtenant property', eg garages, yards, gardens, etc, see section 1(7).

Certain authority and association premises may fall within the terms of Part I of the 1993 Act because it covers flats held on long leases granted, inter alia, under the RTB provisions of the 1985 Act, see section 7(1)(c). The flat must also be held at a 'low rent' under section 8, which is defined in terms of a rent limit which is, in the case of a lease entered into before 1 April 1990, two thirds of the rateable value, and in the case of leases entered into after that date a rent of £1,000 pa (Greater London) or £250 (elsewhere).

However, before the RCE can be exercised a number of conditions must be met:

(a)   the relevant building or part of it must, under section 3(1) be self contained, and the building to be acquired must contain two or more flats occupied by 'qualifying tenants' (RTB long leaseholders will *generally* 'qualify', though not if their immediate landlord is a charitable housing trust, see section 5);

(b)   the total number of flats held by such 'qualifying tenants' must not be less than two thirds of the total number of flats contained in the premises, see section 3(1)(c);

(c)   the qualifying tenants must also for acquisition purposes satisfy, under section 6, a 'residence condition' which is that tenants must have occupied their flats as their only or principal homes for the last 12 months or for periods amounting to three years in the last ten years. By virtue of section 13(2) not less than one half of the qualifying tenants who begin the RCE process must satisfy this residence condition;

(d)   furthermore the application claiming RCE must be given by not less than two thirds of the number of qualifying tenants in the flats who between them occupy not less than half of the flats in the building in question.

These conditions will make the application of the RCE to authority and association property very limited. Under RTB many more houses than flats have been sold. There will not be many blocks of flats where the requisite number of qualifying tenants will be found. For example if a block contains 48 flats, not fewer than 36 would have to be occupied by 'qualifying tenants'. To exercise RCE, 24 of those qualifying have to support the application, and 12 of those have also to fulfil the residence qualification. In parts of London these circumstances may be found satisfied: it is unlikely to be the case elsewhere. Professor Kenny in his annotations to the Current Law Statutes version of the 1993 Act predicted the legislation would in any case prove too complex and expensive to attract much interest. The early evidence supports his contention. By February 1994 not one tenant had appeared able to exercise RCE, see (1994) Times 22 February. Interested readers are referred further to Professor Kenny's work.

Further reading

Audit Commission   *Who Wins? Voluntary Housing Transfers* HMSO, 1993

Department of the Environment   *Housing Action Trusts. A Consultation Document* DoE/HMSO, 1987

English, J (Ed)   *The Future of Council Housing* Croom Helm, 1982

Evans, A   'Voluntary Transfer: Weighing up the Pros and Cons' *Housing and Planning Review* Vol 44, No 1 February 1989, p 14

Forrest, R and Murie, A   *Right to Buy? Issues of Need, Equity and Polarisation in the Sale of Council Houses* Working Paper No 39, University of Bristol, School of Advanced Urban Studies, 1984

Forrest, R and Murie, A   'If the Price is Right', *Roof*, March/April 1986, p 23

Forrest, R and Murie, A   *Selling the Welfare State: The Privatisation of Public Housing* Routledge, 1988

Jones, P and Hillier, D   'Privatising Local Authority Housing', *Housing and Planning Review*, Vol 41, No 4, August 1986, p 20

Karn, V   'Remodelling a HAT: the implementation of the Housing Action Trust legislation 1987-92', in *Implementing Housing Policy* (eds) Malpass, P and Means, R, Open University Press, 1993

Knight, M   'When Owning Becomes a Nightmare', *Roof*, November/December, 1983, p 23

Lynn, P   *The Right to Buy: A National Follow-Up Survey of Tenants of Council Homes in England*, London, DoE/HMSO, 1991

Owens, R   'If the HAT fits', *Roof*, January/February, 1992, p 17

Woodward, R   'Mobilising opposition: the campaign against Housing Action Trusts in Tower Hamlets', *Housing Studies*, Vol 6, No 1, 1991, p 44

Chapter Three

Social housing: its allocation, the rights and status of its tenants

This chapter is primarily concerned with the rights of secure and assured tenants (STs and ATs respectively). But before those rights can be enjoyed a person must have the status of 'tenant'. Both authorities and associations operate in situations where, for a variety of reasons, 'clients' are not tenants, but licensees.

The basic distinction between a tenancy and a licence is that the former is a legal estate in land which, though limited in time, confers a package of rights on its holder, the most basic being the right to have exclusive possession of relevant property. The latter is a purely personal right which simply allows its holder to be on or in a property and which may be terminated simply by giving reasonable notice. A person may be a licensee either because of the quality of premises occupied – some premises are effectively incapable in certain modes of occupation of supporting a tenancy – or because of the nature of the legal relationship between the parties. In all cases it is for the law to decide the nature of the right of occupation: the matter is not to be decided on the basis of the claimed intention of the parties. Since *Street v Mountford* [1985] AC 809, [1985] 2 All ER 289 generally a situation where a person has exclusive occupation of premises for *a term* (which may be on a fixed time or periodic basis, eg a week) at *a rent* is a tenancy. The courts normally lean in favour of finding a tenancy when there are disputes as to the residential status of an occupier. Indeed in *Family Housing Association v Jones* (1990) 22 HLR 45 (since otherwise overruled) it was doubted whether *in ordinary circumstances* it is possible to create a licence which gives exclusive occupation of a self-contained, separate residential unit in return for a money payment. Even so there are exceptional cases:

1) where a person is accommodated in a long stay hotel, *Luganda v Service Hotels Ltd* [1969] 2 Ch 209, [1969] 2 All ER 692;
2) where accommodation is provided in an old person's home, *Abbeyfield (Harpenden) Society Ltd v Woods* [1968] 1 All ER 352, [1968] 1 WLR 374;

3)   where the licensor is itself only a licensee of the premises, *Shepherds Bush Housing Association Ltd v HATS Co-operative* [1991] EGCS 134, and *Tower Hamlets London Borough Council v Miah* [1992] QB 622, [1992] 2 All ER 667;

4)   where the occupier is only a lodger whose contract allows the licensor to have total access to and use of the premises in order to provide the attendance and services;

5)   where the occupier is living in a hostel and does not live in separate accommodation within that hostel, *Central YMCA Housing Association Ltd and St Giles Hotel Ltd v Goodman* (1991) 24 HLR 109, CA and *Westminster City Council v Clarke* [1992] 2 AC 288, [1992] 1 All ER 695. Here C was placed in temporary hostel accommodation as a vulnerable homeless person as the first stage of discharge of homelessness duties. The hostel was used to accommodate single homeless men, including some with personality disorders or physical disabilities. There was a resident warden with a resettlement team of social workers. C was given a 'licence to occupy' and paid a weekly accommodation charge. His licence gave him no right of exclusive occupation of a particular room or accommodation which might be allocated to him. The licence gave the authority power to change allotted accommodation and to require C to share accommodation with any other person. The House of Lords took into account the need of the authority to retain total control over all rooms in the premises in order to discharge their homelessness duties, the very considerable limitations on the occupier's ability to enjoy any room allotted to him, the need for him to obtain approval before he could entertain guests, and for him to comply with instructions from resident staff and concluded his occupation could only be as a licensee;

6)   where a licence is granted as a temporary expedient to a squatter or where a person stays on in a property where he/she lived with the tenant after that tenant moves out, even where a charge is levied, *provided* it is made clear that no intention to create a tenancy ever exists, *Westminster City Council v Basson* (1990) 23 HLR 225 and *R v Barnet London Borough Council, ex p Grumbridge* (1992) 24 HLR 433. Informal arrangements whereby secure tenants share their accommodation with others will generally not give rise to any rights for those others vis a vis the landlord. This will be so even where those others occupy parts of the property and pay a contribution towards costs. The court will be slow to infer in such cases that the tenant intended to create a sub-tenancy, *Monmouth Borough Council v Marlog* [1994] 44 EG 240. However, authorities can be caught by their own inaction. In *Tower Hamlets London Borough Council v Ayinde* (1994) 26 HLR 631, a secure tenant invited the defendant into a council flat, and later wrote to the authority stating a decision to leave and not return

and requesting a transfer of the flat to the defendant, who thereafter paid rent which was accepted. The Court of Appeal found the letter from the original tenant to be a surrender which the authority had accepted and a new tenancy had been granted from the authority's knowledge of the situation and its acceptance of rent from the defendant.

However, it should be noted that when an authority grant an exclusive right to occupy certain living accommodation, eg a 'bed sitter', with cooking facilities (even with shared toilet facilities) that is likely to be, even if not a tenancy, a *secure licence* falling within section 79(3) of the 1985 Act and so subject to statutory protection.

To obtain the status of 'tenant' a person must also be allocated a property.

Allocation policies (council housing)

Section 21 of the Housing Act 1985 gives authorities power to pick and choose their tenants at will. It is true that section 22 currently states that authorities shall ensure that in selecting tenants (including existing tenants wishing to transfer) a reasonable preference is given to persons who are occupying insanitary or overcrowded houses, have large families or are living in unsatisfactory housing conditions and to persons towards whom they are subject to a duty under the homelessness provisions. Nevertheless the general selection and allocation powers of local authorities are subject to very little legal supervision, see per Lord Porter in *Shelley v LCC* [1949] AC 56 at 66, [1948] 2 All ER 898 at 900. Though the court may intervene in allocation decisions by way of judicial review, it is loath to do so, but will, for example, where an authority is clearly failing to do its reasonably practicable best for applicants for housing or where there is clear unlawfulness affecting the whole of an allocation scheme, *R v Newham London Borough Council, ex p Watkins* (1993) 26 HLR 434 and *R v Brent London Borough Council, ex p Sawyers* (1993) 26 HLR 44.

This does not mean that authorities have total *carte blanche* to allocate as they will: they must behave reasonably, and are subject to the general principles of administrative law. In *R v Canterbury City Council, ex p Gillespie* (1986) 19 HLR 7 a woman and her child lived in overcrowded and unsatisfactory situations following a relationship breakdown. The authority refused for almost three years to rehouse her, or even place her on a housing 'waiting list' unless she relinquished the joint tenancy she held with her former cohabitee. But the landlord authority for that tenancy would not accept the surrender because of rent arrears, and she could not take proceedings against the man as that could render their other child living with him homeless. It was held that the authority were rigidly adhering to a policy of not rehousing a person who had a share in a joint tenancy, and had fettered their discretion in not considering the applicant's peculiar circumstances. Similarly a rigid rule whereby tenants with rent arrears are not considered for rehousing, even where they have a good medical case for a transfer, is illegal, *R v Islington London Borough Council, ex p Aldabbagh* [1994] EGCS 156.

Authorities must not allocate homes for arrantly political reasons to enable a person to develop a residence into a 'power base' for a ward election, *R v Port Talbot Borough Council, ex p Jones* [1988] 2 All ER 207, 20 HLR 265, and should not refuse to house persons who owe them money particularly where other means of obtaining that money are available, *R v Forest Heath District Council, ex p West and Lucas* (1991) 24 HLR 85, nor should they *automatically* exclude from consideration for rehousing all owner occupiers *irrespective of need*, *R v Sutton London Borough Council, ex p Alger* (1992) Legal Action, (June) p 13 and *R v Bristol City, ex p Johns* (1992) 25 HLR 249. Furthermore allocation schemes must be fairly, rationally and even-handedly operated, *R v Tower Hamlets London Borough Council, ex p Mohib Ali* (1993) 25 HLR 218. Even so, authorities have virtually complete control over the process whereby they select their tenants. Section 22 gives no enforceable rights to individuals, and lays down no procedural requirement for authorities to follow, and it appears there is no general obligation for them to give reasons for allocation decisions in any great detail, *R v Newham London Borough Council, ex p Dawson* (1994) Legal Action, (September) p 10.

Residence qualifications

To operate allocation procedures authorities maintain what are officially termed 'housing registers' – more colloquially, and correctly, referred to as 'waiting lists'. Some authorities impose conditions for the entry of an applicant's name on the waiting list: for example a condition that an applicant must be living in the district at the time of application. Others achieve the same result by operating two waiting lists – a 'live' list made up of applicants with a real chance of being housed and a 'deferred' list made up of those considered not to be in serious need. Such pre-conditions for inclusion on housing waiting lists have been repeatedly criticised. Restrictions were criticised by the Central Housing Advisory Committee in 1949, 1953 and 1955, and in the 1969 report, *Council Housing: Purposes, Procedures and Priorities*, and in the 1978 Housing Services Advisory Group's Report *Housing for People*. However, since then other restrictions have been discovered. In some authorities there has been pressure to introduce an 'income bar', with those earning in excess of a certain sum being 'advised' to consider house purchase rather than council accommodation. Other authorities have very strict residence qualifications, coupled with income criteria. Some authorities additionally exclude single people from their normal allocations procedures, unless they are over a particular age, or have some special medical need. The 1983 Shelter Study *Restrictive Practices: Waiting List Restrictions and*

Housing Need found that 85% of authorities had residence requirements based on residence or employment within their districts. Similarly many authorities have 'minimum registration periods' before an applicant can receive an offer of accommodation, may be for up to 12 months. Even where an 'open' policy is adopted with regard to allowing anyone to register on a housing waiting list, actual *consideration* of an application made may still be affected by restrictive considerations. Such policies and practices fail to take into account people's need to be able to change accommodation in order to be able to take up employment in new areas.

The last point is particularly important in times of high unemployment when many may wish to move to parts of the country where new industries are creating employment opportunities. Home ownership may not always be open to such would-be migrants on grounds of cost, and so it is necessary to have some social housing available. Since 1981/82 local authorities and housing associations have participated in a *voluntary* mobility scheme now known as the Housing Organisation Mobility and Exchange Scheme (HOMES). This is open to tenants of participating bodies, and to others high on the waiting lists of those bodies, or in pressing need to move to a new area. They may apply to move under the scheme provided: they have obtained permanent employment beyond reasonable travelling distances from their existing homes; or they need to move on social grounds. The scheme operates at both county and national levels. At county level a number of lettings are made available by participating bodies on a quota basis designed to ensure that the number of moves *into* an area within a county is approximately equivalent to the numbers *from* that area rehoused elsewhere in the county. Nationally each participating body makes available 1% of annual lettings for persons needing to move to its area from beyond its county, and also makes available further lettings equal to the number of persons *from* its area who are rehoused *beyond* its county.

The scheme is operated bilaterally and receiving bodies apply their normal eligibility criteria to those wishing to move into their areas under the scheme, minus, of course, residence requirements.

Selection schemes (local authorities)

Even when an applicant's name is on a housing waiting list there is no guarantee of speedy rehousing. Some authorities allocate houses according to date order on a 'first-come-first-served' basis. A small number of authorities use merit schemes to allocate houses. Here tenants are selected according to the knowledge of councillors as to individual applicants. Such schemes have been criticised in the past, for example by the Housing Services Advisory Group in *Housing for People* [1978] and in *Council Housing: Purposes Procedures and Priorities*, which stated at paragraphs 122 and 123: 'Without [a clearly defined and publicised selection policy] it is difficult to achieve fairness and even more difficult to demonstrate it: particularly in small authorities and, in scattered rural areas members will be subject to pressure from applicants and officers will be subject to pressure from individual members'.

Most authorities allocate houses according to some sort of points system. Once applicants are registered the speed with which they are rehoused depends on the number of points they amass.

The general statement about points schemes obscures their vast diversity in practice. Their working varies, often quite dramatically, according to the factors selected for 'pointing' and according to the number of points actually allocated under each head of entitlement. The possibility of variation has been a cause of considerable concern to the critics of municipal housing practice. Factors frequently selected for the 'pointing' include:

1) the date of application;
2) the number of bedrooms needed by an applicant;
3) the size of the family involved;
4) whether the applicant is living in rooms as opposed to a self-contained house or flat;
5) whether the applicant has a separate living room;
6) whether the applicant, having children, occupies only a bed sitting room;
7) the existence of illegal overcrowding;
8) the enforced splitting-up of a family because of accommodation difficulties;
9) sexual embarrassments arising out of unsatisfactory sleeping arrangements;
10) ill-health or disability;
11) lack of amenities;
12) sharing kitchen facilities;
13) being forced to occupy badly located accommodation;
14) age of applicants;
15) the length of time of registration on the waiting list;
16) the suitability of the applicant for the accommodation sought;
17) other factors, such as hardship, or desire of the applicant to be accommodated near to friends or relatives.

Some authorities at discretion simply 'add on' extra points in individual cases, or otherwise vary points awarded so as to promote or retard an applicant's progress up the waiting list. Points schemes have been criticised for giving too much weight to factors which have no real relevance to housing *need* while other factors, for example disrepair, are not considered 'pointable'.

Other factors leading to variation in allocation procedures include different practices in collecting information about applicants: only 30% of authorities obtain information about ethnic origins. *Most* authorities know the number of elderly applicants they have, but a minority know how many applicants have children under 16. *Most* authorities review waiting lists annually to remove 'dead wood' applicants and also disagregate the list into various groups wanting housing, then allocating housing within groups by points schemes.

It is probably impossible to create one national housing allocation scheme because the needs and resources of authorities vary so much. Likewise some matters, such as cases of severe ill-health, or illegal eviction, or where the social services authority is involved, etc, cannot be dealt with by the routine points system, but must be dealt with by special allocations procedures. It also must be noted that in some areas 'ordinary' allocation of council housing has virtually ceased as properties are taken up under homelessness allocations: the priority need groups (see below Chapter Six) then become, somewhat ironically, effectively nationwide criteria for housing allocation. DoE research (*Routes into Local Authority Housing,* Prescot-Clarke, Clements and Park, 1994) indicates that nationally, homelessness is a factor contributing to allocation of council houses in 59% of cases, 78% in London. Some authorities, however, strive to retain some allocations to those on the waiting list and try to maintain a balance between their needs and those of the homeless: frequently there is considerable local political pressure to do this.

When a person has qualified to be housed by amassing a sufficiently large number of points, or by falling within the rehousing obligations of an authority, he/she will not be offered a free choice. Such a choice is impossible because factors such as the numbers of bedrooms needed have to be taken into account in the allocation process. Some authorities, however, base allocations on the reports of housing department officials who pay visits to potential tenants before the offer of a house is made.

These reports are frequently used to grade applicants, and, in general, the better the grade the applicant receives the better will be the choice of housing offered to him. See Murie, Niner and Watson in *Housing Policy and the Housing System* pp 125 to 126.

There is considerable debate amongst housing professionals about the use of such grading techniques. Some are very opposed to anything approaching 'vetting' of potential tenants and warn of the dangers of segregating those who may be considered 'less desirable types', and the consequent creation of stigmatised areas and estates. This is a powerful argument in the context of moves towards housing management being a social service rather more than simple property management.

The discretionary powers conferred on authorities can thus be used in a wide variety of ways. When Parliament confers discretionary power it intends authorities to make decisions. It would be wrong to argue that discretion should be entirely replaced by rigid legal rules which would be too inflexible to meet the variety of circumstances with which authorities have to cope. Nevertheless there is room for central guidance and/or model allocation schemes designed to iron out the most extreme variations that may be caused as a result of the adoption of differing selection and allocation practices.

The Housing Act 1985 took a few tentative steps in this direction. Section 106 states that every landlord authority (eg housing authorities) must publish summaries of rules for determining priorities between applicants in relation to the allocation of housing, and governing cases where secure tenants wish to move. An authority is not required to give an indication of how long an applicant may have to wait to be housed. Sets of allocation rules must be maintained by such bodies and made available for public inspection.

The reasoning behind this provision is that 'publicity is control'. As authorities are democratically elected bodies their electors may reject them at the polls should they disapprove of policies and procedures published for discussion and comment. That is the theory; whether local elections are conducted quite in that way is open to doubt! It can also be argued that public disquiet over a particular policy or procedure, especially as aired in the local press, *might* lead to a change on the part of the authority.

So far as an individual applicant for housing is concerned, section 106(5) of the 1985 Act provides:

> 'At the request of any person who has applied to it for hous-
> ing accommodation, a landlord authority shall make available
> to him, at all reasonable times and without charge, details of the
> particulars which he has given to the authority about himself
> and his family and which the authority has recorded as being
> relevant to his application for accommodation'.

This provision enables applicants to check that authorities have recorded the relevant details of applications (as supplied by those applicants) correctly. It does *not* entitle applicants to see any other facts, opinions, assessments or gradings recorded. Neither does it cover any right to change or challenge any particulars other those which *'he* has given to the authority'.

This right is supplemented by a greater one to have access to personal files under the Access to Personal Files Act 1987. Authorities keeping records containing 'personal information' are subject to requirements allowing personal access by virtue of regulations made under that Act. 'Personal Inform-ation' is that which relates to a living person identifiable from the information, including expressions of opinions, but not indications of an authority's intentions with regard to the individual, see sections 1 and 2 of the 1987 Act. Regulations are made under section 3 of the Act. Currently SI 1989/503 allows tenants, past tenants and would be tenants of authorities to obtain access to *certain* information concerning him/her, or a family member, held by an authority. Information relating to other identifiable persons cannot in general be obtained nor can certain confidential health information. Otherwise, on application in writing, and on receipt of the appropriate fee, an authority must inform a tenant whether it has accessible information on him/her, allow access to, and supply copies of it. Inaccurate information and erroneously formed opinions may be corrected or erased.

Allocation policies (housing associations)

Housing associations who are 'landlord authorities' within section 114 of the 1985 Act, ie registered housing associations (other than co-operative associations) and housing trusts that are charities fall within the ambit of section 106 as to the publication of information about housing allocations. Associations have to have their own selection and allocation rules, bearing in mind Housing Corporation advice on such matters, and counsel from the National Federation of Housing Associations. It is important for associations to make their selection criteria clearly public as they are not democratically answerable bodies yet are in receipt of considerable public funding, though the objects which an individual association was set up to achieve may constrain its selection and allocation policies. But within such constraints policies must be fairly and lawfully applied.

Particular guidance to associations has been issued by the Corporation under section 36A of the Housing Association Act 1985 as 'The Tenants' Guarantee' which, inter alia, stresses the need for equal opportunities policies to be pursued, see also Housing Corporation Circular HC 22/85 which further stresses that special measures may have to be taken to promote the interests of minority groups because they are often over represented amongst those in urgent housing need.

Reform

The Government's 1994 consultative paper *Access to Local Authority and Housing Association Tenancies* proposed radical changes in the legal basis of selection and allocation schemes for social housing organisations. So far as authorities are concerned it is proposed to replace section 22 of the 1985 Act with a provision requiring *all* authorities to maintain a housing waiting list, with *all* allocatees to secure tenancies and nominees to association tenancies being drawn from those lists, while allocation policies should be subject to terms and conditions laid down by Parliament. Thus while it is clear that social housing will be targetted primarily at low income groups, in allocating tenancies housing organisations will have to take account of individuals' housing circumstances, and the length of time they have been waiting to be rehoused. The replacement section 22 would accordingly:

(i) require authorities generally to grant secure tenancies and make nominations to associations' tenancies solely by reference to a 'nominated housing waiting list' held by authorities or their agents; for the operation of the list could be contracted out;

(ii) lay down principles in accordance with which priority for rehousing would be determined;

(iii)   lay down limits to the discretion of authorities to prescribe who may/ may not appear on the waiting list, eg by way of residence or age requirements;

(iv)   require publication of allocation rules *and* adherence to the rules once published;

 (v)   take as a determinant of allocation policy the need to balance time spent on a waiting list against intensity of need for rehousing;

(vi)   empower the Secretary of State (possibly) to issue guidance to authorities on detailed local application of allocation principles.

It was not clear at the time of issue of the consultative document whether the waiting list should include both new applicants for housing *and* existing tenants seeking transfers/exchanges. It was also hinted that authorities might be given some freedom to grant tenancies other than secure tenancies if this would ensure greater management flexibility. So far as associations are concerned the current policy of the Housing Corporation is that they should make available half their net lettings to tenants nominated by authorities. The new law would revise associations' obligations to authorities to reformulate them in a way appropriate to the new framework of authority powers and duties, particularly with regard to homelessness, see below Chapter Six. This reformulation would lead to revision of the Housing Corporation's regulatory standards and the Tenants' Guarantee (see below). Both associations and authorities would be expected to engage in a regular dialogue about allocation policy, and joint waiting lists between authorities and associations would be encouraged. Such joint lists would have to satisfy the requirements of the replacement section 22 but could also incorporate advice and support mechanisms, making provision for applicants to be directed to other sources of housing provision appropriate to them, such as the private rented sector. Ministers are keen that such 'one stop shops' methods of dealing with housing applications should develop.

In July 1994 the Government announced its intention to proceed with the proposal that for *new* applicants authorities should *only* allocate secure tenancies, or exercise nomination rights to association stock, through a waiting list. Authorities will only have discretion over allocation policies to the extent allowed by law, but it appears that the law will *not* involve itself in detailed regulation of allocation policies. What will be outlawed are, for example, what are regarded as discriminatory practices such as requiring five years' minimum residence qualifications before rehousing can take place. The object of the law will be to secure fairness and consistency. Associations and authorities will be encouraged to establish joint waiting lists, but these will not be compulsory. On a non-statutory basis authorities will be encouraged before the introduction of new legislation to develop more rational allocation systems. No proposed legislation to implement those measures was, however, included in the Queen's Speech in 1994.

Discrimination in housing allocation

Black people have fared badly in relation to housing in both sectors. The Commission for Racial Equality's (CRE) 1984 report *Race and Council Housing in Hackney* found in particular that white applicants were more likely to be housed in houses and maisonettes than blacks, who were more likely to be placed in flats, very often on the sixth floor or higher. White applicants were also much more likely to receive new properties from the local authority than blacks. The inequality of treatment could only be attributable to racial discrimination. The earlier report *Allocation of Council Housing with Particular Reference to Work Permit Holders* (CRE, November 1982) found discriminatory practices in providing housing for short stay foreign workers on work permits by the Greater London Council and two London Boroughs. Note also the 1989 Central Government report on housing discrimination *Response to Racial Attacks and Harassment* (HMSO).

Black people have suffered for a variety of reasons: language problems and a lack of knowledge, experience and negotiating ability in applying for public sector housing; poor existing housing leading to low expectations of what the public sector can offer, both factors tending to lead landlords to offer less desirable housing; allocations systems disadvantaging ethnic groups, for example rules barring owner-occupiers from eligibility for rehousing which can operate against those who live in small, poor quality houses in inner city areas; the housing construction system which provides units apt for western families.

In a multi-racial society, both the law and administration of housing must operate to promote equal housing opportunities. Section 71 of the Race Relations Act 1976 makes it the general duty of authorities to work towards the elimination of discrimination and to promote good race relations and equal opportunities for all. Under section 75(5) of the Housing Associations Act 1985 the Housing Corporation has a similar duty. Other provisions are also relevant to housing. Section 21 of the 1976 Act provides:

'(1) It is unlawful for a person, in relation to premises...of which he has power to dispose, to discriminate against another –
    (a) in terms on which he offers those premises; or
    (b) by refusing his application for those premises; or
    (c) in his treatment of him in relation to any list of persons in need of premises of that description.
(2) It is also unlawful for a person, in relation to any premises managed by him, to discriminate against a person occupying the premises –
    (a) in the way he affords him access to any benefits or facilities, or by refusing or deliberately omitting to afford him access to them; or

(b)   by evicting him, or subjecting them to any other detriment'

Unlawful discrimination can happen in two ways.

Direct racial discrimination

This is the act of treating another less favourably on grounds of colour, race, nationality or ethnic or national origins, see sections 1(1)(a) and 3(1) of the Race Relations Act 1976, for example to refuse an applicant's name for rehousing because he/she is black.

Good housing practice will reflect the requirements of the non-discrimination notice issued by the CRE to Hackney London Borough Council under section 58 of the 1976 Act:

1)   landlords should record the ethnic origin of all applicants for housing, and those they house, and monitor records regularly in relation to the quality, type, age and location of properties offered to applicants;

2)   there should be a review of procedures, practices and criteria used in allocation and transfer matters, and such procedures, etc, should be clearly relevant to housing need and applied equally;

3)   housing staff should be trained to avoid discriminatory practices, to inform applicants of all options available to them, to consider the special needs and preferences of applicants, and to apply only criteria relevant to housing need in allocation decisions, particularly where a number of applicants are effectively competing for an available dwelling.

It is also wise for landlords to know the racial composition of the communities within their areas, provide facilities for communicating with members of minority groups in their own languages, understand the cultural and family patterns of ethnic groups, and where possible, to provide appropriate accommodation within their housing stock for extended families. Similarly it should not be assumed that all black people will wish to live in the same area.

However, though direct discrimination is suffered by black people in housing, it is more common to encounter indirect discrimination which unintentionally leads to housing disadvantage.

Indirect racial discrimination

This is the act of applying to a person a requirement or condition which applies equally to persons of *other* racial groups but which is:

1)   such that the proportion of persons of the *same* racial group as that of the person affected who can comply with the condition is considerably smaller than the proportion of persons not of that group who can comply;

2)   not *justifiable* irrespective of the colour, race, nationality or ethnic or national origins of the persons to whom it applies; and

3)   is to that person's detriment because he cannot comply with it. See section 1(1)(b) of the 1976 Act.

The following are examples of indirectly discriminatory practices:

1)   a requirement that applicants for authority housing must have been resident in an authority area for a specified period because fewer numbers of ethnic minority groups could comply with the residence requirements than could members of the host community, or;

2)   a requirement that housing points can only be given for children actually living with an applicant, as this works to the detriment of immigrants part of whose families have yet to join them;

3)   use of racial stereotypes;

4)   steering particular people to particular areas on racial assumptions;

5)   applying criteria which result in single parent families being accorded low priority on housing waiting lists.

Those authorities who apply residence qualifications should certainly review them to ensure that they do not result in indirect discrimination. Indeed it is arguable that a landlord operating a residence requirement might have to justify it under the terms of the legislation; in other words show that it is supported by adequate reasons which would be accepted by right thinking people as sound and tolerable, see *Ojutiku v Manpower Services Commission* [1982] ICR 661, [1982] IRLR 418. It is not enough to argue a practice is needed because it is practically convenient or preserves a particular image of a service, see *Kingston and Richmond Area Health Authority v Kaur* [1981] ICR 631, [1981] IRLR 337. Landlords should consider carefully whether residence requirements result in recognisable discrimination, and assess how serious is that effect.

They should ask what purpose they seek to achieve by the requirement and whether that could be achieved by non-discriminatory or less discriminatory means. Then they must weigh and balance all these issues and ask whether residence requirements can be objectively considered to be reasonable and equitable.

Section 47 of the Race Relations Act 1976, as amended by section 137 of the Housing Act 1988, provides for the introduction of Codes of Practice to eliminate *racial* discrimination and promote equal *racial* opportunities in housing, such codes are admissible as evidence in proceedings under the Race Relations legislation, and must be taken into account in deciding whether unlawful discrimination has taken place where relevant provisions of the Code are not adhered to. The Race Relations Code of Practice begins by outlining the relevant general law and gives examples of good equal opportunity practices. It then exhorts housing organisations to pursue declared equal opportunities policies with regard to access to, and *quality* of housing, and the delivery of housing services, and to keep practices and procedures under constant review so as to eliminate any form of discrimination by way of record keeping and monitoring. Training should thus be given to staff to ensure they understand equal opportunities policies and the needs of minorities. The policy should further extend to combating racial harassment and the support of victims of such harassment. Monitoring records should be undertaken and the unmet needs of minority groups considered so that action may be taken in respect of them. Organisations are further counselled to adopt clearly non-discriminatory selection and allocation procedures and to avoid practices that smack of racial discrimination – eg asking a person to produce a passport as a means of identification. The delivery of services to tenants should also be non-discriminatory so that repairs and housing advice are not provided for the host community faster than for tenants from a minority group.

NB It should be noted that section 35 of the Race Relations Act 1976 while not permitting positive discrimination does allow positive or affirmative action to assist in redressing imbalances between racial groups by making it lawful for members of particular racial groups to have access to, inter alia, housing services and facilities to meet special needs in respect of education, training or welfare, etc. Under this section the Positive Action Training in Housing (PATH) initiative has been taken to encourage members of ethnic minorities to pursue education and training in housing. How far action under section 35 could go is debatable. Arguably it would cover encouraging more ethnic minority applications for social housing, ensuring the proportion of applications is proportional to representation in local populations, making ethnic minorities fully aware of social housing opportunities, and developing housing programmes attuned to minority needs. These are all matters which associations could certainly address, and in this connection see also Housing Corporation Circular 22/85.

For provisions relating to sex discrimination see sections 1 and 30 of the Sex Discrimination Act 1975, for women of all races suffer particular discrimination in housing.

For an exhaustive treatment of the issue of racial and sexual discrimination in housing see Handy, *Discrimination in Housing*, 1993.

Tenure of council dwellings

The rights of secure tenants are contained in Part IV of the 1985 Act. Sections 79 to 81 define tenancy as secure where the following conditions are satisfied:

1)   the dwelling must be let as a separate dwelling-house; there must be no sharing of 'living accommodation' (for example kitchens, but *not* bathrooms or lavatories) with other households, see *Neale v Del Soto* [1945] KB 144, *Cole v Harris* [1945] KB 474 and *Thompson v City of Glasgow* 1986 SLT (Lands Tr) 6 where a single bedroom in a multi-

storey block run for single men which had no cooking or washing facilities and where the occupant did not carry out all his 'living' was held *not* to be 'separate';

2)   the landlord must be a local authority, eg a county or district council, a London Borough council, an urban development corporation, or a housing action trust.

NB Until 15 January 1989, secure tenancies could also be granted by registered associations and the Housing Corporation. Such tenancies granted before that date remain secure;

3)   the tenant must be an individual, or in the case of a joint tenancy each joint tenant must be an individual, and he/she, or in the case of joint tenants at least one of them, must occupy the dwelling as his/her only *or* principal home; a tenant may thus have more than one home, but only a *principal* home, which is an issue of fact in each case, can be the subject of a secure tenancy; furthermore a tenant need not be physically present in a dwelling provided there is an intention to return and to retain possession which may be evidenced by the presence of furniture, *Crawley Borough Council v Sawyer* (1987) 20 HLR 98.

4)   the tenancy must not fall within the excepted classes as laid down in Schedule 1. These are:

a)   long tenancies, that is a tenancy granted for a term certain exceeding 21 years;

b)   premises occupied by the tenant as a requirement of a contract of employment directed to the better performance of his/her duties; it is for the landlord to show the exemption exists, *Hughes & Hughes v London Borough of Greenwich* (1992) 24 HLR 605; there is no presumption automatically arising from the mere fact of employment, someone may continue to live in a property originally subject to a service tenancy and yet do another job which does not require residence, in which case the exemption ceases to apply, *Little v Borders Regional Council* 1990 SLT (Lands Tr) 2 and *McEwan v Annandale and Eskdale District Council* 1989 SLT (Lands Tr) 95. Conversely where a person takes a tenancy of a dwelling and subsequently accepts employment in consequence of which residence in that dwelling is a contractual requisite, the exemption applies, *Elvidge v Coventry City Council* [1993] EGCS 140. Retirement *may* not, however, automatically destroy the exemption, once it applies, *South Glamorgan County Council v Griffiths* [1992] EGCS 10;

c)   where (i) the tenant is a member of the police and the dwelling is provided rent free under the Police Act 1964, or where (ii) the tenant is a fire authority employee *and* his/her contract of employment requires him/her to live close to a particular fire station, *and* the dwelling was let by the fire authority in consequence of that requirement, or where (iii) within the period of three years immediately preceding the grant of the tenancy the police, or fire authority conditions above, or the conditions in (b) above have been satisfied with respect to *a* tenancy of the dwelling, *and* before the grant the landlord notified the tenant in writing of the circumstances, stating that the tenancy would fall within this exemption; but in this case the tenancy is only non-secure until the periods during which the conditions are not satisfied with regard to the tenancy amount, in aggregate, to *more* than three years;

d)   where the house stands on land acquired for development and is only being used as temporary housing accommodation, it will, however, be a question of fact in any given case whether an intention to redevelop land survives an extended period during which no action is taken and at the end of which there is little prospect of redevelopment, *Lillieshall Road Housing Co-operative Ltd v Brennan and Brennan* [1991] EGCS 132; however, a simple change in planned development will not be enough to destroy the exemption, *Attley v Cherwell District Council* (1989) 21 HLR 613, neither does the *immediate* landlord have to have an intention to develop, provided that is the owner's intention, *Hyde Housing Association Ltd v Harrison* [1990] EGCS 122;

e)   where accommodation has been provided temporarily for a homeless person under section 63, 65(3) or 68(1) of the 1985 Act, the tenancy cannot become secure before the expiry of a period of 12 months beginning with the date on which he/she receives notification of the local authority's findings as to his homelessness, unless he/she is notified otherwise within that period;

f)   accommodation *specifically* granted to a person who was immediately before the grant not resident in the district, and having employment or the offer thereof, within the district or its adjoining districts, to meet a need for temporary accommodation in order to work there, and also to enable him/her to find permanent housing, cannot be subject to a secure tenancy before the expiry of one year from the grant unless the tenant is otherwise notified within that period;

g)   where the landlord has taken only a short term lease from a body incapable of granting secure tenancies, for example a private individual, of a dwelling for the purpose of providing temporary accommodation, on terms including one that the lessor may obtain vacant possession on the expiry of a specified period or when he requires it, there is no secure tenancy for *their* lessees,

and the position is the same where the property has been *licensed* to the landlord, *Tower Hamlets London Borough Council v Miah* [1992] QB 622, [1992] 2 All ER 667;

h)   a tenancy is not secure if it is of a dwelling made available for occupation by the tenant while works are being carried out at his/her own former home, *and* provided the tenant was *not* secure in that home;

i)   where the tenancy is of an agricultural holding under the Agricultural Holdings Act 1948 and the tenant is a manager;

j)   where the tenancy is of licensed premises;

k)   where the tenancy is one granted specifically to a student to enable attendance on a designated course at a university or further education establishment;

l)   where the tenancy is of business premises falling within Part II of the Landlord and Tenant Act 1954;

m)   where the licence to occupy the dwelling was granted by an alms-house charity.

All tenancies excluded from 'secure' status simply exist at common law and, in general, may be terminated by four weeks written notice to quit, *Cannock Chase District Council v Kelly* [1978] 1 All ER 152, [1978] 1 WLR 1 and *Sevenoaks District Council v Emmott* (1979) 39 P & CR 404

Security of tenure

The basic rule contained in section 82 of the Housing Act 1985 is that a secure tenancy cannot be brought to an end at the landlord's behest without an order from the court (that is the county court by virtue of section 110).

NB *Tenants* may bring tenancies to an end by simply giving notice to quit in due form, ie by complying with any term governing notice in their agreements, and, generally, section 5 of the Protection from Eviction Act 1977 will require there to be four weeks notice in writing to expire at the end of a tenancy period, see further Chapter Five below.

The court may not entertain proceedings for an order unless the landlord has first served on the tenant a notice in correct ministerially specified form stating the ground on which the court will be asked to give possession, but the ground may be altered with the leave of the court, see sections 83 and 84. In the case of a periodic tenancy the landlord's notice, which will have a currency of 12 months, must also specify a date after which possession proceedings may be begun. That date must not be earlier than the date on the which the tenancy could, apart from the Act be brought to an end by notice to quit given on the same day as the landlord's notice.

A notice not containing all requisite information (see SI 1988/2201) will be defective leading to dismissal of proceedings, *Swansea City Council v Hearn* (1990) 23 HLR 284. Note also the requirements of section 48 of the Landlord and Tenant Act 1987 that *landlords* generally must furnish tenants with an address at which notices may be served on the landlord by the tenant – a requirement relevant to the inception of possession proceedings.

The court may not, however, grant a possession order outside the parameters fixed by the legislation, even if the parties agree to it, *Wandsworth London Borough Council v Fadayomi* [1987] 3 All ER 474, [1987] 1 WLR 1473. Furthermore, the Notice of Intention to Seek Possession (NISP) must make it clear to its recipient what is needed to amend the situation leading to an action, eg by specifying the level of arrears in question, but a mere minor error in these particulars will not invalidate the notice, *Torridge District Council v Jones* (1985) 18 HLR 107 and *Dudley Metropolitan Borough Council v Bailey* (1990) 22 HLR 424.

The grounds on which possession may be given are found in Schedule 2 of the 1985 Act. Their substance is as follows.

Ground 1

Where any rent lawfully due from the tenant has not been paid, or where any obligation of the tenancy has been broken or not performed. The use of possession action to deal with arrears of rent will be considered below. Note that an authority may apply for a mandatory prohibitory injunction to enforce a negative covenant (eg a 'no pets' clause) in a tenancy agreement. Such a remedy is discretionary and the tenant may resist on the basis that greater hardship would flow from granting the order than would follow from denying it, *Sutton Housing Trust v Lawrence* (1987) 19 HLR 520. Injunctive relief can only be obtained under this ground to enforce terms of a tenancy already imposed, not to rewrite an existing agreement. Some authorities, however, make use of their power to prohibit racial harassment by means of a tenancy obligation and possession has been obtained in cases of breach. Where a breach of covenant is admitted, and there is clearly an intention to continue the breach the court will only rarely refuse to grant a possession order, *Sheffield City Council v Green* [1993] EGCS 185. Clauses forbidding harassment by tenants are the most common methods used by authorities to prevent racist behaviour on estates, coupled with well publicised policies on violence and harassment, and it appears a majority of authorities are now prepared to at least threaten possession proceedings against tenants who perpetrate racist incidents, though many authorities are also prepared to move victims of such abuse as a matter of priority – this may be seen as 'rewarding' a perpetrator whose desire was to drive away a neighbour. For further details see Love and Kirby *Racial Incidents in Council Housing: The Local Authority Response* (HMSO, 1994).

Ground 2

Where the tenant or any person residing in the dwelling has been guilty of acts of nuisance or annoyance to neighbours, or has been convicted of using the house for illegal or immoral purposes. However, there is no implied term in a secure tenancy obliging the landlord to enforce the tenant's obligation not to commit a nuisance, the remedy is an action in nuisance on the part of those aggrieved, see *O'Leary v Islington London Borough Council* (1983) 9 HLR 81. A local authority landlord is not *in general* liable for nuisance committed by a council tenant, see *Smith v Scott* [1973] Ch 314, [1972] 3 All ER 645.

Increasing use of this ground is expected as landlords respond to pressures from other tenants to take action against those whose conduct affects others' use and enjoyment of property. For the ground to be made out it must be shown either that the tenant has been guilty of acts or nuisance or annoyance to those who are 'neighbours' though they need not be physically contiguous neighbours, *Cobstone Investments Ltd v Maxim* [1985] QB 140, [1984] 2 All ER 635, *or* that someone residing with the tenant has committed such acts and the tenant took no reasonable steps to prevent the activity, eg by eviction of the wrongdoer, *Commercial General Administration Ltd v Thomsett* (1979) 250 Estates Gazette 547. Alternatively the tenant must have been convicted of using the house for immoral purposes, such as a brothel, or for illegal purposes, such as using the dwelling to make explosive devices. It is not enough to show a dwelling was simply the place where an offence was committed, *Schneiders & Sons Ltd v Abrahams* [1925] 1 KB 301, while the tenant took no active part in the illegal activity, *Wandsworth London Borough Council v Hargreaves* [1994] EGCS 115.

As with Ground 1 injunctive relief may be obtained, either on a final or an interim (interlocutory) basis, to restrain the commission of nuisances, and an authority may be able to obtain such an order to prevent a dispossessed tenant from returning to the dwelling to continue a nuisance, see *Liburd v Cork* [1981] CLY 1999. Note also *Woking Borough Council v Bystram* [1993] EGCS 208 where a suspended possession order was granted in respect of a continuing nuisance arising from the defendant's use of foul and abusive behaviour which other residents on his estate found menacing.

Ground 3

Where the condition of the dwelling or any common parts of a building comprising the dwelling have deteriorated as a result of the tenant's waste, neglect or default or as a result of the acts of any person residing in the dwelling-house whom the tenant (if that person is a lodger or sub-tenant) has unreasonably failed to remove from the dwelling.

Ground 4

Where the condition of any furniture provided by the landlord for use under the tenancy (or in any common parts of a building as the case may be) has deteriorated as result of ill treatment by the tenant or any person residing in the dwelling.

Ground 5

Where the tenant obtained the tenancy knowingly or recklessly by false statements.

Ground 6

Where the tenancy was assigned to the tenant, or to the tenant's predecessor in title being a member of the tenant's family and residing in the dwelling, by virtue of exchange under section 92 *and* a premium was paid in connection therewith.

Ground 7

Where the dwelling is comprised within a building held by the landlord mainly for non-housing purposes and consisting mainly of non-housing accommodation, *and* the dwelling was let to the tenant in consequence of employment by the landlord, or the local authority etc, *and* the tenant, or a person residing in the dwelling, has been guilty of conduct such that, having regard to the purpose for which the building is used, it would be wrong for the tenant to remain in occupation.

Ground 8

Where the tenant, being a secure tenant of another dwelling which is his/her home and which is subject to works, has accepted the tenancy of the dwelling of which possession is sought on condition that he/she would move back to the original home on completion of the works in question, and where the works have been completed. *Tower Hamlets London Borough Council v Abadie* [1990] EGCS 4 indicates that a tenant may defend under this ground by showing the original accommodation is not being offered.

Ground 9

Where the dwelling-house is illegally overcrowded.

Ground 10

Where the landlord intends within a reasonable time to demolish, or reconstruct or carry out works on the dwelling, etc, and cannot do so without obtaining possession. Here a mere desire simply to remove a particular person from a particular dwelling is not enough: the landlord must show a clearly defined and settled intention to do major works which cannot be done without possession being obtained, *Wansbeck District Council v Marley* (1987) 20 HLR 247.

Ground 10 A (Introduced by the Housing and Planning Act 1986)

Where the dwelling is in an area subject to a ministerially approved re-development scheme under Part V of Schedule 2 and the landlord intends to dispose of the dwelling under the scheme within reasonable time of obtaining possession.

Under Part V of Schedule 2 approval may be given for schemes of disposal and redevelopment of areas of dwellings. Landlords must first serve notice on affected tenants stating the main features of the scheme, that they intend to apply for approval, the effect of approval in relation to possession proceedings, and giving the tenants at least 28 days to make representations. Landlords must not apply for approval before considering representations made. In considering whether to approve a scheme the Secretary of State must particularly consider the effect of the scheme on housing accommodation in the area, the proposed time scale of the scheme, the extent to which housing to be provided under the scheme is to be sold or let to existing tenants and other representations made to him or brought to his notice. Approval may be given subject to conditions. Suitable alternative accommodation must be available.

Ground 11

Where the landlord is a charity and continued occupation by the tenant would conflict with its objects.

Ground 12

Where the dwelling is sited in a building held by the landlord mainly for non-housing purposes and consisting of mainly non-housing accommodation, *and* the dwelling was let to the tenant in consequence of employment by the landlord, or the local authority etc, *and* that employment has ceased *and* the landlord reasonably requires the dwelling for some other employee.

Ground 13

Where the dwelling has features which are substantially different from those of ordinary houses so as to make it suitable for occupation by a physically disabled person, and where there is no longer such a disabled person living in the house, while the landlord requires the dwelling for occupation by such a person.

Ground 14

The landlord is a housing association or trust which lets dwellings to persons whose non-financial circumstances make it difficult for them to satisfy their housing need, and *either* there is no longer such a person residing in the dwelling, *or* the tenant has received an offer of a secure dwelling from a local authority, *and* the landlord requires the dwelling for occupation by a person with special needs.

Ground 15

Where the dwelling is one of a *group* which it is the practice of the landlord to let for occupation by persons with special needs, and also:
1)   a social service or special facility is provided in close proximity to the dwellings in order to assist those with the special needs;
2)   there is no longer a person with those needs residing in the house, and
3)   the landlord requires the house for someone with those needs.
   Note that a *'group'* cannot be made up of a number of dispersed properties all of which have the special features in question, *Martin v Motherwell District Council* 1991 SLT (Lands Tr) 4.

Ground 16

Where the tenant, being a successor (other than a spouse successor), by virtue of being a member of the deceased previous tenant's family, is under occupying the dwelling, in that it is too large for reasonable requirements. Notice of intention to commence possession proceedings must be served *more* than six months, but *less* than twelve months, after the date of death of the original tenant. In determining whether to make an order under this ground the court must consider, inter alia, the tenant's age, the period of occupation of the dwelling and any financial or other support given by the tenant to the previous tenant.
   The court is not to make a possession order on Grounds 1 to 8 unless it considers it reasonable to do so; on Grounds 9 to 11 unless it is satisfied that suitable accommodation will be available for the tenant on the order taking effect, and on Grounds 12 to 16 unless *both* conditions are satisfied.

What is to be regarded as 'suitable accommodation' for the purposes of granting possession is defined by Schedule 2, Part IV of the 1985 Act.

Accommodation is suitable if it is to be let as a separate dwelling under a secure or assured tenancy, and the court considers the accommodation is reasonably suitable to the needs of the tenant and his/her family. The court must consider the nature of the accommodation usually let by the landlord to persons with similar needs; distances between the accommodation and relevant places of work or employment and the home of any member of the tenant's family if closeness between the parties is essential to the well-being of either; needs and means of the tenant; terms on which the accommodation is available; where furniture was provided in the former tenancy, whether furniture will be provided in the new accommodation.

General considerations affecting discretionary grounds of possession

Under section 85 of the Act the court has extended discretion as to ordering possession.

Where possession proceedings are brought under Grounds 1 to 8 and 12 to 16 above, the court may adjourn the proceedings for such periods as it thinks fit. Where a possession order is made under any of the above grounds its execution may be stayed, suspended or postponed for such period as the court thinks fit. Where the court exercises this discretion it must impose conditions with regard to the payment of any arrears of rent, etc, unless it considers that to do so would cause exceptional hardship to the tenant or would be otherwise unreasonable. Other conditions may be imposed. Where these conditions are fulfilled the court may rescind or discharge the order. A tenant's spouse or former spouse having rights of occupation under the Matrimonial Homes Act 1983, and in occupation of a dwelling, the tenancy of which is terminated by possession proceedings, has the same rights with regard to suspensions and adjournments, etc, as if his/her rights of occupation were not affected by termination. In those cases where the court must be satisfied that it is reasonable to make a possession order, *Woodspring District Council v Taylor* (1982) 4 HLR 95, an action under Case 1 should be noted. The tenants had maintained a satisfactory rent record for over 20 years, and then ran up arrears as a result of unemployment and disability. The court held that it is for the landlord to show why it would be reasonable to grant possession.

Landlords should not assume that a tenant vacating a dwelling while owing rent is evidence of surrender of the tenancy, *Sutton London Borough Council v Swann* (1985) 18 HLR 140. In such circumstances landlords should seek possession on the statutory grounds, *Preston Borough Council v Fairclough* (1982) 8 HLR 70.

The court may also take into account the homelessness consequences of making a possession order, *Rushcliffe Borough Council v Watson* (1991) 24

HLR 124. Where a suspended possession order is granted failure by the tenant to meet its conditions means the tenancy is ended, *Thompson v Elmbridge Borough Council* (1987) 19 HLR 526, though even here the county court retains jurisdiction to suspend execution of the order, *R v Ilkeston County Court, ex p Kruza* (1985) 17 HLR 539. *R v Newham London Borough Council, ex p Campbell* [1994] Fam Law 319, 26 HLR 183 indicates, however, that once a tenancy is lost by breach of a suspended order, making a further suspension does *not* revive the tenancy: the tenant simply has a personal status of irremovability while the terms of the suspension are complied with (and until they are discharged). This is a most untidy situation, and many landlords – let alone tenants – are unlikely to understand the consequences of breach of a suspended order.

It is possible to set a suspended order aside or to appeal against the making of such an order, *Peabody Donations Fund Governors v Hay* (1986) 19 HLR 145. Even after an order has been executed it may still be set aside on appeal provided the landlord is not prejudiced, *Tower Hamlets London Borough Council v Abadie* (supra).

Once a possession order has been granted the landlord may proceed to execute it by obtaining a county court warrant, and no need exists to inform the tenant of an application for warrant, *Leicester City Council v Aldwinckle* (1991) 24 HLR 40. Once the order has been executed, the warrant for possession may not be set aside or suspended unless: (a) the possession order itself is set aside; (b) the warrant has been obtained by fraud, or (c) there has been some abuse of process or person during execution, see *Peabody Donation Fund Governors v Hay* (supra). The lack of notice to the tenant has been the subject of adverse judicial criticism, *Hammersmith and Fulham London Borough Council v Hill* [1994] 35 EG 124.

Where the court makes a possession order on grounds where the reasonableness of the issue is not a deciding factor, discretion is limited by section 89 of the Housing Act 1980 (still in force). So far as secure tenancies are concerned this provision is relevant where recovery of possession is sought under Grounds 9 to 11. In such circumstances the giving up of possession cannot be postponed (whether by the order itself, or any variation, suspension or stay) to a date later than 14 days after the making of the order unless it appears to the court that exceptional hardship would be caused by requiring possession to be given up by that date. In such cases the giving up of possession may be suspended for up to six weeks from the making of the order but for no longer. The provision also applies to non-secure tenancies.

Use of possession proceedings in cases of arrears

The great majority of possession actions brought by authorities concern arrears of rent. Such actions may frequently go through the county court 'on the nod' with suspended orders being granted, but they have the disadvantage of putting the tenancy at risk. Where arrears of rent are the basis for an action they must be specified in the NISP and proved in court, *and* the landlord must still convince the court it is reasonable to make a possession order taking into account the conduct of both parties and the public interest in the matter. The arrears must exist at the date proceedings commenced, and a refusal to accept rent tendered will mean there are no arrears, while a tender of arrears after the commencement of proceedings is likely to persuade the court against making an order save where the tenant has a history of persistent late payment, see *Bird v Hildage* [1948] 1 KB 91, *Haringey London Borough Council v Stewart and Stewart* (1991) 23 HLR 557 and *Taylor v Woodspring District Council* (supra). The arrears must have been run up by the tenant in question, *Tickner v Clifton* [1929] 1 KB 207, while disputes as to the amount of rent owed may reduce the likelihood of an order being make, *Dun Laoghaire UDC v Moran* [1921] 2 IR 404. The court will also consider the nature of the arrears, eg are they recent, and the reason for their existence, and whether the landlord is itself in breach of any of its obligations.

However, how does the law work in practice? The research study *'Taking Tenants to Court'* Leather & Jeffers (DoE 1989) discovered that orders are most often sought for rent arrears, and that authorities have evolved their own procedures for such cases involving:
1) identification of the problem;
2) issuing a NISP;
3) allowing a minimum period of 28 days before seeking a county court summons;
4) the setting of the hearing date, and finally
5) the judgement – which, if for an order, is usually suspended.

On average the number of NISPS served as a percentage of housing stock was 8.7%, though the figures varied from a high of 21% to a low of 3%. There is an enormously wide variation in the numbers of court cases as a percentage of NISPS. On average that percentage was 29.7%, but the high was 74% and the low 8% – clearly there is a wide variation in practice between authorities as to what happens after a NISP has been served and before action starts. Equally there is variation as to what level of rent arrears will lead to a case being taken to court, with the figure for one authority being as low as £169 while the highest figure was £988. Most authorities are generally successful in gaining orders where they seek them.

Though some suspended orders are discharged, many tenants do not comply with conditions and discharge their debts, which suggests limited effectiveness for such orders. However, an application for a warrant to evict tends to produce a flurry of response, either in the form of some payment, or with the tenant leaving voluntarily – often with no forwarding address. This suggests that from the authority's point of view possession proceedings are not truly effective as a means of dealing with arrears. Certainly from the tenant's point of view they are unsatisfactory. It has a long been argued, and the 1989 survey confirms this, that most tenants in arrears served with a NISP do not realise their tenancies are in danger. Tenants rarely know how to respond in such circumstances, lack independent advice on how to act, are intimidated by courts, and especially by public hearings. Many do not attend their actions, sometimes because they are encouraged not to, having reached an informal agreement that the authority should have a suspended order from which has grown the myth of the 'consented possession order'.

A procedure which *did not* put the tenancy at risk was the Rent Action, introduced in 1971 under the County Court Rules to enable recovery of rent from a tenant, including one still in occupation of a dwelling. The action was little used, and most authorities argued possession proceedings were more efficacious (Duncan & Kirby, *Preventing Rent Arrears*, HMSO, 1983). The action was abolished in 1993 (SI 1993/2175).

Distress is the other remedy for arrears of rent. It was characterised as 'archaic' by Lord Denning in *Abingdon RDC v O'Gorman* [1968] 2 QB 811, [1968] 3 All ER 79, and is subject to severe restrictions in relation to assured tenancies under the Housing Act 1988. In 1986 the Law Commission, in an interim report recommending its abolition, concluded the remedy was riddled with inconsistencies, uncertainties, anomalies and archaisms. However, in 1978 105 authorities used distress regularly as a remedy and 32 used it exceptionally. In 1986 CIPFA concluded from its postal survey of all 405 English and Welsh authorities (which received a 68% response) that amongst English shire districts use of distress was evenly matched by non-use. Further research carried out for the Certificated Bailiffs' Association in the late 1980s revealed a total then of 102 English and Welsh authorities using distress – 1 inner London Borough, 7 outer London Boroughs, 2 Metropolitan districts, 86 shire districts and 6 Welsh districts. Not all authorities using distress in 1978 were still using it in 1986-88. Authorities may take up use of distress and then refrain from it over a period of time. The pattern of use is not necessarily connected with the party 'colour' of an authority.

However, what is distress? Very briefly it is a remedy which allows the landlord to obtain satisfaction of rent in arrears by the seizure and sale of certain goods found on the premises in respect of which rent is due. Only certain goods may be the subject of distress – clothing and bedding are, for example, exempt up to certain values. Survey evidence suggests the sort of goods usually taken are easily transportable and saleable items, such as electrical goods, and luxury items such as cameras and jewellery. The actual procedure for levying distress is exceptionally technical. Those levying distress may not break into a house or enter by force, though they may enter by a door which is closed but not fastened. Once inside, however, inner doors may be broken open during the levying process. Bailiffs may also enter via *open* windows, and may climb over walls and fences from adjoining premises –

these are merely some of the minutiae of the technical rules. However, these detailed rules are, it has been repeatedly alleged, often overlooked. Many complaints have been made of the behaviour of bailiffs.

DoE Circular 18/87 did not counsel against the use of distress, however, and it is unlikely that the present government will take up the Law Commission's 1991 final proposal to abolish the remedy. Nevertheless of all the legal remedies for arrears considered it is the most unsatisfactory.

1) It is discriminatory in that it is effectively available only against authority tenants.
2) Its use is geographically uneven.
3) Where authorities do use it there seems to be little concern as to how and when. Some are long term users, adopting it as a well publicised part of a managerial stance on arrears, others resort to it only rarely, perhaps as a short, sharp shock, others use it as a threat.
4) The amounts levied by distress often bear no resemblance to the amounts owed.
5) There is no long term evidence to suggest that distress prevents the build up of arrears where these are caused by misfortune and poverty.
6) Bailiffs are subject to weak regulation, and yet the evidence suggests they can act in an abusive, intimidatory and illegal manner.

If distress is to continue in use as a remedy for arrears measures need to be taken to remove at least the worst abuses. These could include stricter guidance from the DoE on the use of distress, if necessary backed up by legislation; the use of distress only after a policy decision to that end has been taken by the full council, who thereupon become democratically answerable for their decision; and a stricter regulation and examination of the qualifications of bailiffs to act. Failing these steps it is hard to see how the continued use of an arcane, medieval remedy can be countenanced.

Other individual rights of secure tenants

Subletting and assignment

Section 93(1)(a) of the Housing Act 1985 makes it a term of secure tenancies that tenants may allow any person to reside as lodgers. Section 93(1)(b) goes on to state the tenants must not, without written consent, sublet or part with possession of a part of their dwelling-houses. Such consent is not to be unreasonably withheld, see section 94. In any dispute over consent it is for the authority to show refusal was not unreasonable. The county court has jurisdiction in such matters. Possible overcrowding, and also any proposed carrying out of work on the house in question may be taken into account when determining whether a refusal was unreasonable. Consent may not be given conditionally. If a tenant applies for consent in writing the authority must give consent within a reasonable time or it is deemed withheld. If they withhold consent they must give a written statement of reasons.

Secure tenancies *cannot be assigned.* (Neither can a secure tenant part with possession of or sublet the whole of a dwelling let on a secure tenancy, without the tenancy *ceasing to be secure*.) See sections 91 and 93(2) of the Act of 1985. To this there are three exceptions:

1) where the tenancy is assigned under section 24 of the Matrimonial Causes Act 1973; or
2) where the assignment is to a person who would be qualified to succeed the tenant if the tenant had died immediately before the assignment; or
3) where the assignment is by way of exchange, or is part of a chain of assignment, under section 92.

Secure tenants may, with the landlord's consent, assign tenancies to another secure tenant or to an assured tenant of the Housing Corporation, Housing for Wales, a registered association or Housing Trust which is a charity (see section 92 (2A), provided that other has his/her landlord's written consent to the operation. Consent, which may not be given conditionally (save as to conditions requiring the payment of rent arrears or the performance of tenancy obligations) may only be withheld on the grounds set out in Schedule 3 of the 1985 Act. These are that the tenant or proposed assignee is subject to a possession order; possession proceedings under Grounds 1 to 6 of Schedule 2 have begun; the proposed assignee would unreasonably under-occupy the dwelling; the dwelling is not reasonably suitable in extent to the assignee's needs; the dwelling is comprised within a building held mainly for non-housing purposes and was let to the tenant in consequence of his being in the landlord's (etc) employment; the assignee's occupation of the dwelling would conflict with the landlord's charitable status; the dwelling has features substantially different from ordinary dwellings designed to make it suitable for occupation by a physically disabled person, and the result of the assignment would be that such person would no longer reside there; the landlord is a housing association or trust letting dwellings to persons whose non-financial circumstances make it difficult for them to satisfy their housing needs, and if the assignment were made such a person would no longer reside; the dwelling is one of a group normally let for occupation by persons with special needs and close to a social service or special facility provided therefor, and if the assignment were made such a person would no longer reside, the dwelling is subject to a management agreement with a qualifying tenants' association and the proposed assignee is unwilling to be a member of the association. To rely on any of these grounds the landlord must serve notice specifying and particularising the ground in question on the tenant within 42 days of the tenant's application for consent.

Improvements

It is a term of secure tenancies under section 97 that a tenant may not make any improvement without the landlord's written consent, though such consent is not to be unreasonably withheld. 'Improvement' covers any alteration in, or addition to a dwelling and includes additions to or alterations to the landlord's fixtures and fittings, and alterations, etc, to the services to the house; the erection of wireless or television aerials, and the carrying out of *external* decoration. If a dispute arises over the withholding of consent it is for the landlord to show (section 98) that it was reasonable. The county court may take into account in disputes:

1) whether the improvement would make the dwelling or any other premises less safe for occupiers;
2) whether it would be likely to involve landlords in otherwise unlikely expenditure, or
3) whether it would be likely to reduce the price of the house if sold on the open market, or the level of the rent at which it could be let.

Where a tenant applies in writing for the necessary consent the landlord must give it within a reasonable time, otherwise it is deemed withheld, and must not give it subject to an unreasonable condition, otherwise consent is deemed unreasonably withheld. A refusal must be accompanied by a written statement of reasons for refusal. Consent *unreasonably* withheld is treated as given.

Consents may be given retrospectively to work already done, and may be given conditionally, though it is for the landlord to show the reasonableness of conditions. Under section 99 failure to comply with reasonable conditions is treated as breach of a tenancy obligation. This may render the tenant subject to possession proceedings, as will carrying out improvements without consent.

Section 99A of the 1985 Act, inserted in 1993, applies prospectively to work where the landlord, being an authority, gave written consent to an improvement, or is treated as having done so, *and* at the time the tenancy comes to an end it is secure and the landlord is an authority. The section gives the Secretary of State power to make regulations *entitling* 'qualifying persons' at the time when the tenancy ends to be paid compensation by the landlord. It is generally for the landlord to determine the amount of compensation (see below).

Particular provision is made as to when a secure tenancy shall be *treated* as coming to an end by section 99A(8). Such will be the case where the tenancy ceases to be secure because the landlord condition is no longer satisfied, or where it is assigned with the consent of the landlord to another secure tenant under section 92, or to a secure tenant under section 92(2A). But *no* compensation is payable under the regulation (see below) where a tenancy comes to an end on possession being ordered, or on exercise of RTB etc.

To be a qualifying tenant under section 99B a person must fit one of a number of definitions. Thus a person must be the tenant at the time the tenancy comes to an end *and* either the improving tenant, or a joint tenant with that person, or a successor to the improver by succession, devolution or assignment, or a transferee under matrimonial legislation.

The detailed rules on this right to compensation are contained in SI 1994/613. A formula provides for calculation of compensation whereby the cost of listed qualifying improvements are to be 'written down' in value over a specified number of years and the written down value is to be deducted from the actual cost to produce a compensation figure at the time compensation is payable. No compensation less than £50 or more than £3,000 is payable, and compensation may be further reduced in specified cases, eg where the tenant owes the landlord money.

Where a secure tenant begins and makes an improvement to a dwelling after 3 October 1980 and this (a) has received the landlord's consent, and (b) has added materially to the dwelling's sale or rental value, section 100 of the Act gives the landlord *power* to make such payments to the tenant as they consider appropriate at the end of the tenancy. The amount payable must not exceed the cost or likely cost of the improvement *after* deducting the amount of any grant paid under Part XV of the Housing Act 1985. Under section 101 of the Housing Act 1985 the rent of a dwelling let on a secure tenancy is not to be increased on account of a tenant's improvements where the tenant has borne the *whole* cost, or would have so borne that cost but for a grant paid under Part XV of the Act. If, irrespective of grant aid, only part of the cost is borne by the tenant, a pro rata increase in rent can be made. (For the 'right to repair' see Chapter Seven below.)

The distinction between sections 99A & B and 100, is of course, that the former create a *right* to compensation for improvement, the later now provides merely a residual discretion to cover cases outside its predecessor's scope.

The collective rights of secure tenants

The rights described above are 'individual' in the sense that their exercise by a tenant affects only the relationship of landlord and tenant between the parties on a one to one basis. The rights that follow are those where the exercise of powers by a landlord affects *all* their tenants, or where it is the sum total of exercises of options *or* rights by tenants, or a group of them, which has an effect on the landlord.

Variation of terms and publicity

Under section 102 of the 1985 Act the terms of a secure tenancy, other than those implied by statute, and *other* than with regard to rent etc, may be varied, deleted or added to by agreement between the parties. In the case of a periodic tenancy terms may also be varied under section 103 by the landlord serving notice on the tenant. The notice must specify the variation, and the date on which it takes effect. The period between service and the coming into effect of the change must not be shorter than the rental period of the tenancy, nor shorter than four weeks. Before notice of variation is served, the landlord must serve a preliminary notice on the tenant stating the proposed changes and effects and inviting comments within a specified time. Comments received must be considered. When the variation is made it must be explained to the tenant. A variation will not take effect where the tenant gives a valid notice to quit before the arrival of the date specified in the notice of variation. A change in premises let under a secure tenancy is *not* a variation.

Section 104 of the 1985 Act imposes duty to publish, and thereafter to update, information about secure tenancies. This must explain in simple terms the effect of the express terms (if any) of secure tenancies, the provisions of Parts IV and V of the Housing Act 1985, and of sections 11 to 16 of the Landlord and Tenant Act 1985 (implied covenants of repair). Every secure tenant must be supplied with a copy of this information, and also with a written statement of the terms of the tenancy so far as not expressed in a lease or tenancy agreement or implied by law. This written statement must be supplied on the grant of the tenancy or as soon as practicable afterwards. Note also section 104 (3), inserted in 1993, which imposes yearly obligation to supply secure tenants of authorities with copies of current information published under section 104.

Tenant participation in housing management

This chapter has shown that the rights afforded to tenants are, in law, essentially individual and this is despite the fact that the management of the dwellings and very often the built environment are collective in form. Indeed, such is the distinctiveness of council housing in this regard that since the inception of the first estates there is a record of a collective response to the experience of living there. This has often taken the form of the establishment of tenants' associations and there is considerable literature which records the activities and charateristics of a tenants' 'movement'. We make brief reference to this record here as it usefully locates the current legal position concerning tenant participation and underscores the somewhat anomalous situation of the essentially individual nature of landlord-tenant relations as it stands in law, compared to the social and political reality.

The inter-war period saw the growth of thousands of tenants' associations on new estates. These were created mainly in response to initial problems with local services, housing management and a wider socialisation process. The distinctive geographical and social environments inhabited by 'council tenants' was recognised during the earliest stages of the post-1919 building programme, as we saw in Chapter One. The sociology of these communities was, indeed, documented on several occasions, notably by Durant in her study of a new estate in North London (Durant, R *Watling: A Survey of Social Life on a New Housing Estate*, London, P S King, 1939). In this and other similar studies the growth of tenants' associations as part of the life of these new communities is commonplace.

After the Second World War the tenants' movement became more widely established with the appearance of a number of local federations and several attempts to organise a national body. For example, the Association of London Housing Estates, established in 1957, represented a large number of socially orientated associations and has been continuously active since that time. Regional and national organisations were, however, difficult to sustain, requiring funds from uncertain sources and needing to establish credibility with associations which were essentially local bodies.

Through the 1950s most associations were socially oriented providing the management of tenants' halls and programmes of social events. But from the 1960s to the end of the 1970s there was a considerable politicisation of the tenants' movement due to opposition to higher rents, mirroring the PRS, and which was accompanied by means tested rent rebate schemes. The most studied and best documented example of this type of activity was the case of a rent strike in Sheffield (Hampton, W A *Democracy and Community*, Oxford University Press, 1970; Lowe, S G *Urban Social Movements: The City After Castells*, Macmillan, 1986).

On a national scale the tenants' movement reached a zenith between 1968 and 1973 in the context of resistance to the Housing Finance Act 1972 and there was evidence of concerted action including rent strikes in over 80 local authority areas (Sklair, L 'The Struggle Against the Housing Finance Act', *Socialist Register*, London, Merlin, 1975). After the collapse of the campaign against the 1972 Act the tenants' movement went into decline. A degree of activity re-emerged in the late-1970s in response to some new issues – the possibility of a Tenants' Charter, problems of dampness in flats and over repairs. However, the key issue of rent levels and rebate schemes had been decisively lost and in the main disappeared from the agenda of the movement particularly as more and more tenants became eligible for housing allowances. A conference sponsored by the National Consumers' Council (NCC) in 1977 reinvigorated the idea of regional federations but this initiative made little impact. Over a decade later in 1989 a National Tenants' and Residents' Association was set up 'to promote and protect public housing and tenants' rights in the face of hostile legislation' (cited in Cole and Furbey, 1994, p 158). This body secured some 40 affiliations from associations around the country but failed to make any impact on national legislation.

This pattern has continued into the 1990s and there is little evidence of spontaneous activity which was common among council tenants in the past. Associations tend to have been institutionalised and as we describe above the rights conferred on tenants through the Tenants' Charter provisions of the Housing Act 1985 are essentially individual rights for redressing grievances with limited consultation procedures and certain rights to periodic information. A recent study by Glasgow University based on nationwide interviews found that only 20 % of tenants believed that authorities always or usually consulted them on important issues. According to the study, consultation is often limited to narrow issues such as modernisation proposals whereas many tenants would like more formal consultation on key issues such as repairs and rent-setting (Centre for Housing Research, *The Nature and Effectiveness of Housing Management in England*, HMSO, 1989, p 93).

Indeed, authority support for tenants' associations and federations is very limited and only in a handful of larger authorities has finance for the administration of such organisations been made available (Institute of Housing/ Tenants' Participation Advisory Service, *Tenant Participation in Housing Management*, IOH/TPAS, 1989). The only funding from national resources occurs under section 16 of the Housing and Planning Act 1986 but this money is channelled to support government initiatives or government approved bodies, particularly Priority Estate Programme schemes or bodies such as the Tenants' Participation Advisory Service (TPAS). TPAS was set up in 1988 with the assistance of the NCC to help associations or groups of tenants to establish tenant management organisations by providing training to tenants' representatives and advising authorities and associations on the feasibility of such management organisations. In 1990-91 £3.25 million was made available by the DoE under section 16 and the majority of this funding was used to sustain these secondary organisations rather than to support local initiatives.

The life-cycle of tenants' associations

The sociological studies referred to earlier reveal that the mobilisation of tenants as a collective force is characterised by a high degree of associational spontaneity and informality. For this reason the social science literature has not found it easy to chart or evaluate how the associational networks operate. Nevertheless the life-cycles of tenants' associations appear to move from early agitational activity to a more settled routine of social events which conceals inter alia a range of functions. Lowe sums up this type of development,

> 'The early formation of a tenants' association is characteristic of the initial moving-in phase – to counteract the hostility of nearby private residents, or to deal with complaints about the estate, and generally as a means for facilitating social contact. Later these associations change their functions or disintegrate as the local networks become established and the socialisation function gives way to more specialised organisations.'
> (Lowe, 1986, p 65)

Associations which begin in the throes of radical campaigns using rent strike tactics tend either to disipate once the issue has defused or they go on to adopt the more typical features of the established associations. The evidence suggests that the rent strike tactic is very difficult to sustain because, unlike an industrial dispute, it depends on individuals in the privacy of their own homes. Tenants may be claiming to withhold rent when, under threat of eviction, they are in fact paying it.

It is often the case that authorities attempt to defuse the threat posed by such spontaneous associational activity by channelling their efforts towards responsibility for a tenants' hall or community centre. There is some evidence that it is indeed difficult to sustain more overtly political action from such a base compared to an estate with no institutional roots (Lowe, 1986, p 110). However, it is also clear that where there is an established association a range of functions typically associated with voluntary associations are being played out – overcoming loneliness, advocacy on behalf of individual tenants or groups of residents, pastoral and so on. As Goetschius observes from his 15 year study of associations in London:

> 'They provide direct recreation and social welfare services to their members…secondly, the groups represent the membership and the estates in discussion with statutory and voluntary bodies…thirdly, their work involves the development of social life on the estates.'

(Goetschius, G W *Working With Community Groups*, Routledge and Kegan Paul, 1969)

It is also clear that some characteristics of estates affect the propensity of associations to form or fail; the size of an estate certainly appeared to influence the stability and survival of associations in Goetschius's study and some practical considerations such as the presence or absence of a meeting place or the existence of potentially competing associational activity (such as a workingmen's club) is also a significant. Other factors to do with the specific history and characteristics of an estate can all affect whether or not an association can take root or is likely to fail.

Finally, it is clear that the tactics available to the associations have limited their impact on policy and as Hampton observes, 'The spontaneous eruption of feeling that can shake a city council is not a noticeable influence on national housing policy' (Hampton, 1970, p 273). Tenant participation on decision-making bodies has been of a very limited nature, indeed section 13 of the Local Government and Housing Act 1989 proscribed voting rights for representatives of tenants' associations on local authority housing committees. As we describe below and also in Chapter Two there is a very restricted place for tenant involvement through Tenants' Choice procedures, the decisions on LSVTs and in compulsory competitive tendering for council house management. All these are essentially government inspired or legislative requirements which are highly controlled despite the language of consumer and 'customer' choice. Indeed this form of parlance underpins our view of the essentially individualistic rights afforded to tenants, who in law are *not* consumers or customers in the normal way because their tenure is governed by a tenant-landlord relationship. As with so much of public housing policy, the recent phase in the history of tenant participation is a long way from the rent strikes and militant campaigns which were a recurrent feature in earlier decades. There is nevertheless a thriving network of associations around the country. TPAS, for example, currently includes in its list of affiliated member organisations well over 400 individual tenants' associations and some 50 tenants' federations (*TPAS Annual Report 1994*). In this light we now move on to outline the current position in law of tenants' involvement in housing management beginning with the duties of authorities to inform tenants on a variety of issues.

Section 105 of the 1985 Act requires that certain authorities shall maintain such arrangements *as they consider appropriate*, to enable secure tenants who are likely to be substantially affected by matters of housing management to be informed of proposed changes and developments, and also to ensure that such persons are able to make their views known to the authority within a specified time. Matters of 'housing management' are defined by section 105 to include matters which, *in the opinion of the authority,* relate to management, maintenance, improvement, or demolition of municipal dwellings, or are connected with provision of services or amenities to such dwellings, *and* which represent new programmes of maintenance, improvement or demolition, or some change in the practice or policy of the authority, *and* which are likely to affect substantially all an authority's secure tenants or a group of them. A 'group' is defined as tenants forming a distinct social group, or those who occupy dwelling-houses which constitute a distinct class, whether by reference to the kind of dwelling, or the housing estate or larger area in which they are situated. However, see *Short v Tower Hamlets London Borough Council* (1985) 18 HLR 171 where the Court of Appeal held that a decision taken 'in principle' to market the sale of certain council properties was not a matter of 'housing management' requiring consultation. The obligation to consult arises where there is a real question of *implementing* a change.

A matter is *not* one of housing management in so far as it relates to rent payable or to any charge for services or facilities provided by the authority. It is the duty of an authority to *consider* any representations made by secure tenants before making any decisions on a matter of housing management.

Landlord authorities must publish details of their consultation arrangements. A copy of any published material must be made available for free public inspection at their principal offices during reasonable hours. Copies must also be available for sale at reasonable charges. 'Landlord authorities' for the purposes of this provision *include* district and London Borough councils.

The statutory power to vary the terms of a tenancy will supersede the terms of a tenancy entered into before the statute was enacted, *R v Brent London Borough Council, ex p Blatt* (1991) 24 HLR 319. Duties to consult tenants and licensees generally may arise outside the context of section 105 where the law considers it would be procedurally unfair to allow an authority to proceed with a proposal without taking into account the view of occupiers likely to be affected by it – such instances are likely to be rare, however, *R v Devon County Council, ex p Baker* (1992) Times, 20 October and *R v Durham County Council, ex p Curtis and Broxson* (1993) Times, 21 January.

Practice varies greatly as to the involvement of tenants in management. Some authorities have joint estate management committees (JEMS) to transfer a measure of power to tenants, or to have created area or district committees of tenants, members and officers to discuss relevant housing issues. Consultation rights and procedures may or may not be mentioned in tenancy agreements or tenants' handbooks.

It was possible from 1975 to transfer authority housing management powers to housing co-operatives, but little use was made of this power. Section 27 of the 1985 Act, as amended, allows authorities to transfer specified management functions over specified properties to 'another person' subject to ministerial consent. Such devolutions are made by 'management agreements' which must contain any provisions specified in regulations made by the Secretary of State. Ministerial approval is needed for such devolutions, but that may be given on a block basis to authorities generally or on an individual basis. This legislation further enables authorities to put management functions out to tender in line with the philosophy of Compulsory Competitive Tendering (CCT) which was introduced generally under the Local Government Act 1988. This broadly requires where an authority wishes to allow its own staff to carry out a particular activity they must first put that activity out to tender, ie authority staff have to compete for contracts to provide particular services. Section 2(3) of the Local Government Act 1988 empowers the Secretary of State to list activities subject to CCT, and housing management was a candidate for inclusion in the CCT process from April 1994, while some authorities had already put their estate management out to tender from the private sector on a voluntary basis using their section 27 powers.

The Secretary of State exercised these powers by the Local Government Act 1988 (Competition) (Defined Activities) (Housing Management) Order SI 1994/1671 which laid down that certain housing management activities could only be carried out by authorities provided they had previously been put out to competitive tender. See also SI 1994/2297 which requires authorities to subject specified proportions of housing management work to competitive tendering. The activities in question are:

1) dealing with applications for housing *once a property has been allocated* to the applicant *until* immediately after the tenancy has been entered into;

2)   dealing with assignments under section 92 of the 1985 Act;
3)   informing authority tenants of the terms of tenancies *and* taking steps to enforce such terms;
4)   collecting rents and service charges, collecting arrears, negotiating payment of arrears and monitoring compliance with agreements to pay off arrears;
5)   keeping records of sums of rent etc collected;
6)   arranging for the vacating of dwellings once a tenancy/licence has ended;
7)   inspecting vacant properties and assessing works needed before the next letting, ensuring such works are done and reporting thereon to the authority;
8)   taking steps to secure voids against vandalism and trespass;
9)   taking steps to remove unlawful occupiers of relevant property;
10)   assessing the condition and maintenance etc requirements of the common parts of relevant property;
11)   assessing repair requests, and ensuring necessary works are done;
12)   carrying out surveys of the physical condition of relevant property, and checking on its occupation;
13)   assessing compensation issues under the 'Right to Repair' under section 96 of the 1985 Act (as substituted);
14)   operating reception and security services provided at the entrance to local authority housing;
15)   taking action to control disturbances in local authority housing, dealing with inter neighbour disputes, and dealing with dispute resolution agencies.

Section 131 of the Leasehold Reform Housing and Urban Development Act 1993, inserting section 27A into the 1985 Act, provides for cases where the Secretary of State makes an order under section 2(3) of the 1988 Act including housing management within the framework of CCT. Regulations may be made to deal with cases where, in consequences of CCT, a management agreement has to be made, and these will apply a consultative framework similar to that which applies under a voluntary transfer under section 27 of the 1985 Act.

The consultative framework that applies to a management agreement under section 27 is supplied by section 27AA as substituted in 1993. This replaces, so far as management agreements are concerned, the provisions of section 105. Authorities proposing to make agreements must make appropriate arrangements to enable affected tenants to be informed of the terms of agreements (including standards of service to be supplied), the identities of managers and any other centrally prescribed details. Those tenants are entitled to make their views known and those views must be taken into account before decisions are taken, but there is no *right* on the part of tenants *under the Act itself* (as amended) to block a proposed management agreement (but see below) though a judicial review could surely be sought in a case where an agreement was being pursued in clear breach of the general requirements of administrative law, eg where the agreement was being made *solely* to enrich a particular management organisation, though *not* where an agreement is being made solely because that represents the political policy of the authority in question.

Once agreements are made section 27A(2) requires authorities to maintain such arrangements as they consider appropriate to enable tenants of relevant properties to make their views known on standards of service achieved by managers under agreements, and before making any decisions on enforcing standards required by agreements to take into account tenants' views.

But what of proactive tenant involvement in the above process? Section 27AB of the 1985 Act, as inserted in 1993, empowers the Secretary of State to make regulations requiring authorities to take steps to respond where any tenant management organisation (TMO) serves written notice proposing that the authority should enter into a management agreement with the TMO. Those regulations are the Housing (Right to Manage) Regulations 1994, SI 1994/627. Under these a TMO may serve a right to manage notice (RMN) on an authority where it is a representative and accountable body, eg it must be open to any tenant of a relevant dwelling to joint the TMO and the TMO must pursue an equal opportunity policy. It must serve a defined geographical area and have a membership of at least 20% of *both* secure tenants and of *all* tenants of houses, flats, hostels etc belonging to the authority within the designated area. The TMO must take a democratic decision to serve a RMN by delivering a copy to each affected dwelling, and authorities are able inter alia, to refuse a RMN relating to fewer than 25 dwellings let on secure tenancies. Only members of the TMO can vote, and a majority of members must back the proposal. If a notice is accepted the TMO will select a training agency and the authority is expected to support the TMO with accommodation and office facilities, and the TMO will select a training agency (an 'approved person') from a list maintained by the DoE and a feasibility study funded by a grant under section 429A of the 1985 Act by the Secretary of State will be undertaken. This study will be in two parts, the full study can only proceed if the initial study indicates to the approved person it is reasonable to proceed, and at that point the authority will arrange for a ballot or poll of *all* affected tenants. (It is not reasonable to proceed where it is concluded a TMO is unlikely to progress towards full tenant management, or where it appears a TMO is not representative of its community and will not reform itself.) If the ballot is in favour by a majority of all tenants and a majority of all secure tenants, the full study proceeds. A further training agency *then* selected by the TMO from the DoE list will proceed to develop a programme of management skills for the TMO by reference to the range of functions the TMO wishes to assume: a training programme – *Preparing to Manage* – has been developed by the DoE for this purpose. 75% of these development costs will be met by Section 429A grants, the rest will come from authorities (see also the TMO Modular Management Agreement, HMSO 1994).

If, however, the training agency concludes the development programme is unlikely to result in the TMO assuming a range of management functions, a timely report should be made to the TMO, the authority and the Secretary of State, and if the TMO accepts the conclusion its proposal is deemed withdrawn and no further similar proposal can be put forward for two years. But when a programme is successful the TMO will need registration as a company or an individual or provident society so as to provide a legal 'person' with whom the management agreement can be made. Only when the training agency certifies a TMO has reached the requisite level of competency for the functions it wishes to discharge can matters proceed. If the agency decides against the TMO on this point, the TMO may submit the issue to arbitration. If, however, the TMO is certified to proceed then within two months the authority must inform affected tenants of the terms of the proposed management agreement with the TMO, *and a ballot will then be held in prescribed form*: all tenants of affected dwellings must be given the chance to vote and a vote must be given to each tenant. If the TMO gains a majority vote from all tenants including a majority of secure tenants, the proposed management agreements must be entered into; a failure to obtain a majority result is the deemed withdrawal of the proposal and a moratorium of two years on similar proposals. For further guidance see DoE Circular 6/94.

Note, however, that it is possible for authorities to enter into management agreement with TMOs voluntarily, provided the Secretary of State approves the form of the agreement and the requirements of sections 27 and 27A are complied with. It is also possible for a TMO to invite an authority to nominate one or more people to be directors/officers of the TMO where the authority have entered into or propose to enter a management agreement with the TMO.

The first virtually total takeover of an authority's housing is likely to be in Kensington and Chelsea where 93% of tenants have voted for a TMO management agreement likely to be in operation by 1995. The TMO, which will become the employer of the authority's housing staff, will assume responsibility for rent collection, lettings, caretaking and repairs. Individual TMO agreements were, by April 1994, in place for 11 estates with a further 67 well advanced. It is government policy that authorities should divest themselves of direct housing management by 1996 and it is likely that large scale voluntary transfer of management (LSVT) to associations or TMO transfers will be the preferred means for authorities to achieve this.

Tenure of housing association dwellings

In Chapter One we described the rise of associations after their position had been transformed by the Housing Act 1974. This enabled them to build new properties or renovate existing stock using Housing Association Grant (HAG). By 1990 associations owned and managed some 600,000 homes compared to only 170,000 in 1970. We showed that a second phase of housing policy began in 1987 heralded by the publication of the White Paper *Housing: the Government's Proposals* Cm 214, HMSO. One of the central aims of these proposals was to move housing associations away from their status as quasi-public sector organisations to being a more fully fledged part of the private sector, known at that time as the 'independent rented sector'. The deregulation of the PRS was applied also to associations. The introduction of mixed funding and extending the reliance of associations on private finance aimed to reduce their reliance on public funding. The aim was to reduce the imbalance between the PRS and the associations.

A new funding regime brought in a much greater emphasis on 'value for money' and in effect associations had to compete with each other for funds on a cost efficiency basis and with sharply reduced levels of HAG funding and increased private finance. The incentive for the associations to enter this new world of private finance and competition was a very large increase in the annual Approved Development Programme (ADP), said to triple by the mid-1990s when the vast majority of the ADP would be for mixed funded schemes. This programme spells out the total spending available to housing associations in any one year. Actually the ADP for 1994/95 was severely curtailed in the 1993 Budget and Autumn Statement following which total spending on social housing, including the element of private finance, has fallen *in fact* to its lowest for several decades.

Housing associations have taken over as the main suppliers of general needs 'social' housing in the public sector while the authorities have become 'enablers' working through and with other agencies instead of making direct provision themselves. The consequences of this change of role for the associations have been dramatic. These were summed up by Page as:

1)   provision of housing for fewer old people, single people and those with special needs (the 'traditional' focus of association provision) in favour of families with children and homeless households, the latter currently in receipt of 50% of provision of new dwellings;

2)   the size and type of dwellings have changed with fewer flats and one-bedroomed units being built in favour of family houses with two to four bedrooms;

3)   the type of developments mounted have changed from an emphasis on rehabilitation and improvement of existing stock and small specialist developments on in-filling sites to large estates often built by volume builders.

(Page, D *Building for Communities: a study of new housing association estates*, Joseph Rowntree Foundation, 1993)

Traditionally associations developed schemes on a one-off basis but in order to meet the stringent cost requirements of the new finance system they now buy conventional houses built by volume construction companies for sale into owner occupation. During the slump in house prices over the last seven years builders, especially in the south of England have been only too pleased to sell 'off the peg' housing to associations; for their part associations are able to buy housing cheaply due to the absence of normal development costs when they start a scheme from scratch.

A high proportion of nominations to this housing has been from local authorities due to deals which involved building on authority land and the Housing Corporation's requirement that 50% of new houses should be let to homeless households. One consequence of this, according to Page's study, is that the average income of new association tenants on the new large estates is only 33% of the national average. A range of problems has arisen from this, particularly that associations' 'traditional' managers are not well equipped to cope with the problems that arise and vulnerable tenants are often housed in unsuitable situations.

Association tenants are thus drawn from far more diverse groups of people than in the past and the tenancies also span the 'old' and the 'new' regimes. Rents have been increased to a so called 'affordable' level to meet the costs of sponsoring private finance and less well-off tenants are protected at the moment by their entitlement to individual housing benefit.

Consultation papers issued by the DoE before the Housing Bill 1987 was published made it clear that *existing* association tenants would continue to enjoy statutory security of tenure and the other rights enshrined in the Housing Act 1985. Future association tenancies would be on the new assured tenancy basis. Some 70,000 new lettings are made by associations each year and these new lettings are virtually all on the 'assured' basis.

After the commencement of the 1988 Act the fair rent provisions of the Rent Act 1977 Part VI do not *generally* apply to new tenancies granted by associations. Furthermore association tenancies entered into after commencement are not *generally* secure. *New* association tenants do not have the rights of secure tenants (including the right to buy) instead they are *Assured Tenants* under Part 1 of the 1988 Act. A tenancy entered into after commencement is not a 'housing association tenancy' as previously defined by Part VI of the Rent Act 1977 *unless:*

a)   entered into by virtue of contract made *before* commencement, *or*

b)   granted to a person who (solely or jointly) was a housing association tenancy holder immediately before grant, *and* is granted by person who was landlord under that tenancy, *or*

c)   it is granted to a person who prior to grant was previously in possession of a dwelling subject to a possession order subject to section 84 (2) (b) or (c) of the Housing Act 1985, *and* the grant is of premises which are suitable accommodation for the purpose of those provisions, *and* in the possession order the court directed the tenancy to be a housing association tenancy.

Assured tenancies: the basic position

Under section 1 of the 1988 Act a dwelling (including a flat) is let on an assured tenancy (AT) if it is let (ie the relationship of landlord and tenant must exist) as a separate dwelling (ie a unit capable of supporting the functions of living such as eating and sleeping). 'Separate' bears the meaning it has in the corresponding provisions of the 1985 Act, see above, *save* that under section 3 of the 1988 Act where a tenant enjoys exclusive occupation of some accommodation with persons *other* than the landlord, and that is the *only* reason why assured status would be denied, the accommodation the tenant has is deemed to be a dwelling let on an AT. The tenant, or if there are joint tenants, each of them, must be an individual, and *must* occupy the dwelling as his/her only or principal home. Occupation of some other dwelling as the only or principal home will cost a tenant his/her security. The requirement of residence may be satisfied by one of a number of joint tenants. The dwelling must also not fall within the excepted classes of Part 1, Schedule 1 of the 1988 Act, ie tenancies:

a)   entered into before, or pursuant to a contract made before, 15 January 1989;

b)   at high rents, ie £25,000 per annum;

c)   at *no* or low rents, ie £1,000 per annum in London or £250 elsewhere;

d)   within the provisions of Part II of the Landlord and Tenant Act 1954 (business lettings);

e)   of licensed premises;

f)   of agricultural land or agricultural holdings;

g)   granted to students intending to follow specified courses of study by specified educational bodies (for out of term lettings see Ground 4 below);

h)   which are holiday lettings, ie those where the purpose is to confer on the tenant the right to occupy the dwelling for the purpose of a holiday;

i)   granted by resident landlords, ie in general tenancies where the landlord, who must be an individual, has granted a tenancy of a dwelling which forms only part of a building which is *not* a purpose built block of flats, *and* the landlord resided in some other part of the building as his/her only or principal home at the time of the grant and has so resided ever since and the tenancy must *not* have been granted to a person who immediately previously was an assured tenant of the same dwelling or of another dwelling in the building, *and* the landlord is the same in relation to each; but such an exemption is not available to a company landlord, even where a director resides in the building, and would be unavailable to an association, see *Barnes v Gorsuch* (1981) 43 P & CR 294;

j)   which are granted by the Crown or a local authority.

Where the tenancy is excluded from AT status *and no other legislation applies*, it will be a tenancy at common law, and subject only to control under section 3 of the Protection From Eviction Act 1977 which requires that possession can only be obtained by court order.

The great majority of tenancies granted by associations since 1989 are thus 'assured'. However, in some cases an association may decide to grant an 'assured shorthold tenancy' (AST), for example where it holds short life property it wishes to have occupied on a temporary basis. An AST is an AT in all respects (eg as regards recovery of possession) save that its creation is subject to certain formalities which must be complied with before a prospective tenant is allowed into possession and its security is limited to a great degree. An AST is, according to section 20 of the 1988 Act, a tenancy:

a)   for an initial *fixed* term of not *less* than six months, which runs from the date of grant and which cannot be backdated, see section 45(2) of the 1988 Act – thus an AST cannot initially be granted on a periodic basis, though one may be granted *after* the termination of the initial term, or by virtue of the statute on a periodic basis, see further below;

b)   where the *landlord* has no power to end the tenancy earlier than six months from the start of tenancy, and

c)   where due notice in prescribed form giving certain information, and clearly stating the tenancy is to be an AST, has been served by the landlord on the tenant *before* the tenancy is entered into, and thus it is at least advisable for the notice to be given to the tenant in good time for it to be read before the actual signing.

So far as the landlord's power to determine the tenancy is concerned, wherever a lease is granted subject to a *break* clause which entitles *the landlord* to terminate the term before the initial six months is up that lease cannot be an AST. However, under section 45(4) of the 1988 Act a *forfeiture* clause (for example one entitling the landlord to bring a lease to an end for non payment of rent) does not infringe the prohibition on break clauses, and a landlord could only rely on such a clause during the initial six month term. Thus an AST can be granted *where the tenant* only can exercise a break clause in the agreement (if there is one) on notice at any time, while the landlord can only rely on such a clause *after* the initial six months is over. Forfeiture clauses are excepted, though the combined effect of sections 5(1), 7(6) and 45(4) of the Act is to create a statutory system which has to be relied on where a landlord wishes to rely on a forfeiture clause, see further below. Turning to the pre-tenancy notice, it is essential that inaccuracies are avoided, otherwise the notice could be ineffective. Minor errors such as obvious slips of the pen will be ignored, but a substantial error, such as inserting in the notice a date for termination earlier than that in the actual tenancy agreement itself will not be allowed to pass. The Assured Tenancies and Agricultural Occupancies (Forms) Regulations 1988, SI 1988/2203 must be complied with in addition to the requirements of statute. The pre-tenancy notice must be in writing, even though an AST for less than three years may escape the need for a formal written lease as a tenancy in possession at the best rent available under section 54 of the Law of Property Act 1925.

However, it should be noted that where a tenant has an existing AT a new AST of the dwelling cannot in general be granted in substitution by the same landlord, see section 20(3).

If an AST comes to its end and a new tenancy – which may be *either* fixed term or periodic (unlike the initial AST) – of the same, or substantially the same, premises arises by express grant *without a break of time* whereunder both landlord and tenant are the same, the new tenancy will be an AST, irrespective of whether the conditions referred to above for creating such a tenancy have been observed. Where, additionally, an AST simply expires a statutory periodic assured shorthold tenancy (SPAST) arises under section 20(1) of the 1988 Act; the periods of this tenancy will be determined according to how rent *was* paid under the original tenancy – eg monthly. Termination of such subsequent shortholds may take place according to special procedure – see below.

Security of tenure

ATs have a degree of security of tenure, for under sections 5(1), 7(7) and 9(3) the basic rule is that the tenancy can only be brought to an end by a court order following service of Notice of Possession Proceedings (NOPP). Thus if an AT is for an initial fixed term a periodic tenancy arises under statute, see section 5(2) of the 1988 Act, on its expiry, while a periodic AT will continue until terminated in legal form, and a mere notice to quit *from the landlord* will have no effect, though the tenant may exit via this route.

The application of the rules of security is thus dependent upon whether the AT is initially periodic or fixed term.

Periodic tenancies

The position here is that the AT can only be brought to an end by means of a NOPP and a court order, see sections 5(2) and 9(1).

Fixed term tenancies

Here the tenancy can come to an end by:
a)   surrender (including clear long term abandonment) by the tenant;
b)   where the tenancy contains a break clause ie a power for the landlord

to determine it in certain circumstances, the exercise of that power *followed* by NOPP and court order – mere exercise of power to determine alone is not enough;
c)   by effluxion of time, ie the tenancy runs out, *and* there is a NOPP and a court order.
    A number of points need to be noted.
1)   In the case of a fixed term AT which is still current provided there is a 'break clause' enabling the landlord to determine in particular circumstances, exercise by the landlord of that clause in those circumstances will bring the AT to an end but the tenant will remain in possession under the SPT (statutory periodic tenancy) which automatically arises under section 5(2). To gain actual possession the landlord will then need to proceed by the NOPP route and will thus have to prove that one of the statutory grounds for possessions applies.
2)   In the case of a fixed term AT which is still current where the tenant is in breach of obligations, *and* tenancy conditions make provision for it to be brought to an end – by way of re-entry, forfeiture, determination by notice or otherwise – on the basis of facts falling within Grounds 2 or 8 (mandatory) or Grounds 10 to 15 (discretionary) of Schedule 2 to the 1988 Act (see below, but effectively serious rent arrears or breach of condition) the court may, under section 7, entertain possession proceedings. In other situations the AT will subsist until its contractual expiry.
3)   Where a fixed term AT expires, provided the landlord follows, and can follow, the NOPP route, the court's power to order possession will bring to an end any SPT as from a specified date.
    Though associations may only rarely grant fixed term ATs it is clearly crucial that their terms are carefully drafted so as to comply with the above requirements.
    Where a fixed term tenancy expires and there is *no* NOPP and a court order the tenant will be entitled to stay in possession of the dwelling by virtue of the SPT. This, as stated, takes effect immediately on the end of the fixed term and is deemed granted by the landlord to the tenant in respect of the dwelling on broadly comparable terms, save that the only means of obtaining possession is NOPP and a court order see sections 5(1) and (2). Not later than one year after the former tenancy is succeeded by a SPT either party may serve on the other notice in prescribed form proposing terms for the SPT different from those implied under the 1988 Act, see section 6.

Procedure for obtaining possession

The county court is the appropriate forum (see section 40 of the 1988 Act) and the NOPP procedure *must* be used, see section 8. The landlord must serve notice in prescribed form (see SI 1988/2203) informing the tenant that:

a)   the landlord intends to begin proceedings for possession on one or more
      of the grounds specified in the notice (which may be added to or altered
      only with the leave of the court), and
b)   proceedings will not begin *earlier* than a date specified in the notice,
      and will also not begin *later* than 12 months from the date of service of
      the notice. The *general rule* is that proceedings may not begin *earlier*
      than two weeks from the date of service of notice, however, where
      possession is sought on the basis of Grounds 1, 2, 5, 6, 7, 9 and 16 (for
      which see below) proceedings may not begin *earlier* than two months
      from date of service of notice nor, in the case of a periodic tenancy,
      earlier than the date the tenancy could have been ended by notice to
      quit. The requirement for a NOPP may be relaxed if the court considers
      it just and equitable, though this dispensing power does not exist where
      the landlord is relying on Ground 8.

The actual grounds for possession are specified by section 7 and Schedule
2 of the 1988 Act. Two types of grounds are provided, mandatory and
discretionary. Part 1 of Schedule 2 contains the mandatory possession grounds.
If the ground is made out and all other requirements are complied with the
court here has no option but to order possession.

Ground 1

Not later than the beginning of the tenancy (ie the day it was entered into) the
landlord gave the tenant *written* notice that possession might be required *and*
some time before the tenancy the landlord occupied the dwelling as his/her
only or principal home, *or* the landlord *requires* the dwelling as his/her or
his/her spouse's only or principal home, *and* the landlord did *not* acquire the
dwelling for value over the sitting tenant's head. Clearly this ground is
inapplicable to an assured tenancy granted by an association.

Ground 2

The dwelling is subject to a mortgage granted before the commencement of
the tenancy and the mortgagee is entitled to exercise the power of sale and
desires possession to exercise that power. Again notice must be given before
the tenancy commences if this ground is to be relied on, though the court has
a dispensing power if, for example, an adequate verbal warning has been
given, see *Bradshaw v Baldwin-Wiseman* [1985] 1 EGLR 123 and *Fernandes
v Parvardin* (1982) 264 Estates Gazette 49.

Ground 3

The tenancy is for a fixed term of not more than eight months, and written
notice was given before commencement that this ground might be relied on

and at some time within the period of 12 months ending with the beginning of the tenancy the dwelling was occupied for holiday purposes.

Ground 4

The tenancy is for a fixed term not exceeding 12 months *and* written notice that possession might be sought was given before commencement, *and* some time within the period 12 months ending with commencement the dwelling was let as student accommodation by specified educational bodies or persons. This provision facilitates vacation lettings of student accommodation.

Ground 5

The dwelling is held for the purpose of being available for occupation by a minister of religion as a residence from which to perform clerical duties *and* written notice that possession might be sought was given *and* the court is satisfied that the dwelling is required for occupation by such a minister.

Ground 6

The landlord must intend to demolish or reconstruct the whole or a substantial part of the dwelling, or to carry out substantial works on the dwelling or any part of it, or any building of which it forms part, *and* in addition:
a)   the intended work must be incapable of being carried out unless possession is obtained , *and* either
   (i)   the tenant is unwilling to agree access to enable the work to be done, *or*
   (ii)   the nature of the work is such that granting access alone would be insufficient to enable it to take place, *or*
   (iii) the tenant is unwilling to forgo possession of that part of the dwelling as would allow the landlord to carry out the work reasonably, *or*
   (iv)   the nature of the work is such that it is not practicable for the tenant to be left with a tenancy of part only of the dwelling.
b)   It is further required that landlords must demonstrate a settled intention to do works of demolition/construction and that they have reasonable prospect of carrying them out. (See above the similar Ground 10A under the Housing Act 1985.) Where possession is ordered under Ground 6 the tenant's reasonable removal expenses must be reimbursed by the landlord, see section 11(1).

Ground 7

The tenancy is *periodic* (including a SPT) and has devolved by will or intestacy on the death of the previous tenant, *provided* proceedings are begun not later than 12 months after the death of the former tenant. The acceptance by a landlord of rent from a new tenant after the death of the former tenant is not to be regarded as creating a new periodic tenancy unless the landlord agrees to a change, in writing with regard to rent, the period of the tenancy, the premises or the terms of the tenancy. This ground of possession does *not*, however, affect any statutory succession rights given by the Act itself, see below Chapter Five.

Ground 8

To rely on this ground *both* at the date of service of the NOPP *and* at the date of the hearing there must be substantial rent in arrears, ie:

a)   where the rent is payable weekly or fortnightly, at least 13 weeks' arrears;
b)   where payable monthly, at least three months' arrears are owed;
c)   where payable quarterly at least three months arrears of that quarter are owed;
d)   where payable yearly at least three months rent must be more than three months in arrears.

Discretionary grounds

Ground 9

Suitable alternative accommodation is or will be available – this is further defined in   Schedule 2, Part III as either:

a)   a certificate from the local housing authority that they will rehouse;
b)   premises which are to be let as a separate dwelling on an assured basis (but not as an AST or any dwelling subject to such notice as would allow mandatory recovery of possession), or
c)   premises which will afford security equivalent to that of an AT.
    The premises must also be reasonably suitable to the needs of the tenant and his/her family as regards proximity to place of work and must also be *either* similar as regards rent and extent to authority properties in the area provided for persons with needs similar to those of the tenant, *or* reasonably suited to the means and needs of the tenant and his/her family as regards extent and character. A property is not suitable if occupation would result in statutory overcrowding. Suitability will be determined by considering the tenant's *housing* needs, as opposed to cultural and spiritual matters see *Siddiqui v Rashid* [1980] 3 All ER 184, [1980] 1 WLR 1018.

Ground 10

Some rent lawfully due must be unpaid on the date on which possession proceedings are begun and must have been in arrears at the date of service of the NOPP.

Ground 11

Whether or not there are arrears, this applies where the tenant has persistently delayed paying rent lawfully due. What constitutes 'persistent delay' will be a question of fact in each case – but the delay may arise for reasons outside the tenant's control – eg as a result of delayed housing benefit.

Ground 12

There has been a breach of a tenancy obligation (see the similar ground above in relation to secure tenancies).

Ground 13

Where the condition of the dwelling, or of any common parts, has deteriorated owing to acts of waste by, or the neglect or default of, the tenant or of any other person residing in the dwelling, provided in this latter case the tenant has failed to take such steps as he/she should to remove the wrongdoer.

Ground 14

Where the tenant or any other person residing in the dwelling has been guilty of conduct which is a nuisance or annoyance to adjoining occupiers, *or* has been convicted of using the dwelling, or of allowing it to be used, for immoral or illegal purposes; see the similar ground above in relation to secure tenancies.

Ground 15

Where the condition of furniture provided under the tenancy has deteriorated owing to ill treatment by the tenant or by residents in the house whose wrong-doing the tenant has failed to prevent by removing them from the dwelling.

Ground 16

Where the dwelling was let to the tenant in consequence of employment by landlord and that employment has ceased.

The discretionary grounds require the reasonableness of granting possession to be made out by the landlord – as with secure tenancies – and the court will then take into account all the factors in the case – eg the length of time the tenant has resided in the dwelling. Also in relation to the discretionary grounds, section 9 of the 1988 Act grants the court extended discretion to adjourn for such period as it thinks fit any proceedings for possession. Likewise where an order is made under the discretionary grounds the court may stay or suspend its execution or postpone the date of execution. However, conditions are to be imposed with regard, inter alia, to the payment of any arrears of rent, unless the court considers that such an imposition would cause *exceptional* hardship to the tenant or would otherwise be unreasonable. Where these conditions are complied with the court may then rescind or discharge a possession order.

Security of tenure: ASTs

Where an AST expires under section 20(4) and, for example, the tenant 'holds on' a new AST will arise as described above. Apart from that, however, there is little long term security for the holder of an AST.
1)   All the mandatory and discretionary grounds applicable to ATs also apply.
2)   Note the special ground for obtaining possession provided by Section 21 of the 1988 Act as amended.
      Once the end of an AST *which was for an initial fixed term* has come, the court *must* make a possession order if satisfied:
1)   that the initial AST has come to an end and that no further assured tenancy of *any* sort is for the time being in existence (*other* than an AST including a SPAST) see section 21(1A), and
2)   the landlord has given the tenant not less than two month's notice stating that he/she requires possession of the dwelling.
      The court has no discretion in the matter once satisfied the AST is expired and that there is no further existing AT other than an AST (statutory or not) and that the requirement of notice has been complied with, see section 21(1) of the 1988 Act. Note also that the notice may be given once the initial fixed term has expired, or before or on the expiry date, even though a SPAST would arise on that date, for where possession is ordered any such tenancy ends automatically the day the possession order takes effect, see sections 21(2) and (3).
      Likewise the court *must* make a possession order in respect of a dwelling let on a AST which is a periodic tenancy following the initial fixed term AST under section 20(4) where satisfied:
a)   that the landlord has given the tenant a notice stating that after a specified date (such a date marking the end of a period of the tenancy, and not being earlier than two months after the date of the notice) that possession of the dwelling will be required, *and*

b)   that the date specified in the landlord's notice is not earlier than the earliest day on which at common law the tenancy could have been brought to an end following notice to quit.

Only one notice to gain possession under section 21 need be served. The court, it must be remembered has no discretion in relation to such issues, save as provided by Section 89 of the Housing Act 1980 – ie power to postpone a possession order for only 14 days save in cases of exceptional hardship where postponement for up to 6 weeks is allowed.

Modification of the assured tenancy regime for association tenants

With the introduction of assured tenancies for new association tenants as from 15 January 1989, it was clearly necessary to ensure their position was not radically different from existing association *secure* tenants, and also to make provision to ensure a measure of continuity for *authority secure* tenants becoming *association assured* tenants on any transfer, see below.

Section 49 of the Housing Act 1988 inserted section 36A into the Housing Associations Act 1985, which enabled the issue of guidance by the Housing Corporation on the management of housing by registered associations, either generally or more specifically. Particular guidance may be given on housing demand for which provision should be made, selection and allocation procedures, tenancy terms, principles for determining rent, maintenance and repair standards and practices, and consultation and communication with tenants. Such guidance may be issued from time to time, but before issue or revision consultation must take place with bodies representing associations, and a draft of the advice submitted to the Secretary of State for approval. In deciding whether associations are being well (or badly) managed the Corporation may consider whether they are (or are not) complying with section 36A advice.

A resume of the rules relating to association tenancies over the years

1)   Before 1980 associations were subject only to the 'fair rent' provisions of the Rent Act 1977, the security provisions did *not* apply, and the tenurial position was governed by the common law only – even judicial review was not available.
2)   From 1980 to 15 January 1989 associations were 'hybrid', security of tenure applied to tenants as 'secure', rents were 'fair rents' under the 1977 Act. Association tenancies granted during or before that period are still generally subject to that regime.
3)   From 15 January 1989 new association tenancies are, in general, on an AT basis both as to security and rent levels. An association cannot grant an old style hybrid or 'Housing Association tenancy' unless:

a)   it was granted under a contract made before 15 January 1989 *or*
b)   granted to a person who immediately before the grant was an association tenant and is granted by the same association who was his/her landlord before.

Hence an association tenant can move from dwelling to dwelling of an association and remain 'secure', but if he/she goes to *another* association the tenancy status changes from ST to AT. Likewise authority tenants who transfer to an association landlord under Part IV of the Housing Act 1988 (a PAL scheme) move from ST to AT status, but an association ST who exchanges tenancies with another ST retains that status.

However, because associations are 'social landlords' the dramatic nature of the change is somewhat modified. Under section 36A the Housing Corporation has issued 'The Tenants' Guarantee', whose object is to create additional rights for association ATs. Extra rights are conferred in respect of: repairs; in relation to complaints procedures; rents; exchanges, taking in of lodgers, carrying out of improvements; being consulted about changes in management. None of this causes any legal problems; the rights given (in addition to those given by the 1988 Act to ATs) are similar to those of STs, and are given by contract, see the model tenancy, initially drawn up in consult-ation with the NATFED. Problems, however, arise where the tenancy document seeks to *take away* from the provisions of the 1988 Act. The model tenancy states the landlord will *only* rely on Grounds 10, 12, 13, 14 (all discretionary grounds) and Ground 7 (mandatory). The model tenancy in effect binds the landlord *not* to use any of the appropriate mandatory grounds apart from 7 (ie 2, 3, 4, 6, 8). The question is can the landlord 'contract out' of powers under statute? In the context of the Rent Acts it was well established that tenants *cannot* by contract deprive themselves of protection, see *Baxter v Eckersley* [1950] 1 KB 480, [1950] 1 All ER 139, *Barton v Fincham* [1921] 2 KB 291, *Brown v Draper* [1944] KB 309, [1944] 1 All ER 246, *Solle v Butcher* [1950] 1 KB 671, [1949] 2 All ER 1107 and *Mauray v Durley Chine (Investments) Ltd* [1953] 2 QB 433, [1953] 2 All ER 458.

But can a landlord contract out? Note the following: 'Parties cannot of their own volition oust or reduce the jurisdiction of the courts to grant orders for possession', per Lord Asquith, in *Rogers v Hyde* [1951] 2 KB 923 at 931, [1951] 2 All ER 79.

Is this a rule of general application? Arguably yes, for parties cannot increase the jurisdiction of the court by agreement, see *Wandsworth London Borough Council v Fadayomi* [1987] 3 All ER 474, [1987] 1 WLR 1473. The effectiveness of the initial model tenancy with regard to use of the mandatory grounds of possession is therefore dubious, and the DoE acknowledged this to the National Consumer Council in 1988. The DoE thought a landlord *could* rely on the mandatory grounds but might have to pay damages for doing so for breaking the tenancy agreement. But could this be so: can a landlord be made to pay damages for exercising a right given by Parliament? We do not know. The Local Government and Housing Act 1989 has *partly* dealt with the problem. Where an association has acquired housing under a PAL scheme and a tenant has therefore gone from ST to AT status no reliance is possible on Ground 6 of Schedule 2 to the 1988 Act (substantial reconstruction) but otherwise the position is most unsatisfactory. Early evidence indicated that not all associations were using the model tenancy agreement.

The 'Tenants' guarantee' further provides:

1) associations registered with the corporation should consult with tenants about the proposed changes in management maintenance policy, changes in the environment of their dwellings, and the extent and cost of any services provided;
2) regular consultation arrangements should be set up;
3) associations should encourage tenants' groups;
4) associations should inform tenants of management participation opportunities where these exist;
5) there should be complaints procedures and provisions for appeals.

This guidance is not mandatory, but is likely to be adhered to as non adherence will be taken into account by the Corporation when allocating finance (see also Housing Corporation Circular 29/91).

The accountability of social landlords

There are a variety of methods to ensure that landlords are accountable to their tenants. In the most extreme cases of illegal activity (and such cases are very rare) a local authority landlord may be made subject to judicial review, while associations are subject to the very considerable investigative and monitoring powers of the housing corporation under section 28 of the Housing Associations Act 1985. Associations are also subject to the Corporation's 'power of the purse' by virtue of its powers under section 79 of that Act.

The Housing Corporation's regulatory powers in practice

The way in which the Corporation exercises its powers was examined by Day, Henderson & Klein in *Home Rules: Regulation and Accountability in Social Housing* (Rowntree Foundation, 1993). They discovered that since 1988 the Corporation has radically revised its operating procedures so that, for example, there is now much greater scrutiny of associations applying for registration. This has resulted in the number of new registrations declining; but 'sifting' would-be registrees is now an essential part of the regulatory system designed to ensure that inexperienced organisations are prevented from getting themselves into problems. Once registered every major association is inspected by corporation staff in detail every three to four years. Some of these associations receive an 'update' visit once a year when some specific aspect of policy will be examined. Medium sized associations are given a 'partial, management only visit' every four years and other visits if needed. The programme of visits is drawn up by the corporation's regions and time is left free to deal with emergencies or to visit associations causing alarm by their performance. Newly registered associations are regularly checked and visited. Since 1993 the Corporation has received quarterly financial returns from all associations which are actively developing housing and any others deemed to need regular scrutiny: these returns enable the Corporation to identify any associations 'at risk' and therefore in need of inspection.

The Corporation further uses its powers to ensure that associations maintain adequate standards of service provision for their tenants, and that national social policy objectives are implemented, and a number of documents have been issued to further this objective. Thus, for example, quite detailed guidance has been given on the pursuit of equal opportunity policies, though Day, Henderson and Klein consider much of the guidance given to be somewhat subjective and insufficiently precise, while in other cases it may result in extremely difficult decisions having to be made. For example associations are urged to involve tenant groups in participating in management but are then told to withdraw recognition from any group which fails to follow equal opportunity policies.

When a corporation inspector visits an association it will be graded on a four (A-D) point scale – the lowest positions indicating a good or generally satisfactory performance needing a few minor improvements. Other grades indicate either the need for major change or that Corporation intervention is needed. Where major change is needed a realistic time scale (between three and six months) for improvement will be agreed. If, however, the Corporation has to intervene it will first draft in new committee members to strengthen the association and oversee to its workings under section 17 of the Housing Associations Act 1985. Where, however, an association continues to act badly, generally illegally or unconstitutionally, the Corporation will use its 'last resort' powers under section 28 and order an inquiry.

Section 28 empowers the Corporation to conduct inquiries into the affairs of registered associations, and the person who is appointed, who may not be an actual or former member of the Corporation's staff, may require the production of books, accounts and other documents relating to an association's business for the purpose of conducting the inquiry. A special audit of accounts for the inquiry may be undertaken under section 29. Where the Corporation are satisfied that there has been misconduct or mismanagement in an association's affairs, they may, under section 30, remove or suspend those responsible from membership and/or office, order banks or others holding an association's money or securities not to part with them without Corporation approval, and generally restrict the powers of the association to enter into transactions. Due notice of an intention to remove a person from office, etc must be given to the person and the association and the person have rights of appeal to the High Court.

Where an inquiry or audit has uncovered mismanagement or misconduct in the administration of a registered association which is also a society registered under the Industrial and Provident Societies Act 1965, *or* the management of the association's land would be improved if transferred to another association, the Corporation may direct the transfer to another registered association.

Though section 28 powers are extensive they are not as rapidly effective as those of the Charity Commission under the Charities Act 1960 for there is no power to enter premises or to 'freeze' activity in order to prevent further malpractice. In such circumstances a more useful deterrent is the power of the Corporation to halt building programmes by withholding funding.

In practice corporation visits are concentrated on the quite small number of associations which collectively provide most of the stock. Most are given a clean bill of health, though in 1990/1 37% of those inspected were graded C or D. There were, however, regional variations in ratings with some areas having no 'Ds' while others had up to 17% – this *may* reflect differences in regulatory style encountered by Day, Henderson and Klein in the survey, or local differences in the composition of associations. The survey evidence indicates 'management only' associations as being more likely to be graded unsatisfactory especially with regard to equal opportunity policies, while larger associations tended to receive the most satisfactory gradings. On the other hand new 'developing' associations were most likely to be lowly graded with regard to finance and management control.

The objects of the Corporation are to ensure that associations are publicly accountable for the money they are given, that they are good stewards of their assets and that they fulfil social policy objectives. Financial viability is a precondition to achieving these objects, but not all viable associations will otherwise reach required standards. Day, Henderson & Klein concluded that the device of concentrating most inspection effort on the largest associations mean most of the stock is subject to effective oversight at low cost, but this can result in less than effective supervision of smaller associations. It was also discovered that most effort is devoted to inspecting managerial structures and processes by looking at files and minutes as opposed to physical investigation of actual properties. To strengthen oversight, however, the research applauded the decision of the Corporation to create an ombudsman for associations, see below, and argued for a more comprehensive complaints system being created.

Currently inspection reports are written for the private consumption of associations concerned, but their public use is spreading as sources of private finance for development often wish to see reports – as do authorities who have land for development. In the future reports may become public property. This raises the issue of whether some form of common public regulatory system for both associations and authorities is desirable. This could take the form of National Housing Agencies, which would fund *all* social housing, and a new Standards Agency to assess and ensure quality of management amongst social landlords. Such bodies would, however, be non-elected which could result in a diminution in tenant participation. Common standards, performance indicators and publicity requirements for *all* social landlords could, however, be developed. In the past such techniques of regulation have been used for diverse purposes: in the case of authorities to make them more accountable to electors; in that of associations to make them responsive to central oversight via the Corporation. But in practice this distinction is blurred and the various techniques could be made to converge so that the performance of all social landlords in managing and providing housing could be compared nationally and locally.

One note of caution needs to be sounded about the creation of too many standards and requirements. There is already evidence that over rigid insistence on social policy objectives – for instance equal opportunities – may result in a loss of diversity and flexibility amongst associations: increasingly rigorous regulation results in homogeneity. Secondly there could be regulatory overkill with associations in particular being subject to investigation by both the Corporation and other agencies – for example with regard to community care. Thirdly there can be a considerable amount of latitude in the interpretation of certain policy requirements, and ambiguity about how a particular policy is to be achieved. What, for example, is an 'affordable rent' (see further Chapter Four) particularly when the parameters for deciding this are fixed externally by Central Government decisions on social security and housing benefit. Likewise how does one take account of tenant views on management issues when these may run directly counter to equal opportunity policies. (See further below on complaints mechanisms.)

However, on a day to day basis something less drastic than these powers outlined above is needed to ensure that social landlords always bear in mind the fact that while the freehold of units of accommodation they provide is legally theirs, those dwellings are other people's homes. What is provided to achieve this is a range of measures some of which are adjudicatory, some provide channels of complaint while others are informatory.

Adjudicatory systems

These are the various ombudsmen systems and arbitration. It is convenient to deal with arbitration first. A tenancy agreement may provide for tenants to be able to refer disputes with their landlords to independent arbitration under the terms of the Arbitration Acts 1950 and 1979. The procedure can be cheap, speedy and less risky than litigation, and allows tenants to conduct their own cases. However, arbitration is only available in respect of those matters dealt with by the arbitration agreement and there is no legal obligation on any landlord to provide such an agreement.

Ombudsmen

Local government has been subject to the supervision of the Commission for Local Administration (the 'Local Ombudsman' or LO) since the Local Government Act 1974, see especially section 25(1)(a).

The 1974 Act section 34(3) provides that nothing in the Act authorises or requires the LO to question the *merits* of a decision taken without maladministration by an authority in the exercise of a discretion vested in it. This does not prevent the *investigation* of the merits of a decision, but it prevents the LO from criticising a decision as *wrong in substance* when there was no procedural flaw in the process leading up to the decision. The maladministration must, by virtue of section 26(1) of the 1974 Act, arise 'in connection with action taken *by or on behalf of* a local authority'. This is wide enough to cover the acts and decisions of members, officers and other employees, and also agents of an authority. The LO also has jurisdiction over Housing Action Trusts.

'Maladministration' is an elusive concept, which certainly has a procedural aspect, seeming to extend, penumbra like, from cases where an authority has clearly behaved illegally to instances of excessive delay in dealing with matters, biased or hearsay influenced decision making, victimisation or oppression of those subject to administrative powers, bad or non-existent procedures, making misleading statements about policy or practice, breaking promises, failing to respond to justifiable complaints, imposing harsh requirements on applicants for housing, and generally behaving in an inappropriate and heavy handed way.

The complaint must also claim to have sustained injustice in consequence of maladministration. 'Injustice' is not legislatively defined but covers a wide range of matters from loss consequent upon refusal to make a financial grant through to annoyance, disturbance or frustration caused by maladministration. No financial loss need be proven.

There are certain sorts of failings and practices that regularly result in findings of maladministration causing injustice. Authorities should beware of:

1) delay in taking appropriate action, for example, with regard to processing grant applications, or applications for housing benefits, or claims to exercise the right to buy, or in transferring anti-social tenants to other accommodation or otherwise failing to deal with nuisances caused by such tenants, or in pursuing programmes of repair and modernisation;

2) failure to comply with legal requirements or otherwise to keep promises or implement undertakings given in relation to housing matters, or to

compensate tenants for damage suffered as a result of an authority's fault in relation to their obligations;

3) not making adequate information or advice available or failure to explain policies on housing issues clearly, or failing to make clear the effect of obtaining alternative accommodation on a waiting list application;

4) failing to investigate matters properly or to consider medical or overcrowding evidence in relation to rehousing applications;

5) general inefficiency in processing housing applications etc, or in providing services where stipulated in a contract of letting, or in failing to give a tenant an opportunity to reply to complaints made about his behaviour by other tenants;

6) behaving inappropriately in cases of relationship breakdown. When an authority deals with the consequences of a relationship breakdown, they should act in an even handed and open fashion, not reaching unjustified assumptions about the parties' whereabouts and intentions. They should act on the basis of verified information, doing nothing to prejudice the rights of the parties until a court has dealt with the matter. Likewise it is unacceptable for an authority to require the taking of particular legal steps – steps that the parties are not by law required to take – as a pre-condition for rehousing.

Procedure

There is a strict procedure, laid down in section 26 of the 1974 Act, to be followed before a complaint will be entertained. The LO will not investigate any complaint until it has been brought to the attention of the authority complained against, either by the person aggrieved or by a member of the authority on behalf of that person, and until the authority has had a reasonable time in which to reply to the complaint. Since June 1992 this provision has been particularly strictly applied. A complaint intended for reference should be made in writing to a member of the authority complained against with a request that it should be sent to the LO. It should state the action which it is alleged constitutes maladministration. If the member does not refer the complaint to the LO, the person aggrieved may ask the LO to accept the complaint direct.

The current operating procedures were laid down in 1991.

1) Complainants complete forms which are sent to the LO's office. If the LO decides a complaint cannot be investigated the complainant is told, with reasons, in writing. If an investigation is to take place the complainant is also told.

2) The LO communicates with the Chief Executive of the authority in question and asks for comments on the matter.

3) Officers of the authority will then usually supply details of the matter to the Chief Executive who will then respond with the authority's view.
4) A decision is then taken whether to investigate further; a decision to proceed indicates suspicion of maladministration and injustice.
5) An investigating officer will speak to the complainant and also visit the authority to carry out a detailed investigation which will involve studying files and interviewing appropriate members and officers.
6) A decision and report will then be made and issued.

The effectiveness of the LO in providing a remedy

Certain matters are excluded from the ambit of the LO's investigations; for example there cannot normally be an investigation of a matter if the complainant has or had a right of appeal or a right to go to the courts but has not used it, Local Government Act 1974, section 26(6). Similar exclusions apply where there is a right of appeal, reference or review to any statutorily constituted tribunal, or where there is a right of appeal to a minister. These exclusions are subject to the proviso that the LO may conduct an investigation if satisfied that in the particular circumstances it was reasonable for the complainant not to have used other legal remedies, for example, because the cost of pursuing a remedy in the High Court would be prohibitively high. The Commission has a general discretion to investigate complaints, the exercise of which was considered by the Court of Appeal in *R v Local Comr for Administration for the North and East Area of England, ex p Bradford Metropolitan City Council* [1979] QB 287, [1979] 2 All ER 881.

The decision confirmed:
1) although the LO cannot question the merits of a decision taken without maladministration, a complaint about the decision can be investigated to see whether there was maladministration in the process of making it;
2) the fact that a complaint is about the exercise of 'professional judgement' does not prevent investigation by the LO;
3) a complainant should not have to specify any particular 'piece' of mal-administration. It is enough to specify the action of the authority in connection with which the complaint arises;
4) because the complainant might be able to voice the complaint in court proceedings, the LO is not barred from investigating questions of injustice and maladministration which will not be directly at issue in those proceedings.

A perceived weakness of the LO's work is that there is no obligation on authorities made subject to a report of maladministration to implement recommendations, though authorities must report to the LO any action taken or to be taken. Where no such report is received, or where it is unsatisfactory, the LO may issue a second or 'further' report indicating what would be an appropriate response. From 1981/2 to 1988/9, 1,574 reports finding injustice caused by maladministration (*not* just in housing cases) were issued, 121 further reports, were issued from which satisfactory settlement was subsequently achieved in 33 cases (Local Ombudsman, Annual Report 1988-1989). Since 1988, authorities have been under an obligation to make reports of action they propose in response to further reports, and, under section 26 of the Local Government and Housing Act 1989, where no satisfactory response to a further report is made, the authority in question is under an obligation to issue public statements as to the LO's recommendations and, if they wish, a statement of why they do not intend to implement them; this can cost more than putting right the initial injustice, and it remains a feature of the office that many authorities fail to implement specifically recommended remedies. The *Citizens Charter* of 1991 did not rule out the possibility of making the LO's recommendations specifically enforceable.

The evidence to hand suggests that most cases where maladministration causing injustice was found were remedied satisfactorily. The general rarity of further reports in housing cases indicates that the activities of the LO have *some* effect on authorities and *may* contribute to the better administration of discretion. Against this it should be said that some authorities have from time to time been made the subject of multiple complaints by numbers of individuals. The evidence here suggests that there may be pockets of resistance to the introduction of good housing administration policies.

Remedial action is likely to fall under one, or more, of the following four headings: giving an apology; redressing the actual grievance; a compensatory payment; and improvement of administrative procedures. Steps taken to redress the cause of a complaint will satisfy the complainant. However, there are times when correcting one wrong may well cause the other problems, for example where rehousing a complainant raises allegations of unfair treatment in relation to other persons awaiting accommodation. In such circumstances an authority is justified in considering the wider issues and their implications before deciding what response to make.

In some cases making a monetary payment may be the best course of action. Section 1 of the Local Government Act 1978 allows authorities to make payments to or provide other benefits for persons who have suffered injustice because of maladministration. It may not, however, always be easy to satisfy the loss caused by maladministration. Some authorities have resorted to the services of an independent expert to quantify the amount of the payment to be made. In 'Local Authority Response to the Local Ombudsman' [1979] JPL 441 Christine Chinkin revealed that sums of up to £20,000 have been paid as compensation. Over the years the LO has become more willing to make specific suggestions in reports as to the best way to ensure that the act of maladministration has been remedied.

The receipt of a finding of maladministration may, of course, lead to a change or improvement in an authority's administrative workings so as to minimise the risk of future complaints. Some authorities now have schemes to monitor their further performance in relation to their statutory functions, and others have created special subcommittees to deal with specific problems.

The LO is generally agreed to be quite effective in securing a means of redress for *some* grievances on the part of authority tenants, but the procedures adopted act as a sieve through which only a certain number and type of complaints pass. In addition, the level of public awareness of the LO's service generally remain low. Many tenants are simply unaware of its existence, and even where tenants have heard of the service most will not know how to contact it, while some potential complainants perceive the LO as 'too important' to approach. Knowledge of the LO's service, and of how to contact it is markedly higher in 'advantaged' areas than in 'deprived areas'.

It is not, however, simply authority tenants who may utilise an ombudsman service.

The Housing Association Tenants Ombudsman Service (HATOS)

In the first annual report on the Citizen's Charter, Ministers declared an intention to create an ombudsman service for association tenants to:

1) provide an accessible, fair and effective means of resolving complaints against associations by those they serve;
2) *seek* redress where a complaint is found justified;
3) identify deficiencies in service delivery and to improve associations' quality of service; clearly a point of distinction from the Commission for Local Administration.

After consultation the Housing Corporation set out its proposals for HATOS in 1993, and the service has been operational since 1994. The service is non-statutory and is established by the Housing Corporation. However, to underscore the independence of HATOS the corporation undertook to: restrict their power to remove the ombudsman within the first three years of service; set up an independent expert panel to advise the ombudsman; allow direct access for the ombudsman to the Chairman of the Corporation; locate the service in a building not occupied otherwise by the corporation or any association. HATOS has no power to *enforce* its recommendations, but derives its powers from the Corporation's extensive investigative and other regulatory powers, for example under section 27A of the Housing Associations Act 1985. Where associations refuse to collaborate with HATOS a request can be made to the corporation to step in and use its own powers.

HATOS has no access to confidential information about associations held by the Corporation, but the latter may be asked to supply relevant information in respect of a complaint investigation.

HATOS will receive complaints on the following basis:

a)   they must be from (or made on behalf of) those who receive direct services from registered associations eg as a tenant, licensee, etc or a disappointed applicant for housing by an association;

b)   there must be evidence of a breach in the relationship between the parties usually, but not exclusively, in consequence of possible maladministration, which is characterised as delay, muddle, bias, failure to follow procedures and bad decision making;

c)   internal complaints procedures must have been exhausted;

d)   complaints must not fall within excluded classes, eg rent and service charge matters, neighbour disputes, 'old' complaints, ie those known to the complainant more than 12 months before it was drawn to the association's attention or the Ombudsman's, matters already taken to court, matters more effectively remedied in court, cases falling with other ombudsmen's jurisdiction, complaints against the corporation, vexations or frivolous complaints, anonymous complaints, though identities will be kept confidential for as long as possible.

HATOS follows a number of paths in seeking to resolve disputes laid before the service.

Mediation is a technique overseen, but not provided by HATOS, and is encouraged as a way of resolving disputes by communal arrangement between the parties as opposed to an imposed third party solution. The 'mediation route' is an entirely private arrangement between the parties and the end result is not binding on either. Where mediation is agreed on a matter within the jurisdiction of HATOS the service is free and is provided by specialist mediation agencies.

Arbitration again depends upon the agreement of the parties, though here the decision of the arbitrator is binding in law, and once the process has begun neither party may abandon it unilaterally. HATOS *may* agree to act as an arbitrator, subject to pressures on resources, and will in such cases make only a nominal charge, otherwise an external arbitrator has to be appointed at an appropriate fee.

'Good Practice' is the title of the NATFED's collected guidance on the handling of tenant complaints by associations. The adoption of the best practices of individual associations by all will, it is believed, result in more complaints being satisfactorily handled.

Investigation will take place where a matter within jurisdiction (see above) is referred to HATOS and it cannot be resolved informally by the above techniques, and the ombudsman decides to carry out a full investigation leading to a report. A complaint duly received will be examined to see if it falls within the terms of reference, whether there is prima-facie maladministration, and to see how it may be progressed. Further information from one or both of the parties or the Corporation may be required at this stage. Where a straight-forward informal resolution cannot be reached and mediation/arbitration is not acceptable investigation will follow and the original complaint and subsequent correspondence will be copied to the association, unless the complainant has requested anonymity. An investigation will gather all relevant facts ensuring that all concerned are able to put forward their views. The facts will be passed to the ombudsman who will review the case and prepare a draft report which will be sent to the parties for comments on its factual accuracy. A final report is produced in the light of comments received, and copies are sent to all those directly involved and the corporation: the complainant's real name will not be used in the report. The report will give the association a final compliance date for remedial action if maladministration is found, but, of course, HATOS cannot enforce its findings.

Formal complaints about associations may still be made to the Corporation. When such complaints fall within HATOS terms of reference they will be forwarded there, otherwise the Corporation will continue to see what it can do to resolve complaints.

It is clear that HATOS has a more flexible approach to its functions than does the LO because of its non-statutory constitution and because it is the product of thinking which accepts the need for a wide variety of approaches to be provided to deal with tenant complaints. HATOS further proceeds on the basis that complaints and their resolution are both performance indicators of the level and quality of service provided to tenants as 'consumers' by their association landlords.

Complaints mechanisms

The LO service is not simply concerned with investigating individual allegations of maladministration, but also with promoting overall good practice amongst authorities. Thus in 1978 the Local Authority Associations and the Local Commission issued a Code of Practice on complaints, urging all authorities to have a written procedure for dealing with all complaints about their activities. In their 1988/89 annual report the Local Commission expressed their expectation that all authorities would have an internal complaints procedure, and stated a failure to have such a procedure, or reliance on a faulty procedure, would be itself good evidence of maladministration. Further guidance on such procedures was issued by the service in 1992, and members of the public are in general expected to utilise their authorities' internal procedures before taking allegations to the LO. Since then there has been widespread adoption of local complaints systems by authorities. It is further a feature of the 'Citizens Charter' approach to public administration that not only should management be open and co-operative in nature but that there should be a complaints service with provision for compensation to be paid in cases where complaints of a serious nature are shown to be justified and loss has been suffered, see further *The Council Tenant's Charter*, DoE 1992.

The basic hallmarks of a complaints system are that it should be 'user friendly', it should possess clearly defined stages through which complaints should proceed, and should be promptly responsive to problems. The service should also be objective, confidential and comprehensive in operation. All complaints mechanisms should have definitions of what constitutes a complaint, who is able to complain, when and how complaints may be made, how they are to be processed and who is charged with taking appropriate action, see further, Hughes, Karn, Leabeater, Lickiss, and Ward *Housing Complaints Procedures: Principles of Good Practices for Social Landlords*, National Consumer Council, 1991.

A number of authorities currently operate a complaints service – some under the terms of their tenancy agreements, others as a free standing service or 'guarantee' thereof. There is no one national standard model complaints mechanism.

So far as association tenants are concerned the Tenants' Guarantee, see above, indicates that associations should have complaints procedures, and there is evidence to suggest the Housing Corporation expects monitoring of complaints to be part of overall self assessment of their service by associations. Certainly associations are expected to be responsive to tenants' complaints. Though there is no prescribed model of a complaints mechanism for associations there is no reason why the principles applicable to authority mechanisms should not apply.

The Corporation has indicated that it will investigate complaints made to it by association tenants once they have exhausted internal complaints mechanisms, and this it does as part of its supervisory task, though only serious complaints in practice will receive the corporation's attention. Nominated complaints officers in regional officers receive complaints, provided they are in writing, and once a complaint is formally made the complainant's consent is sought so that the corporation may approach the association in question. An appropriate officer will be assigned to investigate a complaint, and in due course the corporation will inform the complainant of its view of the matter. Where legal action is called for the corporation will advise a complainant to seek legal advice, or to consult the CRE or EOC in appropriate cases.

Informatory systems: reports to tenants

Tenants of authorities receive annual reports from their landlords detailing housing managerial performance which must be sent to them within six months of the end of the previous financial year – effectively by the end of September in each calendar year. A copy of such a report must also be sent to the Secretary of State, see Section 167 of the Local Government and Housing Act 1989. The philosophy here is that publicity is a form of accountability and the objectives for reports are that they should provide up-to-date information about housing performance to promote tenant interest and involvement, and thus to enhance management standards by stimulating customer demand and interest. Though specific management targets do not have to be set under the statute, ministers *expect* authorities to do so, and thus the system is designed to be a form of self discipline, see DoE Circular 10/94.

The content of reports is determined by ministers by direction under section 167(1) of the 1989 Act and the current direction is contained in Circular 10/94. Currently authorities are required to report on: the status of the housing stock, including the number of dwellings and those that are houses, flats or maisonettes, and the numbers of dwellings by number of bedrooms; rents, including average weekly rents and the percentage of those owing over 13 weeks' arrears; repairs including priority cases, target response times and compliance with such times; allocations, including those to new tenants, nominations to associations, allocations to priority homelessness cases, dwellings empty and available for letting, or awaiting only minor repairs and average re-let times of such dwellings, average weekly management costs per dwelling per year. This is the minimum content of reports, authorities may provide more information if they wish, and may set it in the context of local circumstances.

Reports should provide information in understandable forms, and may be in languages other than English where appropriate. Information should be given on qualitative as well as quantitative matters – eg on the delivery of services. Reports should be simple and inexpensive and authorities are urged by ministers to disaggregate information on an estate by estate basis where-ever possible. Under the terms of the 'Tenants' Guarantee' (HC circular 29/91, para G4) association tenants are also entitled to yearly reports on rent levels, and collection performance, speed of effecting repairs, voids and rates of reletting, and to whom re-lets are made.

An overall management philosophy

In addition to the foregoing mechanisms, the general policy stance of landlords should reflect, in terms of securing accountability, recommendations made by Bines, Kemp, Pleace and Radley in *Managing Social Housing* (HMSO, 1993). These included statements that:
1)   housing management targets and objectives should be internally discussed with housing staff;
2)   tenants should have a greater voice in determining the way in which they may participate in housing management;

3)   there should be enhanced dissemination of information about participation arrangements and existing tenants' group to tenants;
4)   allocation policies should be regularly reviewed to ensure that groups in need are not excluded;
5)   applicants for housing should be regularly informed of their progress towards rehousing, and the likely timescale for this;
6)   allocation and lettings services should be more carefully monitored by the collection of more statistical information on allocation, and special steps should be taken to monitor the reletting of empty properties.

Conclusion

Despite a long historical tradition of English Law which has allowed the ownership and control of property to be 'parcelled out' among a number of persons in the form of the trust and the settlement of land, the dominant position with regard to the provision of rented housing has been to vest both ownership and control in the landlord. How to modify that, particularly in relation to social housing, has been a matter of legal and policy concern since the 1960s. It was then recognised that, as the private rented sector declined, society was becoming polarised in housing terms, between owner occupiers (the larger group) and (then) authority tenants, with the tenurial position of the latter being, in terms of legal rights, very weak. Strengthening that position, and that of the increasing number of association tenants, has led legislators down a variety of paths. From 1980 onwards the position of authority tenants was legally revolutionised – that term is not too strong – by the introduction of the secure tenancy. However, that package of rights was primarily individual in nature in that the rights conferred affected most of all the relationship between *individual tenants and their landlords*. Furthermore the principal right, namely to buy, was a right to *cease* to be a tenant.

Collective rights where the sum total of tenants' exercises is what affects a landlords' behaviour were scarcely well developed in the 1980 legislation. The Callaghan Government's 1979 Housing Bill, on which the Thatcher Government's 1980 Housing Act was largely based in so far as it created the notion of a secure tenancy (though not with the right to buy), did contain the notion of the Joint Estate Management Committee (JEM). These would have been required nationwide within authorities, and would have ensured a measure of representative tenant democracy in housing. Some authorities have set up JEMs on a voluntary basis: some have encouraged the development of vigorous and local tenants' associations, but there is no single national mechanism for enabling tenants' views even to be ascertained, apart from the weak requirements of section 105 of the 1985 Act.

Thus since 1980 there has been a diverse search to find means whereby landlords may be made more responsive generally to their tenants; but the search has not produced an even pattern across the sectors. Arguably within the local authority sector the chosen 'model', under the Citizen's Charter and Council Tenant's Charter, has been that of a company where an authority is like a board of directors making reports to, and seeking the views of, tenants who are thus likened to shareholders. Turning to associations the model is rather more that of a public utility where the Housing Corporation has increasingly adopted the role of an external regulator such as OFGAS or OFWAT. In the meantime some authorities have followed another model, namely that of a retailer offering a complaints mechanism as a service to tenant 'consumers' or 'customers'.

It may be asked whether any of these models is appropriate to the world of housing coming as they do from commerce and industry. None of them address the fundamental issue of how to divide ownership and control so that the landlord's ownership of 'the house' and the tenant's possession of 'the home' are held in an equitable balance which further recognises the landlord's need to intervene from time to time to ensure harmonious neighbour relationships and tenants' collective wishes for the future of their local environments. The most recent developments under the 'banner' of CCT to transfer specified management functions to TMOs is perhaps, the most significant steps so far in the direction of responsible, democratic tenant control of housing. How far that initiative can and will go must remain an issue for speculation.

Further reading

In addition to the books and articles noted in the text, the following should also be consulted.

General Policy
Donnison, D and MacLennan, D (eds) *The Housing Service of the Future*, Longman/Institute of Housing, 1991
Cole, I and Furbey,R *The Eclipse of Council Housing*, Routledge, 1994 Chapters 5 and 6
Lambert, Paris & Blackaby *Housing Policy & the State* (Macmillan , 1978) Chapter 3
Merrett, S *State Housing in Britain* (Routledge & Kegan Paul, 1979) Chapter 8
Murie, Niner, & Watson *Housing Policy & The Housing System* (George Allen & Unwin 1976) Chapter 4

Racial Discrimination
Race Relations & Housing Cmnd 6252 (HMSO)
Housing in Multi Racial Areas (Community Relations Commission, 1976)
Handy, C *Discrimination in Housing* (Sweet & Maxwell, 1993)

Love, A-M and Kirby, K   *Racial Incidents in Council Housing: The Local Authority Response* (HMSO, 1994)

Smith, D   *Racial Disadvantage in Britain* (Penguin, 1977) Part 3

Smith & Whalley   *Racial Minorities & Public Housing* (PEP, 1975)

CRE   'Homelessness and Discrimination: Report of a formal investigation into Tower Hamlets', London, 1988, CRE

CRE   'Housing Allocation in Oldham: Report of a formal investigation', London, 1993, CRE

Allocation Policies

Corina, L   *Housing Allocation Policy and Its Effects* (Department of Social Administration, University of York, 1976)

Hughes, D and Jones, S   'Bias in the Allocation and Transfer of Local Authority Housing' (1979) *Journal of Social Welfare Law* 273

Lewis, N   'Council Housing Allocation: Problems of Discretion and Control' (1976) 54 *Public Administration* 147

Prescot-Clarke, Clemens and Park   *Routes into Local Authority Housing* (HMSO, 1994)

Tenants' Rights

Chinkin, C   'Local Authority Response to the Local Ombudsman' [1979] JPL 441

Chinkin, C   'The Power of the Local Ombudsman Re-examined' [1980] JPL 87

Hoath, D C   'Council Tenants' Complaints and the Local Ombudsman' (1978) 128 NLJ 672

Hughes, Karn, Leabeater, Lickiss and Ward   *Housing Complaints Procedures* (National Consumer Council, 1991)

Luba, Madge & MaConnell   *Defending Possession Proceedings* (Legal Action Group, 1992)

Karn, Lickiss, Hughes and Crawley   *Neighbour Disputes* (Institute of Housing, 1993)

Markson, H E   'Investigating Local Maladministration' (1981) 131 NLJ 844

Tagliavini, L   'Setting aside a warrant for possession after execution' (1994) *Legal Action* (July) 18

Ward, C   *Tenants Take Over* (Architectural Press, 1974)

Williams D W   'Social Welfare Consumers and their Complaints' (1979) *Journal of Social Welfare Law* 273

Reports

Audit Commission   *Managing the Crisis in Council Housing*, HMSO, 1986

Centre for Housing Research   *The Nature and Effectiveness of Housing Management in England*, DoE, HMSO, 1989

Kirkby, K, Finch, H and Wood, D *The Organisation of Housing Management in English Local Authorities*, DoE, 1987

Institute of Housing *Tenant Participation in Housing Management*, IOH/ Tenants' Participation Advisory Service, 1989

Maclenna, D and Kay, H *Moving On, Crossing Divides* DoE, HMSO, 1994

Chapter Four

Rents and subsidies

The financing of authority and association housing has undergone major change over the last 20 years, broadly speaking reflecting the transition of social housing to a more overtly residual function within the housing system as a whole. This period of change culminated in the introduction of a 'new financial regime' in the Local Government and Housing Act 1989 but much of the logic of this system – and many of the policy instruments – were put in place over many years and some appreciation of these earlier arrangements is necessary to understand fully the new regime. The first part of this chapter highlights the main elements from the post 1919 system and puts in context the beginning of the period of fundamental change to the 'traditional' system, which can be dated from the Housing Finance Act 1972, notwithstanding that that legislation itself had a lengthy gestation. The chapter then unravels in turn the capital and the revenue sides of the financial arrangements for both authorities and associations, although it will rapidly become apparent that the elements of capital and revenue (current expenditure) are very closely connected, not least because, in the case of the authorities, a large share of current spending is the repayment of loans and debt charges arising from past capital projects. Finally the chapter makes a brief statement of the law regarding the administration and payment of housing benefit.

In deference to the overall structure of the book and to the more purely economic scholarship on this complex and controversial subject we refer readers to the texts of: Hills, J *Unravelling Housing Finance*, Clarendon Press, 1991; Gibb, K and Munroe, M *Housing Finance in the UK*, Macmillan, 1991; Merrett, S *State Housing in Britain*, Routledge and Kegan Paul, 1979; and Malpass, P *Reshaping Housing Policy*, Routledge, 1990

The law on social housing finance is relatively easily stated, providing a framework for the policy process. Compared to other strands of housing policy discussed in this text, however, *implementation issues* exert a crucial influence on the outcomes, witnessed in the very great diversity of stocks of social housing in different parts of the country and the wide range of rents paid for dwellings that are to all intents and purposes the same, built in some cases by the same construction company. This historic diversity has important implications for the present day system of finance and is one of the reasons for the much greater control which central government now exerts over authorities' capital programmes and revenue accounts. To a considerable degree the struggle over the practice of housing finance has been waged on a central–local government battlefield with the law shaping and honing the weapons but very much circling round the protagonists. It is a field on which politicians and accountants have held sway. It follows that a considerable part of this chapter is about changes in inter-governmental relations and the policy implementation process.

Arrangements under the 'traditional' system

One of the most important points to grasp about the modern period of social housing finance, which we take to mean the post 1919 era (see Chapter One), is that the financing of authority housing has been based for most of the time on an historic cost principle, that is to say the value of each dwelling has been set according to the initial costs of building it and buying the land. The loans needed to undertake construction were therefore defined according to prices at the 'historic' point in time and the repayment burden was distinctly 'front loaded'(ie high at the beginning of the repayment period but tapering off in real terms). As time went by this allowed authorities to charge lower rents than would be necessary under the *current value* convention which operates in the private sector. Private landlords generally expect to receive a rental income which reflects the current market value of the property and have no economic incentive to invest capital unless this is so. Thus there are two quite distinct forms of renting which in this country have been the basis for the division of the rental market into two separate systems. Indeed it was precisely the harmonisation of the two systems, by reference to the private sector 'current capital value' model, that the 'new financial regime' was designed to achieve. There was no inevitability about this outcome and the decisions leading to it were largely defined within the party political system and the central civil service. In other European countries, notably Sweden and Germany, the *public sector* has defined the terms of the rental market and harmonistaion has occured creating a unitary rental system driven through the influence of the public sector (see Kemeny, J *Housing and Social Theory*, Routledge, 1992).

The British subsidy system which lasted from the 1923 Act in practice up to the Housing Act 1980 was based on the payment to authorities by the central Exchequer of a fixed annual amount of cash per dwelling built and given to them over a specified period of time, typically 40 to 60 years. (Note that the 1919 Act had a somewhat different system due to authorities' financial liability being limited to the product of a penny rate. The central Exchequer aborted the subsidy in 1921 on the grounds that it was too expensive.) The subsidies under the various Acts (together with rental income and any rate fund payments) were accumulated into each authority's Housing Revenue Account (HRA), a system which was imposed by the Housing Act 1935 to avoid the complexity of keeping separate accounts for money received under each item of legislation. Payments of interest on capital loans and management and maintenance costs were therefore paid out of a single unified account and this system remains a basic instrument of local authority housing finance to this day.

It was through the very literal 'bricks and mortar' investment subsidy that central government sought to exert leverage on authorities to build in line with prevailing central policy, whether for general needs housing or other needs such as slum clearance. By varying the generosity of each subsidy it was possible to engineer a general response, as exemplified in Chapter One with the development of certain types of high rise construction which were encouraged by subsidies available in the Housing Subsidies Act 1956. At the same time this system still gave individual authorities a considerable degree of autonomy to decide what to build and how much rent to charge for 'their' property. Authorities also had duties to ensure that their accounts balanced and this they could do by controlling rent setting and topping up their HRAs from local rate fund contributions. It should be remembered that before the introduction of the present system of financing local government – the council tax which effectively levies a charge per head of the population in an area by reference to certain 'bands' of property values – local authorities derived a proportion of current income from rates. These were a form of property tax by which, each year, 'ratepayers' had to contribute sums of money to their local authorities by reference to the rateable value of their homes. Rateable values were determined by District Valuers, who based their calculations on the sum of money a 'hypothetical tenant' would be prepared to pay as rent for a given dwelling. Once such a value was established the yearly rate was set as a proportion or percentage of it. Rates were unpopular as the liability to pay bore no relationship either to household size or income. Payments from its ratepayers went into an authority's 'general rate fund' from which money could be taken to subsidise the HRA. This was perceived as unfair because it was widely believed that only owner occupiers paid rates. This was not so: council houses were themselves rated, but the rate payments were simply subsumed into the payment of rent.

In an era when the main task of housing policy was to overcome the absolute shortages of dwellings such an investment centred subsidy system worked well. Authorities knew how much money they would receive each year from the centre and so could calculate how much they would need to transfer from the rate fund, if at all, and in particular what level of rent would need to be set in order to balance the HRA. It had the distinct political and administrative advantage of allowing different governments to frame the emphasis of their housing policies without having to restructure the subsidy system from scratch and the Treasury commitment was relatively predictable. In addition until the creation of the Housing Investment Programme (HIP) at the end of the 1970s, there were no central limits on authority capital spending and this further encouraged local councils to expand their housing stock. Above all these financial mechanisms were sufficiently flexible to sustain a long-term balance between the demands of national policy change and a locally administered system of 'council' houses.

However, once the era of overall shortages of dwellings drew to a close during the 1970s the logic and stability of this system increasingly began to be questioned, particularly as council housing came to play a more residual role in the nation's housing strategy; the main aim being the expansion of home ownership (see Chapter One). Accordingly the subsidy system evolved away from an investment orientation towards supporting the incomes of individual households least able to afford access to the private market. This shift was accompanied by the idea of abandoning HRA calculations based on the actual services supplied with a high degree of autonomy for authorities in rent setting. Instead a deficit subsidy was devised which reflected central government's own notions about the expected cost of managing and maintaining stock rather than what actually was happening. The purpose of the HRA subsidy came to be to make this 'notional' account balance. Thus as Malpass and Warburton observe, '...the shift from investment to deficit subsidy systems can be seen as embracing a parallel move from historic cost pricing to current value pricing...' (Malpass, P and Warburton, M 'The New Financial Regime for Local Authority Housing' in P Malpass and R Means *Implementing Housing Policy*, Open University Press, 1993, p 93)

The Housing Finance Act 1972 introduced during the Conservative Heath government (see Chapter One) attempted to move towards a more market oriented rent system with a deficit subsidy for HRAs calculated by reference to 'fair rent' assessments rather than outright capital value. It did not work well because the system was too rigid and by abandoning almost entirely local control over rent setting was too adversarial in its approach to the subtle and enduring balance between central and local government.

Though the 1972 Act was repealed in 1975 the point for now is that abandonment of 'bricks and mortar' investment subsidy, which has taken place since the return to power of the Conservatives in 1979, in favour of a 'current capital value' approach – with market-level rents paid in conjunction with a system of targeted *means-tested* housing allowances – has switched the emphasis in housing finance towards individual assessment of tenants' incomes parallel with, and eventually integrated into, the social security system.

It should be noted *en passant* that such targeting was also a major mechanism by which home ownership was able to expand rapidly in the 1960s-1980s through *non means-tested* income support in the form of tax relief on mortgage interest, the abolition of Schedule 'A' taxation in 1963, and exemptions from the payment of capital gains tax on the sale of principal residences. Schedule A tax, for those happily young enough not to remember it was a form of income tax charge on notional income. It was based on the idea that owner occupiers received a benefit from not having to pay rent for their homes, and so they should pay tax on that benefit. Tax relief was, however, given to those who were buying their homes with the assistance of a mortgage. When Schedule A tax was abolished mortgage interest was not, thus giving mortgage payers a considerable 'hidden' subsidy in that part of their liability to pay income tax was taken away.

It is now widely accepted that these tax reliefs underpinned not only the expansion of the tenure but also the damaging inflationary spiral in house prices. They also caused considerable financial inequities between the tenures. Indeed one of the main findings of the Duke of Edinburgh's *Inquiry into British Housing* (National Federation of Housing Associations, 1988) was the inequity in the level of financial support targeted at owner occupiers and council house tenants with the balance overwhelmingly in favour of home owners during the 1980s. We note this point and return to the main purpose of the chapter which is to unravel *social* housing finance, although in a sense all housing is 'social' as we have pointed out elsewhere (Lowe, S and Hughes, D (eds) *A New Century of Social Housing*, Leicester University Press, 1991, pp 184-186).

Local authority capital spending

Capital spending generally refers to investment programmes in housing infrastructure particularly for new building. But as we describe in Chapter Seven the renovation and rehabilitation of *existing* older housing stock which thereby lengthens its life span can also be considered as capital spending. Such works might, however, also be regarded as essential for landlords to keep their houses lettable and thus in reality are *current* expenditure, the cost of which should properly fall on the revenue accounts drawn from rental income. Whether repair work was capital investment or recurrent revenue expenditure was, as we shall see, an issue of considerable controversy between central and local government in the 1980s in relation to spending capital receipts raised from the sale of council houses.

There were some controls on the use of capital f*or housing improvement* introduced under the Housing Act 1974 and this is indicative of the increasing need of governments of all policital complexions to control public spending. In 1976 this system of central 'allocations' was extended to all housing investment programmes (HIPs) and from 1977/78 each authority was required to submit an annual HIP to the DoE based on an assessment of local housing needs and costed capital programmes. Permission to borrow necessary capital was then given on the basis of HIPs, see further below. The original aim of the HIP system was to strength central control over the capital programme at a time of financial constraint, but also with the intention of giving authorities greater freedom in forward planning and allowing them to set priorities for spending locally. In practice the most important feature of the HIP process has been to control borrowing on a year by year basis which has severely curtailed the development programme and made forward planning *more* difficult. In retrospect it is clear that the aims of the original HIP process were somewhat contradictory and, although established during a period of Labour government, have been used to constrain and then virtually eradicate municipal house building under the Conservatives. Following restrictions on HIP allocations from the early 1980s the level of spending on new building by the end of the decade was down to very low levels and the share of public sector building was less than 30% of total housing construction (see Chapter One). In this respect the policy instrument was very effective. Moreover in the 1980s when the receipts from the sale of council houses began to accrue to authorities the HIP system became the instrument for restricting the use and reinvestment of these massive capital receipts (amounting to nearly £20 billion since 1980).

Under the post-1977 system the total capital spending programme was allocated in theory according to an assessment of local needs, said to be captured in a set of indices which together formed the General Needs Index (GNI), and by reference to previous years' spending . This system was never very satisfactory because the indices were themselves subject to considerable local variations which reflected individual authorities' policy stances. For example, one index was a count of statutory homeless households but this figure could be low in areas which had a liberal policy which aimed to assist families in housing need before they became actually homeless. There was also a very large element of discretion in the final allocation of borrowing permission for capital projects which reflected the central government's own prorities rather than the GNI measurement.

During the 1980s the practice of 'top-slicing' the capital programme was also increasingly influential in asserting support for favoured central programmes. Money was taken out of programmes and re-allocated elsewhere, for example, into the Priority Estates Initiative and Estate Action projects designed to revive inner cities and regenerate 'difficult to let' estates. This form of targeted spending clearly further reduced local control and is now an overt mechanism for making authorities compete against each other for borrowing permissions under the HIP system.

In making a HIP bid an authority sought permission to borrow money– the 'net allocation' – but also was able to spend a certain proportion of the receipts from the sale of council houses and other assets such as land. The capital programme was financed from these two sources and during the 1980s the rapid increase in the receipts from the sale of council houses had a considerable impact on the balance of advantage between the centre and the local level.

Under arrangements made through the Local Government, Planning and Land Act 1980 authorities were, however, permitted to spend only a fixed proportion of their capital receipts. Following the introduction of the RTB in the 1980 Act this was set at 50% of receipts but was subsequently reduced as receipts built up. After 1985/86 the proportion was reduced down to only 20%. Nevertheless, the expenditure rules allowed authorities to spend during each year the same proportion of remaining accumulated receipts and under this so called 'cascade' effect authorities in England and Wales would eventually have been able to spend all their receipts. One of the main purposes of the reform of the 1980s system in the Local Government and Housing Act 1989, was to deal with this issue by compelling authorities to use their accumulated receipts to pay off historic debts.

The use of capital receipts was one of the most bitterly fought and controversial features of housing policy in the 1980s with many authorities critical of government control over what they regarded as their own money. On the other hand the centre did not wish to do anything which detered council house sales. A total prohibition on the use of receipts would have inhibited the sales programme – particularly sales on a voluntary basis – which by the mid 1980s was already past its initial peak. As receipts built up and the cascade effect developed many authorities were able to undertake a considerable programme of capital spending, often not on building houses but in renovating their existing stock. Although not technically considered to be 'capital' spending, this system of 'capitalising repairs' was widespread and caused central government concern that public spending limits were being breached by creative accountancy and the redefinition of what were or were not capital works. It should be remembered, however, that many authorities did not wish to build new houses so this apparent defiance of central policy did not amount to a breach of core political doctrine. It does, though, illustrate that the balance between central and local levels was not at all one-sided through most of the 1980s.

The accumulation of capital from receipts varied very considerably from authority to authority, and where large numbers of council house sales took place the balances were so great that the *interest* received on this deposited money became a significant source of income to the HRAs. 12% of total HRA income was derived from this source in 1988/89 (Gibb, K and Munroe, M *Housing Finance in the UK*, Macmillan, 1991, p 73). The scale of capital receipts thus caused distortions in the revenue side of the financial system (see further below). Moreover due to the distribution of sales this system tended to favour already affluent areas, particularly suburban authorities in South East England, where housing needs were relatively less acute. The DoE's strategy for distributing borrowing permissions through the HIP proposals and the GNI was also very much distorted by the uneven distribution in the volume of RTB sales and the whole logic of a national distribution of resources, including weightings towards areas of particular housing stress, fell apart. In 1980/81 HIP allocations accounted for over 80% of expenditure while capital receipts accounted for less than 20% . By the late 1980s this position was completely reversed with only 28% of total spending accounted for by HIP borrowing permission (Gibbs and Munro, 1991).

It is against this background of faltering central control due to the 'cascading' of receipts, the uneven patterns of expenditure round the country, and the problem of what to do with the massive accumulation of capital receipts that the government moved in the late 1980s to reform the housing finance system and thereby strengthen their grip over local authority investment programmes and to re-establish their policy instruments on the revenue side which they had progressively lost, as many authorities by this time received no central subsidy.

The new regime for capital spending

The Local Government and Housing Act 1989, which came into effect in April 1990, introduced very considerable changes in both the capital and the revenue sides of funding arrangements.

The new regime for capital spending restricts the definition of 'capital' to prohibit the capitalisation of repairs, although improvement of property to enhance its life expectancy is within the definition. The system controls much more tightly the ability of authorities to spend capital receipts. The major change to the 1980's system is that only 25% of capital receipts can be spent on capital projects and all the rest must be used to pay off debt charges or, if sufficient capital is available, to pay the interest on an equivalent amount of debt. Either way the new regime effectively ends the 'cascading' of resources and stops authorities from spending three quarters of capital receipts. The initial response of authorities, having been alerted to this change in a consultation paper (*The New Financial Regime for Local Authority Housing in England and Wales*, DoE, July 1988) was a considerable surge in capital spending (by about 25%) in the financial year 1989/90 prior to the introduction of the new system. But subsequently the level of expenditure fell sharply and the setting aside of receipts for debt redemption resulted in an estimated £3,200 million reduction in authority housing debts in 1990/91 (Malpass and Warburton, 1993 p 97). In the Autumn Statement of 1992 authorities in England and Wales were given a capital receipts 'holiday' and allowed to spend 100 % of receipts from November 1992 to the end of 1993. While this gesture certainly boosted the planned expenditure for council house investment during that period receipts were in fact very low and in the three years up to 1994/95 the real level of investment was lower than in 1991/92 and lower than at any time during the 1980s (Joseph Rowntree Foundation, *Social housing investment and the 1992 Autumn Statement*, Housing Research Findings No 79 March 1993).

Rules for capital controls over local authority house building

The detailed rules on borrowing generally are now found in Part IV of the Local Government and Housing Act 1989, see particularly section 43(8). Section 428 of the Housing Act 1985 (which must be read subject to the terms of the above Act) is also relevant in this context. Section 428 grants a general power to authorities to borrow in so far as that relates to the execution of repairs and works by them, and also with regard to clearance and re-development. Local authorities also have power to borrow for the purposes of providing housing accommodation, housing grants and mortgages.

Approval for loan finance may be withheld or given subject to restrictions whenever central government feels it necessary to reduce or contain public spending, and also to reduce the housing provision role of authorities. However, as we described above, not only is borrowing capital subject to control, the expenditure of other capital derived for example from RTB receipts is also stringently centrally controlled.

Part IV of the 1989 Act aims generally to keep the total amount of net authority capital spending in a given financial year within central government expenditure plans, to enable central government to target allocations of spending and borrowing allocations, having considered the resources authorities have; further to ensure that some capital generated by the sale of assets goes to repay existing debts, and to require authorities to make provision for repayment of debt.

Housing authorities fall under the post 1989 Act system by virtue of section 39, while housing capital expenditure is 'caught' generally by virtue of section 40, borrowing powers, as already noted, are brought within the system under section 43, further limits on powers to borrow apply under sections 44 and 45. Section 62 of the 1989 Act provides for the calculation of an 'aggregate credit limit' for each authority, and powers to borrow may not be generally used so that the aggregate credit limit is exceeded. Section 53 empowers the Secretary of State to issue annually 'basic credit approvals' (BCAs) to authorities which are, inter alia, the base authority for capital spending purposes. They further have the effect of limiting authorities' borrowing powers. Sections 55 and 56 lay down the criteria to be used in issuing BCAs, making the system very much subject to the discretion of the Secretary of State; likewise the way in which authorities are to use BCAs have been allocated. In addition to the annual BCAs the government indicates the likely limits for the next two years so that an element of forward planning can occur and such Supplementary Credit Approvals (SCAs) can be set for specific purposes as decided by the government. Section 58 proceeds to control the capital receipts an authority may receive – for example from RTB sales. Section 59(2) particularly provides that where council dwellings are sold 75% of the receipts must be 'reserved' to meet 'credit liabilities', ie to redeem past debts. As we outlined above this clearly is a major limitation on the powers of authorities to reinvest RTB receipts in the provision of new housing.

Under the 1989 system – which is described in full in DoE Circular 11/90 – authorities now have very limited annual capital programmes. See further SI 1990/432 (as amended) and SI 1990/767 (as amended) which lay down detailed rules on the expenditure and borrowing of capital.

Current expenditure

The new regime for current expenditure also develops out of the system that was put in place by the Housing Act 1980 and a brief explanation of the 'old' system is a prerequisite to the discussion of the 1989 Act. In general it can be said that the new legislation was designed to overcome the problems inherent in the 1980's system notably that, by the middle of the decade, a majority of authorities were no longer in receipt of general housing subsidy. As a result the centre had in effect lost their leverage over authorities' HRAs especially with regard to rent setting. The 1989 regime, therefore, represents a tightening of control by central government over the revenue side of local authority finance to mirror constraints on capital spending.

The 1980s system

The 1980 Act implemented a set of arrangements designed to achieve control over the level of local authority housing subsidy, but in this case without giving the appearance of destroying local autonomy. As we saw above the idea of relating subsidy to a centrally directed 'fair rent' system would have completely abandoned the local authority role in rent setting which is why the Housing Finance Act 1972 was so bitterly contested. The right of authorities to set their own rents was restored to them by the Labour government in 1975. The innovation in the 1980 Act was to base HRAs on a centrally controlled model, a so called 'notional HRA', rather than the actual income and expenditure as before. This notional HRA was based on central government's own ideas of annual costs and notably the expected income from rent. Authorities were still able to use their rate funds and could spend in theory whatever they wanted on management and maintenance costs but as the government withdrew general subsidy so rents were forced up to compensate for the shortfall on the notional HRA. As Malpass and Means observe,

'The adoption of the notional HRA gave the centre considerable power... (and) was a highly potent and successful device for reducing subsidy and raising rents.'
(Malpass and Means, 1993, p 94)

The main impact of this system was felt largely on the income side of the HRA. Expenditure in the new system remained much as it had been and continued to form the basis of the 'new financial regime' in the 1990s. The main expenditure items within the HRAs are loan charges (accounting for nearly 44% in 1988/89), capital expenditure (a very small amount), management costs on such items as staff and offices (18% in 1988/89), repairs and maintenance, covering planned programmes and small works (24%) and a variety of other smaller costs. Some authorities in the 1980s also transferred HRA surpluses into their rate funds (RFCs).

The main source of income to the HRA is rents for which in the 1980s there were two sources; the rents paid in cash directly by tenants (net rents) and the rent paid in the form of a rent rebate under the housing benefit system to low income households. Currently net rents account for only about half the total rent paid with housing benefit topping up HRAs. Together these sources of rent accounted for nearly 65% of HRA income in 1988/89. (An important change, however, in the new financial regime is that housing benefit becomes part of the HRA subsidy and so is incorporated into the 'notional' model. In this way *only* net rents (rent paid directly by tenants) are counted as income (see below for further explanation).) Other sources of income were interest from deposited capital receipts – the second largest source of HRA income in 1988/89 – and rate fund contributions.

One other main source of income under the 1980s system was the general subsidy paid by the centre to authorities. Each authority was in effect given notional HRA figures while the housing subsidy was a sum to balance such accounts annually. The calculation of subsidy was based on the rather simple mechanism of taking last year's subsidy payment and adding on estimates for changes in expenditure on debt charges and the cost of management and maintenance (M and M). In the absence of any other way of doing it M and M was also calculated on the average *actual* costs of a number of previous years. This amount was then adjusted according to the central government's calculation of the expected increase in income from rents, the rate fund and the rent rebate subsidy. The notional HRA and subsidy calculation drawn up by central government was thus a mixture of actual costs, estimates of some costs and a series of assumptions about the level of income to be generated, particularly from rents. Authorities had very little alternative than to acquiesce in this notional system, furthermore as central government withdrew general subsidy so rents were 'levered up'. It was a very successful arrangement in this regard and average rents increased in 1981 by 48% and 18.5% in 1982. By 1989 the average authority rent in England and Wales was £20.64 compared to only £7.71 in 1980 (Gibb, K and Munroe, M *Housing Finance in the UK*, Macmillan 1991, p 90). The problem, however, from the point of view of central government, was that with the rapid withdrawal of subsidy the leverage over authorities to increase rents was gradually lost. Indeed by 1988 only 95 authorities (out of over 400 in England and Wales) received housing subsidy into their HRAs and in total this was only 5% of total HRA income.

Thus during the 1980s there was a dramatic collapse of income to the HRA from housing subsidy and an equally dramatic increase in income from net rent and rent rebates. The expenditure side of the account – M and M, loan repayments etc – was much less changed.

One of the consequences of the increase in rents was a further differentiation between different types of authority, and against the steeply upward trend of rents considerable variations emerged between individual authorities, as exemplifed by the London Boroughs of Redbridge and Tower Hamlets where average rents in 1989 were £35.90 and £20.97 respectively. Authorities varied quite considerably in their response to the 1980 Act system with some authorities driving up rents in order to create surpluses on their HRAs (then transferred into the rate fund) while others resisted pressure to increase rents by the risky strategy of transferring money *from* the rate fund to support the HRA. It was also discovered that some authorities still in subsidy at the end of the 1980s were *transferring* money *from* the HRA *into* the rate fund suggesting that the system was extremely poorly targeted in terms of housing needs. The government thus needed to improve targeting and above all from their point of view to regain control of what happened at the local level.

The new financial regime (revenue)

As is commonly the case with changes of policy direction, the Conservatives announced their reform of public housing finance in a 'consultation' paper (*New Financial Regime for Local Authority Housing in England and Wales*, DoE, 1988). It was argued that the subsidy system needed to be simpler, more equitable between authorities and tenants, and to encourage improved management practice. As with the 1980 system entitlement to subsidy is based on notional calculations about levels of expenditure and on rents and the so called 'deficit' on this account is met by a new combined Housing Revenue Account subsidy.

HRA subsidy, introduced in section 79 et seq of the 1989 Act, replaces not only the old housing subsidy but also rent rebate (housing benefit) subsidy and excludes contributions from the rate fund. A crucial part of this realignment of HRA subsidy is that the new unified subsidy includes an estimate for rent rebate payments for the following financial year. By bringing rent rebates into the new HRA subsidy the government in effect changed the definition of how HRAs balance. Rent rebates instead of being an item of income along with net rent are now in effect counted as expenditure against net rental income. As a result virtually all authorities instantly come back 'into subsidy' and by this very simple mechanism the government solves its problem of how to exert leverage on rents which they lost during the 1980s. One effect of this is that any surplus made on the HRA by increases in net rents will be offset against rent rebates. Thus tenants paying full net rent will be paying some of the housing benefit of those of their neighbours who are in receipt of the benefit.

The overall effect of the new regime is to re-establish government control over HRAs. Income to HRAs is limited to net rents and the unified HRA subsidy with rate fund contributions eliminated as a source of balancing the account. Expenditure is much the same as before consisting of loan charges, M and M and *surpluses* from the HRA transferred to the general fund (now called the 'general' fund). It is now no longer permissible to draw on the rate fund to help balance the HRA which *must* balance and on a yearly basis a *planned* deficit cannot occur, see section 76 of the 1989 Act. Unforeseen circumstances may result in an unplanned deficit in any given year and such a deficit has to be carried forward to the next year as a debit. (The detailed rules on maintaining HRAs will be examined below.)

Thus apart from the continuing ability to transfer surpluses to the general fund the revenue side is completely self-regulating, an arrangement sometimes referred to as 'ring-fencing'. In the new regime the government had intended to change the way rents are calculated and provision was made to do this by applying a notional rent increase for *each* authority based on the capital value of property in the area. This figure is derived from the value of houses sold under the RTB. However, the range of rents so determined was so dramatic – with massive increases in areas in the south of England where house prices were high and actual decreases in rents in the north – that the government had to introduce a system of 'dampening' whereby decreases were not allowed and an upper ceiling was put on increases. No authority was allowed to impose an increase of more than £4.50 in the first year of the new system. So called guideline rent increases of between £1.38 and £2.50 were set in 1991/92 and £1.20-£4.50 in 1992/93. As Malpass and Warburton observed there appeared to be no rational explanation for these levels of increases but the effect of dampening the very high increases in the South of the country was to drag up the lower limits elsewhere, notably in parts of the Midlands and the North (Malpass and Warburton, 1993, p 96). Once again a pattern of differentiation came unwittingly into the system to the detriment of areas of relatively higher housing stress.

Another almost certainly unforeseen consequence of the new regime was the considerable difference between the DoE's guideline rents and the actual rents being charged, these being often considerably *above* the guideline. Amounts claimed in the rent rebate part of the HRA subsidy were then forced higher, and the cumulative effect of this was for the DoE's estimate of rebate subsidy to have been considerably underestimated. Indeed in 1990/91 a special payment of over £600 million was made from the Treasury's contingency reserves to deal with this problem. This example suggests that although the central government has clearly tightened its grip on authority housing finance and once again has policy instruments capable of delivering rent increases, the extent to which they remain securely in control in the face of local practices and tactics remains an open question. Inequalities in the system are still manifest and there remain a number of insuperable problems which are inherent in the historical context, and in the daily administration, of this essentially local service. It remains, for example, very difficult to measure management efficiency – the improvement of which is a stated aim of the new regime – and so far as there is an element of the calculation of M and M expenditure in the HRA which depends on *previous practices* there is no direct connection between the intention and the effective outcome of the policy.

The Local Government and Housing Act 1989

Having outlined the broad policy sweep of the change from the 1980 Act system to the new financial regime we move on to consider the main duties of authorities with regard to the keeping of a HRA under the 1989 legislation. Section 74 of the 1989 Act imposes on authorities a duty to keep a HRA of sums 'to be credited and debited' in respect of their housing stock, even where an authority no longer possess any stock, unless exempted by the Secretary of State, see section 74(4). Though six classes of property are capable of being 'stock' for HRA purposes, the most important are: houses and other buildings provided under Part II of the 1985 Act, ie council houses and flats and ancillary shops and other buildings; buildings and housing purchased but not yet in use, land required or appropriated for Housing Act use, houses which have been purchased as unfit under section 192 of the 1985 Act but which are repairable at reasonable expense and any other land, houses or buildings specified centrally.

Section 75 and Schedule 4 of the 1989 Act lay down the rules for keeping a HRA. As we described above the account is 'ring-fenced' from other authority accounts, ie it must internally balance itself, and cannot be generally subsidised by the authority. Authorities have very little discretion as to what can or cannot be excluded save where an item is on the borderline of a definition. Even then the Secretary of State has powers under section 87 of the 1989 Act to give directions on the issue. See generally *R v Ealing London Borough Council, ex p Lewis* (1992) 24 HLR 484.

As credits to the HRA authorities must include rents and charges (eg for heating) in respect of houses etc within the account. 'Rent' includes notional amounts for those dwellings where the actual cost of the rent is met by housing benefit. Any HRA subsidy (HORAS) payable under section 79 of the Act of

1989 is also to be credited to the HRA, likewise any subsidy for rent rebates on HRA dwellings under the Housing Benefit Scheme (see below). Credit may be given to the HRA from the Housing Repairs Account which authorities have a discretion to keep under section 77 of the 1989 Act; however, only exceptionally may credit be given from authorities' general funds, and then only at the direction of the Secretary of State.

As was shown above debits to the HRA remain much as they were under the 1980 Act system; costs of repair, maintenance, supervision and management of HRA properties, though not all 'housing related work' will qualify, for example initial work done on assessing a homelessness application. (But see below on 'special cases'.) Also included are rents, rates and other taxes an authority may have to pay on relevant property, as are rent rebates paid to tenants. Any sum paid to a Housing Repairs Account must also be a debit, as must unpaid rents, etc, considered to be 'bad' or 'doubtful' debts.

In certain 'special cases' sums may be credited to the HRA, for example sums received by an authority in respect of facilities such as shops, recreation centres etc, provided by them under housing powers (such as section 12 of the 1985 Act). Such facilities confer benefits not just on tenants but on the community as a whole, and an amount to reflect the community's share of that benefit is to be credited to the HRA, see generally *Hemsted v Lees and Norwich City Council* (1986) 18 HLR 424. Also included is income from certain welfare services provided in connection with housing, eg housing advisory services, warden services, etc, under section 11A of the 1985 Act, see section 127 of the Leasehold Reform, Housing and Urban Development Act 1993. The cost of providing the services is also debited to the HRA as a 'special case'.

Under the new system the Secretary of State has, under section 80 of the 1989 Act, virtually total discretion as to drawing up formulae from which subsidies are calculated – even to the extent of fixing a negative amount of subsidy for given authorities: in which case an equivalent positive amount has to be taken from the HRA and placed in another fund (usually the general fund) but the HRA must still be made to balance after the debit, meaning increases in the credits to it, ie rents. Before making a determination the Secretary of State must consult such representatives of local government and relevant professional bodies as seem appropriate to him, and if he makes, as he has power to, an individual determination for an individual authority, he must consult them, see section 87. The matters taken into account in determining HORAS include: the fixed sum the Secretary of State will receive from the Treasury in respect of the subsidy fixed under central government's spending rules; any actual loan charges on capital borrowing an authority has, and changes therein; numbers of tenants receiving rebates; changes in the size of the housing stock. The Secretary of State may also make assumptions annually about rent levels and management and maintenance costs and fix subsidies accordingly.

At this point it is necessary to consider what sums an authority may charge by way of 'reasonable rents' to tenants.

Reasonable rents

The notion of 'reasonable rent' goes back to the Housing Act 1935, the same legislation that introduced HRAs. Attempts had been made before to equate rents for council houses with those prevailing in the PRS but there were several problems. New council dwellings were very different in age and character from the mainly pre-1919 urban housing stock, while authority 'cost' rents were far higher than anything at the lower end of the PRS. Moreover rent control was still in place for much of the PRS and this also caused problems when making comparisons between the private and public rental systems. The 1935 Act introduced the idea of a 'reasonable' rent which authorities were to charge, but it was not defined in the Act and in practice authorities were given very wide discretion to charge a rent which suited the type and age of property. There has been no successful legal challenge to the basic concept, and reasonable rents have come to mean nothing more than the actual rents set by authorities having regard to the subsidies from the centre, rate fund contributions to HRAs and latterly rent rebate subsidies; though an authority abusing the system may be challenged. The current position in law regarding reasonable rents is outlined below.

Reasonable rents – the current legal framework

Under section 24 of the Housing Act 1985 authorities may make such reasonable charges for the occupation of their houses as they determine, but must from time to time review their rents. This does not give an absolute discretion as to fixing rents. See generally *Belcher v Reading Corpn* [1950] Ch 380, [1949] 2 All ER 969. Authorities are entitled to pursue social policies in fixing rent levels, provided they do not behave unreasonably, see *Mandeville v Greater London Council* (1982) Times, 28 January and *R v Greater London Council, ex p Royal Borough of Kensington and Chelsea* (1982) Times, 7 April. The courts will intervene in the rare cases where an authority comes to a clearly perverse decision on its policies and considers immaterial policy matters. An authority can, however, consider the existence of a subsidy when fixing rent levels, see *R v Secretary of State for Health and Social Security, ex p City of Sheffield* (1985) 18 HLR 6. The courts thus exercise little effective supervision over the day to day administration of authority rent policies, and will only intervene in certain unusual circumstances. Indeed there appears to be only one recorded instance of an authority's discretion being overturned. This remains true even after the 'ring fencing' of housing revenue following the 1989 legislation, though that does limit an authority's ability to decide what ranks as 'housing expenditure', see *R v Ealing London Borough Council, ex p Lewis* (1992) 24 HLR 484. See also *Hemsted v Lees and Norwich City Council* (1986) 18 HLR 424.

The general lack of a statutory method of fixing rents for authority dwellings has also been somewhat addressed by section 24(3) and (4) of the 1985 Act inserted in 1989. Authorities are required in fixing their rents to have regard to the principle that the rents of houses/flats of any class or description should bear broadly the same proportion to private sector rents (ie rents under assured tenancies) as the rents of other houses of any other class or description. This somewhat unclear provision introduces the notion of 'relative desirability' which is a device to ensure that rents for authority dwellings should bear some comparison with those for comparable assured tenancies.

As we suggested above such comparisons are very difficult to sustain in practice because of the different characteristics of the stocks of dwellings. In general the idea is to let the market define the difference in cash terms between rents on dwellings on, say, difficult-to-let estates and those in more desirable areas. However, with such a high proportion of tenants in receipt of housing benefit such logic is meaningless because the tenant response is to seek the most desirable properties irrespective of rent because that, to them, is a zero marginal cost. In addition the level of rents now charged for more desirable properties, because it partly depends on geographical area, equates very closely to levels of mortgage repayment for the discounted prices of RTB dwellings. This convergence of the levels of rents and mortgage repayments seems likely to have the effect of stimulating an increase in RTB sales rather than the stabilisation of a 'market' based rental system.

Increasing rents

By section 24(2) of the Housing Act 1985 'the authority shall from time to time review rents and make such changes, either of rents generally, or of particular rents, as circumstances may require'.

With regard to *secure* tenancies (other than association tenancies) sections 102 and 103 of the Housing Act 1985 allow variations of rent to be made either by agreement between landlord and tenant or in accordance with any terms in the lease or the agreement creating the tenancy. In the case of periodic tenancies variations may also be effected by the landlord serving a notice of variation on the tenant. This notice must specify the variation it makes and the date on which it takes effect; and the period between the date on which the notice is served and the date on which it takes effect must not be shorter than the rental period of the tenancy nor in any case shorter than four weeks. Where such a notice is served and, before the arrival of the date specified in it, the tenant gives a valid notice to quit, the notice will not take effect unless the tenant, with the landlord's written consent, withdraws the notice to quit before the relevant date.

Tenancies which are not secure tenancies fall to be dealt with under section 25 of the Housing Act 1985. This provision gives authorities power to increase rents for their houses let on weekly or other periodical tenancies by means of the service of a 'notice of increase'.

Challenging rents

The normal mode of challenge to a decision on rent fixing by an authority will be by way of judicial review, provided a breach of public law principles can be shown, and the remedy sought will be a declaration that the scheme of rents is unreasonable, coupled with an injunction to prevent implementation of the scheme. A tenant has a 'sufficient interest' in such a matter to bring an action by virtue of being an affected rent payer. Alternatively where a tenant is the subject of possession proceedings for arrears of rent, the validity of the rent may be questioned as a defence, *Wandsworth London Borough Council v Winder* [1985] AC 461, [1984] 3 All ER 976.

Rent arrears

Despite the existence of the statutory housing benefit scheme (see below) many authority tenants still get into arrears with their rents either because of an unforeseen financial problem, such as unemployment, desertion by a spouse, illness, or general poverty, or, much less probably, because of unwillingness or incapacity to manage their financial affairs in a satisfactory way.

As long ago as 1983 Duncan and Kirby's *Preventing Rent Arrears* pointed out that *serious* rent arrears, ie at 1980/81 levels, £50 or more, affected one in twenty authority tenants, but arrears were not evenly distributed among authorities. Serious arrears are found in cases where there is a low income, a sudden income drop, eg as a consequence of unemployment, or unexpected heavy demand on finances. Families with dependent children and single parent families are the most likely households to be in arrears, with a crisis, such as the departure of a wage earner, precipitating arrears. Tenants in arrears often live in flats and maisonettes and are dissatisfied with their housing, and the highest rates of arrears are often found on unpopular 'difficult to let' estates, especially where rents are above average. Tenants in arrears frequently experience other budgeting problems, experiencing other forms of debt, yet rarely do such tenants live extravagantly or possess cars and other expensive commodities.

A recent study commissioned by the DoE confirms these earlier findings (DoE, *Rent Arrears in Local Authorities and Housing Associations in England*

1994). Rent arrears are very widespread and almost half authority and association tenants are 'behind with their rent'. One in seven authority tenants owes more than four weeks rent. The research found that households with dependent children and single adults are most likely to be in rent arrears. It suggests a number of closely associated problems which cause a propensity to fall into arrears – living in areas of multiple social deprivation, other debts, and the age of the head of household (with young heads being most at risk). The tenants themselves identified unemployment, changes in domestic circumstances and having other debts as the reasons for their arrears problem.

The study was critical of authority handling of arrears cases with legal remedies often being invoked far too early. The research recommended the establishment of specialist teams of housing department officers to deal with arrears problems by better counselling of tenants and better information systems so that arrears problems can be identified at an early stage and before the problem gets out of hand. They should ensure that all tenants who are entitiled to housing benefit are receiving it and that tenants are fully aware of the authority's policy on arrears and the ultimate consequences of withholding rent.

The Duncan and Kirby Report, the Audit Commission's 1986 Report *Managing the Crisis in Council Housing* and the recent DoE study between them recommended:

1) authorities should ensure, by campaigns and other informative processes, that tenants take up as many benefits as possible and that monetary counselling is available for tenants with many debts, with housing staff receiving training to identify those in need of such counselling;

2) authorities should consider using door-to-door collection of rent (which has been abandoned in many areas for security reasons), as this reduces arrears, and consider tenant representations about methods of rent payment, trying to ensure that, consistent with economy, it is as easy as possible for tenants to pay;

3) use of 'rent-free' weeks helps to prevent arrears, as tenants in arrears can be visited then and back rent collected;

4) there is a need to identify tenants with mounting arrears in respect of whom action is, or ought, to be taken: tenants should be clearly told how much they owe;

5) accounting practices should be examined to prevent the creation of 'technical arrears', eg accounting periods which close mid-week when many tenants pay on Fridays, and rent collecting and accounting should be undertaken by one department;

6) authorities should fix specific levels at which action in respect of arrears is taken, allocate sufficient staff to deal with arrears, should give tenants more information about rent payment options, and how to cope with arrears, should monitor performance in dealing with and reducing

7) arrears: members should set clear policy guidelines on control of arrears; good staff training in dealing with arrears and those in arrears is most important: specialist staff may be needed;

8) effective liaison with the courts and local DSS offices can help in dealing with tenants against whom action has to be taken;

9) early, firm and fair action over arrears is useful in reducing arrears, though no action should be threatened that an authority is not prepared to follow up; interviews with tenants in serious arrears are also useful;

10) policies on the allocation of dwellings and on transfers should reflect the need to prevent, or reduce existing arrears, with tenants informed in advance of the likely cost of running a dwelling, and the least well off not being placed, or required to stay, in the most expensive housing.

It is the general tenor of central advice that distress for rent and actions seeking possession from those in arrears, see Chapter Three, are remedies of last resort.

Housing association finance

We outlined in Chapter One information concerning the growth and changing role of associations. Here the focus is on the funding arrangments introduced in the Housing Act 1988 and subsequent developments in procedure. As with authorities we describe first the capital and then the revenue elements of this 'new financial regime'. Once again a brief survey of the old funding system is a prerequisite to the discussion especially because in this case the basic structure of the system remains the same. The consequences of the new regime are, however, dramatic and the housing association movement has undergone a fundamental transformation in character over the last five years.

The 1988 Act stated the government's intention to establish a much expanded 'independent' rented sector in which the associations were to play a central role. The Act reflected the anxiety that associations had become too identified with the mainstream public sector of housing and sought by introducing greater 'market' disciplines to create a more efficient and revitalised supply of rented accommodation. The 1988 Act also restructured the Housing Corporation (HC) and set up two new agencies, Housing for Wales ('Tai Cymru') and Scottish Homes to organise housing west of Offa's Dyke and north of the border.

Mirroring the withdrawal of subsidy from authorities the government also sought progressively to withdraw subsidy from associations and thereby encourage a more business-like and 'risk' oriented ethos. A principal feature of this policy was to replace public subsidy under the system created in the Housing Act 1974 with increasing amounts of private finance in the capital programmes.

The pre-1989 HAG system

Under the old system a high proportion of development costs was written off by a once and for all central government subsidy, Housing Association Grant (HAG). The calculation was based on the Rent Officer's 'fair rent' assessment of the properties in the scheme at the end of the development process (for legal details of 'fair rents' see below). The fair rent income was then used to pay M and M charges with any residual amount used to sponsor, ie repay principal and interest only, that share of the outstanding loan it was capable of supporting. Until 1989 this would result in HAG payments which typically covered 80%-90% of the costs of the scheme, and cases of 100% HAG were not uncommon. This flexible approach meant that associations could develop projects in the knowledge that there was no risk involved because the HAG calculation was done at the end of the project and the vast majority of the borrowing would be written off by the subsidy (an approach to public subsidy quite different from that for authorities).

Each year the HC would announce the framework for the capital programme in its Approved Development Programme (ADP). Associations bid for a share of the ADP to support their projects, although the ADP was very indicative of the types of development it would support. The funds were distributed through the regional offices of the HC to which associations made bids. The regional offices received their share through a modified version of the DoE's General Needs Index for authorities. This index was heavily criticised in the late 1980s and has now been replaced by a new Housing Needs Index (HNI) which may well be even less appropriate. The HNI includes, for example, an indicator of regional house prices as well as measuring homelessness and it has been argued that this procedure in effect counts the same problem (high house prices) twice and thus skews the HNI to areas in the South of England where house prices remain generally highest (see Barnett, R and Lowe, S 'Measuring housing needs and the provision of social housing' in *Housing Studies* Vol 5 No 3, 1990). This process remains the basic system for the allocation of ADP funds.

With, however, the desire to reduce public expenditure on housing and the drive to increase association reliance on borrowed private capital, modifications were made in the grant system by the 1988 Act whose provisions replaced those of the Housing Associations Act 1985.

The 1988 capital regime

The main ideas behind the new regime – increased numbers of mixed funded schemes, increased value for money and more business-like management through higher risks and incentives – were announced in a consultation paper *Finance for Housing Associations, the Government's Proposals* 1987 (DoE).

Following the 1988 Act the number of mixed funded schemes was to be increased so that by 1994/95 over 90% of HAG funded projects would be required to draw in private finance through the new 'fixed' HAG regime. At the same time the proportion of private finance was increased, beginning in 1989/90 with HAG set at an average of 75% of initial costs (a proportion that was planned to decline, and is in the current year 1994/95 65%). Associations had to make up the remaining share from private financial sources and had to bear the whole risk of increases in costs as the scheme progressed. Rents for new lettings were deregulated from 15 January 1989 in line with the assured tenancy regime in the PRS. The logic of the new regime is that the flexible element in the system is now the ability of associations to increase their rents to meet their higher loan costs, while the financial risks are borne by the associations themselves and ultimately their tenants. Under the old system, it was HAG that was the flexible element but this is now a fixed proportion of the intial cost of the scheme.

A new part of the capital regime requires associations to fund major repair works from a sinking fund which they must set up. Instead of using HAG for this purpose as was the case under the old system associations must now set aside 0.8% of their current income to cover future major repairs. The system divides association property into two categories; Block A and Block B. As the sinking fund builds up associations gradually reclassify their properties from A to B categories. 'B' properties are those which are deemed most likely to need major repair work. Associations therefore have little control over how their sinking funds can be used and it is quite likely that a significant share of their properties will remain in Block B and therefore can only be repaired using the difficult route of new fixed HAG funding.

Under the new regime, because private investment was not counted as public spending, there appeared to be the possibility of a considerable increase in housing output for less public spending. However, in the event the expected boom in association output did not materialise. This was partly to do with an initial transitional cash crisis during the first year of the new regime which was unforeseen by the HC. The problem appears to have been caused by changes in the rules on the HC's approvals procedures in order to speed up the administration of grants. In the the first year HAG was claimed by associations more quickly than had been anticipated and the HC ran out of money before the end of the financial year. In January 1989 the government had to allow £120 million from the 1990/91 allocation to be brought forward and the expected expansion of production was stalled.

In the financial years 1989/90 and 1990/91 £1.4 billion of public subsidy was drawn down to the development programme with some £370 million of private loans. Private finance reduced average HAG payments from 85% to 75% of scheme costs and resulted in 4,700 more units being built than would otherwise have been provided. Mixed funded projects have subsequently risen within the overall ADP for new houses to rent, but the 1990/91 approvals were lower than for the previous decade and the 1994/95 programme has a projected output of only 30,000 units which is similar to low output in the late 1970s under the old flexible HAG system and but a small fraction of the annual output achieved by local authorities year on year for over half a century. It is now clear that associations have lost their favoured status with the government (see Chapter One) and the ADP has been an easy target in the current round of public spending cuts.

The new regime, as we have shown, significantly increased the financial risk for housing associations and this led to a series of mergers between smaller associations trying to defend themselves from the dangers inherent in the new regime. More recently there has been a strong trend for the bulk of the ADP to be taken up by a small number of very large associations operating at the national level.

In order to achieve maximum 'value for money' associations have been forced to change the type of people housed from those they have traditionally catered for, and also the type of accommodation provided. Recent research by Page showed that associations were doing less rehabilitation work (now less than 20% of the ADP compared to over 50% in 1988) and few small schemes and instead were developing large estates built by volume builders. It was found that there were considerable savings to be made by buying 'off the peg' housing from speculative builders rather than undertaking more costly 'design and build' schemes which were characteristic of association development under the old flexible HAG system. As a result fewer flats and one-bedroom units were being built in favour of 'family' housing. Moreover the space standards of these buildings were on average 10% lower than pre-1989 dwellings. Fewer older people and those with special needs were being catered for in favour of families with children and homeless households. (Page, D *Building for Communities: A study of new housing association estates*, Joseph Rowntree Foundation, 1993.) This lower risk type of development has moved associations away from their traditional involvement with inner-city renewal and has created additional problems for associations because of their relative inexperience of managing large estates.

One of the most worrying problems to emerge from the recent experience of the new capital regime has been the disinclination of many of the major sources of private capital to invest in associations' mixed funded schemes. This is a significant flaw in the logic of the system at a time when associations have become dependent on this source of finance for their projects. Virtually no lending has come from pension funds or insurance companies, and of the banks and building societies a very high proportion of lending has been accounted for by only a handful of organisations: in the first two years of the new financial regime 21 building societies were involved but three of these accounted for over 85% of total lending (Randolph, B 'The re-privatization of housing associations' in *Implementing Housing Policy* (eds) Malpass and Means, Open University Press, 1993, p 53).

Housing Association capital and revenue (HACR)

The main statutory sources of control over association capital spending and revenues are now described.

Section 50 of the 1988 Act provides that the Housing Corporation and Housing for Wales are the grant aiding bodies for associations in England and Wales, and they may determine procedures and circumstances for the payment of HAG and the mode of its calculation and payment. HAG may be made conditional. Section 52 further grants to the Corporations powers to reduce, suspend or cancel grants, or to require their repayment on the happening of certain 'relevant events' which trigger powers of 'claw back', for example a failure to comply with grant conditions. The Corporations have power to make 'general determinations' or individual ones as to the exercise of these grant aiding powers under section 53 of the 1988 Act, but a general determination requires the approval of the Secretary of State and the consent of the Treasury, while an individual determination will simply require ministerial approval. Similarly before a general determination is made the Corporations must consult bodies representative of associations, and must publicize such determinations once made so that associations may understand their position. The Corporations must, of course, comply with the general principles of administrative law in the formulation and implementation of determinations, ie they must behave within their powers, and in a rational and procedurally proper fashion.

The Corporations may also, under section 51 of the 1988 Act, pay Revenue Deficit Grants (RDG) to associations whose expenditure exceeds their income for specified periods. Again general determinations as to the principles concerning payment of RDG can be made under section 52. It seems likely from this that RDG will only be paid in very exceptional circumstances and will certainly not be paid to associations that have reserves which could be used to cover deficits.

The current general determinations on HAG, etc, are to be found in Housing Corporation Circulars 16/89 and 19/89.

Section 55 of the 1988 Act should also be noted. This applies to associations which have received HAG. Such associations must show separately in their accounts any surpluses arising from increased rental income for specified periods. This then constitutes a Rent Surplus Fund (RSF), and the Secretary of State may require payment to him of such funds from time to time, with interest, or direct their application to other purposes. Determinations as to the way in which a RSF is to be calculated are to be made by the Secretary of State, who may delegate the power to make determinations to the Corporations, which has in fact been done. Consultation with appropriate representative bodies must take place before a determination is reached. See Housing Corporation Circulars 18/92, 5/93, 12/93 and 32/93.

As was the case under the old system all surpluses thus have to be identified in association accounts but in the new regime surpluses can be retained for the purpose of building up their major repairs funds. However, there appears to be very little incentive to do this because associations have to pay 50% of RSF to the HC who monitor this procedure very tightly – ensuring that surpluses do not find their way into lower rents or increases in M and M costs.

The general position on the revenue part of association accounts is one of continuing central control and scrutiny and thus the rewards for having to engage in more risk taking and a de-regulated rent regime are very slender indeed. Surpluses appear either to be paid directly to the HC or used to subsidise withdrawal of grant from other areas of association activity.

Housing association rents

Existing secure tenants continue to benefit from the 'old' rent system based on fair rent assessment and the detail of this entitlement is described below.

Rents for secure tenancies granted before 1989

Part VI of the Rent Act 1977 applied to 'housing association tenancies', and still does to tenancies granted before 15 January 1989, to ensure that their holders are charged only 'fair rents'. Section 87 lays down that there shall be a part of the register under Part IV of the 1977 Act in which rents may be registered for dwelling-houses let under housing association tenancies and that sections 67, 67A, 70, 70A, 71 and 72 and Schedule 11 apply to that part of the register. Under section 88 a rent limit exists for these association tenancies, excess rent above the limit being irrecoverable from the tenant. That limit is, where a rent is registered, the registered rent or, where there is no registered rent, whichever of the following applies is the limit:

(a)   where the lease or agreement creating the tenancy was made prior to 1 January 1973, the rent recoverable thereunder;

(b)   where the lease or agreement was made after 1 January 1973, and not more than two years before the tenancy began the dwelling was subject to another tenancy, the rent is that recoverable under that other tenancy's last rental period;

(c)   otherwise the rent originally payable under the lease or agreement is that which is recoverable.

Under section 94 where a tenant has paid 'irrecoverable' rent, that tenant is entitled to recover the relevant amount from the landlord, and may do this by deduction from rent payable, though no such amount is recoverable at any time after the expiry of two years from the date of payment. Housing association periodical tenancy rents may, under section 93, be increased, without the tenancy being terminated, from the beginning of a rental period by a written notice of increase, specifying the date on which the notice is to take effect and given by the landlord to the tenant not later than four weeks before that date.

Under section 67 of the 1977 Act application for registration of a fair rent may be made to a rent officer by either landlord or tenant, or jointly. However, as was stated earlier the pre-1989 practice was for associations to refer rent fixing on new developments to the Rent Officer at the end of the development process and the determination of the 'fair rent' then had implications for HAG. Applications (now, of course, limited to cases where it may be that the parties are not satisfied as to the 'fairness' of rent) must be in prescribed form, and must specify the rent it is sought to register, sums payable in respect of services and such other particulars as are prescribed. In general once a rent is registered, no application by *either party alone* for registration of a different rent for the dwelling may be entertained before two years have expired from the date on which a registered rent took effect, or, where a registered rent has been confirmed, the date on which its confirmation took effect, unless there has been such a change in the condition of the dwelling (including improvements), the terms of the tenancy, the quantity, quality or condition of furniture provided under the tenancy, or any other circumstances taken into account when the rent was registered, as to make the registered rent no longer fair. However, a *landlord* alone may make an application within the last three months of the period of two years.

The procedure in respect of determining a rent is laid down in Schedule 11. Where an application to register is received the Rent Officer may obtain information relevant to the application from the parties. On a joint application the Rent Officer may register the rent specified in the application without more ado if he/she considers it fair. In other cases the Rent Officer invites the parties whether they wish him/her, in consultation with them, to consider what rent ought to be registered. The party who did not make the application must be served with a copy of the application. Where no response is made in due form to the Rent Officer's invitation, he/she may consider what rent ought to be registered, and register a rent, or new rent, or confirm the existing as the case may be, or serve notice of intention to fix a rent. Where the officer's invitation results in a written response from either or both parties that they wish the rent to be considered, the officer must serve notice of the time and place at which he/she proposes in consultation with the parties, or such as appear, to consider what rents ought to be registered etc, for the dwelling. At the consultation the parties may be represented. Thereafter the officer may determine, or confirm, as the case may be, the rent and register it, informing the parties by notice. They then have 28 days in which to lodge an objection, and the matter is then referred by the officer to a rent assessment committee (RAC).

The RAC may obtain further information from the parties, and must allow them to make representations, either in writing or orally. It is the committee's duty to make such inquiries as they think fit and to consider information supplied and representations made, and then to determine whether the rent officer reached a correct fair rent, or whether the rent was not fair, in which case they determine the fair rent. Their decision is notified to the parties and the officer, who makes an appropriate entry in the register of fair rents.

In determining a fair rent under section 70 regard has to be had to all the circumstances, other than personal circumstances, and in particular to the age, character, locality and state of repair of the dwelling, and the quantity, quality and condition of any furniture provided under the tenancy. Certain matters may not, however, be taken into account, for example improvements or defects attributable to the tenant affecting the dwelling or furniture provided under the tenancy. Furthermore where demand for dwellings exceeds supply thus giving them a 'scarcity value' a discount of that element in the rent has to be made, see section 70(2). The amount to be registered as rent under section 71 must include any sum payable for the use of furniture or services, whether or not those sums are separate from the sum payable in respect to occupation of the dwelling, or are payable under a separate agreement. Where any sums payable include sums varying according to the cost from time to time of services provided by the landlord, or works of repair carried out by the landlord, the amount to be registered as rent may, where the rent officer, or RAC as the case may be, is satisfied that the terms as to variation are reasonable, be entered as an amount varying in accordance with those terms.

Under section 72 the registration of a rent takes effect, where determined by the rent officer, from the date of registration, and, where determined by the committee, from the date of their decision, and similarly for confirmation of existing rents.

The new law of renting under the Housing Act 1988

Cm 214 promised the de-regulation of private sector lettings, and this policy was enshrined in the 1988 Housing Act, though this did not entirely translate into legal form the White Paper proposals. However, the basic philosophy of the White Paper is contained in the Act: higher rents *will call forth an increased supply of rented accommodation*. The ability of the new financial regime to deliver the hoped for gains in output and value for money hinges on the deregulated rent regime introduced in the 1988 Act. Under the new system rents are set by individual associations for most of their new lettings and there is no specific guidance from the HC about the principles behind this new form of rent setting. In HC Circular: HC 60/89 associations are urged to maximize rental income while at the same time keeping rents 'affordable' for people in low paid employment. These somewhat contradictory objectives have in fact been resolved by increasing pressure on the housing benefit system and the income of tenants in new lettings.

Average weekly rents for new lettings increased in the first two years of the new system from £18 to nearly £33 (an increase of 81%) and rents for newly built homes increased by 104%. These figures compare with an increase in the Retail Prices Index of only 26% over the same period (Randolph, B 'The Re-Privatization of Housing Associations' in *Implementing Housing Policies* (eds) Malpass, P and Means, R, Open University Press, 1993 p 45). Higher rents do not appear to have drawn in more affluent tenants but have had the effect of deepening the very considerable benefits trap experienced by unemployed and low income tenants. New tenants have to spend an increased proportion of their income on rent *in addition* to claiming higher levels of housing benefit. As Randolph's analysis of the affordability problem shows, '…the growth of housing benefit take-up has not stopped the proportion of income spent on rent for new tenants rising steadily since the Act. Housing benefit has only partially "taken the strain" of higher rents' (Randoph, 1993, p 48). Thus rents in this new system are nowhere near being 'reasonably affordable' for the traditional tenants of housing associations and it is the social security system and an additional burden on the income of tenants themselves, paying excess rent *above the HB tapers*, that have shored up the new system.

The new era for associations

Between 1989 and 1994 associations were propelled into a new era in which they became the main providers of new social housing but in the context of a more highly commercial financial system and under a government intent on reducing public spending. Problems have arisen because the affordability of rents has been severely jeopardised for associations' traditional tenants. The housing benefit system (which itself has been redefined) has not compensated for the underlying increase in rents arising from the new financial regime. On the capital side the continuing drought of private finance calls into question the logic of a regime based on increasing levels of such an input. The associations' world has changed out of all recognition with mergers and insecurities of many types for the majority of small traditional associations. Meanwhile the mission of the new era to deliver a more cost-effective and rapidly increasing supply of new dwellings has failed abjectly.

The next three portions of this chapter deal with the basic law with regard to rents for assured tenancies, assured shorthold tenancies and, finally, an outline of the legal structure of the administration of housing benefit. As we have outlined above HAG still has a considerable influence on the level of rents charged by associations to their tenants, but the *legal* structure of rent determination is the same as that for 'pure' private landlords.

Assured tenancies (AT)

The basic law is contained in sections 13-14 of the 1988 Act and depends on the principle of sanctity of contract; both sides are bound by what they have agreed. There is no limit to what can be charged by way of the initial contract and the principle of market forces applies, save that where a tenancy is granted by an association the notion is one of 'affordable rents' because of the cushioning effect of HAG though even here, as we have seen, new lettings are at rent levels substantially above the old fair rents associations used to charge.

With regard to a fixed term AT there is no legal limit to what can be contractually charged, and no outside agency can interfere with the level of rent. The ability to increase rent will depend upon whether the tenancy agreement makes provision for this.

Where a statutory periodic tenancy has arisen (ie after the end of the initial assured contractual period) or where there is *no* rent review clause governing a periodic AT, the landlord may increase the rent by serving on the tenant a notice in prescribed form proposing a new rent to take effect at the beginning of a 'new period' of the tenancy specified in the notice. That new period must be a period beginning not earlier than:

(a)   in relation to yearly tenancies, six months;
(b)   in relation to periodic tenancies of less than a month, one month, and
(c)   in relation to any other case, the period of the tenancy, *but*:
   (i)   the new rent period can *generally* only begin as from the end of the first anniversary of the date on which the first period of the tenancy began, and
   (ii)   in a case where rent has previously been increased by the statutory method a further notice of increase can only be served once one year has expired from the taking effect of the new rent.

Effectively this means the landlord has a statutory right to increase the rent at the end of a fixed term tenancy, or at the end of the first year of a periodic tenancy provided there is no other rent review clause – it is likely that properly drafted tenancy agreements will contain such clauses, and they will then govern the situation, see section 13(1)(b). Notices of increase can generally only be served under the statutory system once every 12 months and the notice can only come into effect at the end of whatever is the appropriate minimum period. However, under section 13(5) the landlord and tenant may *agree* at any time to vary the rent.

Where a statutory notice is duly served the new rent will take effect *unless* before the beginning of the new period as specified in the notice the tenant refers the issue in prescribed form to the relevant Rent Assessment Committee (RAC), *or* the parties together agree on a variation of rent different from that proposed, or agree *not* to vary the rent. Notice that the onus is on the tenant to take action, a failure to act is taken as assent. The effect of a notice *not* in prescribed form is unknown. If the tenant accepts it and pays the revised rent there is no statutory right to recover any payment. On the other hand it may be possible to ignore notices not in due form.

Where the matter is referred to the RAC under section 14 of the 1988 Act they are under a duty to determine the rent at which they consider the dwelling might reasonably be expected to be let on a willing landlord and AT basis in the open market. In particular they are to work on the basis, inter alia, that the AT will be periodic, having the same periods as the current tenancy, and will have the same terms as that tenancy. The RAC must, however, disregard:

(a)   any effect on the rent attributable to the existence of a sitting tenant;
(b)   any improvements carried out by the tenant which have increased the value of the dwelling;
(c)   any failure on the tenant's part to act in accordance with the terms of the tenancy which has reduced the value of the dwelling.

The personal circumstances of the parties are irrelevant, and scarcity value will be relevant (contrast the position under the Rent Act 1977). To assist in their deliberations RACs may obtain information from the parties under section 41 of the Housing Act 1988. 'Rent' does *not* include any service charge but *will* include, inter alia, any payments made for use of furniture. The parties may under section 14(8) agree in writing to withdraw the reference from the RAC, and nothing in either section 13 or 14 affects the rights of the parties to vary any term of an AT (including terms as to rent) by agreement.

There is little case law to show how this system is working in practice. Evidence of negotiated rents is relevant to the work of RACs, and they have to use their own knowledge of general rent levels in their areas, though of course for many years a free market in rents did not fully exist. What a landlord *hopes* to get by way of rent is not conclusive evidence of market rent, but is evidence of what the market may take. Wage levels in an area may also be relevant considerations, as may returns on capital investment. The age, character, condition and locality of the dwelling may also be relevant, and the existence of repairing covenants over and above those implied by law may also affect rent levels. The rent as determined by the RAC will not be a rent limit for the dwelling as was the case with fair rents under the Rent Act 1977 and the parties may subsequently agree a higher rent in any case. The rent fixed by the RAC will come into effect on the date originally specified by the landlord in the notice to the tenant, unless the RAC decides a later date is, under section 14(7), justified on grounds of hardship to the tenant.

A duty is laid under section 42 of the 1988 Act on the president of every rent assessment panel to keep and publicise in a manner specified by the Secretary of State information about rents for ATs, which includes ASTs, which have undergone scrutiny by RACs (see SI 1988/2199). This may over time lead to the 'going rate' for market rents for ATs within any given area becoming known. Section 43 further empowers authorities to publish information about the AT system for the benefit of landlords and tenants. Apart from this authorities do not play a part in the rent fixing process as they could do under the Rent Act 1977.

Unlike the Rent Act 1977 there is no prohibition on charging a premium for the grant of a tenancy on an assured or assured shorthold basis, nor any limit on what may be charged by way of premium.

Rents for assured shortholds (ASTs)

Again the basic principle is sanctity of contract, the tenant is bound by what he/she has agreed. However, the tenant under an AST may, by virtue of section 22 of the 1988 Act, refer the rent to the RAC for their determination of what the landlord could reasonably expect to receive by way of rent. The application must be made in due form, see SI 1988/2203. Such a right will be of use to the tenant where the rent is 'significantly higher' than rents payable for similar tenancies of similar dwellings (whether on a shorthold basis or not) in the locality (an indeterminate area). However, there are a number of restrictions on the powers of the RAC and hence on the tenant's rights.

(a)   No application may be made if the rent is a rent previously determined under section 22 ie the right is on a 'once only once' basis.

(b)   No application may be made where the AST in question is a periodic one that has arisen at the end of the previous AST's initial fixed term.

(c)   The RAC may not make a determination unless they consider there is a sufficient number of dwellings in the locality let on ATs and ASTs to enable them to make a comparison, nor may they make a determination unless they consider the rent in question is significantly *higher* than what the landlord could reasonably expect to obtain having regard to comparable rents for comparable properties.

Where the RAC do determine a rent for an AST under section 22, the new rent, which may only be a reduction of that contractually agreed, will take effect from the date fixed by the RAC and will operate as a rent limit for the tenancy in question, any excess sums being irrecoverable from the tenant. However, the determination will *not* act as a rent limit for any other lettings of the dwelling, contrast the former position under the Rent Act 1977. Where a determination is made under this provision no notice of increase of rent may be served for one year from when the determination takes effect.

It should be noted that the Secretary of State has power under section 23 of the Act to direct that RACs shall not exercise their section 22 powers in relation to AST rents in designated areas.

Housing benefit (HB)

The law of housing benefit is now too complex a body of rules to be included at length in this work. Interested readers are referred to the specialist yearly works, Zebedee and Ward *Guide to Housing Benefit and Council Tax Benefit* (SHAC/IoH) and Findlay and Ward *Housing Benefit and Council Tax Benefit Legislation* (CPAG) and the Department of Social Security's *Housing Benefit and Council Tax Benefits Guidance Manual* (HMSO). However, some brief outline and assessment of the legal structure has to be given simply because of the enormous importance 'HB' has for the management of social housing, and also because, without doubt, it is the classic example of a subsidy given to individuals as opposed to the older form of subsidy given to 'bricks and mortar' to keep housing costs down for everyone.

This chapter will therefore include a brief examination of the *basic* rules relating to HB, but not other similar benefits such as Council Tax Benefit. For the detailed rules see, inter alia, the Social Security Contributions and Benefits Act 1992, in particular sections 130-137, the Social Security Administration Act 1992, sections 1-5, 16, 63, 75, 112, 127, 134-137, the Housing Benefit (General) Regulations SI 1987/1971, The Housing Act 1988, section 121, The Rent Officers (Additional Functions) Order SI 1990/428, the Housing Benefit and Community Charge Benefit (Subsidy) (No 2) Order SI 1993/935 and the Housing Benefit and Community Charge Benefit (Subsidy) Regulations SI 1991/441.

There are two forms of HB for those who rent their homes: rent rebate for authority tenants; rent allowance for those renting from associations, and private landlords. Similarly there are two ways in which HB can be claimed, either at the same time as a claim for income support from the Benefits Agency, in which case the Agency will, after assessing the claim to income support, pass the HB claim on to the relevant local authority for their assessment, or by way of a direct HB claim from an authority. The authority in all cases is the district or London borough council.

HB is closely aligned with income support which is a state benefit for those, generally over 18, neither in full time work nor full time education, whose income (or 'means') is less than their defined 'needs' or 'the applicable amount', and who have no capital above £8,000. Those who are on income support will generally receive HB of 100% of their eligible rent, minus certain deductions. Where people are not on income support they may still receive that 100% benefit if their means are less than their needs, otherwise they will receive a proportionately decreased ('tapered') HB according to the excess of means over needs. Because HB is a personal subsidy it is designed to concentrate the most help on those with the greatest needs – households with very low incomes and/or those whose rents are *unavoidably* high. This feature of the HB system stands alongside generally reduced levels of subsidy paid under the scheme by central to local government.

Outline of the HB scheme

Those who may apply for HB are in *general* those liable to make payments in respect of a dwelling occupied as a home, though excluding those whose income support includes an element in respect of housing costs. Many authority and association tenants fall within this class. To qualify for HB a claimant should normally be *legally* liable to pay rent for his/her dwelling, *but* certain other people may be *treated* as liable and so qualify for benefit, eg the partner of a person legally liable, or a person who has had to make payments to enable continued occupation of the home while the person legally liable does not pay rent, and the actual payer was formerly the partner (ie spouse or cohabitee) of the person liable, or is someone the authority consider it reasonable to treat as liable. Certain persons *cannot*, however, be treated as liable (though their presence may influence the outcome of a HB claim) eg claimants who reside with the person to whom they have to pay rent and that person is a close relative of the claimant, or where liability has been created to take advantage of the HB Scheme, such as in R *v Manchester City Council, ex p Baragrove Properties Ltd* (1991) 23 HLR 337 where landlords were considered to have contrived the payment of high rents by particular groups of vulnerable tenants.

A claimant can *generally* only claim in respect of one home actually occupied, though there are exceptions eg in respect of those forced from their homes by fears of violence from a landlord or where the claimant is a student and must perforce have more than one home, see further Zebedee and Ward pp 53-55.

As stated above the presence of certain persons may influence the outcome of a HB claim. The size and composition of a claimant's household is thus an issue of considerable importance for the computation of any benefit payable. For legal purposes a claimant's household is the claimant, the claimant's family (if any) and any other person living in the dwelling and who is a 'non-dependant' for HB purposes. The claimant may, of course, be a sole person, but may equally be a lone parent or a member of a married or cohabiting relationship. A claimant's family will consist of the claimant's partner (if any) plus any children or young persons (ie those over 16 but under 19 who are not on income support, nor in advanced education) for whom the claimant is responsible and who are members of the household (if any). Non-dependants are those who normally reside with the claimant but who are not liable to make payments in respect of the dwelling, eg adult children, foster children and boarders: their presence will normally result in a fixed deduction from HB paid.

As stated earlier there are two ways in which HB can be claimed, with or without income support.

Where income support (IS) is claimed from the Benefits Agency, which acts on behalf of the DSS the claimant will be invited to apply for HB contemporaneously on appropriate forms. When these forms are received back by the agency they are checked, but no reminders are sent to those who fail to complete and return forms. Once a claimant's IS entitlement is determined the agency will endeavour to send the HB claim to the relevant local authority within two working days. Delays can occur, however, and in such cases an application for HB may be made direct to the authority. The forms give certain information as to the claimant, his/her partner (if any), their address, people living with the claimant and whether any persons fall into classes relevant to the consideration of non-dependant deductions (see below). If a claimant has been awarded IS that is proof that he/she satisfies the conditions for receipt of the maximum benefit, *R v Penwith District Council Housing Benefits Review Board, ex p Menear* (1991) 24 HLR 115. However, it is not proper for an authority to simply rubber stamp the benefit agency's findings on a claimant because some IS claimants may be ineligible for HB, and therefore authorities should generally make determinations on entitlement. The benefits agency does, however, monitor claimants to the extent that where it hears of changes in a claimant's circumstances which could affect HB entitlement it will inform the relevant authority, though this does *not* supersede the duty which lies on claimants to notify such changes themselves.

Claims for HB may be made direct to the local authority, and this is the normal route for those not claiming IS. Where, however, it is believed a claimant should have IS the authority applied to should advise him/her to claim it. There is no single national standard application form, but the forms used should be designed so as to elicit the information needed to determine the claim. More than that is unnecessary and detailed accounts are not required, though any reasonably required certificates, documents and other like evidence may be demanded. Claims must be made in writing, however, and on approved forms, duly completed, though authorities have discretion to accept other written forms considered sufficient in the circumstances of the case. Where claims are insufficiently made authorities are required to inform the claimant and to take steps to request the requisite information, allowing at least four weeks in which the claimant is to respond. Claims may be amended before they are determined and also withdrawn before determination.

It is important to determine on a claim what the 'date of claim' is for this influences the day on which entitlement to HB begins: the date of claim is *normally* the day on which the HB claim is received by the authority. 'The first day of entitlement' will, *in general*, be the Monday at the start of the first benefit week after the 'date of claim'. Once awarded HB is payable only for a fixed period to be determined by the authority up to a maximum period of 60 benefit weeks from the first week of benefit entitlement. At the end of this period the benefit will run out on the Sunday at the end of the fixed period's final benefit week, though in certain circumstances a change of circumstances may bring a benefit period to a premature end. At the end of a benefit period the claimant should be invited to make a 'repeat claim', though a claimant may make a repeat claim at any time, and the authority will have a duty to act on it *provided* it is made within the 13 week period before the benefit period expires.

Backdating of HB for up to a year previous to the date of claim is provided for in the regulations, for further details see Zebedee and Ward, op cit, pp 97-100.

With regard to the amount of HB a claimant receives the basic notion is very simple: the higher a claimant's income the less HB is received. A claimant on IS, for instance, may thus qualify for the maximum level of assistance – subject to reductions if there are non-dependants in his/her household in respect of whom deductions have to be made.

To make a HB entitlement calculation an authority will therefore, in general, need to know: who are the members of the claimant's household; the eligible costs of housing, ie the household's share of the eligible rent; whether there are non-dependants for deduction purposes; what the claimant's capital resources are; what the claimant's net income is. In the case of an applicant on IS no questions as to capital need be asked as the benefits agency will have dealt with this matter and the authority's question will be directed to the details of the eligible rent and the presence of non-dependants (if any).

The basic formula for calculation benefit is:

$$HB = WER - (NND + \frac{EI \times 65}{100})$$

where: WER = weekly eligible rent;
  NND = any non-dependant deductions;
  EI = any 'excess income' (but only where a claimant is not on IS).

The maximum benefit available is WER – NND, and that, for instance, will be the benefit paid to those on IS. Those not on IS will receive a lower, or 'tapered' benefit and if they have capital of over £16,000 they will not receive any benefit at all. The starting point in cases of non IS claimants is to determine whether their income is less than the appropriate 'applicable amount' (see below). If the answer is 'yes' the maximum benefit is payable, If 'no' then there will be 'excess income', and the benefit will be accordingly reduced by a percentage or 'taper', which is 65% in the case of HB. The practical result is that HB is reduced by 65 pence in the pound for each pound of excess income. HB of less than 50 pence per week is not payable.

Some brief explanation of the various terms used above must now be given.

Eligible rent and other costs

To be 'eligible' rent is the actual rent payable for a home, including rent for any garage, but excluding any business premises, minus amounts in respect of charges for water, fuel, any meals etc charged for in the rent, and minus a

further sum where a rent is considered unreasonably high or the accommodation unreasonably large. With regard to this latter deduction, the
determination is one for authorities to make. However, in many cases
(excepting an authority's own lettings) there is an obligation on authorities to
refer claims for HB to the Rent Officer for a determination, inter alia, whether:
the claimant's rent is reasonable; or what a reasonable market rent would be;
whether the claimant's accommodation is of reasonable size. The Rent Officer
determines whether a given rent is 'significantly higher' than what the landlord
might reasonably be expected to obtain and whether certain size criteria have
been exceeded. The Rent Officer's determination of a 'reasonable market
rent' has consequences for the *benefit awarding authority*, for it establishes
whether there will be a reduced payment of HB subsidy to the authority in
respect of the relevant claimant's HB.

Where, for example, the Rent Officer determines a rent is unreasonably
high it is then for the authority to determine whether or not to reduce HB, and
by what amount they consider appropriate. Each case has to be treated on its
merits and authorities should not simply 'rubber stamp' the rent officer's
findings, see generally *R v Housing Benefits Review Board for East Devon
District Council, ex p Gibson and Gibson* (1993) 25 HLR 487. However, an
authority may not reduce the amount of rent 'eligible' b*elow* that payable in
respect of comparable alternative accommodation, see *R v Brent London
Borough Council, ex p Connery* [1990] 2 All ER 353, (1990) 22 HLR 40.
Authorities are also not to take into account the effect of the subsidy rules on
their own finances.

Non-dependant deductions

A deduction is generally made in the amount of HB in respect of each non-
dependant living in the claimant's home. A non-dependant is defined, in a
ridiculously cumbersome fashion in SI 1987/1971 as, effectively, adults who
live with close residents; those who live with others and who make payments
to them for their accommodation on a non-commercial basis; those who are
parties to an agreement designed to take advantage of the HB system, a former
non-dependant who claims to be a joint tenant where the authority concludes
a change of status was undertaken to take advantage of the HB system. Though
such non-dependants usually make a contribution to household expenses it is
important to note that a deduction has to be made even in respect of a non-
dependant who pays nothing at all. Certain persons are, however, not non-
dependants, eg children under 16 and young people of 16-18, boarders, carers
provided by voluntary agencies. Similarly where a non-dependant falls within
a particular group no deduction will be made, eg non-dependants on IS who
are aged under 25, non-dependants who are full time students, those who
have been in hospital for more than six weeks etc.

Where a deduction has to be made the amount varies according to whether the non-dependant is/is not in 'remunerative work' (ie work of 16 hours or more each week for which payment is made) and the level of income received. Where, for example, a non-dependant is in remunerative work with a gross income of £135.00 per week or more a deduction of £21 is made: for someone *not* in such work the deduction is £4.00.

Excess income

Excess income arises where a claimant's income is in excess of, that is over, the 'applicable amount', ie a sum determined to reflect the claimant's basic living needs.

The applicable amount is made up of personal allowances and, possibly, one or more 'premiums' ie amounts determined to reflect particular needs if certain conditions are fulfilled, for example where a claimant has responsibility for a disabled child, or is a carer. Some premiums can be enjoyed together, eg those in respect of having a family, having a disabled child, having severe disability, while others (the 'overlapping' premiums) are restricted in that a claimant may only be awarded the most valuable of those for which he/she qualifies. The personal allowances vary according to whether the claimant is single, or a lone parent, etc.

In addition a claimant's capital may be relevant in determining HB entitlement in respect of those claimants not in receipt of IS. As stated above if a claimant has more than £16,000 capital there is no entitlement to HB, capital sums of less than £3,000 are ignored and thus in respect of sums between £3,000 and £16,000 a claimant is deemed to be deriving an income ('tariff income') from the capital and this is relevant for HB purposes. 'Capital' is not statutorily defined, but DSS guidance indicates it is property with a clear monetary value reasonably available to the claimant, and that includes cash and savings, Savings Certificates, Premium Bonds, shares, landed property, trust funds. Certain items of capital are, however, 'disregarded' eg rights to income under annuities, social fund payments and personal possessions such as furnishings and cars, save where these have been purchased with a view to taking advantage of the HB system.

'Income' is also not specifically defined, but any regular periodic payment is likely to be treated as income. For HB purposes the 'income' that counts is the net weekly income of the claimant from all sources (including tariff income if applicable, see above), though certain specific 'income disregards' are not taken into account for this purpose and are deducted from net earnings to produce the assessable earned income. Certain state benefits are also totally disregarded. In certain cases, however, a 'notional income' may be attributed to a claimant even though he/she does not actually possess it, for example any income a claimant has deprived him/herself of to take advantage of the

HB system. A claimant's income will also include that of his/her partner, and that of a child or young person who is a member of the household and for whom the claimant is responsible.

Administering HB

In general once an authority possesses all the information reasonably required from a claimant it should make a determination within 14 days or as soon as possible thereafter, and all those affected should then be notified and the first payment made within 14 days though authority tenants will receive rebates of rent rather than cash sums. Authorities should only exceed the time limits where they are entitled to do so eg because a claim has been incorrectly made, or requisite information has not been supplied. However, there is evidence that authorities do not meet time limits, and there is ample room for disagreement between claimants and authorities.

The mode of payment of any HB in the form of a rent allowance, eg to an association tenant, is largely at the discretion of the authority, though in some cases claimants have the right to a fortnightly payment. Payments will normally be made to claimants, but direct payments to a landlord have to be made where part of a claimant's IS is being paid to the landlord in respect of arrears, or where a claimant has arrears of rent of eight or more weeks. There is a *discretion* to make payments direct to a landlord where: a claimant requests, or consents to, such payments; the authority consider such a mode of payment is in the claimant's interest; benefit is owed to a claimant who has quit his/her dwelling in arrears of rent. In certain other circumstances HB payments may be withheld, eg where an authority is reasonably satisfied the claimant is failing to make regular payments of rent.

Once a claimant is in receipt of HB he/she is under a duty to inform the paying authority of any relevant change of circumstances, ie any change the claimant might reasonably be expected to appreciate could affect his/her entitlement to HB, the amount or method of payment of HB. Certain changes need not be notified, eg an authority tenant need not inform the authority of rent increases they impose. However, changes of address, of the status of non-dependants, changes in capital and income, etc, have to be notified so that the authority may revise HB, or, in some cases, end payment of HB, for example where a claimant ceases to be entitled to IS.

Where a dispute arises as to a HB determination, a claimant has the right to appeal (a 'review'). This will have two stages: an 'internal review' by officers of the authority, and a 'further review' by a 'review board' at a hearing. The internal review leads to a 'determination' of the dispute and if this does not satisfy the appellant the matter proceeds at his/her request to a review board who will make a 'decision' on the matter.

All those affected by an initial determination of a HB claim are entitled to be notified of the decision, and all such are further entitled to seek 'a review', eg claimants, non-dependants whose capital or income is treated as being the claimant's, or a landlord in certain circumstances, eg where there is an issue as to whether HB should be paid direct to the landlord.

In general any matter relating to a HB determination can be subjected to the review procedure, and a dissatisfied claimant has six weeks from the date of notification of determination to make such a request in writing, though this time limit may be extended. The stage one internal review – which should be carried out by senior officers or at least officers different from those who made the initial determination – is to be completed within 14 days, or as soon as is reasonably practicable. The outcome of this review must then be notified to the appellant within 14 days, or as soon as reasonably practicable, together with information as to further appeal rights. A disappointed appellant then has four weeks to apply in writing for a further review *giving the ground on which it is sought.* This time limit may be extended. The meeting of the review board, which will be composed of at least three members of the authority, should normally take place within six weeks of the request for a further review, or as soon as possible thereafter. Some procedural requirements are laid down for the conduct of review boards, for example to ensure both claimant and authority have the right to be heard, and to call evidence and to examine and cross examine it. Claimants have the right to be accompanied by a friend or legal representative. Where a landlord requests a further review the HB claimant has the right to be a full party to the proceedings. Certain travelling expenses of claimants may be paid by authorities, but legal aid is not available for review board representation.

The rules of natural justice require review board proceedings to be fairly and even-handedly conducted: a failure to observe this requirement could be the subject of judicial review proceedings, for review boards are generally subject to the supervisory jurisdiction of the High Court, see generally *R v Sedgemoor District Council Housing Benefit Review Board, ex p Weaden* (1986) 18 HLR 355. Though the procedure at a review board is inquisitorial, with members being expected to inquire into points made by the parties, the overall requirements of fairness still apply. A weakness of the system is that the regulations are unspecific about what constitutes the conditions for a fair procedure, but Zebedee and Ward point to the need to consider whether: Review Board members should also be members of council committees otherwise responsible for HB administration; members should receive training; there should be a clerk to advise members, and, if so, who should that person be; documents should be available before a hearing; procedures should be formal/informal, public/private; the claimant or the authority should speak first and how questions should be asked.

Once a Review Board has reached its decision, which may be by majority vote, with the chair having a casting vote if necessary, that decision must be recorded, with a statement of the findings of fact, the interpretation of the relevant law, and the reasoning of the board. Failure to do this lays the decision open to judicial review, see *R v Sefton Metropolitan Borough Council, ex p Cunningham* (1991) 23 HLR 534. In this context the reasons must be sufficiently clear to enable the parties to understand how the decision has been reached and why they have failed/succeeded. The obligation is on the chair of the review board to record the necessary elements of its reasoned decision. It is not appropriate for a clerk to a board to draw up a reasoned case for a decision for the chair subsequently to approve. Where a finding adverse to a claimant is reached it is of critical importance for the reasoning to be set out and for the evidential basis of the finding to be identified, see *R v Solihull Metropolitan Borough Council Housing Benefits Review Board, ex p Simpson* [1994] Fam Law 380, 26 HLR 370. The review board's decision must be notified in writing to the parties within seven days of the decision, or as soon as possible thereafter, and there are certain limited circumstances in which a review board may set aside its decision if requested to do so, ie where a relevant document was not received by a person affected by a determination, where a person affected was absent from the review board hearing or where the interests of justice otherwise require it. Such a request has to be made in writing within 13 weeks of notification, and other interested parties have to be informed and given an opportunity to make representations before reconsideration takes place.

Little use appears to be made generally of appeal procedures concerning HB, and the DSS has encouraged authorities to give greater publicity to the issue by means of leaflets and information sheets. Even so the procedures have been subject to criticism both as to their structure and operation, see *Housing benefit reviews: an evaluation of the effectiveness of the review system in responding to claimants dissatisfied with housing benefits decisions*, Sainsbury and Eardley, DSS Research Report Series No 3, HMSO, 1991.

Further reading

Cope, H *Housing Associations: Policy and Practice* (Macmillan, 1990).
Davey, M *Residential Rents* (Sweet and Maxwell, London, 1990), Chapters 1, 2, 5, 7, 8, 9, 10, 11, 14, and 15.
Gibb, K and Munro, M *Housing Finance in the UK* (Macmillan, 1991).
Hills, J *Unravelling Housing Finance* (Clarendon Press, 1991).
Malpass, P *Re-shaping Housing Policy* (Routledge, 1990).
Malpass, P and Murie, A 'Local Housing Finance' Chapter 7 in *Housing Policy and Practice*, 3rd edn (Macmillan, 1990).

Chapter Five

Housing and relationships

Over the last few decades patterns of 'family life' and the relationships between and within the sexes have undergone some radical changes. These changes are partly to do with the influence of specific developments in the law and social policies and are partly a consequence of the evolution of society and the economy more generally. Law and policy are perhaps more influential in these patterns of change than social scientists are prepared to acknowledge, preferring to account for social change in abstract conceptual forms. But as exemplified in Chapter One, the state – through a range of specific policies – has a powerful role in directing the restructuring of the pattern of housing tenure in Britain during the course of the twentieth century. In a similar manner the legal and policy environment of the last 20 years has had a major impact on the social structure of Britain and on patterns of social behaviour.

This chapter focuses on the legal framework which surrounds and regulates the housing rights of people in the context of their close personal relationships. The rather weak position of women is a salient issue. However, before we consider legal rights it is important to describe the most important of these wider social developments and to indicate how the law and policy have helped create such change.

A very good example of this is the divorce reform legislation of 1969, which becoming effective in 1971 resulted in a surge in the divorce rate. By the mid-1980s divorce had more than doubled and that rate of increase, were it to continue, would lead to about one third of all marriages ending in divorce. Research by Ermisch confirms the commonly held assumption that the risk of relationship breakdown recedes with the length of marriage and also declines significantly after the birth of children to the family (Ermisch, J 'Divorce: Economic Antecedents and Aftermath' in *The Changing Population of Britain*, Joshi H, (ed) Basil Blackwell, 1989). Further detail on trends in divorce and marriage may be found in Haskey, J 'One parent families in Great Britain', *Population Trends*, 45, 1986, pp 5-13. More detail on the incidence of divorce and marriage is discussed later in the chapter drawing on the principal official study by Holmans, AE, Nandy, S, and Brown, AC in 'Housing Formation and Dissolution and Housing Tenure in a Longitudinal Perspective' (1987) 17, *Social Trends* 20.

An important consequence of the increase in divorce is that the number of lone-parent families has risen dramatically during the 1980s. The proportion of one-parent families with dependent children grew from 3.5% of all household types in 1971 to 10% in 1991 (well over one million households), and as a proportion of families with dependent children more than doubled from 8% to over 18%. The proportion of lone-parents who have never been married has also increased but the vast majority of lone-parenthood, about 70%, is attributable to the breakdown of a marriage. 90% of lone-parents are women.

Remarriages have also increased dramatically with 70% of women aged 25-34 at the end of the first marriage eventually remarrying. The chances of remarrying are considerably enhanced if the woman is in work and also if she has been through some form of post-compulsory education. Ermisch shows that the chances of a woman with 'high' educational attainment remarrying within three years of a divorce is 2.5 times higher than for other women.

Remarriage has repercussions for household formation and housing demand. This is in part due to the increasing incidence of remarried people having second families. In 1961, births to remarried women were 2% of legitimate births but 8% in 1985. Obviously the presence of children, after divorce or remarriage will affect the size and type of accommodation required by the parent with whom they live, and the policy and practice of family legislation is to try and keep children in touch with both their parents by encouraging shared responsibilities. This in itself can create the need for both parents to be able to offer accommodation suitable for children's requirements.

It is from within the group of those women who do not remarry that a core of long-term one-parent families is drawn. Many of these families are very poor. According to the Family Expenditure Survey the average income of lone-parents is about 40% of two-parent families. Such a low standard of living is mainly due to their dependence on state benefits and this issue has become the focus of a much publicised government inspired campaign to link the growth of single-parenthood with welfare dependency. In fact single-parenthood is a complex social phenomenon and is one part of much wider patterns of social change caused among other things by developments in contraceptive technology and new social attitudes about the relationship between the sexes. Far more couples cohabit before marriage and between marriages than in previous generations and many couples opt to remain unmarried. This trend is not as advanced in Britain as it is in some societies, notably in Scandinavia, but the increasing number of children born outside a marital relationship suggests that more cohabiting couples are having children and opting to remain unmarried.

Increasing female wage rates and participation in the labour force throughout the 1980s are particularly important factors in this connection because they have, to a certain extent, increased women's financial independence. This may itself have contributed to the growth in divorce as women become less financially dependent on their husbands. Increased wages and salaries paid to women have important implications for patterns of child-rearing with women opting to delay childbearing and having fewer children.

Indeed, one of the main demographic changes in recent years has been the decline in the birth rate and it is quite conceivable that higher wage rates and increased work opportunities for women partly underlie this trend. In 1973 the birth rate fell below the level needed to replace the population and by the end of the 1980s it had stabilised at 1.8 children per woman, well below the replacement rate. Associated with this has been a considerable decrease in the size of households which have declined from an average of 3.1 persons in 1960 to only 2.5 in the mid-1990s. The decline in household size is also a consequence of the rise in the number of single person households which now comprise 26% of all households.

Despite the declining birth rate the projected population of Britain in the second decade of the 2000s is only a few thousand lower than the current population, due to increased longevity for both sexes. Thus one major change in the population structure in recent decades has been the well-known 'ageing of the population'. In the three decades since 1960 the proportion of those aged 65 years and over has increased from under 12% to nearly 16%, and includes a particularly rapid growth in the number of 'old' elderly people, those aged over 80. At the other extreme the number of children under 16 years old fell by nearly 20% between 1971 and 1991.

This is not the place for a full-blown account of the demographic changes that have been and are shaping the pattern of social life in Britain. We have highlighted a number of particularly salient issues which relate closely to the law concerning housing and relationships – increased levels of divorce and remarriage, the growth in cohabiting, lower fertility rates, the ageing of the population. One of the most accessible and useful of the recent publications in this area is the study by John Ermisch (Ermisch, J *Fewer babies, longer lives*, Joseph Rowntree Foundation, 1990). He explores, inter alia, patterns of family formation and dissolution in the context of the housing market and the demand for social housing and so is particularly informative to students of housing and housing law. He points out, for example, that the boom in house prices in the mid-1980s was partly stimulated by a surge in new household formations arising from the entry of the 1960s 'baby-boom' generation into the housing market. Additional pressure was thus put on the already limited supply of dwellings and prices were, as a result, forced upwards. Because of escalating house prices pressure increased on the social housing sector – to cater for those unable to access the market – at a time, as we saw in Chapter

One, when supplies of public housing were declining through cuts in central funding and the right to buy policy. By the same token the huge increase in unemployment in the 1980s also increased the pressure on the social housing agencies and the rapid increase in homelessness, described in detail in Chapter Six, is closely connected to the undersupply of 'affordable' rental housing in the public sector.

Women and housing

The importance of public sector housing, particularly council housing, to women experiencing a relationship breakdown is clearly illustrated in the study by Holmans, Nandy and Brown. Their longitudinal analysis of OPCS data shows that of men and women married in 1971 and who were at that time local authority tenants, but divorced in 1981, the proportion of male tenants fell but the proportion of women tenants increased considerably. (Holmans, A E, Nandy, S and Brown, A, *Social Trends* 17, 1987.)

The position of women living in owner occupied dwellings at the time of a divorce is often constrained because they may not command the very considerable resources needed to find an alternative home in the open market. If the woman wishes to end the marriage, which frequently is the case – over 70% of divorce decrees are granted to the wife – then her need for accommodation is a crucial issue especially if the matrimonial home is not readily sold or the husband refuses to leave. Even when wives are in possession of a share of the capital from the disposal of the former matrimonial home their chances of accessing adequate housing with mortgage finance is often restricted because of their generally low level of earnings and costly childcare responsibilities. Thus it is frequently the case that relationship breakdown leads women to leave the matrimonial home and turn to the public rented sector for support. This issue and the law which surrounds it are discussed in detail later in the chapter.

Housing difficulties for women caused by relationship breakdown have recently been highlighted in a report published by the Department of the Environment. Bull's research shows that relationship breakdown encompasses a wide variety of experiences and that housing problems varied according to tenure, whether children are involved, and evidence of domestic violence against women, often associated with acute forms of housing crisis, was common all over the country. Legal remedies were found frequently to be limited in effect because of extreme fear of reprisal from the former partner. A sensitive and rapid response to such situations was sadly lacking and many local authorities were found to leave the victims of such violence feeling stigmatised and disbelieved. (Bull, J *Housing Consequences of Relationship Breakdown* HMSO, 1993.)

During the course of this research a 'Relationship Breakdown Working Party' was established in the Homelessness Policy Division of the Department of the Environment specifically to consider the implications for security of tenure of the Housing Act 1985. A series of recommendations were published in December 1993 and included support for the Law Commission's view that the criteria for making an order that one party should leave the home should be altered to make it easier for the victim to remain there, at least in the short term. They further argued in favour of a limited ground for possession in the case of domestic violence with the court assessing the reasonableness of granting possession in such circumstances. The Working Party's overall view was that a package of measures, including administrative changes, good practice guidance and legislative changes would be of great assistance in helping the victims of violent relationship breakdowns and helping local authorities to be more sensitive to the problems (*Relationship Breakdown and Secure Local Authority Tenants : Recommendations of the Relationship Breakdown Working Party*, Special Needs Housing Branch, DoE, December 1993).

The growth of lone-parenthood, the problems of tenants and owner occupiers involved in relationship breakdown, and the growing evidence of women experiencing domestic violence have all increased the pressures on public sector housing at a time when it is least equipped to cope with such problems.

General housing rights within relationships

The law is concerned to regulate housing rights at a number of times within a relationship. While it exists and when it ends there will be legal consequences for a couple's home. These will not follow a common pattern, as the recent research studies have shown. As we have seen everything depends on the mode of tenure of the dwelling, the nature of the relationship between the partners – married, unmarried, gay or lesbian – the legal status of the tenancy held, and whether there are children involved.

Housing rights while a relationship subsists

English law recognises only two marital statuses, married and unmarried (including the bereaved and divorced). There is no such status as 'common law wife/husband' and use of that phrase will be avoided. In this chapter when the rights of those who are in an unmarried relationship are discussed they will be referred to as 'partners' while married persons will be denoted as 'spouses'.

Freehold conveyancing practice tends to treat joint ownership of a house as the norm where property is to be occupied jointly. In municipal housing historic practice assumed where a married couple occupied a council house the husband would be the tenant. The 1976 National Consumer Council discussion paper Tenancy Agreements pointed out it cannot be assumed the male within a couple should automatically be the tenant. In 1977 the Housing Services Advisory Group (HSAG) in its report on tenancy agreements argued that prospective tenants should be given the opportunity to chose between joint and sole tenancies. By 1978 HSAG (report on the housing of one parent families) recommended use of joint tenancies in municipal lettings. It is now quite common for both spouses and heterosexual partners to be given joint tenancies. Practice tends to vary rather more with regard to gay and lesbian relationships.

A joint tenancy gives both parties the right to occupy the home, irrespective of whether they are spouses or partners, while marriage confers on each spouse the right to occupy the matrimonial home irrespective of whose name the tenancy is in. The Housing Act 1985 recognises that authorities may grant joint tenancies. Joint assured tenancies may also be granted by associations under the Housing Act 1988. One pre-1980 practice impossible under current law is that of issuing notice to quit to a deserted joint tenant before granting a new sole tenancy, unless, of course, the landlord can show one of the grounds for possession. For the future it may be hoped that landlords will use joint tenancies when letting to couples, irrespective of marital status and sexuality.

Administrative practice should reflect the legal situation and communications from landlords should be sent to tenants jointly in both names. It should be made clear in the tenancy agreement that the authorisation of either joint tenant is sufficient for the doing of works and repairs by the landlord. Where a joint tenancy is not possible, a couple being allocated a house should be given a choice as to which will be tenant. Before a choice is made it is obviously a matter of good housing management for a landlord to explain the implications of tenancy types to intending tenants.

The rights of non-tenant spouses during the subsistence of marriage

A wife who is not a tenant has the right to occupy and use the matrimonial home because at common law she is entitled to maintenance by her husband.

Legislation goes further than this. Section 1 of the Matrimonial Homes Act 1983 provides where one spouse is entitled to occupy a dwelling by virtue of a beneficial interest, contract or enactment giving him/her the right to remain in occupation, and the other is not so entitled, then that other spouse has rights of occupation in the dwelling; in particular, if in occupation, the right not to be evicted or excluded from the dwelling except by court order, or, if not in occupation, the right to enter and occupy the dwelling by virtue of a court order. Section 1 (5) of the 1983 Act also provides that where a spouse is entitled to occupy a dwelling, any payment made by that spouse in satisfaction of any rent, etc, due from the other spouse shall be treated as if made by that other spouse. In addition section 85 (5) of the Housing Act 1985 provides that where possession proceedings are taken in respect of a secure tenancy, and a spouse or former spouse who has rights of occupation under the 1983 Act is in occupation, and the tenancy is terminated by the proceedings, the spouse or former spouse, so long as remaining in occupation, has rights to apply for adjournments, stays, suspensions or postponements irrespective of the termination, while section 1 (6) of the 1983 Act further provides a spouse's occupation by virtue of the section is to be treated as possession by the other spouse for the purpose of Part IV of the Housing Act 1985 (secure tenancies) and Part I of the Housing Act 1988 (assured tenancies). Thus if a secure sole tenant decamps leaving the other spouse in the matrimonial home, the deserted spouse's occupation maintains the deserter's possession of the property.

So long as one spouse has rights of occupation either may apply for a court order suspending or restricting the exercise by either spouse of the right to occupy the dwelling, or requiring either spouse to permit the exercise by the other of that right. The court has a wide discretion, under section 1 (3), in making orders and is to take into account the conduct of the parties, their needs and resources, the needs of any children and all other circumstances of the case.

The needs of children are not the only consideration, nor are they of paramount importance, in the exercise of this discretion, see *Richards v Richards* [1984] AC 174, [1983] 2 All ER 807, though most commentators agree the courts will give great consideration to advancing the interests of that spouse with whom the children of the relationship are living, particularly if in bad or unsuitable housing while the other spouse occupies the former home alone. However, spouses who have behaved badly may find discretion exercised against them. An order may be made even though violence has not yet broken out between the parties provided it is clear the marriage cannot continue, though mere tension is not enough, see *Phillips v Phillips* [1973] 2 All ER 423, [1973] 1WLR 615.

A court will not, however, make an order merely to aid an authority in obtaining possession of a dwelling where it is clear the wife will not return to the dwelling if the husband is excluded, see *Warwick v Warwick* (1982) 1 HLR 139. Orders will not be made simply to allow 'cooling off' or reconciliation periods between spouses, see *Summers v Summers* [1986] 1 FLR 343, [1986] Fam Law 56, nor as merely routine steps on the way to divorce, see *Burke v Burke* (1986) 151 JP 404, [1987] 2 FLR 71. However, much depends on the facts of each case, see *Lee v Lee* [1984] FLR 243, [1984] Fam Law 243 where the court was persuaded to make an order because of allegations of indecency in respect of his daughter by the husband.

The above rights only apply within marriage.

The rights of non-tenant partners during the subsistence of the relationship

The rights of partners who are not legally tenants of the dwelling they occupy are decided according to common law principles, which, overall, give little protection. With regard to social housing the best a non-tenant partner can hope to hold is a sub-tenancy of part of the dwelling, ie he/she has exclusive occupation of some accommodation and pays rent for it and there is a definite relationship of landlord and tenant between the parties.

It is most unlikely as a matter of fact that such a relationship would exist between parties who are living, eating and sleeping together. In any case by virtue of section 1 and Schedule 1, para 10 of the Housing Act 1988 there can be no assured tenancy granted after 15 January 1989 where there is a resident landlord, while section 93 of the Housing Act 1985 provides in relation to secure tenancies that a tenant will not, without the landlord's written consent, sublet or part with possession of part of the dwelling. It is thus likely a non-tenant partner will be a licencee, ie a person who has the householder's personal permission to be present on land, either gratuitously as a 'bare' licensee or contractually where something is given in return for the license, such as a contribution to rent or outgoings. Only rarely will a contractual license be found to exist where partners are in a relationship. A bare license can be ended simply by the householder asking the licensee to leave, and by giving a reasonable period of notice. What is 'reasonable' will depend on the facts of each case; on matters such as: length of period of occupation; nature of the licensee's personal belongings on the property, and whether children are involved. However, at the end of the period of notice the licensee can be excluded from the property, and, because the situation will be governed by section 3A of the Protection from Eviction Act 1977 (ie the licence will have been one where the licensee has shared accommodation with the licensor) there will be no need for a court order.

What happens where a sole tenant partner leaves his/her dwelling while the other partner remains in occupation? The general attitude of the court towards such 'staying on' situations is that a new tenancy does not arise, even where the remaining partner pays money to the landlord claimed to be 'rent' see *Marcroft Wagons Ltd v Smith* [1951] 2 KB 496, [1951] 2 All ER 271. However, the operative test appears to be whether the partner is staying on with the agreement of the landlord. Landlords should make clear their attitude to the creation of a new tenancy in such circumstances. In *Westminster City Council v Basson* [1990] EGCS 141, a couple were secure tenants and the defendant went to live with them. The couple gave notice to quit, handed in their keys and left the defendant in occupation. The Authority wrote to the defendant informing her of possession proceedings and stating a 'use and occupation charge' would be made, they also stated they did not intend to create a tenancy. It was found that no tenancy had been created.

The rights of joint tenants during a relationship

On the assumption that women are, if in employment, generally less well paid than men, and may well not be 'gainfully employed' at all, there are obvious advantages for women if they have joint tenancies of homes with their male spouses/partners.

(1)   In the event of his death there is no need for her to apply for a transfer of the tenancy to herself, because a joint tenancy passes automatically on the death of one joint tenant to the survivor(s) though there may be particular consequences because of statutory rules relating to succession, see further below.

(2)   In any proceedings for divorce, nullity or judicial separation the court may make an order with regard to the transfer of the property under section 24 of the Matrimonial Causes Act 1973.

(3)   If the relationship breaks up she will be entitled to remain in occupation by virtue of her legal estate.

(4)   Under section 9 of the Matrimonial Homes Act 1983 where each of two spouses is entitled by virtue of joint legal estate to occupy a dwelling which is, or was, their matrimonial home, either may apply to the court with regard to the exercise during the subsistence of the marriage of the right to occupy for an order prohibiting, suspending or restricting its exercise by the other, or requiring that other to permit its exercise by the applicant. The right also applies where the entitlement of the spouses arises by virtue of a contract or enactment.

The disadvantage of a joint tenancy to a woman is that she can be held liable for any rent arrears accrued by the man before his death or desertion, etc.

Housing rights on disintegration of a relationship

There is a need to distinguish between long and short term remedies. In general the former are only available under matrimonial legislation to the married, though the Children Act 1989 and possession of a joint tenancy can result in entitlements for unmarried couples.

A disintegrating relationship may result in a couple being unable to live together under one roof. There may be inter party violence or violence to children. There are remedies in such circumstances available on a short term basis

Domestic violence

'Domestic violence' is the euphemism for spouse/partner battering, usually but not exclusively perpetrated by men on women. The Select Committee on

Violence in Marriage Report (HC 553, 1974-5) recognised this problem and recommended special refuges be set up where women could get away from violent men. Initial target provision should be one family place per 10,000 of the population. Authorities should assist in making this provision and the HSAG report *The Housing of One Parent Families* stated at pp 15-16:

> 'The refuge need not be in the form of a hostel. In fact in rural areas and small towns it will probably be more appropriate to have mutual arrangements between the police, probation services, social services and housing departments for the provision of emergency accommodation and social work support where and when the need arises. In cities, there may be a strong case for hostel-type provision, but this should be only for short stay emergency accommodation and more satisfactory family accommodation should be provided as quickly as possible, even if this is an intermediate step before permanent rehousing'

There were by the mid-1980s some 150 to 200 refuges nationwide (one refuge place per 70,000 of the population) some municipally provided and administered, others provided by various support groups, often run co-operatively. Recent research revealed that by the mid-1990s there had been very little improvement in the situation. A study by the London Housing Unit revealed that there were less than 1,700 places in refuges for women and their children in England whereas there was a demand for over 8,000 such places, estimated to require an additonal 700 refuges. The research further revealed the poor standard of accommodation being provided with overcrowding, lack of privacy and limited facilities being common problems, sometimes resulting in women returning to a violent partner. (*Nowhere to Run: Underfunding of Women's Refuges and the Case for Reform*, London Housing Unit, 1994.)

To protect women in the home the Domestic Violence and Matrimonial Proceedings Act 1976 was enacted. Previously a wife could commence assault proceedings against her husband, and this might result in him being bound over with, perhaps, some supervision by a probation officer. Likewise where a wife had commenced divorce or judicial separation proceedings she could also apply for an injunction excluding the husband from the home. But faster and simpler legal machinery was needed. The 1976 Act provides:

> '1 (1) Without prejudice to the jurisdiction of the High Court, on an application by a party to marriage a court [ie The County Court] shall have jurisdiction to grant an injunction containing one or more of the following provisions, namely,
>
> (a)   a provision restraining the other party to the marriage from molesting the applicant; [an 'anti-molestation' order].
>
> (b)   a provision restraining the other party from molesting a child living with the applicant; [an 'anti molestation' order].

(c)   a provision excluding the other party from the matrimonial home or a part of the matrimonial home or from a specified area in which the matrimonial home is included; [an 'ouster' order].

(d)   a provision requiring the other party to permit the applicant to enter and remain in the matrimonial home or a part of the matrimonial home; whether or not any other relief is sought in the proceedings.

(2) Sub-section (1) above shall apply to a man and a woman who are living with each other in the same household as man and wife as it applies to the parties to a marriage and any reference to the matrimonial home shall be construed accordingly'.

Anti-molestation orders are injunctions forbidding particular conduct, but they do not exclude the injunctee from the joint home, though they are theoretically more effective than criminal prosecutions because behaviour not in itself criminal can be prohibited.

The provision was tested in *Davis v Johnson* [1979] AC 264, [1978] 1 All ER 1132. A young unmarried mother held a joint tenancy of a council flat with the father of her child. She left because of the father's behaviour towards her and applied under the 1976 Act for an injunction to restrain him from molesting her or the child and also excluding him from the flat. The House of Lords held the county court has jurisdiction to grant an injunction excluding a violent person from a home where he has lived, with a woman, irrespective of their marital status, and irrespective of any right of property vested in the person excluded, whether as an owner, tenant or joint tenant. A further illustrative case is *Adeoso (otherwise Ametepe) v Adeoso* [1981] 1 All ER 107, [1980] 1 WLR 1535. The parties moved into a council flat consisting of one bedroom, a sitting room, kitchen and bathroom. They did not marry, but the woman adopted her partner's name. The relationship became unhappy; the man began to resort to violence. The parties slept in different rooms, and the woman ceased to cook or wash for the man. Communication was by notes: they locked rooms they occupied individually. The woman applied for an order under the domestic violence legislation requiring the man to stop molesting her and to leave the flat. The man argued that the 1976 Act did not apply as they were not in fact living together, and because they occupied separate accommodation. The Court of Appeal rejected both contentions. Ormrod LJ said looking at the household from the outside it would be assumed the parties were living together. Also it was impossible to say that the parties were living separately in a flat with only two rooms.

In *Wooton v Wooton* [1984] FLR 871, [1985] Fam Law 31 the court held that orders under the 1976 Act were temporary measures, designed to make stop gap provision in a situation where immediate protection is required pending a property adjustment by the court, and inappropriate where no such order is to be made. This was followed in *Freeman v Collins* (1983) 12 HLR 122. But an order lasting for a longer period may be granted where evidence of continuing violence justifies it, see *Spencer v Camacho* (1983) 12 HLR 130 and *Fairweather v Kolosine* (1983) 11 HLR 61.

The general 'stop gap' nature of orders under the 1976 Act has been continually stressed by the courts, and the considerations which will weigh in their decisions are those mentioned in section 1 (3) of the Matrimonial Homes Act 1983, irrespective of whether parties are married, see *Thurley v Smith* [1984] FLR 875, [1985] Fam Law 31. The court will therefore consider the conduct of the parties, their needs and resources, the needs of any children and the other circumstances of the case.

In *Wiseman v Simpson* [1988] 1 All ER 245, [1988] 1 WLR 35, a man and woman occupied a council flat with, their child, as joint tenants. The relationship deteriorated, but neither wished to leave. The woman changed the locks and excluded the man. He applied under the 1976 Act for an order permitting his return. The woman applied for his exclusion. There was no evidence of violence but the county court judge held it was impracticable for the parties to live together and easier for the man to find alternative accommodation; therefore he should be excluded. The Court of Appeal held this wrong. It is not enough to justify making an order to show one party has a stronger case in housing terms to have the home than the other; before making an order the overriding requirement is it must be shown to be just and reasonable. This is illustrated by two cases.

Wooton v Wooton [1984] FLR 871, [1985] Fam Law 31 was a case of tenanted property. If the man was excluded, he would not be classified as 'homeless'; no order made. But in *Thurley v Smith* [1984] FLR 875, [1985] Fam Law 31 it was considered, despite the fact that if the man were excluded he would not be within the homelessness laws, the position of the woman was so desperate as to justify excluding him, especially as the local authority could give no guarantee of housing the woman. Much will also depend on the nature of the interest of the party to be excluded – the stronger the interest the more evidence is required to justify exclusion, and in this context a secure tenancy is a 'strong' interest.

Section 2 of the 1976 Act provides extra enforcement proceedings for breach of injunctions.

'(1) Where on application by a party to a marriage, a judge grants an injunction containing a provision;
(a) restraining the other party to the marriage, from using violence against the applicant, or
(b) restraining the other party from using violence against a child living with the applicant, or
(c) excluding the other party from the matrimonial home or from a specified area in which the matrimonial home is included, the judge may, if he is satisfied that the other party has caused actual bodily harm to the applicant, or, as the case may be, to the

child concerned and considers that he is likely to do so again, attach a power of arrest to the injunction'.

Where a power of arrest is attached, a police constable may arrest without a warrant any person whom he reasonably suspects of being in breach of provisions included in the injunction. This section applies both to spouses and partners, see *White v White* [1983] Fam 54, [1983] 2 All ER 51.

For unmarried persons the 1976 Act provides domestic violence remedies, married persons may use the route provided by section 1 of the Matrimonial Homes Act 1993 (see above) and indeed following *Richards v Richards* [1984] AC 174, [1983] 2 All ER 807 they are expected to do so.

The 1976 Act only applies where partners are actually living with each other as if married at the time of the incident in question. Where partners are living separately the jurisdiction is not available, contrast *Adeoso v Adeoso* (supra) with *Ainsbury v Millington* [1987] 1 All ER 929, [1987] 1 WLR 379n. It is for the court to decide whether parties are living together. It will not be enough to claim protection to show a couple have had only intermittent sexual relations, or where they ceased to cohabit some time before an application is made, see *Harrison v Lewis* [1989] FCR 765, [1988] 2 FLR 339. The deficiencies of the 1976 Act were recognised in *Pidduck v Molloy* [1992] 1 FCR 418, [1992] 2 FLR 202. Here a man and woman had lived together and had a child. The woman began an action in trespass, assault and battery against the man from whom she had separated and had obtained an injunction against him restraining trespass on her property. The Court of Appeal pointed out the 1976 Act does not apply to former cohabiting couples who have parted and between whom violence then arises, and argued the law should be extended to protect ex cohabitees. However, the declaration of the existence of a separate tort of harassment by the Court of Appeal in *Khorasandjian v Bush* [1993] QB 727, [1993] 3 All ER 669 may do much to provide protection for a person pestered/threatened by an ex partner after a relationship has ended.

Section 16 of the Domestic Proceedings and Magistrates' Court Act 1978 empowers a magistrate's court to make a personal protection order prohibiting a spouse from threatening, or using violence against, the other spouse or any child in the family.

Either party to a marriage may apply to the magistrates under this section. Where the court is satisfied the respondent has used, or threatened to use, violence against the applicant, or a child of the family, and it is necessary for their protection to make an order, one or both of the following 'personal protection' orders may be made; (a) an order not to use or threaten to use violence against the applicant, (b) an order not to use or threaten to use violence against the applicant or a child of the family. Where satisfied that the respondent has used violence against the applicant or the child of the family or the respondent has threatened violence in contravention of a personal protection order, and the applicant or a child of the family is in danger of physical injury by the respondent, the court may make an 'exclusion' order either requiring the respondent to leave the matrimonial home, or to prohibit the respondent's entry, or both.

Provision is made for extremely rapid hearings in such situations. Section 18 of this Act allows magistrates to annex a power of arrest to an exclusion order where satisfied that the respondent has physically injured the applicant or a child of the family, and considers him likely to do so again.

The magistrates in their domestic jurisdiction have powers approximating to those of the county court, but their powers apply only within the context of marriage.

The long term rights of the parties on the break-up of a relationship

Section 24 of the Matrimonial Causes Act 1973 grants the court extensive jurisdiction to adjust property rights of parties on the break up of a marriage, and to order one party to transfer property to the other. The assignment of a secure tenancy in pursuance of a property adjustment order made in connection with matrimonial proceedings is allowed under section 91 (3)(b) of the Housing Act 1985. In the case of a secure tenancy the court has wide powers to order transfer between the parties to a divorce, decree of nullity or judicial separation. Assured periodic tenancies, however, may, in general, only be assigned with the landlord's consent, see section 15 of the Housing Act 1988. The court, however, also has power to transfer, by its own order, secure and assured tenancies. Section 7 and Schedule 1 of the Matrimonial Homes Act 1983 (as amended) provide that where one spouse is entitled singly or jointly with the other to occupy a dwelling by virtue of, inter alia, a secure or assured tenancy, then on grant of a divorce, decree of nullity, or judicial separation, or at any time thereafter, the court may make an order transferring the tenancy, its benefits and burdens, from the spouse entitled to occupy to the other spouse, the transfer to take effect on the date specified in the order. The tenancy has to be in existence when the application for transfer is made, but an attempted surrender thereafter will not defeat the courts' powers, see *Lewis v Lewis* [1985] AC 828, [1985] 2 All ER 449. Though there is an apparent power to transfer a tenancy after divorce this may not be real, in cases where the former spouse/tenant is no longer in occupation of the dwelling. In relation to a secure tenancy, for example, the tenancy is only secure while the tenant occupies the dwelling as his/her only or principal home. If the tenant is no longer in occupation the tenancy is not secure and not within the powers of the court. Some commentators therefore advise transfers should always be sought on divorce while others counsel seeking an order from the court under section 2 (4) of the 1983 Act during marriage that the non-tenant's rights of occupation are to endure after termination.

Under section 22 of the Matrimonial and Family Proceedings Act 1984 the court has the same power to transfer a secure or assured tenancy as it has under the Matrimonial Homes Act 1983, Schedule 1 on the grant of a divorce etc, where leave is given to apply for an order for financial relief, provided the dwelling-house has at some time during the marriage been a matrimonial home, this latter is also a general requirement under section 1(10) of the 1983 Act in proceedings under that Act, see *Hall v King* (1987) 19 HLR 440 where the male spouse rented a dwelling for the female after their separation though they never jointly lived there: it was held the transfer powers did not apply to this non-matrimonial home.

Where the court makes a transfer under the powers of the 1983 Act there is no assignment, hence the consent of the landlord is not required, but under Rules of the Court made under Para 8(i) of Schedule I of the Act the landlord must be given an opportunity to be heard; any arguments put forward by the landlord have to be taken into account before an order is made. What may concern a landlord most is 'Who is liable for rent arrears, if any?' Where a joint tenancy is transferred into a sole name there is no problem, because a joint tenant is 'jointly and severally' liable for past rent. Where, however, a sole tenancy is transferred Para 2 (2) of Schedule 1 of the 1983 Act provides the spouse losing the tenancy is exempt from liability to pay future rent due after the transfer. No specific mention is made of arrears, though by implication that debt lies with the person who incurred it, not with the transferee. Where a joint tenancy becomes a sole tenancy after relationship breakdown, 83% of authorities surveyed by Kay, A, Legg C, and Foot J, for *The 1980 Tenants' Rights in Practice*, had a policy of requiring the burden of arrears to be borne by the resulting sole tenant. Also despite the fact a *new* sole tenant has no legal respons-ibility for arrears, 22% said they would require that tenant to assume responsibility where the previous tenancy had been solely in the other partner's name.

The court may make an order under paragraph 5 of the schedule to direct who is to be responsible for what past debts in respect of the dwelling. It is therefore a dubious practice for a landlord to demand a transferee should discharge rent arrears incurred by a former sole tenant – and in Scotland it is specifically declared illegal, see section 20 (2) (a) of the Housing (Scotland) Act 1987. In England such a practice may be maladministration – see David Hughes's work with Stephen Jones at [1979] Journal of Social Welfare Law 273 at 286-287.

The above jurisdiction only applies to spouses. Save where the Children Act 1989 applies (see further below) courts have no jurisdiction to alter property entitlements of partners; they may only declare their rights under the general principles of the law of property. The result will be that partners will either be found to be joint tenants or one will be the sole tenant while the other is generally no more than a licensee; these matters have already been generally considered. Where, however, the parties are joint periodic tenants, irrespective of marital status, one of them may affect the property rights of both and, with the co-operation of the landlord, go on to achieve the grant of a new tenancy either of the former joint home or another property.

In *Greenwich London Borough Council v McGrady* (1982) 81 LGR 288 it was held that notice to quit from one joint secure periodic tenant was sufficient to determine the rights of both. This ruling was subsequently accepted in *Hammersmith and Fulham London Borough v Monk* [1992] 1 AC 478, [1992] 1 All ER 1. There the defendant and his partner were joint tenants of a council flat on a weekly joint tenancy, terminable by four weeks' notice. The partners quarrelled; the woman left and gave notice to quit in due form without the defendant's knowledge or consent. The House of Lords considered the ordinary rules of contract clearly indicated a joint periodic tenancy at common law may be terminated by one tenant irrespective of whether the other concurs. Notice to quit destroys the consensus necessary for the continued existence of the contract. Notice by one joint tenant (*provided it is in due form*) is, as a general rule, effective to bring a joint tenancy to an end. This is the rule concerning secure and assured tenancies. But the notice to quit must be in due form if the above principle is to be relied on. Thus in *Wandsworth London Borough Council v Brown* (1987) Legal Action, (September) p 13, notice to quit did not comply with section 5 of the Protection from Eviction Act 1977 which says notice must be in writing and must be given at least four weeks before it is due to take effect. The notice was ineffective to determine the tenancy. Note also *Community Housing Association v Hoy* (1988) Legal Action, (December) p 18. On similar facts to the above the notice was ineffective. The departing tenant then served a second notice of correct length, but found the tenancy agreement forbade the unilateral ending of a joint tenancy and therefore, the notice remained ineffective.

Note further *Hounslow London Borough Council v Pilling* [1994] 1 All ER 432, [1993] 1 WLR 1242, which reinforces the necessity for care by andlords in such cases. An authority had granted a weekly secure joint tenancy to a man and a woman. The tenancy agreement was on a standard printed form, the couple were described as the 'tenant', and both were declared to have all rights and liabilities of the tenancy. Clause 14 of the agreement allowed tenants to give four weeks written notice to quit, or 'such lesser period as the council may accept'. The tenancy commenced on Monday 22 April 1991 but, after making allegations of domestic violence, the woman left on Friday 6 December 1991, writing to the authority that she wished to terminate her tenancy 'with immediate effect'. The authority accepted this as notice to quit, informed the man he was no longer a tenant, and in due course sought possession against him.

Was the woman's letter a valid notice to quit? The court began by pointing out that, as the tenancy was weekly and had begun on a Monday, the earliest date on which a notice given on Friday 6 December could take effect was Monday 16 December. In response the Council relied on Clause 14 of the tenancy agreement which enabled them to accept a lesser period of notice than four weeks. The court considered that, though it was said in *Monk* that a secure joint tenancy could be terminated by an 'appropriate notice to quit' by one of two joint tenants, that also means it cannot be terminated by an inappropriate notice. A notice which did not give the period of notice required by the common law or by the terms of the tenancy was an inappropriate notice. But the council argued that the woman's notice was within the terms of Clause 14 . That gave them the ability to accept a lesser period of notice. Not so, said the court. Clause 14 effectively allowed immediate termination by a tenant, even in the middle of a tenancy period. It was therefore a break clause. The woman's letter was not notice to quit, at all but a letter operating the break clause.

The court added the council had to lose because any notice to quit to be effective under the rule in *Monk* must also comply with Section 5 of the Protection from Eviction Act 1977 ie it must be given for a minimum of four weeks before the date on which it is to take effect. The woman's letter did not comply with that rule and should not have been accepted by the council.

Where one of two joint periodic secure or assured tenants wishes to give notice to quit effective to end the rights of both, that notice must be:

1)   in writing;
2)   of a minimum period of four weeks given before the notice is due to take effect;
3)   expressed to take effect at the end of the appropriate contractual period, ie, in a weekly tenancy at the end of a week counting from the day of the week on which the tenancy began;
4)   of the minimum period which, apart from the rule in section 5 of the 1977 Act, is the minimum period required by common law, ie, the period of notice for any periodic tenancy greater in length than four weeks must be a period equal to the length of the tenancy, so for a two monthly periodic tenancy the period of notice is two months;
5)   given in accordance with a term of the tenancy which allows notice to quit only to be given in accordance with the due requirements of law.

Break clauses in local authority tenancy agreements must not be used where it is wished to rely on the *Monk* principle, and it appears they should appear separately from ordinary 'notice to quit' clauses.

There is nothing to prevent the tenant who gives notice to quit from being given a new sole tenancy of the former joint home, or another property. Nor is there anything to prevent the other joint tenant from being given a new tenancy. In theory use of the unilateral termination method entitles the joint tenant whose rights are destroyed to bring an action for breach of trust. Jointly tenanted premises are held on trust by the tenants as trustees for themselves. The notice to quit is a breach of trust for it destroys the trust property. In practice litigation does not appear to have occurred, but in principle an action for damages could be pursued, and might be, for example, where notice to quit frustrated the exercise of the Right to Buy. See further 'Ouster Orders, Property Adjustment and Council Housing', Williams C, 18 Family Law , pp 438-443.

Though local authority landlords cannot prevent tenants from availing themselves of the principle in *Monk*, to accept unilateral notice to quit without giving warning to the other tenant may amount to maladminstration (see further Hughes, D, and Buck, T G *Housing and Relationship Breakdown* (2nd edn Revised, London, National Housing and Town Planning Council, 1993, paras 4.5-4.21).

Marital disputes may also have consequences for other proceedings between landlord and tenant.

In *Wandsworth London Borough Council v Fadayomi* [1987] 3 All ER 474, [1987] 1 WLR 1473 a husband and wife lived in a council flat which was in the husband's name. They lived there with their two children. The marriage broke down and divorce proceedings started. Before their conclusion, the council sought possession under Ground 10, Part II, Schedule 2 of the Housing Act 1985. The court had to decide whether suitable accommodation within para 1, Part IV, Schedule 2 of the 1985 Act would be available for the husband and his family if possession were granted. The wife wished to be joined as a party to the proceedings, but the county court registrar refused this. The wife appealed on the ground that, because of the divorce proceedings, 'suitable accommodation' in the context meant separate suitable accommodation for her and her children. The Court of Appeal considered every member of a tenant's family living in premises subject to possession proceedings has a potential interest in those proceedings. They may wish, for example, to object to alternative accommodation offered. In such circumstances it is appropriate to join them as defendants to the proceedings. In the present case the factors to be established before an order for possession could be made had not been established and the order would be set aside.

Cases falling within the Children Act 1989

It has long been trite law that matrimonial remedies for rearranging property on the breakdown of a relationship apply only between the married. The Children Act 1989 appears to have altered this, at least for partners who also have children. In *K v K* [1992] 2 All ER 727, [1992] 1 WLR 530, the parents of four young children were unmarried. They were joint tenants of a four-bedroomed council house. Their relationship broke down in June 1991 and the mother was granted an order in the county court giving her custody, care and control of the children with staying access to the father. The father remained living in the house and in September 1991, on an application by the mother that came before the same judge in the county court, the father was ordered to transfer his interest to the mother under the provisions of section 11B of the Guardianship of Minors Act 1971, as amended, provisions now found in section 15 and Schedule 1 of the 1989 Act.

These provisions currently state:

'Schedule 1 (1) on an application made by a parent or guardian
of a child, or by any person in whose favour a residence order is
in force with respect to a child, the court may ... make ...

(e)   an order requiring either or both parents of a child:
  (i)   to transfer to the applicant for the benefit of a child; or
  (ii)   to transfer to the child himself, such property to which the
         parent is , or the parents are entitled (either in possession
         or in reversion) as may be specified in the order.
(3)   The powers conferred by this paragraph may be exercised
        at any time.'

Schedule 1, paragraph 16 goes on to include within the definition of 'parent': any party to a marriage (whether or not subsisting) in relation to whom a child is a child of the family, ie 'parent' includes a step parent who has treated a child as his/her own.

Following the county court decision the father appealed. The Court of Appeal found that 'benefit' in the 1989 Act is not confined to benefits of a financial kind. The court can make an order conferring purely welfare benefits on a child; and, accordingly, the court was entitled in appropriate circumstances to order a transfer of rights in a property from one joint tenant to the other for the benefit of their children. However, the court allowed the appeal because of defects in the original judgement. The judge had failed to give proper consideration to all the matters to be taken into account, in particular the father's accrued rights under the 'right to buy' (RTB) provisions in the Housing Act 1985; and accordingly, the case was remitted to the county court.

Schedule 1, paragraph 4 of the 1989 Act details the matters to be taken into account. These include the income, caring capacity, property and financial resources of the parents, both current and future, together with their needs, obligations and responsibilities; the needs, etc of the child, and its physical and mental condition, and the way in which it may be educated.

(1992) Legal Action, (September) p 20 reported that *K v K* had been reheard by the county court. The mother had applied for the transfer of the father's interest to her for the benefit of the children. The county court judge inquired into the father's circumstances and found he would not be able to exercise RTB, and accordingly made the order sought.

In contrast with *K v K*, however, note *Re J (a minor)* (1992) Times, 12 November. A female joint secure tenant applied on behalf of her child for a transfer of the joint tenancy into her sole name. The other tenant was neither her spouse, nor the father of the child. It was held that the case did not fall within the terms of the Children Act 1989 because the male joint tenant did not fall within the meaning of 'parent' in that section.

The limits of the jurisdiction should be carefully noted. In the first place it is discretionary, to be exercised on the basis of certain considerations. Secondly the court may only make orders against those who are 'parents', that is the actual biological parents of the child in question and step-parents who, within marriage, have treated the child as their own. Finally the court may only order a parent to transfer property which that person is able to transfer.

The housing consequences of relationship breakdown.

In the late 1970s and into the 1980s orthodox wisdom on rehousing following relationship breakdown was contained in the HSAG's *The Housing of One-Parent Families.*

1)   Authorities should remember that on the break-up of marriage two tenancies may be needed rather than one. This 'two for one' element should be remembered in computing future housing needs.

2)   Where a man is living in the former matrimonial home with a woman who is not his wife, following the breakdown of marriage, and the court makes an order against him in respect of that home, eviction leads to an increase in the number of homeless persons.

3)   Where the husband has developed no new relationship and is alone following marital breakdown, the authority should attempt to rehouse him bearing in mind the following factors:

    (a)   will the man be living near enough his children to be able to see them;

    (b)   will he need to be able to have them to stay;

    (c)   is he expecting to remarry;

    (d)   is he emotionally upset and unable to cope with eviction on top of losing his wife and children?

The general tenor of the HSAG's findings was that, wherever possible, housing should be provided for parties leaving the matrimonial home.

After marital break-ups where there are children the parent with whom they live will face other problems, in particular those of a financial nature. The HSAG also made recommendations with regard to local authority housing practices in relation to such one-parent families.

1)   The best policy, would be to house one-parent families in ordinary family housing in a mixed development, as such accommodation accords with their needs and helps prevent social stigmatism.

2)   Even where both former partners have been responsible for rent arrears, these may have arisen during a period of stress. Authorities should make arrangements for gradual repayment of arrears, but should not otherwise penalise the parties.

3)   Liaison between housing and social service departments is essential in order to provide all-round support for the one parent family. Though this is difficult where services are administered by different tiers of the local government system, such co-operation is essential if financial and emotional distress amongst one-parent families is to be reduced.

4)   A wife who retains, or is granted possession of, the former matrimonial home may not wish to stay there. Requests for transfers to housing closer to relatives, schools, places of work or nursery facilities, or to the area of another authority, should be treated sympathetically. A transfer request should not be made conditional on a woman paying

off arrears of rent for which her husband was solely responsible. Authorities should be prepared to make rapid housing exchanges in the case of any woman who fears violence from her former husband. Similar conclusions were reached in the Finer Report, Cmnd 5629.

How far can these liberal aims be pursued today by authorities, even with the assistance of associations? As we described in the first part of the chapter the rate of marriage breakdown has increased dramatically and it is not unrealistic to suppose that the rate of dissolution for unmarried relationships is no less than for married. The study by Holmans, Nandy and Brown shows that divorce increases the chance of women becoming local authority tenants and as the number of divorcees are expected to increase by 1.3million between 1987 and 2000 there are implications for the public rented sector in housing.

As we have shown divorce often results in a loss of owner-occupier status, with women in particular becoming authority tenants. Of 145,000 divorces a year, about 65,000-70,000 owner occupier marriages would be dissolved. About 75,000-80,000 divorced persons would continue as owner occupiers, but 30,000 people would become tenants, some 50% of these being authority tenants. (Holmans, AE, Nandy, S, and Brown, AC *Social Trends*, 1987.

The 1987 findings are largely corroborated by subsequent work, see McCarthy, P and Simpson, B, *Issues in Post Divorce Housing*, 1991. They found that the housing system is ill-suited to meet the demand for housing stimulated by high divorce rates. The findings also show that divorce is likely to result in slippage from owner-occupation – younger married women with children in semi or unskilled work being noted as unlikely to remain as owner-occupiers following divorce.

The disposal of 1.5 million public sector dwellings under RTB and other disposals since 1979 has done much to deprive social landlords of the stock to meet demand for housing consequent on relationship breakdown. The dearth of appropriate rehousing properties is a problem compounded by the complexity of the legal issues involved, already examined above, and the lack of a clearly articulated central policy on family housing matters.

The issue of housing and relationship breakdown falls between departmental boundaries. Environment ministers regard the matter as one for the Lord Chancellor's department to deal with via matrimonial law. The Lord Chancellor tends to regard it as an issue in housing law. However, ministers are not prepared to make changes in the law simply to deal with a problem faced by social landlords. They also seem to ignore the position of partners who fall outside the scope of matrimonial law anyway, despite the fact that one in four couples now live together for at least some time before marriage, and one-third of a million women under 50 are cohabitees (1987 figures).

The result of this dislocation between housing and matrimonial law is that housing and legal practitioners have had to 'cobble together' such solutions as they can. In this context the findings of Kay, A, Legg, C, and Foot, J, in *The 1980 Tenants' Rights in Practice* are of great interest.

Their report indicated only 20% of 140 responding authorities would rehouse a partner from a broken marriage who did not have custody of children and who did not otherwise qualify as a homeless person. This fell to 1% in relation to rehousing a childless former cohabitee. Where no children were involved, 85% of authorities would not rehouse both former marriage partners and 87% would not aid former cohabitees. Some authorities required legal evidence of separation or marriage breakdown. 34% of authorities surveyed required settlement of a divorce and associated property issues before a woman could obtain a tenancy. The concept of exclusive custody is now, of course, redundant under the Children Act 1989. Under this legislation the paramount consideration, see section 1 of the Act, is the child's welfare, while the basic notion of section 2 is that parental responsibility for a child is not to be foregone, but is joint between a child's parents. The court may, however, under sections 8 and 10 of the 1989 Act make 'residence orders' which, for the time being, fix with whom a child is to live.

Women often have to show they have taken action under matrimonial legislation before they can receive aid from authorities or associations. The policies of some authorities have been punitive against women and frequently have led to inappropriate demands for court orders. Women have had to occupy unsuitable temporary accommodation during lengthy court proceedings while authorities dealt with the issue of housing.

Authorities who have required tenants with broken relationships to take particular courses of legal action as pre-conditions to obtaining a tenancy, have sometimes been found guilty of maladministration. Tenants should not be required to regulate their private lives to suit the administrative convenience of landlords. If the law does not require the taking of a particular step, then neither should an authority, a practice that was, condemned in *R v Ealing London Borough Council, ex p Sidhu* (1982) 80 LGR 534 and see Hughes, D, and Jones, SR [1979] JSWL 273.

Some authorities have attempted to have a pro-active role in regulating domestic violence. Kay, Legg and Foot discovered a number of authorities had imposed tenancy obligations dealing with and prohibiting actual or threatened domestic violence. Breach of such a condition could lead to possession proceedings being taken. The report, however, could give no instance of such a clause being tested in court. A court might require a considerable amount of proof of violence before accepting it would be reasonable to allow an authority to obtain possession under such a clause.

Otherwise, there is a considerable diversity of practice in relationship breakdown cases between authorities. This is further highlighted by Frances Logan's 1986 study *Homelessness and Relationship Breakdown*. One authority had a detailed written policy on relationship breakdown and housing which in part resulted from external pressure from a housing aid centre. The policy included rehousing both partners on breakdown. Another authority did not rehouse both partners because this would be at the expense of other priority groups. Instead there was an internal appeal system against housing decisions in relationship breakdown cases, but this did not appear to have been very well publicised. One authority with a policy of rehousing both partners had subsequently extended it to cover all cohabitees, couples in homosexual relationships and those living as a unit through other family ties, such as aunt and niece, for example. However, officers of that authority were concerned that implementing such a liberal policy would become increasingly difficult as housing resources became more limited.

Kay, Legg and Foot further discovered liberal policies on paper may not work in practice unless staff are adequately trained in applying the policies and tenants are informed of them. In one case an authority rehoused a woman's ex-partner close to her. She then suffered violence and the authority was found guilty of maladministration.

Some authorities have taken a much more resistant line in assisting those who lack accommodation following relationship breakdown. This is a consequence of the increasing use of Part III of the Housing Act 1985 as a device to ration the supply of housing. Women have been refused rehousing or assistance under homelessness provisions if they have an interest in their current home, or where the authority have instructed them to resort to their rights under matrimonial law. In some cases an offer of rehousing may not be made to a woman unless she first obtains an injunction or ouster order against the man who is abusing her. In other cases a woman forced from her home by violence may be adjudged intentionally homeless unless she obtains a matrimonial or domestic violence order.

The general view already stated is that domestic remedies should normally be used as temporary expedients. Their use is drastic and not routine, only to be used in emergencies. The court may be unwilling to grant a domestic remedy ousting a violent man from the former home where the effect is to place the woman in the one spot where he knows she will be, thus making her particularly vulnerable. It may be unreasonable to expect a woman to stay in a dwelling in relation to which she has little chance of obtaining an order capable of giving her real and lasting peace and security.

McCarthy and Simpson's work casts interesting light on the practice of authorities in discharging the duty to accommodate following homelessness consequent on relationship breakdown, and the responses of applicants in such situations. A number of applicants expressed dissatisfaction with accommodation offered by authorities. Women may particularly voice complaints over accommodation, especially where they fear for its effects on their children because of perceptions of high crime, weak parental discipline, poor schools, etc, in the area. There may also be adverse reactions to moving into accommodation which, though reasonable and suitable from a legal point of view, is dirty, ill-decorated and may be lacking in repair.

Men homeless following relationship breakdown also report that, where they qualify for accommodation, properties offered are frequently of poor quality. This exacerbates already bruised feelings where a man claims he was the 'innocent' party in the divorce. The allocation of single person's accommodation in a stigmatised area of a district can affect the viability of a divorced man's access to his children.

Future argument on how social landlords may best respond to relationship breakdown may polarise. McCarthy and Simpson argue present day approaches are fixated with a 'special needs' view of issues, seeing the single parent family as a group at whom particular resources are targetted, very often as a type of safety net to ensure recipients of benefits do not fall too far into poverty. They argue that children of divorced parents should have equivalent 'life chances' to their contemporaries whose parents do not divorce. (By analogy the argument can be extended to those whose parents never married in the first place.) McCarthy and Simpson's justification is that children are society's future, and they point to the enormously important, but generally hidden, role of women in producing this 'human capital' by their work in the home as mothers. The provision of a range of decent affordable accommodation, some of it by social landlords, to meet the needs of a society where relationship breakdown is increasingly common is thus justifiable, for it especially recognises the role of female parents in producing and caring for the next generation of economically active people.

Obviously, housing provision by itself is not enough, and McCarthy and Simpson acknowledge it must be accompanied by appropriate welfare and employment benefits. They are forced to acknowledge there would be considerable costs incurred in realising their proposals, but claim the cost would be more than met by abolishing mortgage interest relief. Against McCarthy and Simpson's vision, however, is ranged a powerful and emotional argument that the family as an institution needs to be preserved and rejuvenated, and that individuals should learn that their actions have consequences for which they must take some responsibility. This latter argument is attractive to many in the Conservative Party; it is not without Labour supporters. The arguments cut across races, sexes and social classes. There are many who view with dismay what is perceived as a decline in order in many inner urban areas, who find it disturbing that many young men grow up with no model of responsible male parenthood, and who do not find it desirable that society should encourage beliefs that relationship breakdown carries with it no adverse consequences, and that standards of living and lifestyles are not affected by it.

The long term outcome of this matter is beyond prediction. In the short term those who provide social housing must continue to palliate problems, and look to themselves for solutions. They need to establish policies on relationship breakdown and housing. Policies, should wherever possible, include the following principles:

(1)   where resources permit both parties to relationship breakdown should be rehoused, either in the same district or by co-operation with other

    districts, in areas sufficiently separate to prevent recurrent incidents of violence;

(2)   prohibitions on domestic violence should be included in tenancy agreements;

(3)   women who are forced from their homes by violence should not automatically be regarded as intentionally homeless if they do not rely on domestic remedies;

(4)   sympathetic handling is needed of those made homeless as a consequence of relationship breakdown;

(5)   staff must receive appropriate training to implement policy efficiently and sensitively; this includes training in the legal issues, and appointment of specialist officers to ensure relationship breakdowns are appropriately dealt with;

(6)   good practice requires all homes known to be subject to matrimonial disputes should be recorded as such so that inappropriate action with regard to the property rights of the parties is not taken inadvertently;

(7)   parties should not be required to take steps not legally required simply to suit the administrative convenience of landlords;

(8)   landlords' policies must be clearly spelt out to tenants and potential tenants;

(9)   in the provision of accommodation authorities must not discriminate on ground of race or sex, see *R v Tower Hamlets London Borough Council, ex p Commission for Racial Equality* (1991) Legal Action, (June) p 16, neither may an authority plead impecuniousity as a reason for not fulfilling a duty to accommodate under Part III of the Housing Act 1985, see *R v Haringey London Borough Council, ex p Garner* (1991) Legal Action, (September) p 16.

None of the foregoing will remove the need for other national legal and policy changes, but collectively they may alleviate stress locally.

Succession rights

In housing terms death is not 'the only true unraveller'; legal personality survives physical extinction: both are secure and assured tenancies 'property' which can descend to those related to a deceased tenant, while in some cases an inter vivos transfer is possible.

Secure tenancies

A secure periodic tenancy, or a secure fixed term tenancy granted after 5 November 1982, are not capable of being assigned save in three situations;

1)   under the 'right to exchange' provided by section 92 of the Housing Act 1985, see Chapter Three;
2)   pursuant to an order made under section 29 of the Matrimonial Causes Act 1973 (see above);
3)   where the assignment is to a person who would be qualified to succeed if the tenant had died immediately before the assignment. See section 91 of the 1985 Act.

It is possible for a secure tenant to pass on during life his/her home to someone otherwise qualified to succeed after the tenant's death, despite prohibition on assignment in the tenancy, see *Peabody Donation Fund (Governors) v Higgins* [1983] 3 All ER 122, [1983] 1 WLR 1091 though such an assignment might give rise to a possession action for breach of tenancy condition. For example, an elderly tenant could transfer to a single daughter who has lived with him all her life in the house in question, the secure tenancy of a three bedroom council house. The new tenant could not then be subject to possession proceedings on grounds of under occupation following the former tenant's death, see Chapter Three, and section 89 and Schedule 2, Ground 16 of the 1985 Act; the tenancy would exist by way of assignment and not by way of succession.

There are, however, technical requirements before assignment can be effective. In *Crago v Julian* [1992] 1 All ER 744, [1992] 1 WLR 372 a married couple occupied a privately rented flat on a weekly tenancy. On divorce the man gave a written undertaking to do everything necessary to effect a transfer of the flat to his wife; in fact he did nothing. The woman continued to pay rent and dealt with the managing agents; they continued to issue new rent books in the husband's name. In 1987 the agents realised the former husband had given up all interest in the property. They refused to accept further rent and in 1988 commenced possession proceedings. The issue was whether the tenancy had been assigned. The Court of Appeal pointed out the creation and assignment of interests in land are governed by section 53(1) (a) of theLaw of Property Act 1925 which required transfer in writing. To this there was only one exception, namely under section 54 (1) of the 1925 Act under which a lease not exceeding three years taking effect in possession at full market rent may be created by spoken words. But the assignment of any lease requires the written form of deed. As no such deed had been used in the present case no assignment had taken place.

The rule is the same in the public sector, see *London Borough of Croydon v Buston and Triance* (1991) 24 HLR 36 – a deed is required for an effective assignment of a secure tenancy. Deeds must comply with the requirements of the Law of Property (Miscellaneous Provisions) Act 1989 section 1. A deed need not be sealed, but must be: in documentary form; signed and witnessed as a deed; intended to be a deed, and delivered as a deed.

Note that where a fixed term tenancy granted before 5 November 1982 is assigned outside the three cases outlined above, the consequence is that it continues at common law but ceases to be 'secure', nor can it subsequently become 'secure'.

But who are those who are qualified to succeed to a secure tenancy, and how does succession operate ?

Section 89 provides that where a secure periodic tenant dies, and there is a person qualified to succeed (see below) the tenancy vests in that person. Where there is more than one qualified person the successor will be determined by the following rules:

1) the tenant's spouse has priority.
2) where there are two or more other qualified persons they may agree among themselves who is to succeed, otherwise the landlord selects.

Where there is no qualified successor under section 89 (3) and (4) the tenancy ceases to be secure, save where the case may fall within the matrimonial jurisdiction under section 24 of the Matrimonial Causes Act 1973, and cannot subsequently become secure. The effect of the provisions are explained in *Wirral Borough Council v Smith* (1982) 262 Estates Gazette 1298. On the death of a secure tenant, the secure tenancy comes to an end, but a contractual tenancy remains, and to bring that to an end notice to quit (NTQ) in proper form must be served whether by or on the personal representatives (PRs) of the deceased. If there are no PRs the notice should be served on the President of the Family Division at the Royal Courts of Justice.

Where a deceased tenant had a fixed term secure tenancy, the tenancy remains secure under section 90 of the Housing Act 1985 until vested or otherwise disposed of during the administration of the deceased's estate (save where that vesting etc is in pursuance of an order made under section 24 of the Matrimonial Causes Act 1973, or where the vesting etc, is in a person qualified to succeed) or it is known that on vesting etc the tenancy will not be secure, eg it will vest in a person not qualified to succeed. A fixed term tenancy which ceases to be secure cannot become secure, but, of course, will otherwise continue for its contractual term etc.

Those qualified to succeed are identified by section 87 of the 1985 Act. Such a person is one who:

1) occupied the dwelling/house as his/her only or principal home at the time of the tenants' death; and
2) is either the spouse of the deceased tenant, or another member of the deceased's family who has resided with the deceased throughout the period of 12 months ending with the deceased's death, save, in either case, where the deceased was him/herself a successor (see further below).

A 'member of the family' is defined by section 113 of the 1985 Act to include those living together as husband and wife, and those who are the parents, grandparents, children, grandchildren, brothers, sisters, uncles, aunts, nephews and nieces of the deceased, treating relationships by marriage as by blood, the half blood as the whole, step-children as children and illegitimate children as legitimate children of their mothers and reputed fathers.

The effect of these provisions has been considered by the courts. In *Waltham Forest London Borough Council v Thomas* [1992] 2 AC 198, [1992] 3 All ER 244, the defendant lived with his half brother for two and half years in property owned by the authority of which the brother was a secure tenant. On 11 April 1988 they moved to another council house, of which the brother also became a secure tenant. On 21 April the brother died. The defendant claimed to succeed to his brother's tenancy under section 87 of the Act of 1985. The plaintiffs disputed the claim on the ground that the defendant did not reside with his deceased brother in the same premises throughout the requisite 12 month-period. The House of Lords held that section 87 of the 1985 Act required the successor to a tenancy should have resided with the tenant during the period of 12 months ending with the tenant's death, but did not require the residence to have taken place for the whole of that period in the premises to which succession was claimed: and, accordingly, the defendant was entitled to succeed.

In this connection 'residence' connotes making one's home with the deceased. Even where a familial relationship exists, simply for a person to move in with a secure tenant does not automatically make that person a joint tenant with the original tenant, see *Hamilton District Council v Lennon* 1990 SLT 533.

The definition of 'family' in section 113 of the 1985 Act does not extend to lesbian/gay relationships nor to friends living together, nor to an older man/woman living with a younger man/woman unless cohabitation exists between them, see *Harrogate Borough Council v Simpson* (1986) 17 HLR 205.

With regard to secure tenancies there may be only one succession, and section 88 (1)-(3) of the 1985 Act provides a tenant shall be deemed to be a successor, inter alia, where:
1)   the tenancy vested by virtue of section 89;
2)   the tenancy was joint but has become sole;
3)   the tenancy vested on the death of the previous tenant;
4)   the tenancy was assigned, save that a tenant who was an assignee under section 24 of the Matrimonial Causes Act 1973 is a deemed successor only if the assignor was also a successor, and similarly a person who is a tenant by way of exchange under the right to exchange (see section 92 of the 1985 Act) is similarly a successor only if he/she was a successor in relation to the tenancy which he/she assigned under the exchange provisions.

Note also section 88(4) of the 1985 Act which provides that where within six months of the coming to an end of a secure periodic tenancy the tenant becomes possessed of another periodic secure tenancy, and the tenant was a successor under the former tenancy, and under the current tenancy either the dwelling house or the landlord, or both, are the same as before, the tenant is a deemed successor unless the tenancy provides otherwise.

It is not hard to mistake the effect of the foregoing rules as the cases show. In *Epping Forest District Council v Pomphrett and Pomphrett* (1990) 22 HLR 475, in 1948 Mr Pomphrett was granted a tenancy of a council house. In 1978 he died intestate and no letters of administration were taken out. The authority granted the tenancy to his widow in her name. She died intestate in 1985. No letters of administration were taken out, and her children applied to take over the tenancy. The authority claimed a single succession had already taken place. The court held that on Mr Pomphrett's death his tenancy had vested in the President of the Family Division who had no power to assign or vest it in someone else. When Mrs Pomphrett was allowed to stay on a new tenancy was created and she became the secure tenant when the Housing Act came into force. Her children were entitled to succeed to her tenancy. Likewise note *Bassetlaw District Council v Renshaw* [1991] EGCS 71. Mr and Mrs Renshaw were joint tenants of a council house. Mr Renshaw terminated the joint tenancy and thereafter the authority granted a new sole tenancy to Mrs Renshaw. She lived in the house with her son and some years later died. The son claimed successfully to be a successor.

Assured tenancies

Mention has been made of restrictions on assignment of assured tenancies under section 15 (1) of the Housing Act 1988. It is an implied term of every periodic assured tenancy that, save with the landlord's consent, the tenant may not assign the tenancy in whole or in part, nor sublet or part with possession of the whole or any part of the dwelling house. Nor is there any requirement that the landlord must not unreasonably refuse consent to a request to assign. This implied term is superseded under section 15 (3) if there is a specific provision dealing with the position concerning assignments, subletting, etc, and where a premium is required to be paid on the grant or renewal of the tenancy the implied restriction does not apply.

Section 17 of the 1988 Act provides for succession to an assured periodic tenancy by a spouse, which term includes a person living with the deceased tenant as his/her husband/wife, see section 17 (4). The conditions for succession are that immediately before the death of the sole assured tenant the spouse was occupying the dwelling as his/her only or principal home, and the deceased must not have been a successor, ie, under section 17 (2) someone in whom the tenancy had previously vested by virtue of section 17, or someone who became a sole tenant of the dwelling by survivorship following the death of the other joint tenant. If on the death, by virtue of section 17 (4), there is more than one person qualified to succeed as a spouse under the foregoing provisions, section 17 (5) states they may choose who is to be treated as the spouse; in default the county court shall decide.

Housing associations and succession

For association tenants having secure tenancies on 15 January 1989, the position concerning succession is as for authority tenancies. For other tenants the position is 'governed' by the guidance issued by the Housing Corporation as 'The Tenants' Guarantee' under section 36A of the Housing Associations Act 1985, and, to a lesser degree, the National Federation of Housing Association's (NATFED) model tenancy agreement annexed to the original version of the section 36A 'guarantee'. The Housing Corporation first issued its guidance as Housing Corporation Circular No 43/88; this was revised and reissued in 1991 as HC Circular 29/91. Not all housing associations use the NATFED model agreement.

As currently issued the 'guarantee' counsels associations to consider whether they wish to grant, by contract, rights of succession to members of a tenant's family who have been living with that tenant for the year before the tenant's death, and who have been looking after the tenant, or who have accepted responsibility for dependents of the tenant, or who would be made homeless if required to vacate the accommodation. The 'guarantee' advises associations to use tenancy agreements which permit assignment only where a Court order under section 24 of the Matrimonial Causes Act 1973 is concerned, or by way of exchange between limited classes of tenant. Associations are advised to consider whether they wish to permit a right of assignment by a tenant to a person who would be entitled to succeed to the tenancy on death; those associations which are charitable are reminded to consider carefully whether granting such a right would conflict with their charitable objects.

Further reading

Austerberry, H and Watson, S *Women on the Margins. A study of single women's housing problems*, London, The City University, 1983

Bradshaw, J and Millar, J *Lone Parent Families in the UK* (HMSO, 1991)

Bull, J *Housing Consequences of Relationship Breakdown* (HMSO, 1993)

Chapman, T (ed) *Population Matters : The Local Dimension* Paul Chapman, 1993

HSAG *The Housing of One Parent Families*, London. The Department of the Environment, 1978.

Hughes, D J and Jones, S R *Bias in the Allocation and Transfer of Local Authority Housing* (1979) Vol 1 *Journal of Social Welfare Law* 273

Joshi, H (ed) *The Changing Population of Britain* Basil Blackwell, 1989

Kay, A, Legg, C and Foot J *The 1980 Tenants' Rights in Practice*, London, Housing Research Group, The City University.

Levison, D and Atkins, J *The Key to Equality*, London, 1987, Institute of Housing

Logan, F *Homelessness and Relationship Breakdown: How the Law and Housing Policy Affects Women*, London, National Council for One Parent Families, 1986.

McCarthy, P and Simpson, B *Issues in Post Divorce Housing*, Aldershot, 1991, Avebury
Smith, L *Domestic Violence: an overview of the literature* (HMSO, 1989)
Thornton, R 'Homelessness Through Relationship Breakdown: The Local Authorities' Response' [1989] *Journal of Social Welfare Law* 67
Wright, M 'Ouster Orders and Housing Need' (1988) 138 *New Law Journal* 594

Chapter Six

Homelessness

Historical context

Action on behalf of, or rather against, homeless people has been a feature of English local government since the Elizabethan Poor Law. Up to 1948 the Poor Law authorities attempted to curb homelessness by treating homeless people as an 'undeserving poor' and according to the Victorian Poor Law principle of 'less eligibility' the conditions in the workhouse were made deliberately harsh and degrading. Moreover, people not recognised as local could be ejected from the area under the Vagrancy Acts. These two important principles, of less eligibility and the local connection, figure very prominently in contemporary social policy and law and it is somewhat salutory to see how historically rooted are these themes. In the nineteenth century, as Donnison and Ungerson point out, the number of people affected by Poor Law conditions was very considerable. Virtually everyone at that time lived in uncontrolled privately rented accommodation and eviction and homelessness were prevalent. It is very difficult to get a feel for the scale of the problem but even as late as 1911 a quarter of all single men over the age of 65 were living in casual wards of workhouse infirmaries (Donnison and Ungerson, *Housing Policy*, Penguin Books, 1982).

Homelessness is thus a centuries-old phenomenon affecting millions of destitute families, particularly through the operation of the Poor Law. But although a common enough experience, homelessness was only recognised officially as a *housing* problem in the Housing (Homeless Persons) Act 1977.

The aftermath of the Second World War marked an important turning point in the treatment of homeless people, as in so many aspects of national social life. The National Assistance Act 1948 abolished the Poor Law, but continued much of the muddled thinking that characterised that law in failing to see homelessness as a problem in its own right, nor did it create a comprehensive institutional framework to deal with the issue. Section 2(1) of the 1948 Act created the National Assistance Board among whose functions was, under section 17 of the Act, the provision of reception centres for the unsettled. Responsibility for the *wandering* homeless was entrusted to a *national* authority, while the rest of the homeless came within the care of local authority welfare departments under section 21(1) of the 1948 Act: local *housing* authorities had no real responsibility for the homeless.

Administrative confusion was compounded by lack of resources and use of hostel accommodation, while the law gave rise to particular difficulties. Section 21(1)(b) of the 1948 Act created a statutory duty (since repealed) to provide: 'temporary accommodation for persons who are in urgent need thereof, being need arising in circumstances which could not reasonably have been foreseen or in such other circumstances as the authority may in any particular case determine'. In *Southwark London Borough Council v Williams* [1971] Ch 734, [1971] 2 All ER 175, it was held that this imposed no enforceable duty on local authorities.

Neither was there guidance about what constituted 'urgent need' or 'unforeseen circumstances' and local authority practice was highly variable, as it remains to this day, particularly in the application of the test of intentionality. Legal and administrative difficulties became 'confusion worse confounded' following the reorganisation of local government under the Local Government Act 1972. Section 195 and Schedule 23 of that Act converted the duty under section 21(1) of the 1948 Act into a discretion, though reserving power to the Secretary of State to re-impose the duty. The Department of the Environment issued joint circular No 18/74 *Homelessness* (Department of Health and Social Security (DHSS) Circular No 4/74, Welsh Office Circular No 34/74). This stated that: 'suitable accommodation for the homeless should in future be undertaken as an integral part of the statutory responsibility of housing authorities...' However, on 1 February 1974 the Secretary of State for Social Services issued DHSS Local Authority Circular No 13/74. This re-imposed the duty on social services authorities to provide temporary accommodation.

The results were chaotic. The existence of some sort of duty on *social services* authorities encouraged some *housing* authorities to ignore the exhortations of DoE Circular No 18/74. It was obvious urgent changes in the law were necessary, though it was left to a private member, Mr Stephen Ross, to introduce legislation. His Bill was based on a draft already prepared by the Department of the Environment and it achieved a measure of all party support in Parliament. Even so the Bill was considerably amended in Parliament, largely as a result of fears of large numbers of homeless people moving themselves around the country with the object of jumping local authority housing queues.

The 1977 Act was codified with the rest of the housing legislation in 1985 and became Part III of the Housing Act 1985. Hardly was the ink dry before amendments were made by the Housing and Planning Act 1986. In November 1989 the Government published a review of the homeless legislation. This document proposed to keep the existing law broadly as it was. Managerial change was urged to make better use of existing housing stock, closer liaison with associations, preventative advice, and encouragement of those willing to provide lodgings. It was, however, recognised that enhanced central guidance was needed to ensure a greater degree of consistency between local authority homelessness practices.

Further legal changes came under the Children Act 1989 and the National Health Service and Community Care Act 1990, whose details will be considered below. The result is that around the main body of the 1985 Act there is legal provision under:

(1)   Section 21(1)(a) of the National Assistance Act 1948 (as amended) *empowering* (and where the Secretary of State for Health directs, *requiring*) local social services authorities to provide residential accommodation for persons aged 18 or more who are in need of care and attention by reason of age, or other circumstances.

(2)   Section 67(2) of the National Health Service and Community Care Act 1990 which, from 1 April 1993, under SI 1992/2975 extends the above duty to those in need of care by reason of illness or disability.

(3)   Section 20(1) of the Children Act 1989 which requires social service authorities to provide accommodation for children in need within their areas in certain stated circumstances, while other authorities may be *required* to assist in providing accommodation under section 27 of the 1989 Act.

(4)   Schedule 5 of the Supplementary Benefits Act 1976 (as substituted by the Social Security Act 1980) which requires the Secretary of State for Social Security to provide and maintain resettlement units at which those without settled ways of life are afforded temporary board and lodging, and under which the Secretary of State may require councils of counties, metropolitan districts and London boroughs to discharge this function.

By the mid 1990s we are thus in a situation comparable to that of 1972-77. Once again there are overlapping jurisdictions, and the potential for particular applicants to be shuttled between local authority departments. This would seem to be a very likely outcome of the recent proposals to amend the 1985 legislation, with families being forced to move at regular intervals within the PRS. Some local authorities, notably in London, already operate well beyond their boundaries through networks of private landlords. Furthermore no less than three Secretaries of State have an interest in homelessness. This, coupled with a continuing lack of resources, is guaranteed to cause confusion – at the very least.

The nature of homelessness

Before embarking on a detailed description of the law, some space must be given to the wider context of the facts as we know them about homelessness and the policy environment in which the statutes are implemented. The duties originally given to local authorities under the 1977 Act have been relatively unchanged, although as we write are under challenge, and this stability enables a reasonably long view to be taken, particularly regarding the official statistics. Neither should it be forgotten that from the perspective of policy analysis the statutory definition is essentially a rationing device which balances available supply of council tenancies with judgments about 'priority needs.' As a result, homeless people presenting at different local authorities will be faced with very different receptions depending on the policy stance of the particular authority.

Moreover, we have to make clear that the statutory framework with its emphasis on families with children and the elderly not only excludes other groups of people but itself only recognises one form of homelessness. There is an important debate both in policy and, as we will show, in law about what precisely constitutes homelessness. Without some consideration of this debate it will be difficult fully to appreciate the nature of the case law which follows. Is a woman having been driven from her marital home by a violent husband and now living in a women's refuge homeless? Is the accommodation provided by the refuge of such a poor standard as to render it uninhabitable? If so, despite the roof over her head, is she homeless? Does such accommodation happen to be available in the area where she resides? Do the housing advisory services know of its existence and if so will they help her approach the hostel managers?

The official statistics

The emergence of homelessness as a distinctively *housing* issue was triggered by the revelation of a sharp increase in the number of people living in temporary accommodation, particularly but not exclusively, in London in the early 1960s. Evidence of this was collected in John Greve's study *London's Homeless* which was conducted on behalf of the London County Council (Greve, J 1964). This and a subsequent study for the GLC provided very convincing evidence of the gathering tide of homelessness (Greve J et al, *Homelessness in London*, Scottish Academic Press, 1971).

Figure 1 shows that the number of homeless people living in temporary accommodation in Inner London declined after a peak in 1950 but after 1957 numbers rose sharply until the end of Greve's research period – and, as we shall see, this trend continued. Greve showed that the number of homeless families in temporary accommodation in Inner London rose by 51% between

Figure One: Homeless people living in temporary accommodation in Inner London 1949-1970

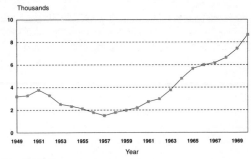

Source: *Greve et al, 1971*

1966 and 1970 and by over 170% in Outer London. Contemporary studies of homelessness in other parts of the country show a similar picture to the London research. A study by Glastonbury, for example, showed a 300% increase between 1963 and 1968 in households entering temporary accommodation in a sample of local authorities in South Wales and the South West of England (Glastonbury, B *Homeless Near A Thousand Homes*, Allen and Unwin, 1971). A feel for the national picture was produced in a study which collated DHSS and Welsh Office data which suggested an increase in people entering temporary accommodation of 120% between 1966 and 1971 (Bailey and Ruddock, 1972). These studies are important because they are the only source of evidence about the rising tide of homelessness and they pre-date the government's own official series of statistics on homelessness which began only in 1971.

As can be seen in Figure 2 overleaf the main feature of the official figures on homelessness is its seemingly inexorable annual increase which continued the pre-1971 trend.

Although the problem has often been associated principally with London all the evidence shows that homelessness affects all authorities' areas, urban and rural. In 1990 nearly 80% of households accepted as homeless were recorded outside London and the place with the highest number of acceptances in relation to total population was Manchester, and it is clear that the fastest rate of increase in officially recorded homelessness has for several decades been outside London (Greve, J *Homelessness in Britain*, Joseph Rowntree Foundation, 1991).

In England and Wales homelessness acceptances have grown since 1978 from 53,000 to nearly 148,000 in 1990. Taking all local authorities in Britain the figure for 1990 alone is nearly 170,000 involving about half a million people, 50% of whom were dependent children. Over the full decade 1980-1990 well over a million households have been accepted by authorities as

Figure Two: Homelessness applications and acceptances by local authorities 1971-1991

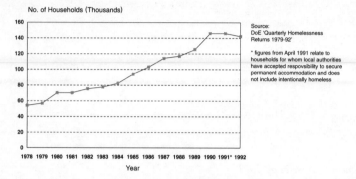

No. of Households (Thousands)

Source:
DoE 'Quarterly Homelessness
Returns 1979-92'

* figures from April 1991 relate to
households for whom local authorities
have accepted repsovsibility to secure
permanent accommodation and does
not include intentionally homeless

Year

homeless and the number of acceptances doubled during the 1980s. These statistics refer only to households housed in some way by authorities and it should be noted that only about half those who apply are accepted and that 80% of these are families with children. None of these figures are, of course, a rigorous measure of the total problem because the net total comprises the year on year additions to the total less those who move out of temporary accommodation.

The proportion of those families statutorily 'rehoused' but placed in 'temporary accommodation' has risen dramatically from under 10,000 per annum in the early 1980s to over 50,000 per annum (140,000 individuals) in the early 1990s. As the supply of council housing has declined during the decade so the number of those placed in temporary habitations has increased. There are three main types of temporary accommodation: bed and breakfast hotels, hostels and the short leasing of private housing. The latter is the largest type and accounts for about half the placements. 'B and B' is the next largest category and over the last five years about 12,000 families per annum have been placed in such accommodation, frequently far from temporary and often in dingy and unsafe premises.

Causes

How do we explain the large national increase in homelessness over the last few decades? We caution against a simplistic, single explanation because it is certain that there are several layers of causality ranging from 'affordability' associated with low income, demographic changes – notably the trend to live in smaller households, the restructuring of the housing tenure system associated in the 1980s with the rise of home ownership and the decline of the rental housing sectors. Policy implementation strategies, particulary through local authority practice, are also likely to have an impact. Above all the obvious is indeed at the heart of the matter; in Britain in the 1990s there is a quantifiable shortage of affordable housing.

The immediate reasons which lead to a situation of homelessness are quite well documented in the local authority statistical returns and the pattern of change over the last 30 years can be examined by comparing the findings in Greve's initial 1964 study – which evaluated the reasons why families were admitted to short-stay accommodation in London – with the data from the local authority annual returns to the DoE.

Figure Three: Causes of homelessness in selected years

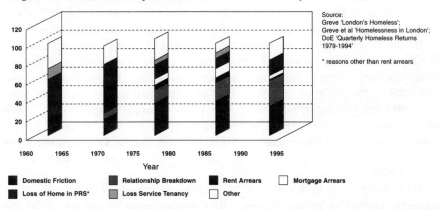

This data concerns only cases of families who were rehoused and it is likely that there will be a different pattern for non-priority cases. The chart also reflects to some extent the evolving pattern of policy over these years regarding the PRS and the switch to more targeted, income-related housing subsidies. One factor which has changed dramatically over the years as a cause of homelessness is the loss of private rented accommodation. This accounted for 44% of total cases in 1961 and was largely due to landlords seeking vacant possession in order to sell the property into owner occupation. Greve suggests that this was almost certainly a consequence of the 1957 Rent Act which reduced security of tenure for many tenants. Greater control through subsequent Rent Acts and the overall decline in the PRS has reduced home-lessness through loss of PRS tenancies to less than 10% by the end of the 1980s.

Rent arrears as a cause has also fallen and this is again due to the decline of both the private and the public rental sectors. However, the growth of problems within home ownership clearly increases and homelessness arising from mortgage arrears is prominent and has grown rapidly in the early 1990s.

The most common cause of homelessness in the 1990s is domestic friction and this has increased rapidly from only 14% in 1961 to over 40% in 1989. There is considerable case-study information which shows that this change is related largely to the underlying problem of separate households having to share accommodation for longer periods of time than was the case in the past.

For example, new households have to spend longer on council house waiting lists and cannot find a temporary home in the PRS because there is so little private rental housing. As a result households live in enforced circumstances with relatives and friends and this clearly is a recipe for stress and tension. Relationship breakdown is also a prominent feature of the more recent statistics. It was not mentioned by Greve but has grown steadily since the early 1970s. As we described in Chapter Five patterns of marriage and divorce have changed dramatically over this period and this is the major reason underlying this trend.

There is also, of course, a range of structural problems which underpin the growth of homelessness. For example, its rapid increase in the 1980s and 1990s is closely connected with problems in the wider macro-economy, particulary the growth of unemployment and widening of income inequalities during the 1980s, as measured, for example, by the government's biannual national sample of the population published in the General Household Surveys. The link between homelessness and unemployment has recently been demonstrated statistically. Bramley concludes from his research that, 'High unemployment is associated with relatively high rates of increase (in homelessness) over the decade (1980-1990)' (Bramley, G 'Explaining the Incidence of Statutory Homelessness in England', *Housing Studies*, Vol 8, No 2, 1993).

Over the post-1945 decades probably the most fundamental cause of the dramatic growth in homelessness is the restructuring of the tenure of the housing stock, described in Chapter One. In particular both the public and private rental sectors have changed considerably, council housing reaching its historic peak in the mid-1970s when it accommodated about one third of households in Britain – now less than a quarter – and the private rental sector (PRS) continuing its long decline under the impact of slum clearance and the persistent failure of housing policies to 'revive' it. For example in 1961 there were 5.2 million dwellings in the PRS but by 1991 less than 2 million, much of which was accounted for by tied accommodation of various types. In the comparable period the right to buy policy resulted in a decline in council housing despite the massive building programmes of the 1960s.

Who are 'the homeless'?

Before considering the 1985 Act in detail it should be noted that the official statistics and the statutory definition of homelessness are very narrowly defined and most of the studies of homelessness do not in fact accept the statutory definition as the only or even the principal focus of the issue. As we discuss below, local authority social service departments have quite separate duties under the terms of the Children Act 1989to provide accommodation for vulnerable young people and children. But there are many other people who fall outside the terms of all the legislative definitions of homelessness and it is clear as Greve et al point out that, '…definitions provided by the legislation are not sufficient to comprehend the nature of homelessness' (Greve, J et al, *Homeless in London*, University of Bristol, School for Advanced Urban Studies, 1986).

One of the most useful ways of understanding homelessness is to consider it as a continuum from outright literal 'rooflessness' to some form of concealment due to an affordability problem. Watchman and Robson identify four main categories:
1) the roofless – sometimes defined as 'rough sleepers';
2) houselessness – people living in institutions or B and B hotels;
3) insecure accommodation – people living in short lease house or in squats;
4) intolerable housing conditions – particularly associated with overcrowded or substandard accommodation.

(Watchman, P and Robson, P *Homelessness and the Law*, The Planning Exchange, 1983).

This broadly based approach is useful in identifying unofficial homelessness and pointing to the types of circumstances involved, but it too has problems. For example, the notion of rooflessness only accounts for people literally sleeping on the streets at any one time whereas it is known that many rough sleepers are only periodically on the streets. The 1991 Census sought to enumerate people sleeping rough and produced a figure of 2,703 in England, but the Office of Population, Censuses and Surveys acknowledges this to be an underestimate. It is thus not a very accurate concept for measuring the most apparently extreme form of homelessness and not a very useful policy-related definition.

Figures for those people living in temporary accommodation – included in Watchman and Robson's 'houseless' category – suggest a considerable and increasing problem, especially for young single people. One form of this is revealed in research produced in 1982 by the DHSS which showed that almost all the supplementary benefits claimants living in so called 'ordinary board and lodging' accommodation (including B and B accommodation, hostels and common lodging houses) were single (cited in Clapham et al, 1990). In 1979 there were 49,000 claimants in this type of accommodation but by 1986 this figure had increased by over 200% to 166,000. (Department of Health and Social Security, *Social Security Statistics* 1987.)

Recently studies of 'housing need' conducted for local authorities – needing information for their Housing Strategy Statements and Local Plans – have revealed a considerable problem of 'concealed homelessness' arising from families and single people being unable to enter local housing markets owing to an affordability gap between their incomes and local house prices. A study in Warwick District, for example, found that nearly 10% of all households contained a concealed household, 60% of these were single, mainly young, adults but many families with children were also affected (David Couttie Associates, *Warwick Housing Needs Study*, DCA, 1993). A recent survey conducted by the Department of the Environment found that 3% of respondents to a national questionnaire were accommodating one or two persons who really need a home of their own (Hedges, B and Clemens, C *Housing Attitude Survey*, HMSO, 1994).

Part III of the Housing Act 1985

The next section considers the definition in law of who is homeless. Here all references, unless otherwise stated, are to Part III of the Housing Act 1985. The legislation does not 'stand alone' and considerable guidance on implementation is given by a Code of Guidance (CoG) third edition issued in 1991 (a revised third edition to take account of the Asylum and Immigration Appeals Act 1993 was issued in 1994) under section 71, which requires authorities to 'have regard' to the CoG in the discharge of their functions. A number of issues concerning the CoG are dealt with initially because they bear directly on the interpretation and implementation of the statute.

The CoG is *not* law: rather it is advice on how law should be implemented. Indeed if a statement in the CoG contravenes either the wording of legislation, or a judicial decision – whether made before or after the Code's introduction – then to that extent the CoG is unlawful and may not be applied, see *Gillick v West Norfolk and Wisbech Area Health Authority* [1986] AC 112, [1985] 3 All ER 402. The CoG is a relevant factor which has to be taken into account, though it need not be slavishly adhered to and authorities are technically free to depart from it. (On the other hand departure may be good evidence of maladministration should a complaint be made to the Commission for Local Administration.)

The *legal status of the current CoG is no different from that of its predecessors* – as a matter of strict law. However, what is different is:
1)   the number of the issues covered;
2)   the degree of detail – or specificity – in which those issues are covered.

It is in practice harder than it was for authorities to depart from the guidance of the CoG, and it may be easier to argue an authority has misdirected itself as to the law on any specific issue on which the CoG has given particular and detailed guidance. There has been some judicial support for this view. In *R v Tower Hamlets London Borough Council, ex p Hoque* (1993) Times, 20 June Sir Louis Blom-Cooper QC, as a deputy judge, appeared to consider the guidance in the CoG amounted to rules, disregard of which was a breach of duty. This was, however, doubted in the Court of Appeal in *R v Brent London Borough Council, ex p Macwan* [1994] 2 FCR 604, 26 HLR 528, and clearly the CoG does not have the force of law and is not mandatory. It is certainly necessary for an authority's decision letter to show that the CoG has been taken into account, see *R v Tower Hamlets London Borough Council, ex p Mahmood* (1993) Legal Action, (March) p 12. Authorities should also rely only on the most recent version of the CoG because of the change in emphasis referred to above, *R v London Borough of Newham, ex p Bones* (1992) 25 HLR 357.

It is important to note that the CoG lays considerable emphasis on *prevention*, with stress being placed on the importance of housing advice and debt counselling services. The need to give advice to young home leavers is also stressed; indeed education on housing issues in schools is to be encouraged, with housing authorities undertaking liaison with LEAs on this matter. The need to give applicants an early statement of any obligations they may be owed is also spelt out. Preventative measures may also involve liaison with other services and departments, see CoG paras 3.7, 10.1 to 10.26, and 15.5 to 15.9.

The homeless in law

Under section 58 (as amended), persons are homeless if they have no accommodation in England, Wales or Scotland. They have no such accommodation if there is no accommodation which they, together with any person or persons normally residing with them as a member of their family in circumstances in which such residence is reasonable, are entitled to occupy: by having an interest in it or under a court order; by express or implied licence; by virtue of any enactment or rule of law. Such persons are also homeless where they have accommodation but: cannot secure entry to it; may be subject to violence or threats of likely violence from some person residing in the accommodation if they occupy it; the accommodation is a movable structure vehicle or vessel and there is no place where it can be located for them to reside in it. Persons are 'threatened with homelessness' where it is likely they will become homeless within 28 days. Obviously the '28 day rule' should not be rigidly interpreted. If an instance of potential homelessness comes to the attention of the local housing authority they should deal with it as soon as possible, see CoG para 5.10.

Section 14 of the Housing and Planning Act 1986 amended section 58 of the Housing Act 1985, inserting subsections (2A) and (2B). Persons are not to be treated as having accommodation unless it is accommodation which it would be reasonable for them to continue to occupy, and regard may be had, in determining the issue of reasonableness, to the general circumstances prevailing in relation to housing in the district of the authority applied to. Applicants should be classified as homeless if the accommodation they have is of such a condition that it would not be reasonable for them to continue to occupy it bearing in mind, inter alia, general housing circumstances in a district. Thus if others are enduring similar housing conditions, it may be 'reasonable' to stay in the accommodation. Much will depend, it appears, on how bad conditions are. It may not be 'reasonable' to stay in a property that is unfit, prejudicial to health and a fire hazard, despite poor housing conditions elsewhere in a district, *R v Kensington and Chelsea Royal Borough Council, ex p Ben-el-Mabrouk* (1994) Legal Action, (September) p 14.

The CoG gives extended guidance on the definition of what constitutes homelessness (para 5.1 et seq). A list of criteria for determining 'reasonableness' for the purposes of section 58(2A) and (2B) is included, for example the seriousness of assaults suffered, the likelihood of further violence, physical conditions and overcrowding, see also *R v Broxbourne Borough Council, ex p Willmoth* (1989) 22 HLR 118. Circumstances must be individually considered and investigated, not pre-judged according to rigid norms derived from other legislation. An illustrative case is *R v Medina Borough Council, ex p Dee* [1992] 2 FCR 691, 24 HLR 562. The applicant had a tenancy of a prefabricated beach hut which was in such poor condition she claimed it was unfit. She was pregnant at the time and was given medical advice that the property would not be suitable for a new born baby. The local authority did not consider the hut statutorily unfit. After the baby was born the applicant joined a squat and applied as a homeless person. The authority, incorrectly, found her not homeless because they considered she had 'accommodation'.

Was it reasonable for the applicant to continue to occupy the accommodation she had? In determining this question the authority had to consider:
1)   the physical condition of the premises;
2)   its suitability for the mother and her newborn baby;
3)   the medical advice given to the applicant.

Section 58, as amended, thus defines the classes of persons to whom the various obligations under the Act can be owed. These *include* those having no physical accommodation, those who have no accommodation which they have the *right* to occupy (for example as owners) or are allowed to occupy under some rule of law, or which they are allowed to occupy by some express or implied licence (for example persons living with relatives). Much in this last case depends on the attitude of individual authorities. Some interpret the Act liberally and classify such people as threatened with homelessness as they have no security of tenure. Where persons are living in premises on a 'grace and favour' basis and are asked to leave with no possibility of resisting the request legally, it would be incorrect for authorities to have rigid requirements that evidence of possession orders must be produced before assistance is given, see *R v Islington London Borough Council, ex p Rahman and Cox* (1989) Legal Action, (December) p 15, and *R v Merton London Borough Council, ex p Ruffle* (1988) 21 HLR 361.

Case law shows how difficult it can be to decide whether a person has 'no accommodation'. A woman living in crisis accommodation provided by a women's refuge was held to be homeless in *R v Ealing London Borough Council, ex p Sidhu* (1982) 80 LGR 534, as was a man whose only roof was that put over him nightly in a night shelter, see *R v Waveney District Council, ex p Bowers* [1983] QB 238, [1982] 3 All ER 727. Authorities, under section 75 of the 1985 Act, must consider whether accommodation is available for occupation by the applicant along with a person who can be reasonably expected to reside with him/her. Persons have 'no accommodation' if what they have is uninhabitable or incapable of accommodating the number of people living in it, *R v South Herefordshire Borough Council, ex p Miles* (1984) 17 HLR 82 and *R v Gloucester City Council, ex p Miles* (1985) 17 HLR 292. A *mere* offer of a room is not enough of itself to constitute 'accommodation'; see *R v Kensington and Chelsea Royal Borough Council, ex p Minton* (1988) 20 HLR 648.

Initial contact with the local authority

When a homeless or potentially homeless person makes contact with an authority there are duties under section 62 to make inquiries. These arise where the person applies in circumstances giving the authority reason to believe the applicant may be homeless or threatened with homelessness. The initial duty is to make inquiries necessary to satisfy themselves as to the applicant's condition.

Authorities should have appropriately trained officers of both sexes responsible for these matters. The Act does not lay down rules for conducting inquiries, and there is no requirement to operate a 24 hour a day, seven days a week service. Cooperation with the social services authority is useful, and progressive authorities have '24 hour-a-day' arrange-ments, as recommended by the CoG (para 3.4). These may consist of telephone numbers of duty officers supplied to appropriate persons and agencies. Once an application is made it must be dealt with: authorities are under duties to take reasonable steps to receive and adjudicate upon applications. What is reasonable depends upon the facts of each case. In populous areas '24 hour' cover may well be necessary, see *R v Camden London Borough Council, ex p Gillan* (1988) 21 HLR 114, and *R v Hackney London Borough Council, ex p Asilkender* (1990) Legal Action, (December) p 15.

The CoG provides guidance as to how inquiries should be undertaken. They should be speedy, sympathetic and conducted in private, with applicants given the opportunity to state cases fully. The assistance of friends and/or interpreters or other intermediaries may be appropriate. The needs of those with inflexible working hours or young children must be borne in mind. Authorities should have standard systems for recording applications, and should adopt target timescales so that initial assessment of eligibility is made on the day of application, or, where application is made out of office hours, on the first following working day. Subsequent inquiries should normally be completed, in 30 working days, with a written decision being given within a further three working days.

There has been considerable litigation on inquiry duties. In *R v Hillingdon Homeless Families Panel, ex p Islam* (1981) Times, 10 February, Glidewell J held that correct inquiries are those necessary to satisfy the authority about the matter in question. It is for the authority to make inquiries and elicit all relevant facts.They must generally behave fairly in doing this. Once told the applicant is homeless and the source of that information, an authority may not refuse to make inquiries, insisting that the applicant furnishes further confirmation of the facts, see *R v Woodspring District Council, ex p Walters* (1984) 16 HLR 73. An officer with delegated authority to make homelessness decisions may rely on interviews conducted by assistants, and does not person-ally have to interview the applicant, though this is desirable, see *R v Harrow London Borough Council, ex p Hobbs* (1992) Times, 13 October. An authority is under no duty to make 'CID' type inquiries, *Lally v Kensington and Chelsea Royal Borough* (1980) Times, 27 March, but they must enable applicants to state their cases, see *R v Wyre Borough Council, ex p Joyce* (1983) 11 HLR 73, and applicants should ensure the authority is informed of what they otherwise might be unable to find out, see *R v Harrow London Borough Council, ex p Holland* (1982) 4 HLR 108. Refusing to be interviewed may prejudice an applicant, *Reynolds v Sevenoaks District Council* (1990) 22 HLR 250, though special provision may be required in respect of those with language difficulties, *R v Westminster City Council, ex p Iqbal* (1990) 22 HLR 215. In conducting inquiries authorities may accept hearsay, where reasonable to do so (though not obvious 'tittle-tattle') and are under no obligation to put any information received 'chapter-and-verse' to applicants, though they must be made aware of the substance of evidence discovered, see *R v Southampton City Council, ex p Ward* (1984) 14 HLR 114. However, information received by an authority during the inquiry process is not confidential, and, it appears, has to be disclosed to the applicant where there is any matter which materially affects the applicant's case, see *R v Poole Borough Council, ex p Cooper* (1994) Times, 21 October. It is not a performance of the obligation to 'rubber stamp' another authority's findings, see *R v South Herefordshire Borough Council, ex p Miles* (1984) 17 HLR 82, *R v Basingstoke and Deane Borough Council, ex p Webb* (1989) Legal Action, (December) p 15 and *R v Tynedale District Council, ex p Shield* (1989) 22 HLR 144.

The inquiry process is a matter for authorities: the courts will only intervene where that process is so defective, or attenuated, that it leads an authority to an unreasonable decision, *R v Kensington and Chelsea Royal Borough Council, ex p Bayani* (1990) 22 HLR 406, and *R v Dacorum Borough Council, ex p Brown* (1989) 21 HLR 405, or where an authority reaches a conclusion so perverse that it flies in the face of all logic, *R v Dacorum Borough Council, ex p Taverner* (1988) 21 HLR 123. Authorities may not change their minds once they have issued a notice of a decision following inquiries unless further inquiries have led them to discover major changes in the circumstances of applicants, see *R v Dacorum Borough Council, ex p Walsh* (1991) 24 HLR

401. The inquiry process, however, must be conducted independently of other housing processes, such as requests for transfers, *R v Sefton Metropolitan Borough Council, ex p Healiss* [1994] 2 FCR 659.

What is an application, and who may apply?

An application need not be formal. An authority may be put 'on notice' via a department other than that which normally deals with homelessness. An application does not have to be made 'in person' by a homeless person; it can be made on a person's behalf, provided it is made clear what the issue is, *R v Chiltern District Council, ex p Roberts* (1990) 23 HLR 387. However, not every *person* is qualified to be an *applicant*.

In *Garlick v Oldham Metropolitan Borough Council* [1993] 2 All ER 65 the House of Lords had to deal with the issue of who is qualified to be an applicant in cases involving applications by two children aged four, and two disabled adults, one aged 24 but with a mental age of 10 to 13, the other profoundly deaf and with no ability to communicate outside the immediate circle of her family. The House of Lords decided the test for whether a child can be an applicant is to determine whether it is independent of parents/ guardians, etc, and has the capacity to appreciate any offer of accommodation and make a decision on it. The House of Lords did not rule out a child aged under 16 being independent, though clearly a very young child is incapable of being independent.

In coming to a decision on a child applicant authorities should consider: whether the child can exercise choices in respect of offers of accommodation made; whether the child is able to act upon advice and assistance given; is of sufficient age and understanding to enter into effective contractual relations in respect of accommodation offered, and can fulfil the duties expected of an occupier. (See, however, below on duties under the Children Act 1989, *R v Northavon District Council, ex p Smith* [1994] 2 AC 402, [1994] 3 All ER 313.)

With regard to adults under disability the test is whether an individual has the capacity to make an application him/herself, or to authorise another to make the application, and has the ability to comprehend and evaluate any offer of accommodation made so as to be able to respond to it.

It is for the authority applied to to decide whether the applicant has sufficient capacity. That is a question of fact in each case which can only be challenged if the decision is based on erroneous considerations, or fails to take into account relevant matters, or is clearly unreasonable or perverse.

Post-initial application inquiries

Once initial inquiries are made section 62(2) places the authority under a further duty to make inquiries to satisfy themselves whether applicants have priority need, whether they became homeless, or threatened with homelessness, intentionally, and, if they think fit, whether applicants have a local connection with the district of another local housing authority in England, Wales or Scotland. If, under section 63, the authority have reason to believe that applicants may be homeless and have priority need, they must make accommodation available to them pending a decision following their inquiries. This duty arises independently of any local connection issue. Where inquiries into intentional homelessness are taking place, an authority may use as an interviewer a person who is aware of the authority's housing shortages, *R v Tower Hamlets London Borough Council, ex p Khatun* (1994) Times, 8 December

Priority need

Whether the section 63 duty is owed depends on whether the applicant is in 'priority need': this is defined in section 59. A number of persons may have such need: pregnant women, or persons with whom such a woman resides or might reasonably be expected to reside (eg the father of the unborn child); persons with whom dependent children reside, or might reasonably be expected to; persons vulnerable as a result of old age, mental illness or handicap or physical disability, or other special reasons, or with whom such a vulnerable person resides or might reasonably be expected to (eg a carer); persons homeless or threatened with homelessness as a result of emergencies such as floods, fires or other disasters.

The definition is far from clear, though considerable guidance is given in the CoG (paras 6.1 to 6.18). Thus, priority arises on pregnancy, irrespective of its length, and a doctor's or midwife's letter is sufficient evidence of pregnancy. So far as dependent children are concerned the legal trend is to move away from highly formal notions of custody, and this is reflected in the CoG. It is the factual issue of which people, and how many of them, have actual 'care and control' rather than who is named in any order which is important. 'Dependent children', undefined by the Act, are those aged under 16, or 16-18 year olds in education or training, and dependency may exist even where a child is not living with an applicant at the time of application, for example because they are abroad. (See further the *Vagliviello* and *McCarthy* cases mentioned below.) Authorities are to avoid, wherever possible, splitting up families with dependents.

Finally note that it appears that when an authority make an assessment of priority need for accommodation, a person on a youth training scheme is not considered a 'dependent child', *R v Kensington and Chelsea Royal Borough Council, ex p Amarfio* (1994) Times, 4 July.

Priority need which arises as a result of vulnerability is also further explained by the CoG, with a list of indicators (not exhaustive) being included to aid authorities. With regard to old age, frailty as a result of age will not be the only criterion, and the age of 60 for both sexes is recommended as a 'bench mark' for determining the onset of old age: authority practice here historically varied considerably. In respect of mental/physical illness and disability the Code stresses:

1) the need for *authorities* to seek necessary medical and social services opinions;
2) the need for confidentiality;
3) the need to make special provision for those discharged from psychiatric care;
4) the desirability of having nominated officers to liaise with health authorities in respect of patients discharged from National Health Service care.

Priority need arising as a consequence of other 'special' reasons extends to cover young people at risk of, inter alia, violence or sexual abuse at home, prostitution, drug taking, etc. Youth alone is not an absolute indicator of vulnerability. It is those who are less well able to fend for themselves as a result of their youth who are contemplated. So far as homelessness in consequence of an emergency is concerned, it appears that a person who has been unlawfully evicted may qualify as being in priority need, *R v Bristol City Council, ex p Bradic* (1995) Times, 6 February.

The advice given is only a matter for consideration; nor does it go far enough. A man just released from prison or some other sort of institution is undoubtedly 'vulnerable', in some sense of the word, yet some authorities argue that he would not fall within the terms of section 59, and the existence of the community care policy alluded to above may confirm them in this view – such a person is 'some other authority's responsibility'. There is no proper definition given to vulnerability by virtue of mental illness; for example, would this cover a homeless alcoholic? In *R v Waveney District Council, ex p Bowers* [1983] QB 238, [1982] 3 All ER 727 an elderly man who suffered from both alcoholism and the consequences of severe head injury was found to be 'vulnerable', and in *R v Bath City Council, ex p Sangermano* (1984) 17 HLR 94 it was said that where a person has mental subnormality, a record of incompetence, and no ability to articulate and communicate, there is evidence of vulnerability. Vulnerability arises where persons are less able to fend for themselves so that an injury can befall them in circumstances where others would be able to cope without ill effects. However, self-imposed disabilities, such as drinking problems, do not generally constitute vulnerability, nor does the presence of vulnerability mean a person cannot be intentionally homeless: though a person *incapable* of managing his/her affairs through mental illness will be vulnerable and may be incapable of being intentionally homeless, see *Ex p B (Homelessness)* (1994) Times, 3 May.

What makes a person vulnerable is a question of fact and degree. Authorities should consider the frequency of any affliction affecting the applicant, see *R v Wandsworth London Borough Council, ex p Banbury* (1986) 19 HLR 76. They should consult relevant experts in housing and social welfare, and not rely on the opinion of a single doctor who has neither seen nor examined the homeless person, and certainly should not 'rubber stamp' his assessment, *R v Lambeth London Borough Council, ex p Carroll* (1988) 20 HLR 142, though a decision which has followed the taking of good medical opinion is hard to upset in court, see *R v Reigate and Banstead Borough Council, ex p Di Domenico* (1989) 20 HLR 153.

Where priority need depends on the presence of dependent children, they need not live exclusively with the applicant, but mere staying access granted to one parent is unlikely to be enough to enable that parent to claim the presence of dependent children. It is for authorities to decide with whom children 'normally reside', see *R v Lambeth London Borough Council, ex p Vagliviello* (1990) 22 HLR 392 and *R v Port Talbot Borough Council, ex p McCarthy* (1991) 23 HLR 207. Authorities should not try to decide the issue by reference to a child's main residence, but by reference to residence with the applicant, considering past, present and future arrangements, *R v Kingswood Borough Council, ex p Smith-Morse* (1994) Times, 8 December.

The duties owed to the homeless

These are contained in section 65. Where the authority is satisfied an applicant has priority need, and is not satisfied he/she became homeless intentionally, it must secure that accommodation becomes available for his/her occupation. Where satisfied of priority need, but also satisfied there has been intentional homelessness, it must, first, secure that accommodation is made available for occupation by the applicant for such period as it considers gives that person a reasonable chance of securing his/her own accommodation, and, secondly, furnish him/her with advice and such assistance as is considered appropriate in the circumstances in any attempts he/she may make to secure occupation. Where not satisfied of priority need the authority must furnish such advice and assistance as it thinks appropriate to aid the applicant in the search to secure accommodation. Section 66 lays down the duties owed to those who are *threatened* with homelessness, and these are generally similar to those listed above, save that the object is to ensure that accommodation does not *cease* to be available for occupation.

These sections create several classes of persons to whom differing duties are owed.

1) A person who is homeless unintentionally and in priority need, to whom the full duty is owed.
2) A person who is threatened with homelessness, and in priority need, and who has not become so threatened intentionally, to whom a duty is owed to secure that accommodation does not cease to be available.

3) A person who is homeless, and who has priority need, but who is homeless 'intentionally' to whom a duty is owed to make available accommodation for such period as the local authority considers will give that person a reasonable opportunity of finding his/her own accommodation. Generally interpreted as a period of 28 days in temporary accommodation, the CoG para 11.4 points out authorities must consider the housing circumstances of their areas in this context: a longer period might be appropriate where accommodation is in short supply.

4) A person who is homeless but who has no priority need, to whom the only duty owed is to give advice and appropriate assistance, see further the CoG paras 14.1 to 14.9.

Much depends on whether the applicant for aid has committed an act of intentional homelessness. Such acts are defined by section 60.

Intentional homelessness

Note the wording of section 60(1) of the Housing Act 1985:

> 'A person becomes homeless intentionally if he deliberately does or fails to do anything in consequence of which he ceases to occupy accommodation which is available for his occupation and which it would have been reasonable for him to continue to occupy.'

An act or omission in good faith on the part of a person unaware of any relevant fact is not to be treated as deliberate, see section 60(3). In determining whether it would have been reasonable for a person to continue to occupy accommodation, regard may be had to the general circumstances prevalent in relation to housing in the district of the authority applied to for aid.

The provision was inserted to quell fears that some might make themselves deliberately homeless with an intent to 'jump' the council house waiting list queue. In practice it has been applied to a much wider range of situations, and has been the subject of considerable litigation, with each 'ingredient' subjected to judicial attention. It is for the authority to satisfy itself whether an applicant falls squarely within the requirements of section 60 before it can treat him/her as intentionally homeless: under section 65(3), the *burden* clearly lies *on the authority* to 'satisfy' itself. Applicants are entitled 'to the benefit of the doubt' where there is any, see *R v Preseli District Council, ex p Fisher* (1984) 17 HLR 147, and *R v West Dorset District Council, ex p Phillips* (1984) 17 HLR 336. Furthermore though an authority should look at all circumstances relating to an applicant's conduct and situation, its decision is most unlikely to be upset provided it can show it reasonably concluded the applicant's condition was *predominantly* intentionally self inflicted, see *R v Newham London Borough Council, ex p Campbell* [1994] Fam Law 319, 26 HLR 183.

Further the CoG, para 7.1, makes it clear decisions on intentionality must follow from inquiries made in individual cases: predeterminations purporting to define intentional homelessness in advance are unacceptable. Authorities do not have to have legal 'proof' on all the issues involved, their task is to come to a reasonable decision in the light of their inquiries. (For the impact on intentional homelessness of section 27 of the Children Act 1989, see below.)

The various portions of the statutory definition must be considered.

Whose act or omission is in question?

Usually the applicant's, it may be that of some member of the applicant's household in which he/she acquiesced, see *Lewis v North Devon District Council* [1981] 1 All ER 27, [1981] 1 WLR 328; especially where the applicant is a joint tenant with the party at fault and fails to defend possession proceedings brought in consequence of that other's acts, see *R v Swansea City Council, ex p Thomas* (1983) 9 HLR 64. Failure to control nuisances committed by members of the applicant's family or lodgers the consequence of which is a grant of possession against the applicant can amount to acquiescence in those acts rendering the applicant intentionally homeless, see *Devenport v Salford City Council* (1983) 8 HLR 54, and *R v Cardiff City Council, ex p John* (1982) 9 HLR 56.

Two cases illustrate acquiescence. In *R v East Northamptonshire District Council, ex p Spruce* (1988) 20 HLR 508 the applicants were joint council tenants evicted for rent arrears. Mr Spruce was found to be intentionally homeless. The authority found Mrs Spruce had shared responsibility for the arrears. Mrs Spruce, however, genuinely believed arrears had been cleared; the authority had not made a correct inquiry in her case. Merely to become aware of debts, etc, when they have become so great they cannot be coped with is not to acquiesce in them. Contrast *R v London Borough of Barnet, ex p O'Connor* (1990) 22 HLR 486. The facts were generally similar to *Spruce*, but Mrs O'Connor had jointly signed a massive mortgage application with her husband. She had grasped the financial situation.

What is a deliberate act or omission?

The CoG (paras 7.4 , 7.5 and 7.7 to 7.9) pointing out applicants 'should always be given the opportunity to explain an act or omission' states certain circumstances should generally not be considered 'deliberate':
1)   acts/omissions occurring while applicants are incapable of managing their affairs;
2)   home loss consequent on real and genuine financial hardship, eg because of loss of employment through redundancy;

3) sale by a mortgagor, or surrender to the mortgagee, before repossession by the mortgagee where it is clear the latter has an unanswerable case to obtain possession;
4) acts/omissions in good faith (see further below).

In *R v Wandsworth London Borough Council, ex p Hawthorne* [1994] 1 WLR 1442, the Court of Appeal stated that where an authority has to decide whether a failure to pay rent is 'deliberate' it is bound to consider also whether that failure was caused by an inadequacy of resources to meet both rent and the needs of the applicant's children. A *conscious* decision by an applicant to devote what resources he/she has to his/her children rather than the payment of rent is not to be treated automatically as a 'deliberate' act, and inability to pay is a relevant matter in deciding whether a failure to pay is 'deliberate'. Note also *R v Southwark London Borough Council, ex p Davies* (1994) Legal Action, (September) p 14 and *R v Wandsworth London Borough Council, ex p Onwudiwe* (1993) 26 HLR 302, CA whence it appears the real question in such cases is to ask 'why is the applicant in his/her present financial predicament?' For example, in a case of homelessness arising from business failure leading to mortgage default, it should be asked did the applicant know the risk he was taking when he used his home as security for his business loan?

'Deliberate' refers to the *doing* of the act, etc, not its intended or desired consequences; indeed, 'voluntary' is not an inapt synonym, for it is not necessary to show that applicants did what they did with the intention of getting themselves dispossessed, *Devenport v Salford City Council* (1983) 8 HLR 54. To fail *deliberately* to pay off mortgage arrears so that the consequence is dispossession is intentional homelessness, see *R v Eastleigh Borough Council, ex p Beattie (No 2)* [1984] Fam Law 115, 17 HLR 168. This also applies to a d*eliberate* refusal to pay rent (but note *Hawthorne* supra on the issue of what is 'deliberate'). However, failure to pay rent or mortgage repayments based on a genuine misunderstanding of material facts, such as a belief that the DSS were making the payment in the applicant's place, would be an act or omission in good faith because of lack of awareness of relevant facts, and so not 'deliberate', see *White v Exeter City Council* [1981] LAG Bulletin 287. Authorities are required to make an inquiry into why the act/omission occurred. Much will depend upon the inquiry process. Authorities must come to reasonable decisions based on the evidence before them, *R v Westminster City Council, ex p Khan* (1991) 23 HLR 230; the court will only intervene where a relevant matter has not been considered if it feels the authority would have reached a different conclusion had it considered the matter, *R v Newham London Borough Council, ex p McIlroy and McIlroy* (1991) 23 HLR 570.

Acts/ommissions which may be considered deliberate include:
1) giving up one's home when in no risk of losing it, *R v Leeds City Council, ex p Adamiec* [1992] 1 FCR 401, 24 HLR 138;
2) home loss consequent upon neglect of advice from qualified persons;

3)   voluntarily relinquishing a home which it would have been reasonable for the applicant to continue to occupy (see further below);
4)   eviction following anti-social behaviour – even the anti-social behaviour of one's children, *R v Rochester upon Medway City Council, ex p Williams* [1994] EGCS 35.
5)   voluntary resignation from a job which carries with it tied accommodation where it would have been reasonable to continue in employment.

What is an act or omission in good faith?

Such occurs where a person is genuinely unaware of some relevant fact, which is not the same thing as a mistake of law or bad advice, though they can be hard to distinguish in practice, see for example *R v Mole Valley District Council, ex p Burton* (1988) 20 HLR 479 where it was held an authority should have taken into account a woman's genuine misapprehension that, under a Trades Union agreement with local authorities, her family would be rehoused following her husband's voluntary resignation from a job carrying tied accommodation. What authorities must look for is an honest mistake, a truly genuine error or misreading of the circumstances, eg a youngster not believing her father when he said he would never take her back if she spent some time living with his estranged spouse, *Wincentzen v Monklands District Council* 1988 SLT 847, or a couple who gave up accommodation in the UK genuinely believing there was a real business opportunity overseas, *R v Hammersmith & Fulham London Borough Council, ex p Lusi and Lusi* (1991) 23 HLR 260. Lack of awareness of a relevant fact is enough provided it is a genuine mistake made in good faith, see *R v Tower Hamlets London Borough Council v Rouf* (1991) 23 HLR 460. Authorities need to ask why did this person act in this way, and what was the true motivation for his/her actions bearing in mind the person's circumstances, beliefs, family background, obligations, knowledge and level of understanding.

Finally note that where a person claims to have been unaware of a relevant fact it is for the claimant to prove the facts. In this context a claim that a person from abroad believed it would be easy to find work in this country may be no more than a statement of hope on his/her part and not a 'relevant fact' within the meaning of section 60(3), *R v Ealing London Borough Council, ex p Sukhija* (1994) Independent, 18 July.

The homelessness must be a 'consequence' of the act or omission in question

Authorities may look beyond the most immediate cause of homelessness, see *De Falco v Crawley Borough Council* [1980] QB 460, [1980] 1 All ER 913, and *Dyson v Kerrier District Council* [1980] 3 All ER 313, [1980] 1 WLR 1205. If there is a 'chain of causation' flowing unbroken from an initial act of intentional homelessness down to the applicant's current condition, the application will be tainted by the initial act. The 'chain' may be broken where applicants obtain some settled accommodation in which they spend a period of time between their initial state of intentional homelessness and their current condition, see *Din v Wandsworth London Borough Council* [1983] 1 AC 657, [1981] 3 All ER 881, but the cases yield few examples of where such a 'break' has been found. *R v Basingstoke and Deane Borough Council, ex p Bassett* [1984] Fam Law 90, 10 HLR 125 shows the 'chain' can be broken by some supervening independent cause of homelessness. Where an applicant seeks to rely on having obtained an intervening period of settled accommodation, what is 'settled' will be a question of fact in each case. Taking a holiday letting will not be enough, *Lambert v Ealing London Borough Council* [1982] 2 All ER 394, [1982] 1 WLR 550, nor will occupying temporary shelter found by relatives in overcrowded circumstances, see *Din v Wandsworth Borough Council* (supra). Accommodation in a hostel where rooms have cooking and washing facilities may be 'settled', however, see *R v East Hertfordshire District Council, ex p Hunt* (1985) 18 HLR 51. Whether there has been such a break is to be determined objectively, not according to the subjective intentions of the applicant. The CoG para 7.8 makes particular mention of periods spent in assured shorthold accommodation, and indicates a distinction can be made between cases where an assured shorthold by its nature cannot have been expected to last for more than its initially fixed term and cases where there could have been reasonable expectation that the tenancy might be allowed to run on following the end of the initial fixed term. The general test is whether the applicant has legally obtained, since the act of intentional homeless, accommodation in circumstances in which it was reasonable to assume it would not be temporary, see *R v London Borough of Merton, ex p Ruffle* (1988) 21 HLR 361. In all cases the matter is one for the authority to decide as a matter of fact, *R v Christchurch Borough Council, ex p Conway* (1987) 19 HLR 238, *R v Swansea District Council, ex p Evans* (1990) 22 HLR 467, *R v Croydon London Borough Council, ex p Easom* (1992) 25 HLR 262, though the length of time spent in the accommodation in question is normally a relevant consideration.

Causation

The authority must be satisfied it is reasonable to regard the applicant's acts or omissions as having caused homelessness. There must be a cessation of occupation that has taken place consequential on the applicant's conduct and in relation to premises that are 'accommodation', *and* which it would have been reasonable for the applicant to continue to occupy. Where an applicant leaves premises that do not constitute 'accommodation' (see section 58, supra) no question of intentional homelessness arises.

Both the accommodation lost, and the act of causing that loss, can be outside the United Kingdom, but authorities should ensure that proper inquiries are made in such cases into the circumstances of the cesser of occupation, see *R v Reigate and Banstead Borough Council, ex p Paris* (1985) 17 HLR 103.

It must be established that the accommodation lost was available for occupation by the applicant. Under section 75 accommodation is 'available' only where it can be occupied by the applicant and by any other person who might reasonably be expected to reside with him/her. In *Re Islam* [1983] 1 AC 688 it was held that a man who had lost his accommodation – a shared room – because he had brought his wife and children to live with him from overseas was not thereby intentionally homeless. Mr Islam had never actually occupied accommodation available to him *and* those persons who might reasonably be expected to reside with him, and the intentional homelessness provisions could not apply to the accommodation he had lost. See also *R v Wimbourne District Council, ex p Curtis* (1985) 18 HLR 79 and *R v Westminster City Council, ex p Ali* (1983) 11 HLR 83. A useful illustrative case is *R v Peterborough City Council, ex p Carr* (1990) 22 HLR 206. Ms Carr, who was pregnant, left her sister's house after her sister had refused to let the putative father of the child move in, and was found intentionally homeless. The court held the accommodation she left was not available for her occupation because it was not also reasonably available to her boyfriend, with whom she could be reasonably expected to reside.

Finally it must be established that it would have been reasonable for the applicant to continue to occupy the accommodation lost, ie the question is not 'was it reasonable for the applicant to leave', but, 'would it have been reasonable for the applicant to have stayed?' See *R v Gravesham Borough Council, ex p Winchester* (1986) 18 HLR 207 and *R v Croydon London Borough Council, ex p Toth* (1987) 20 HLR 576. Section 60(4) of the 1985 Act allows regard to be had to general circumstances prevailing in relation to housing in the district in determining the reasonableness of the applicant's conduct, though factors other than those mentioned in section 60(4) can also be taken into account. Factors an authority may consider in coming to a decision include, first, physical factors such as whether there are other people in the area living in worse conditions than the applicant and the general housing conditions and demands of the area and issues of overcrowding, unfitness, infestation by vermin and inadequacy of size. See generally *R v Gravesham Borough Council, ex p Winchester* (supra).

The CoG, para 7.11, points out it is not normally reasonable for a person to continue to occupy accommodation where he/she has lost the right to occupy because the accommodation was tied to employment which has ended through no fault of his/hers.

The courts have made it clear it is not intentional homelessness to leave property which one clearly has no right to occupy, expulsion from which one could not resist at law, see *R v Hillingdon London Borough Council, ex p Gliddon* [1985] 1 All ER 493, *R v Hammersmith & Fulham London Borough Council, ex p O'Sullivan* [1991] EGCS 110, and *R v Mole Valley District Council, ex p Minnett* (1983) 12 HLR 49.

A question arises whether an assured shorthold tenancy (AST) qualifies as accommodation expulsion from which one cannot resist on the basis of the foregoing cases. Each instance will probably depend on its merits but in *R v Rochester upon Medway City Council, ex p Williams* [1994] EGCS 35 the Court of Appeal indicated that an AST has a potentially infinite duration, and the fact that it is not as secure as a secure tenancy does not mean that its tenants cannot be guilty of intentional homelessness if he/she is responsible for acts/omissions leading to its loss.

Particular problems arise with regard to those who leave home as a result of domestic and other violent disputes and those who apply in this country after giving up homes overseas.

The CoG, para 7.11(b), argues a person who has fled from home in consequence of domestic violence should not be treated as intentionally homeless, for it is not reasonable for that person to remain. It is tempting to advise such an applicant to re-obtain the home by seeking an appropriate order under the domestic violence or matrimonial homes legislation, especially where the applicant is the sole or joint tenant. In *R v Wandsworth London Borough Council, ex p Nimako-Boateng* [1984] Fam Law 117, 11 HLR 95 it was said there can be circumstances where the applicant should reasonably try to seek to stay and restrain the other party by court order rather than apply to the local authority as homeless. However, this would not be reasonable where the applicant stands little or no chance of gaining an appropriate order. In *Warwick v Warwick* (1982) 1 HLR 139 it was made clear that an order excluding the male from the dwelling would not be granted where the local authority had required such an order as a precondition of rehousing, and where it was clear the female had no intention of returning. Likewise in *Charles v Charles* (1984) Legal Action, (July) p 81 the court pointed out that when a woman is forced from her home by domestic violence and her partner is then excluded by a court order, to require her to return to the dwelling puts her in a place where the male knows she is and is thus enabled to further molest and abuse her.

The cases make a distinction between instances of actual domestic violence and other situations. Authorities should very seriously consider whether it is reasonable for someone to continue to occupy property where they have been subject to violence, see *R v Kensington and Chelsea Royal Borough Council, ex p Hammell* [1989] QB 518, [1989] 1 All ER 1202. See also *R v Tynedale District Council, ex p McCabe* (1991) 24 HLR 384. Here a woman fled home on account of her husband's violence. She was rehoused in Newcastle. Her husband discovered her and almost daily visited to threaten or inflict violence. She fled again to her mother's home. After a few weeks she returned to Newcastle to find her house ransacked. She applied to Tynedale District Council who found her intentionally homeless for abandoning the Newcastle tenancy. It was held the authority had failed to make proper enquiries as to the reasonableness of her continued occupation of the Newcastle dwelling.

Women are, as a result of this type of decision and insensitive housing management, particularly vulnerable to hidden homelessness owing to the lack of temporary hostels for women and by being forced to remain in violent relationships against their will due to the lack of alternative accommodation (Greve, J 1991).

With regard to other forms of violence, much depends on the facts of each case, the nature and kind of the violence, and the level and effectiveness of police protection. In *R v Hillingdon London Borough Council, ex p H* (1988) 20 HLR 554, H was an ex soldier who, with his family, left home in Northern Ireland after threats and harassment by terrorists. He applied to the authority as homeless and they held him intentionally so. The court held regard should have been had to the harassment suffered in Northern Ireland. In *R v Northampton Borough Council, ex p Clarkson* (1992) 24 HLR 529, a young woman left her council house because she feared sexual harassment from her brother who was living there temporarily. The authority considered it would have been reasonable for her to stay, but it was held they had failed to have sufficient regard to the sexual harassment issue. Similarly, in *R v Westminster City Council, ex p Bishop* (1993) 25 HLR 459 it was held an authority should consider the issue by taking into account the needs of a dependent child, while in *R v Royal Borough of Kensington and Chelsea, ex p Khassam* (1994) Legal Action, (March) p 14, it was considered the needs of the applicant's carer should be taken into account.

Turning to those who apply in this country having given up accommodation abroad, authorities should take into account the customs, lifestyles and needs of an applicant's community, see *R v Tower Hamlets London Borough Council, ex p Monaf* (1988) 20 HLR 520. Authorities may also consider employment conditions in the place whence the applicant came, though they need not conduct detailed inquiries into local employment conditions there, *R v Royal Borough of Kensington and Chelsea, ex p Cunha* (1988) 21 HLR 16. *R v Newham London Borough Council, ex p Tower Hamlets London Borough Council* [1992] 2 All ER 767, [1991] 1 WLR 1032 indicates authorities should ask whether an applicant's decision to cease to occupy accommodation in the former place of residence was reasonable in the light of the place he/she was leaving it for (and its housing circumstances, and his/her employment prospects there) and also in the light of the applicant's national housing standards.

A finding of intentional homelessness bars the applicant from making further applications to the same authority based on the same facts, see *Delahaye v Oswestry Borough Council* (1980) Times, 29 July. He/she can re-apply *once there is a material change in circumstances*, or new relevant issues come to light, for example a period spent in settled accommodation. There is no fixed 'disqualification period' barring an applicant from re-applying, see CoG para 7.12, and also *R v Ealing London Borough Council, ex p McBain* [1986] 1 All ER 13, [1985] 1 WLR 1351.

What of repeated applications to different authorities? Where a person applies to an authority and they come to a decision that he/she is unintentionally homeless, but has no local connection (see further below) with their area while having such a connection with another authority, the authority may refer the applicant to that authority who come under a duty to the applicant, notwithstanding that authority's earlier determination that he/she was intentionally homeless, see *R v Slough Borough Council, ex p Ealing London Borough Council* [1981] QB 801, [1981] 1 All ER 601. Each authority applied to must make its own assessment of such a repeat application without merely adopting a previous authority's determination. Where an authority use the local connection provisions to refer to another authority a person previously found intentionally homeless by that authority, the 'notifying' authority must make very careful inquiries before concluding deliberations on the application, and if the authority receiving the referral is unhappy about the adequacy of the notifying authority's inquiries they should make a prompt challenge, see *R v Tower Hamlets London Borough Council, ex p Camden London Borough Council* (1988) 21 HLR 197. In *R v Newham London Borough Council, ex p Tower Hamlets London Borough Council* [1992] 2 All ER 767, [1991] 1 WLR 1032, it was held that where an authority refers an applicant to another authority, and that other authority has previously found the applicant intentionally homeless, that earlier finding is a relevant factor which the notifying authority should take into account.

Local connection

A person who is homeless, unintentionally, and who has priority need is, in general, owed the full duty under the law; but the authority applied to *may* inquire whether there is a local connection with the district of another authority in England, Wales or Scotland so they may refer the application to that other authority, see sections 62 and 67 of the 1985 Act. Before such a referral can be made it must be determined that:
1) Neither the applicant, nor any person who might reasonably be expected to reside with him/her has a local connection with the district applied to (the 'notifying authority').
2) That the applicant etc, *does* have such a connection with another district (the 'notified authority').
3) That the applicant etc, will *not* run the risk of domestic violence in the

notified authority's district, ie a risk of violence from a person with whom, but for that risk, he/she might reasonably be expected to reside, or from a person with whom he/she formerly resided, or there is a risk of threats of violence from such a person likely to be carried out. It follows from *R v Bristol City Council, ex p Browne* [1979] 3 All ER 344, [1979] 1 WLR 1437, that the fact an applicant suffered domestic violence in the past does not *necessarily* mean the person runs the risk of such violence in the future. Authorities are required to inquire into the issues, though the duty may be discharged simply by asking relevant questions of the applicant, see *R v London Borough of Greenwich, ex p Patterson* (1993) Times, 27 May. It is not sufficient simply to ask the authority to whom reference is being made whether an applicant's former home has been vacated and relet, see *R v London Borough of Islington, ex p Adigun* (1986) 20 HLR 600.

Questions whether conditions for referral of applications are met are determined by agreement between relevant authorities, or, in default in accordance with arrangements made in directions given by the Secretary of State, see the arbitration provisions of SI 1978/69, and SI 1978/661 and the authorities' own Local Authority Agreement 1979, implementing these requirements. *The Agreement on Procedures for Referral of the Homeless* is reprinted as Annex 2 of the CoG. In *R v Hillingdon London Borough Council, ex p Slough Borough Council* (1980) 130 NLJ 881 it was held arbitrators should consider only the issue of local connection.

'Local connection' is defined in section 61 of the 1985 Act. An applicant may have a connection with an authority's district:
1) because he/she is, or was, normally resident there by choice;
2) because of employment in the district;
3) because of family associations;
4) because of other special circumstances.

All possible bases for finding a local connection have to be explored before a referral is made, *R v Slough Borough Council, ex p Khan* (1995) Times, 30 January.

Whether such a connection exists is a question of fact. In *Eastleigh Borough Council v Betts* [1983] 2 AC 613, [1983] 2 All ER 1111 the House of Lords held applicants must show they have built up and established a real connection with the area of the authority applied to. They may do this by a period of residence, or employment, or because of family associations enduring in the area, or because of other special circumstances. When an application is based on residence alone it is not improper for an authority to apply the guideline in the 1979 Local Authority Agreement that to reside in an area for less than six months during the period of twelve months preceding the application is insufficient to establish such a real connection with an area, provided the guideline is not operated as a rigid rule. During making inquiries as to 'local connection' and negotiations between authorities the authority first applied to is under a duty to accommodate the applicant, see sections 63(2) and 68(1) of the 1985 Act. Under section 68(2) of the 1985 Act where it is determined the conditions for referral are satisfied, the notified authority come under the duties imposed by law, otherwise they remain with the notifying authority. It is for the notifying authority to inform the applicant in writing of the outcome and reasons for the determination, see section 68(3).

Where on a homelessness application an authority conclude a local connection lies only with another authority, they do not have to make a referral, and then they come under the duty to accommodate the applicant under section 65(2). If, however, they do make the referral it is the notified authority who are under the duty to accommodate, and the fact that they make an offer of accommodation which is refused by the applicant will not entitle the notifying authority to claim on a *subsequent* application by the same person who has by that time acquired a local connection with them that they have discharged the duty to accommodate, see *R v Tower Hamlets London Borough Council, ex p Abbas Ali* (1992) 25 HLR 158.

The issue is whether the applicant has no local connection with the notifying authority's area while having a connection with the area of the notified authority, not whether there is a greater local connection with some other authority's area, see *R v Mr Referee McCall* noted in (1981) 8 HLR 48.

A rigid policy of referring all cases of apparent local connection with other authorities is a fetter on discretion. Before making a referral an authority should consider whether it is appropriate to do so, see *R v Harrow London Borough Council, ex p Carter* (1992) 26 HLR 32.

Where an applicant has no local connection with any authority, the responsibility lies with the authority first applied to, see *R v Hillingdon London Borough Council, ex p Streeting* [1980] 3 All ER 413, [1980] 1 WLR 1425. A person who is legally in this country, and homeless unintentionally, and having priority need, is owed the duties under the Act. However, in *R v Secretary of State for the Environment, ex p Tower Hamlets London Borough* [1993] 3 All ER 439 an authority claimed an applicant had obtained entry to the United Kingdom *fraudulently*, by representing that housing was available for him, contrary to the Immigration Rules of 1990. They alleged they owed no duty to assist such a person, to which the Secretary of State replied that issues of fraudulent entry are matters solely for immigration officials, and that once a person has been admitted he/she is entitled to rely on Part III of the 1985 Act. The Court of Appeal held a person is an illegal immigrant once he/she obtains leave to enter the UK by deceit, and it is appropriate for a housing authority to determine whether an applicant under Part III is such an illegal immigrant because false representations have been made about housing matters.

A distinction, however, must be made between illegal immigrants (ie persons who have entered the country by evading immigration control, or who have re-entered after deportation, or who have obtained entry by fraud or have overstayed their period of leave to be in the country) and genuine 'asylum seekers' under the Asylum and Immigration Appeals Act 1993 for whom special provision is made. If an asylum seeker (ie the person fleeing from racial, religious, national or political persecution) makes a homelessness application the 1993 Act, section 4, provides that no duty is owed if the applicant has 'any accommodation however temporary which it would be reasonable for him to occupy', ie where there is some form of suitable accommodation. In determining this issue the authority are to have regard to the general housing circumstances of their area, though where an application relates to a family group, the reasonableness criterion extends to take into account the needs of those who might reasonably be expected to reside with the application. Where, for example, a refugee family is in an assembly or school hall in common with many others, the shelter they have would not qualify as 'accommodation' sufficient to relieve an authority of duties under the 1985 Act. In a case such as this an authority is under a duty to accommodate while the applicant remains an asylum seeker, though the obligation is only to provide temporary accommodation. A successful asylum seeker granted leave to stay should, at that point, be treated as a new homelessness applicant under the 1985 Act, see further section 5 and Schedule 1 of the 1993 Act, and the supplementary CoG on applications from asylum seekers issued by the DoE in 1993. See now the revised third edition of the Code, paras 4.19-4.36, Chapter 16, and annexes 4, 5 and 6.

The duty to accommodate

The duty to accommodate a person who has successfully cleared all the hurdles in the Act is contained in section 65. Section 69 empowers the performance of the duty to accommodate by:
1)   the provision of ordinary council housing;
2)   securing that accommodation will be provided by some other person;
3)   giving such advice and assistance as secures the applicant accommodation from some other person.

(The CoG gives guidance on these duties in paras 11.1 to 11.8, 12.1 to 12.16, which deal with providing permanent accommodation, and 13.1 to 13.14 which detail the various circumstances in which temporary accommodation may be provided.)

Accommodation secured must comply with section 75 and be available not only for occupation by the applicant but also by any other person who might reasonably be expected to reside with him/her. In *R v Newham London Borough Council, ex p Dada* (1994) Times, 29 July it was considered that any property offered to a pregnant woman should be capable of accommodating her child also on its birth. But where a person or body promises an authority to find accommodation for a homeless person, the authority need not be told the exact identity of the proposed accommodation.

Though the duty to accommodate can be discharged in general by making one offer of permanent accommodation, see *R v Westminster City Council, ex p Chambers* (1982) 6 HLR 24, authorities must behave reasonably in making offers. An offer must not be perverse or absurd, either as to the premises involved or the time allowed to consider it, see *Parr v Wyre Borough Council* (1982) 2 HLR 71. Accommodation must be habitable, and habitable by the applicant bearing in mind his medical condition, see *R v Ryedale District Council, ex p Smith* (1983) 16 HLR 66. With regard to time allowed to consider offers note *R v London Borough of Wandsworth, ex p Lindsay* (1986) 18 HLR 502 where the court said it could only intervene in relation to the amount of time allowed where the period was absurdly or perversely inadequate.

Accommodation offered must, as a result of amendments made to section 69 in 1986, be 'suitable'. In determining whether accommodation is 'suitable' regard is to be had to the statutory provisions on unfitness, overcrowding and multiple occupation. An authority may discharge its duty in stages, provided it does its best according to the resources available to 'staircase' applicants as expeditiously as possible towards satisfaction of the duty. There may be more than one move between temporary homes as the authority discharges the duty, *R v Brent London Borough Council, ex p Macwan* [1994] 2 FCR 604, 26 HLR 528. Stages on the way to the discharge of the duty, for example provision of hostel accommodation on a temporary basis, are unlikely to fulfil the duty, though this will be a question of fact and degree in each case. In *R v East Hertfordshire District Council, ex p Hunt* (1985) 18 HLR 51 Mann J considered that, as a matter of fact and degree, the offer of accommodation in a hostel could be of sufficiently settled accommodation to constitute a fulfilment of the duty to accommodate. This was reiterated by the Court of Appeal in *R v Brent London Borough Council, ex p Awua* [1994] 26 HLR 539, now subject to appeal to the House of Lords. It is not tenable to argue that a homeless person always has no 'settled residence' until there is accommodation in suitable permanent accommodation. Each case turns on its facts: bed and breakfast 'lodgings' are clearly temporary, a place in a hostel is likely to be temporary, but much depends on the nature of the person and the hostel. However, though the duty to accommodate can be discharged in stages, if a person is kept in temporary accommodation for a while there must come a point when the failure of the authority to find permanent accommodation is an unreasonable failure to comply with the Act. Such a situation can arise if an authority has a rule that in certain circumstances, for example because of non payment of accommodation charges, an applicant's name is taken off the active rehousing list. Authorities should not penalise non payers in this way, but should proceed by way of an action for debt, see *R v Tower Hamlets London Borough, ex p Khalique* [1994] 2 FCR 1074, 26 HLR 517.

What then, in general, is 'suitable' accommodation? It must be suitable to the person to whom it is offered, bearing in mind all relevant medical, social, employment and emotional factors pertaining to that person as assessed by the authority, *R v Brent London Borough Council, ex p Omar* (1991) 23 HLR 446 and *R v Lewisham London Borough Council, ex p D* [1993] 2 FCR 772, [1993] Fam Law 277. Furthermore accommodation offered must be available at a rent the applicant can afford, either from his/her own resources, or with the benefit of public assistance, *R v London Borough of Tower Hamlets, ex p Kaur* (1994) 26 HLR 597, while where accommodation is offered an authority is under a duty to ensure the applicant can move in and is not kept out, for example, by squatters, *R v Lambeth London Borough Council, ex p Campbell* (1994) Legal Action, (June) p 13. Offers made should take into account whether the applicant may be subject to racial violence if offered properties in particular areas, *R v Tower Hamlets London Borough Council, ex p Subhan* (1992) 24 HLR 541. Where an offer is made and the applicant puts forward arguments that the accommodation is not suitable, the authority cannot discharge its duty unless and until it has considered the arguments, *R v Wycombe District Council, ex p Hazeltine* (1993) 25 HLR 313. Making a suitable offer of accommodation will generally, at that point of time, absolve an authority from the need to do more should the applicant unreasonably refuse the offer, see *R v Hammersmith and Fulham London Borough Council, ex p O'Brian* (1985) 17 HLR 471. That does not mean the applicant is an intentionally homeless person to whom no obligation is owed unless there is an entirely fresh and unconnected incidence of unintentional homelessness. In *R v Ealing London Borough Council, ex p McBain* [1986] 1 All ER 13, [1985] 1 WLR 1351 the Court of Appeal stated that one offer of accommodation unreasonably refused satisfies an authority's obligation *pro tem*: where the applicant can thereafter show a material change in circumstances making the previous offer clearly unsuitable an authority's obligations are renewed. In allocating accommodation to a homeless pregnant woman, an authority is not bound to take account of the unborn child when assessing 'suitability', see *R v Newham London Borough Council, ex p Dada* (1995) Times, 3 February

Once, however, the duty to accommodate is owed it is owed indefinitely, see *R v Camden London Borough Council, ex p Wait* (1986) 18 HLR 434, irrespective of the fact that the applicant previously occupied a dwelling under licence in a property with a destined short life which he would have had to vacate at the end of his licence period to allow substantial reconstruction of the building.

In making offers of accommodation authorities must avoid racial and sexual discrimination, see *R v Tower Hamlets London Borough Council, ex p Commission for Racial Equality* (1991) Legal Action, (June) p 16; monitoring applications and offers is clearly important in this context and to remove such safeguards may be evidence of an arbitrary and random mode of allocating accommodation to the homeless which can be struck down on grounds of unfairness and irrationality, see *R v Tower Hamlets London Borough Council, ex p Ali (Mohib)* (1993) 25 HLR 218. Likewise though an authority is allowed to charge for accommodation, charges must be reasonable and not levied disproportionately on particular homeless persons, *R v Ashford Borough Council, ex p Wood* (1990) Legal Action, (December) p 16. Similarly accommodation provided, even temporarily, must not be cancelled 'in terrorem' to coerce an applicant, *R v Islington London Borough Council, ex p Byfield* (1991) Legal Action, (March) p 14.

Authorities may request other housing and social services authorities and registered housing associations to assist them in discharging homeless functions. Such a request, under section 72, places the requested body under a duty to provide reasonable assistance. The CoG, para 12.7, points to the existence of agreements between associations and authorities for the former to take nominated homeless persons as tenants as evidence of this provision in operation. However, figures released by the Housing Corporation indicate that, though associations are rehousing more homeless persons, less than 20% of their lettings go to the homeless, see Miller, K, 'The Let Down' [1993] *Roof* March/April, p 20.

Where a homeless person is accommodated, questions arise as to the legal nature of the person's interest in the accommodation. The first issue is to determine whether premises are capable of supporting a tenancy. Where the person accommodated could not have exclusive possession of them, or part of them, no issue of a tenancy arises. Where the premises are self contained residential property which constitute a separate dwelling and exclusive occupation is granted in return for a periodical money payment, it appears that, irrespective of the name given to the transaction, a tenancy is created.

Where premises are capable of supporting a tenancy and one is granted in *pursuance of the duty to house a homeless person pending inquiries into apparent priority need*, ie where section 63 applies, or *where a homeless person is housed pending determination of whether a referral under the local connection provision* (section 68) is to be made, the tenancy is *not secure*, though it is a tenancy at common law. The position is similar with regard to tenancies granted under section 65(3) where temporary accommodation is found for an intentionally homeless person. Furthermore the tenancy cannot become secure before the end of a period of 12 months which begin on the date the tenant received the notification required under either section 64(1) or section 68(3), as appropriate, of the decision(s) on homelessness (threatened or actual) priority need, and intentionality, or as to a 'local connection' referral. Authorities should not 'stretch out' the period within which they take the decision on the 'pending' issue in question where they have all the information needed, see *Restormel Borough Council v Buscombe* (1982) 14 HLR 91. However, before the expiry of the 12 months post notification period the authority may inform the tenant the tenancy is secure. A similar situation applies where an authority places a person in private sector premises in pursuance of interim duties, see section 1(6) of the Housing Act 1988.

But where an authority accepts a duty to accommodate under section 65(2) or section 68(2) and gives notification to the applicant, *and then* moves that person into local authority accommodation, other than that in which the person previously was, there will, *in general*, be a secure tenancy of that new property. See the CoG paras 13.13 and 13.14.

In practice, however, many local authorities have become unable to fulfill even their most minimal duties to rehouse due to the dramatic shrinkage of the council housing stock over the last 15 years. The legal duty and the practical reality stand in stark contrast. The problem is readily demonstrated from the data which compares the supply of council lets with the demand arising from their duties to house certain homeless households. As Figure 4 shows the number of relets within the English local authority housing stock has remained stable at about 200,000 per annum, despite the overall decline in council housing due to sales arising from the right to buy policy – a decrease of about 1.5 million tenancies since 1980. However, the collapse of the local authority building programme has had a dramatic impact at a time when home-lessness acceptances have reached record proportions (Bramley,1994).

Figure Four: Homelessness and the supply of local authority lettings

England (1978-1990)	1978	1982	1986	1990
Homeless acceptances	53,100	74,800	103,600	147,790
Re-lets	203,000	217,000	210,000	200,000
New and acquired	100,000	38,000	33,000	24,000

Source: Bramley, 1994

The table shows that homeless acceptances in 1978 were about 17.5% of combined relets and new building (available supply) but in 1990 acceptances were over 65% of available supply. As a result of this allocations policy in many local authorities has been seriously distorted, particularly in London, with an ever increasing share of relets allocated to homeless households at the expense of applicants on the waiting list. Indeed in some London boroughs waiting lists are effectively closed as a route to council housing.

The impact of this position is severe for low income households who in the past commonly sought accommodation through the council waiting lists. The chance of being housed in the normal way was so severely curtailed that there was an immediate stimulus to the number of households presenting through the homelessness procedures. The decline in the supply of council housing caused homelessness to rise.

Duties of notification

Various duties of notification are imposed by section 64. When certain determinations are made they, and the reasons for them, must be given to the applicant.

These are:
1)   whether the person is homeless or threatened with homelessness;
2)   whether there is priority need;
3)   whether there is intentional homelessness;
4)   whether there is a 'local connection' with another housing authority.

Notices must be given in writing, and if not actually received by the applicant, are treated as given only if made available at the offices of the relevant authority for a reasonable period for collection by the applicant or on his/her behalf.

In giving notice it is insufficient simply to repeat statutory wording. The applicant must be informed why and how the case has been determined in a properly articulated decision, *R v Islington London Borough Council, ex p Trail* [1994] 2 FCR 1261, and reasons must be stated in such a way that the recipient can see *why* a decision has been reached, and is thus in a position to mount a challenge if the reasoning is deficient, see *R v Northampton Borough Council, ex p Carpenter* (1992) 25 HLR 349. The authority's conclusions of fact should be clearly stated as such, and these must be separated from other relevant considerations and judgements the authority has reached, *R v Islington London Borough Council, ex p Hinds* (1994) Legal Action, (September) p 15.

Offences

Various offences are created by section 74. Where a person, with intent to induce a belief on the part of an authority in connection with their homelessness functions as to his/her, or another's state of homelessness, threatened homelessness, priority need or unintentional homelessness, knowingly or recklessly makes statements false in material respects, or knowingly withholds information reasonably required by the authority, that person commits an offence. Applicants are required to inform authorities of material changes in circumstances arising before they receive notification of determinations. Authorities are required to explain this obligation to applicants in ordinary language.

Protecting the property of the homeless

Where an authority is under a duty to an applicant under sections 63, 65(2), 65(3), 66(2), or 68, and they have reason to believe there is danger of loss or damage to an applicant's personal property by reason of inability to protect it and that no other suitable arrangements have been made, they must take reasonable steps to prevent or mitigate loss or damage to the property in question. A *power* exists to protect property where duties under the foregoing provisions are not owed. Authorities are given wide powers to deal with property, including powers of entry. They may decline to take action save upon such conditions as they consider appropriate, for example as to the recovery of charges for having taken action. The duty ceases when the circumstances that gave rise to it cease to apply, and authorities must notify applicants of that fact.

Challenging decisions made under the Act and enforcing the duties

A disappointed applicant may complain:
1)   to a senior officer of the authority who may be able to review the initial decision;
2)   to local councillors, or MPs, who may seek to have the matter reopened;
3)   to the Commission for Local Administration where there is maladministration which arises out of failure to fulfil obligations, or unreasonable delay or inefficiency, etc, causing injustice. Failure to follow the provisions of the CoG could be a prima facie instance of maladministration.

Despite calls for an appellate system for homelessness decisions, the CoG, para 9.6, merely *recommends* creating a system of internal review, within an initial stage dealt with by a senior officer, and possibly an appellate panel with councillors as members and an independent chair. In 1990 some 30% of authorities had such a system. (See 'Internalising Rights of Appeal' Robson, (1990) 140 *New Law Journal* 712.) The existence of an appellate system does not prevent judicial review being sought. This can extend to the appeal decision itself, see *R v Sheffield City Council, ex p Burgar* (1990) Legal Action, (June) p 16. It should be made clear what sort of appeal system an authority is using (either a complete de nuovo examination of the case or a review of a decision in the light of any new information/arguments available) so that the applicant may know what is required of him or her, see *R v Tower Hamlets London Borough Council, ex p Hoque* (1993) Times, 20 June. Certainly an appeal system must be flexible and must not impose harsh and unreasonble requirements on a homeless person as a condition of receiving an appeal, see *R v Newham London Borough Council, ex p Gentle* (1993) 26 HLR 466. Nor may an appeal decision be reached without each of the matters raised by the appellant being investigated, see *R v Newham London Borough Council, ex p Laronde* (1994) Times, 11 March.

Recourse to the courts will be rarely available as a remedy since they have shown they wish to leave the day to day administration of the Act to local authorities, and will only involve themselves on points of law. It might be thought the very large number of decisions on homelessness indicates considerable judicial intervention in homelessness practice, but this is illusory. *Judicial Review in Perspective* (1993) Sunkin, Bridges and Mezzaros, members of the Public Law Project, indicates generally only 30% of judicial review applications reach a final hearing with one in six resulting in a ruling by a public body being challenged. Leave to apply for judicial review is needed and obtaining leave is something of a lottery, often depending upon which judge deals with an application, and corporate and institutional applicants are more successful in obtaining leave than are individuals. The courts will only intervene if they find an authority has erred in a point of law, ie it has clearly misinterpreted the wording of the Act, or has behaved in a procedurally improper manner, or has exceeded its powers; or has failed to obey the rules of natural justice in dealing with applications fairly; or has been random and arbitrary in the application of policies; or has behaved perversely by dealing with applicants in a gratuitously oppressive fashion; or has taken into account irrelevant factors, or failed to consider those that are relevant; or has fettered its discretion by adopting rigid rules as opposed to flexible guidelines, and certainly so where these have been developed by ad hoc groups not having formally delegated authority from their authority, see *R v Tower Hamlets London Borough Council, ex p Khalique* [1994] 2 FCR 1074, 26 HLR 517. Even where error is encountered the court may decline to provide a remedy if it concludes the applicant has not suffered substantial prejudice.

The burden of proof being on the challenger, a challenge under RSC Ord 53, r 1 and section 31 of the Supreme Court Act 1981 is the preclusive means of challenge to the actual decision of an authority, see *Cocks v Thanet District Council* [1983] 2 AC 286, [1983] 3 All ER 1135. It might still be possible to rely on *Thornton v Kirklees Metropolitan Borough Council* [1979] QB 626, [1979] 2 All ER 349 in an extreme case and bring an action for breach of statutory duty where a plaintiff could show that some right in private law had been infringed by the authority, see *Mallon v Monklands District Council* 1986 SLT 347 where a lack of accommodation was found to have contributed to psychiatric illness, likewise *Puives v Midlothian District Council* (1986) SCOLAG 144 where damages of £438 were awarded following breach of an undoubted duty to accommodate. The possibility of private law rights to sue was accepted in *South Holland District Council v Keyte* (1985) 19 HLR 97, but they can only arise after an authority has taken a decision and cannot be used to force decision taking, nor to question the validity of decisions, see *R v Lambeth London Borough Council, ex p Barnes* (1992) 25 HLR 140. However, breach of the duty to make inquiries into a homelessness application is a public law matter only, and gives no right to seek damages, see *R v Northavon District Council, ex p Palmer* (1994) Times, 16 March, (1994) Independent, 2 February. The matter of the suitability of accommodation, irrespective of how it arises, is one of public law only, see *Ali v London Borough of Tower Hamlets* (1992) 24 HLR 474, *London Borough of Tower Hamlets v Abdi* (1992) 25 HLR 80 and *Hackney London Borough v Lambourne* (1992) 25 HLR 172. (For a criticism of this line of development see Cowan, D, 'The Public/Private Dichotomy and "Suitable Accommodation" under Section 69(1) of the Housing Act 1985' [1993] JSWFL 236.) It is, however, possible for damages to be awarded in judicial review proceedings provided they are claimed along with one of the other remedies and 'arise out of any matter to which the application relates', see section 31(4)(a) of the Supreme Court Act 1981.

Under section 31 of the Supreme Court Act 1981 applications for orders of certiorari, mandamus, etc, must be made to the High Court whose leave (as already noted) must be obtained before application is made. Generally a person challenging a decision will also need interim or 'interlocutory' relief to keep accommodation over his/her head pending resolution of the issue and a final order. Interlocutory relief by way of injunction may be sought. In *De Falco v Crawley Borough Council* (supra) Lord Denning argued that to obtain such relief the applicant should be able to show a strong prima facie case that the authority is in breach of obligations. In *R v Cardiff City Council, ex p Barry* (1990) 22 HLR 261 the Court of Appeal indicated that the normal course of action where a decision is susceptible to challenge should be to grant interim relief; but only where the applicant can show there is a strong prima facie case the challenge will be successful, *R v Westminster City Council, ex p Augustin* [1993] 1 WLR 730.

With regard to final orders Lord Bridge made it clear in *Cocks v Thanet District Council* (supra) that courts do not sit to substitute their decisions for those of authorities, though, in practice, a court's finding that no reasonable authority could have come to the decision actually reached may be enough to settle an issue. Certiorari will be the principal remedy to quash a decision wrong in law, and mandamus will also be appropriately awarded to require a redetermination of issues. But in any case specific issues of illegality must be pleaded as no order of mandamus will be granted simply to make an authority perform its homelessness obligations generally, see *R v Beverley Borough Council, ex p McPhee* (1978) 122 Sol Jo 760.

Costs may be awarded in a review application once leave is granted, and authorities who concede cases before judgment usually pay costs voluntarily, though it appears the court may award costs even on an application for leave where an authority concedes, see *R v Secretary of State for Wales, ex p Rozhon* (1993) 91 LGR 667.

Duties under the Children Act 1989

Section 20(1) of the 1989 Act provides that social services authorities must provide accommodation for children 'in need' in their areas who appear to them to need accommodation as a result of: there being no persons having responsibility for them; their being lost or abandoned; persons who have been responsible for caring for them being prevented from providing suitable accommodation or care. Children, according to section 105(1) of the 1989

Act, are persons under the age of 18. Section 20(3) imposes a duty on social service authorities to provide accommodation for any 'child in need' within their areas who has reached the age of 16 and whose welfare they consider is likely to be seriously prejudiced if they do not provide him/her with accommodation. Section 27(1) enables a social services authority to request the specified aid of another authority (including a housing authority) in discharging the above functions, and subsection (2) requires an authority whose help is requested to comply with that request if it is 'compatible with their own statutory or other duties and obligations and does not unduly prejudice the discharge of any of their functions'.

Under section 20 the duty is primarily to accommodate the child in question, but there is no specific exclusion of accommodating the child with the rest of his/her family. However, in *R v Tower Hamlets London Borough Council, ex p Byas* [1993] 2 FLR 605, 25 HLR 105, the Court of Appeal considered that where an obligation is owed to a child under the 1989 Act that does not extend automatically to its parents, particularly where they are intentionally homeless. Second, the section 20(1) duty is owed in respect of children who are both 'in need', and who appear to need accommodation in *specified circumstances*. This definition is not the same as that of a homeless person under the 1985 Act. A child in need is defined by the 1989 Act as one who is disabled, or who is unlikely to achieve or maintain a reasonable standard of health or development without the provision of social services support, or whose health or development is likely to be significantly impaired without the provision of such support. The duty under section 20(3) in respect of general provision of accommodation to those aged between 16 and 18 is owed in respect of those who are 'in need', and whose welfare is likely to be 'seriously prejudiced' if they are not accommodated. Thus not every person aged between 16 and 18 will be able to rely on the obligation, even if 'in need', though a young person discharged from care may look for assistance to a social service authority under section 24(2) of the Act provided he/she was accommodated after reaching 16.

Survey evidence (*Plans No Action: The Children Act and Homeless Young People*, CHAR, 1992, and *Housing our Children: The Children Act 1989*, Centre Point, 1993) indicates that 62% of social services authorities accepted that being 16 or 17 and homeless placed a child 'in need', but 18% did not, while 12% were formulating a policy on the matter and 6% had no policy. In London over half the 32 social services departments had no procedure to make an assessment of a young person for the purposes of section 20, 77% had no accommodation suitable for 16-17 year olds and 44% did not consider homelessness alone a sufficient reason to provide accommodation under section 20. Only 33% of social services authorities have increased their supply of accommodation, mostly in supported lodgings, children's homes and bed and breakfast hotels (even though the wishes of children accommodated are to be taken into account in providing accommodation, see section 20(6)), while 75% of authorities have not taken steps to assess the needs of 16 and 17 year olds in their areas.

So far as section 27 of the 1989 Act is concerned, judicial guidance was given in *R v Northavon District Council, ex p Smith* [1994] 2 AC 402, [1994] 3 All ER 313 by the House of Lords. Mr and Mrs Smith, parents of five children aged under ten, had been found intentionally homeless. The Smiths then sought aid under the 1989 Act on behalf of their children from the social services authority who approached the District under section 27 and requested assistance for the Smiths in securing accommodation either by providing a full tenancy of a type commensurate with their needs, or by at least delaying their eviction from their temporary accommodation. The District refused to comply, and Mr Smith sought judicial review. In the House of Lords it was pointed out that when Mr Smith had made his homelessness application he was also entered on the housing waiting list under section 22 of the 1985 Act. But there were already 2,632 names on that list and he could expect a two and a half to three year wait before rehousing: to advance Mr Smith's rehousing would have been unfair to over 2,000 other persons. As a homeless person Mr Smith's case had been duly considered, and he had been found entitled only to a period of temporary accommodation. He was not entitled to any priority under section 22, and the County had no power to require the District to exercise rehousing powers. When responding to a request under section 27 of the 1989 Act an authority must judge that request in accordance with the various duties it has under the 1985 Act. The appropriate response is one of co-operation. Certainly a District must consider what it can do in response to a request, and must decide what help it can give, but the duty to co-operate must not unduly prejudice the discharge of housing functions, and where a District finds it cannot lawfully co-operate with a County request any duty to accommodate children in need remains with the County. Furthermore in *R v Tower Hamlets London Borough Council, ex p Byas* (supra) the Court of Appeal held that section 27 only applies *between* authorities, *not* between departments of *unitary* authorities: an authority cannot seek aid from itself, see also section 29(9) of the 1989 Act which allows for inter-authority reimbursement of costs incurred in providing accommodation under section 27.

Even so there remains room for conflict between authorities. Further clarification is needed of what is meant by the statutory concepts 'compatible with their statutory or other duties and obligations' and undue prejudice to the discharge of functions. For example it is arguable that where an authority tenant with children has been evicted for grossly bad behaviour involving violence or racial abuse towards neighbours in breach of a tenancy condition, it would be incompatible with that authority's duties etc, if they were then required to rehouse that tenant by virtue of a section 27 request, and in such cases the duties to the children will remain with the social services authority.

Outside of cases like that if a housing authority wished to resist a request for assistance it would not be enough for them merely to reiterate the statutory formulae in section 27. They would have to produce clear evidence as to the housing problems they face, and show that *in consequence* of those problems incompatibility with other duties or prejudice to their functions would be the necessary result of compliance with the social service authority's request. In fact that is what was done in the *Smith* case.

It appears, nationally, that 50% of social services departments have attempted to set up joint section 27 policies with housing departments, but only 21% had, by 1992, arrived at joint policies.

Duties under the National Assistance Act 1948 – care in the community

As we saw above the application of the strict definition of homelessness excludes very large numbers of households in severe housing need. Among these groups the most prominent are young single people, defined as being over age 18 although in reality there is considerable blurring in the 16-18 age groups. *Young* single people and couples represented only 7% of acceptances by authorities nationally although rising to 20% in Metropolitan authorities (Evans, A and Duncan, S *Responding to Homelessness: Local authority policy and practice*, HMSO, 1988). Young single people are the largest group of the 'hidden' homeless and are by definition difficult to quantify. The most recent attempt to review the scale of single homelessness in Britain concluded, 'There is no reliable estimate of the scale of single homelessness ... it is a national problem ... not confined to London or major cities' (Anderson, I *Access to Housing for Low Income Single People*, Centre for Housing Policy, University of York, 1993, p 1).

We have to rely therefore on the research findings of individual projects to point us to the magnitude of the problem. For example, a study of single homeless people in London conducted by the National Federation of Housing Associations estimated that there were 74,000 people living unwillingly in other people's households, 11,000-12,000 living in hostels, 10,000-12,000 in short-life housing, 19,000 in squats, 4,000-5,000 in bed and breakfast accommodation and up to 3,000 rough sleepers; in total about 100,000 single homeless people in London alone. This, of course, is only a snapshot at a particular point in time and as with all the statistics on homelessness fluctuates according to a variety of factors, primarily the state of the economy. A similar study commissioned by the London Boroughs Working Party on single homelessness estimated 50,000 single people living in temporary accommodation, squats or on the streets, and 74,000 seeking an independent home but currently living against their will in another household (Eardley, T *Move-on Housing: The Permanent Housing Needs of Residents of Hostels and Special Needs Housing projects in London*, SHIL, National Fedaration of Housing Associations, 1989).

Another recent study of the young single homeless has shown that certain groups of young people are particularly vulnerable to becoming homeless. These include leavers from local authority or other forms of care homes, young ex-offenders, and young people with psychiatric problems. This study also showed that a large proportion of young single homeless people said they became homeless due to arguments with their parents, often concerning their parent's alcohol abuse and related violent behaviour. 13% of the sample said they had been sexually abused at home (Stockley, D *Young people at risk of homelessness* Joseph Rowntree Foundation, 1993).

Provision for such people is at best scanty and at worst in some authority areas almost totally non-existent despite the, albeit contradictory and confusing, duties imposed on them through the National Assistance Act and recent legislation concerning the attempt to develop a system of community care. Here we consider the formal duties regarding vulnerable young adults and others.

Under the National Assistance Act 1948, and the amendments made by the National Health Service and Community Care Act 1990 and the Community Care (Residential Accommodation) Act 1992, social services authorities may, under section 21 of the 1948 Act (and must if directed by the Secretary of State) make arrangements for providing residential accommodation for those aged over 18 who by reason of age, illness, disability or any other circumstances are in need of care and attention not otherwise available to them. Regard must be had to the welfare of those accommodated and different types of premises should be provided according to their differing needs. Authorities may provide accommodation in their own premises, or they may, under section 26, as amended, make arrangements with voluntary organisations (including housing associations) and other persons for accommodation to be provided, for example in premises registered under the Registered Homes Act 1984. Section 24 of the 1948 Act empowers social services authorities to provide residential accommodation for persons in their areas who have no settled residence, or though not ordinarily resident in their areas, are in urgent need of residential accommodation.

Community care of those discharged into society from institutional accommodation fits into the pattern of residential accommodation established under the foregoing provisions – at least in theory. Section 46 of the National Health Service and Community Care Act 1990 requires social services authorities to make and keep under review plans for the provision of community care services in their areas. In making plans authorities are to consult, inter alia, with relevant housing authorities and voluntary housing agencies. Section 47(1) of the 1990 Act further requires, where it appears to a social services authority that any person for whom they may provide community care services is in need of such, they shall assess his/her needs and decide in consequence whether services shall be provided. Section 47(4) empowers the Secretary of State to give binding directions as to how assessments are to take place, otherwise they are to be carried out as authorities consider appropriate. Section 47(5) allows for provision of services without assessment in cases where a person's condition requires services as a matter of urgency.

Community Care as a policy is in its infancy, but there was in mid-1993 public disquiet about its implementation. This centred on high profile incidents in which discharged psychiatric patients were involved in alleged murders, assaults or self-inflicted injuries, including suicide. There was also cause for concern relating to the policy's housing implications. Many of those discharged may qualify under the 1985 Act as priority need cases because they are vulnerable; indeed of 35,529 homelessness acceptances in the third quarter of 1992, 23% were because applicants were 'vulnerable', 7% being due to mental illness and 'other' reasons for vulnerability. The CoG ,para 6.11, gives guidance on procedures applicable to those discharged from institutional care. This counsels involving social services departments in the assessment of the case.

Early evidence suggested little liaison had taken place nationally between authorities. Central government stressed the need for co-operation between housing authorities and associations and social services agencies, see DoE Circular 10/92, including need for housing providers to assist in assessment procedures and the development of referral procedures between departments, with nomination of liaison officers being suggested. The impact of Community Care policies on housing strategies should also be considered by housing authorities, and appropriate provision reflected in the composition of Housing Investment Programmes. However, the policy creates 'no new category of entitlement to housing' and housing needs consequent on the policy are to be considered alongside existing processes and local priorities. Homelessness duties are, moreover, only briefly touched on in the annex to the Circular, though one item of advice is that individuals subject to Community Care should not be given unsuitable accommodation such as rooms in unsupervised hostels.

There is ample room for conflict. What, for example, of a person who applied to a district council as homeless and vulnerable following discharge from institutional care, and who was considered by that authority not vulnerable? If the person proceeds to apply to the social services authority and they make an assessment and determine they are under a duty they may request the district council to reconsider the case, but no more. What of a district council which encounters homeless applicants and tenants unable to cope without social services support? In many cases referral will be made to the social services authority, but those in need of assistance may not get help because they get lost between authorities, or they may obtain inappropriate or incomplete aid by way of cross referrals and liaison not taking place. Some authorities have introduced new means of assessing housing need, while a number of associations are considering a role as both housing and care providers. In some metropolitan areas housing and social services departments have been merged in an attempt to improve housing and care services. However, institutional rearrangement is of little worth unless it is accompanied by the creation of appropriate housing units for those with special needs, and resources to provide those units are conspicuous by their increasing absence.

Affordable housing as a response to homelessness

Lack of housing that people of modest incomes can afford is a cause of homelessness, and it has been recognised by planning policy that: 'it may be desirable ... that new housing developments on a substantial scale in both urban and rural areas should incorporate a reasonable mix and balance of house types ... to cater for a range of housing needs' (Planning Policy Guidance Note (PPG) 3, March 1992, para 38). Planning authorities are asked to assess the need for affordable housing and to reflect this in plan making, and may negotiate with developers under section 106 of the Town and Country Planning Act 1990 (as amended in 1991) to secure the inclusion of such housing in development schemes. Planning authorities are counselled against preferring particular forms of tenure or price levels for such housing, and against seeking to impose quotas of affordable housing on all residential schemes. Planning law does not generally permit planning authorities to restrict the tenure, price or ownership of housing, hence PPG 3 counsels involving housing associations in schemes including affordable housing. An association may be able to purchase the low cost elements of a housing development which will then be available for long term renting.

The law and homelessness: an assessment

Homelessness cannot be erradicated by passing laws. The most the law could do would be to create a framework within which resources can be justly and equitably divided. At the moment there is not even an integrated, internally coherent legal structure seeking to provide appropriate accommodation for all in need. Rather we have a number of measures designed to deal ad hoc with aspects of homelessness. Part III of the 1985 Act is designed to provide assistance only to limited numbers of people who manage to satisfy certain criteria. Despite attempts to ensure consistency of practice nationwide, it is clear the application of the law of homelessness varies considerably between authorities. Initially this had a great deal to do with whether authorities had accepted voluntary responsibility for the homeless in 1974. Since then the issue has been confused by the interaction of a range of issues: attitudes of officers and councillors, local political pressures to ensure some housing stock is retained for allocation to those on the 'normal' waiting list; size and composition of the available housing stock; numbers of homelessness applications received.

It has been powerfully argued by Ian Loveland that the influence of the law in such circumstances is not nearly so great as lawyers might wish, with administrative practice counting for much more than might be supposed, see 'Administrative Law, Administrative Processes, and the Housing of Homeless Persons' [1991] Journal of Social Welfare and Family Law (JSWFL) 1, and 'The Politics, Law and Practice of "International Homelessness" Parts 1 and 2' [1993] JSWFL 113 and 185. But the law does have an undoubted part to play, and experience of working with authorities throughout the East Midlands indicates that the influence of the law varies according to levels of training received by relevant staff, the nature and quality of relationships between authorities and local campaigning organisations, and the availability of legal advice to applicants either through law centres or specialist firms of solicitors.

The real problem, however, lies with the general shortage of social housing. Society has since 1945 undergone radical changes. Extended families living together have largely disappeared; the single adult unit (with or without children) is much more common. The pattern of housing demand has changed dramatically: less so the pattern of housing supply. There has also been a blithe official assurance that rising real incomes would enable more and more people to purchase their own homes; the trend throughout the century. The official mind has further been fixated since 1979 with questions of who should own social housing, and has not properly addressed the question of how much, and what sort of, social housing is needed. Not everyone wants to be, or can be, an owner occupier. It is no sin not to own one's home, nor is it a great offence to find that one needs assistance to obtain reasonable accommodation. There will always be a constituency for social housing: the homeless are the most obvious manifestation of that demand.

Homelessness – the future?

Far from regarding the claims of the homeless as being the prime housing need, the government in its 1994 consultative proposals – *Access to Local Authority and Housing Association Tenancies* – appeared set on returning the law to virtually its pre-1977 position. Arguing that the automatic priority accorded to the homeless over other applicants for council housing has made it almost impossible in some areas – particularly in London – for an 'ordinary' applicant to obtain housing, the Government condemned the 'homelessness route' as an 'attractive way into subsidised housing for those wishing to be re-housed'. They then proposed certain changes, the most important of which would require new legislation.

The first major change would be to redefine authorities' duty to the homeless as one solely to provide emergency assistance, ie the duty would be to help those who, unintentionally, have no accommodation of *any sort* available for occupation, and that duty would not formally commence until an authority had made an assessment of the circumstances and was satisfied the applicant met the legal criteria. This would equate homelessness with rooflessness. Second, the extent of authorities' duties would be restricted to securing accommodation for a limited period while applicants found something for themselves from an association, the ordinary waiting list or a private landlord. How short a period would be involved in this restricted duty was a cause of some speculation. Ministers argued it could be statutorily limited in length, or left to authorities to determine, either *prospectively* at the time of application (in which case they would determine a period at the outset of each application which would be a 'reasonable' time to find accommodation) or *retrospectively* once they concluded an applicant had had a reasonable time to find a dwelling. Either of these latter methods depends on the exercise of subjective discretion and thus are open to challenge by way of judicial review. In the exercise of that discretion authorities would have to take into account difficulties in finding private accommodation in their areas and the average length of time needed to secure accommodation in social housing, and there would be a duty to give warning to an applicant that the duty to accommodate was considered drawing to an end. This duty to provide emergency assistance would, however, recur if a household continued to meet all the necessary criteria, save, that where an applicant turned down an offer of suitable accommodation while being temporarily accommodated an authority would be entitled to consider that no further duty would arise.

A third major change in the law related to persons eligible for assistance. First, a person asked to leave his/her home by family or friends should no longer be *automatically* entitled to assistance, and it was argued that authorities might require such applicants to show court orders against them granting possession before providing assistance. This would not be the case, however, where a person was fleeing from domestic violence of whatever form. Second, authorities would be under no duty to persons who had any form of accommodation available, however temporary the tenure, though criteria of space, health and hygiene would apply to determine whether shelter constituted 'accommodation'. Third, persons would not be in need of assistance where alternative accommodation was generally available. This would require authorities to ask applicants whether they have tried to help themselves, whether they have put their names on housing waiting lists, and to direct them to particular vacant accommodation considered suitable, with a failure to respond disentitling the applicant to assistance.

Further changes under consideration to the rules on priority need and intentional homelessness would likewise restrict eligibility. For example 'very young single mothers' might be made subject to special housing provision requirements such as living in supervised hostel or in shared housing, while a failure to take up an offer of suitable alternative accommodation that is reasonably available would be regarded as intentional homelessness invalidating a claim to assistance. Particular restrictions would also apply to persons from abroad. The government proposed there should be a statutory rule that persons admitted to the UK on the understanding they will not be a burden on public funds should have no entitlement to emergency housing assistance. It was further proposed that those who have lived overseas (whether or not they are UK citizens) and who still have accommodation in those countries which they can reasonably be expected to occupy should also be excluded from cover under the new law. It is clear such an exclusion would bear down hard upon members of ethnic minorities who are used to splitting their time between the UK and other parts of the world.

So far as discharging the duty to offer emergency accommodation is concerned ministers proposed that a guiding principle should be that authorities should ensure 'value for money' in securing accommodation. Associations would be placed under obligations requiring them to give reasonable assistance to authorities in relation to providing emergency accommodation.

Ministers also invited views on whether authorities should be required to have an appeals system for homelessness decisions which would have to be used before a remedy could be sought in court. They were uncertain whether this appellate system should be internal to authorities or exist independently of them. They were also concerned that judicial review is the only route of legal challenge to homeless decisions and proposed to consider whether alternative means of challenge should be available. One matter on which they were certain was that current informal appellate systems are not working in a clearly satisfactory way: it is strange that in its 1989 review of the homelessness legislation a government of the same political colour rejected both a formal requirement for an appeals system and the possibility of allowing the county court to have some sort of appellate jurisdiction with regard to homelessness issues.

Some 10,000 responses were received to the consultation paper, as a result of which some modifications were made in the government's proposals, though there was no alteration in the central contention that the current form of the law allows homeless applicants to gain priority in the housing queue over those having comparable underlying housing needs. What the governement did accept was that to give *greater* discretion to authorities in dealing with homelessness applications could lead to too great a burden on individual authorities. Accordingly the proposals are that:

(1)   as at present a duty to a household in need of assistance will begin when an authority has reason to believe a person may be homeless and in priority need;

(2)   there should be a *new* duty to secure accommodation including shorthold tenancies in the PRS for those in priority need who have no suitable accommodation available, provided that situation has arisen unintentionally, for a minimum period of one year, during which time

they may be able to (and may be encouraged to) find accommodation for themselves, or during which they may qualify on the 'normal' waiting list for an authority or association tenancy;

(3)   If at the end of the minimum period assistance is still needed the duty to assist will recur subject to a review of an applicant's circumstances which should take place within two years;

(4)   the duty to assist should extend to people in refuges, direct access hostels and other short stay accommodation;

(5)   the provision concerning intentional homelessness will be modified to enable authorities to consider why accommodation is being withdrawn in a case where a person is homeless having been asked to leave by family or friends;

(6)   those admitted to the UK on the understanding they will have no recourse to public funds will not be entitled to assistance under the new law;

(7)   local authorities will be required to have their own formal appeals mechanisms for handling homelessness disputes, and this it is hoped, will lessen the incidence of judicial review, with the government proposing to consider how the new appellate system will relate to legal challenges by way of review;

(8)   there will be no change in the current law relating to local connection issues;

(9)   authorities will be placed under a duty to provide housing advisory services to assist those seeking accommodation and to prevent homelessness.

On a non-statutory basis authorities will now be encouraged to develop partnerships with the private sector to deal with homelessness. Development of the system of giving guarantees for rent, or rent deposits, to private landlords by authorities to enable people to take up private sector tenancies is to be undertaken while the private sector's involvement in rehousing the homeless within the constraints of current legislation is also to be examined.

It seems likely therefore, writing in the summer of 1994, that the government will adopt a major policy change based on their consultation paper. This approach will certainly throw into relief the position of the PRS to which the government is looking to take the strain from the local authorities. But the PRS is a fragmented tenure divided between tied accommodation for nurses, the police, agricultural workers and so on, a residual 'traditional' rent controlled sector mainly occupied by elderly people, an 'up-market' for well-off single people and families, and a sub-sector mainly occupied by young mobile people frequently in receipt of housing benefit and in which, as a result of the low rental stream, housing standards are poor (Kemp, P *The Future of Private Renting*, University of Salford, 1988). For the latter group the continuation of this sub-sector may arguably be a solution to immediate

housing needs and so prevent homelessness but the absence of a widely dispersed PRS is a peculiar feature of the Britsh housing system and its near absence in some parts of the country is undoubtedly a major underlying cause of homelessness. As we understand it the government is proposing to reinvigorate the use of the PRS as a temporary staging post for homeless households to re-enter the housing market or to provide 'holding' accommodation while such families await their turn in the local authority waiting list. It seems almost inevitable in such circumstances that many of the worst features of the PRS might re-appear. At the very least homeless families will find themselves in the highly unsatisfactory situation of living in a series of temporary private lets. By October 1994, however, the government appeared to have had a, temporary at least, change of mind. The homelessness proposals were not included in the Queen's Speech on legislative proposals.

Further reading

Articles

Birkinshaw, P 'Homelessness and the Law – the Effects and Response to Legislation' [1982] *Urban Law & Policy* 255

Bryan, M 'Domestic Violence: A Question of Housing' [1984] JSWL 195

Ghosh, S 'Community Care or Carelessness' (1994) *Roof* March/April 11

Hoath, D 'Split Families and Part III of the Housing Act 1985' [1987] JSWL 15

Hoath, D 'Homelessness Law After the Housing and Planning Act 1986: The Puhlhofer Amendments' [1988] JSWL 39

Loveland, I 'Legal Rights and Political Realities: Governmental Responses to Homelessness in Britain' (1991) *Law & Social Inquiry* 249

Loveland, I 'Square Pegs, Round Holes: The "Right" to Council Housing in the Post War Era' (1992) 19 *Journal of Law & Society* 1

Robson, P and Watchman, P 'The Homeless Persons' Obstacle Race' [1981] JSWL 165

Sunkin, M 'Trends in the use of Judicial Review before and after Swati and Puhlhofer (1987) 137 *New Law Journal* 731

Sunkin, M 'What is happening to applications for Judicial Reviews?' (1987) *Modern Law Review* 432

Watchman, P 'Heartbreak Hotel' [1988] JSWL 147

Reports

Anderson, I Access *to Housing for Low Income Single People* 1994, University of York, Centre for Housing Policy

Anderson, I, Kemp, P and Quilgars, D *Single Homeless People* 1993, London, HMSO

Arnold, P, Bochel, H, Brodhurst, S, Page, D   *Community Care: The housing dimension* 1993, York, Rowntree Foundation
Association of District Councils   *Homelessness: Meeting the Tide* 1987, London, ADC
Association of District Councils   *Homelessness: A Review of the Legislation* 1988, London, ADC
Evans, A, and Duncan, S ˙ *Responding to Homelessness: Local Authority Policy & Practice* 1988, London, HMSO
Garside, P   *No Place Like Home* 1990, London, HMSO
Greve, J   *Homelessness in Britain* 1991, York, Joseph Rowntree Memorial Trust
National Audit Office   *Homelessness* 1990, London, HMSO
Niner, P   *Homelessness in Nine Local Authorities: Case Studies of Policy & Practice* 1989, London, HMSO
Randall, G and Brown, S   *Private Renting for Single Homeless People: An Evaluation of a Pilot Rent Deposit Fund* 1994, London, HMSO
Thomas, A, and Niner, P   *Living in Temporary Accommodation: A Survey of Homeless People* 1989, London, HMSO

Books
Hunter, C, and McGrath, S   *Homeless Persons: Arden's Guide to the Housing Act 1985*, 4th Edition, 1992, London Legal Action Group

Chapter Seven

Housing standards

Historical context

The issue of housing standards and the renewal of the housing stock became important issues during the nineteenth century due to the public health consequences of rapid urbanisation. Appallingly high mortality and morbidity was endemic in Victorian slum housing. As we described in Chapter One the insanitary condition of urban housing was one of the principal reasons for state intervention in the housing market. As early as 1868, in The Artizans' and Labourers' Dwellings Act (the Torrens Act), local authorities with populations over 10,000 were granted considerable powers to enforce compulsory unfitness notices against landlords, and so provided for the closure and demolition of dwellings unfit for human habitation. There was, of course, at this time no financial assistance and improvement grants did not become available in urban areas until after World War Two. The Housing (Rural Workers) Act 1926 gave authorities in rural locations discretion to award grants and make loans for improvements but these powers were rarely used.

In the Artizans' and Labourers' Dwellings Improvement Act 1875 (the Cross Act) authorities were given powers to clear and redevelop *areas* of unfit housing but they had very limited possibilities to rebuild even after the Housing of the Working Classes Act 1890 and, in the absence of any significant central government funding until the conclusion of the 1914-18 war, far more slums were cleared than were rebuilt. Individual closures and the redevelopment of whole areas of housing have been enshrined in the issue of housing standards ever since.

For most of the twentieth century renovation and improvement of existing housing stock was subsumed under both the slum clearance programme and the drive for new building. It was not until the end of the 1960s that investment in the renovation of existing property became more cost effective than demolition and rebuilding due to the decline in the absolute shortage of housing stock. Renovation of existing property is, of course, one way in which new supply can be achieved – by giving existing dwellings a longer life expectancy than they would have otherwise (Needleman, L 'The comparative economics of improvement and new building' *Urban Studies* Vol 6 No 2, 1969 pp 196-209). Under the different circumstances of the 1920s the renovation and reconditioning of existing housing was promoted as an *alternative* to local authority building by the opponents of municipal housing. Bowley estimates that between 1919 and 1930 some 300,000 houses *per annum* were rehabilitated by forcing private landlords to recondition and improve their property by statutory orders against them (Bowley, M *Housing and the State*, Allen and Unwin, 1945). Renovation of housing in the PRS thus made a considerable contribution to the inter-war drive to increase housing supply but the standard of improvement was frequently poor and many rehabilitated houses were later demolished as slums. Improvement of this stock up to the very basic standard inherited from late-Victorian housing legislation was not, therefore, an adequate response to the problem of slum housing. Accordingly a specific subsidy for slum clearance and their replacement by new houses was adopted in the Labour Government's Second Housing Act 1930. This legislation was not as some commentators argue a major break in policy but, seen in the light of the reconditioning of housing in the 1920s, can be viewed as an extension of existing concern about the state of the PRS.

This is not the place for a detailed evaluation of the slum clearance programme and we refer readers to Chapter Two of Gibson and Langstaff's *An Introduction to Urban Renewal* (Hutchinson, 1982) for a full account. The clearances were of massive dimensions and some two million dwellings have been demolished since the Housing Act 1930 (Greenwood Act) with the built environment of almost every major town and city changed as a result. Clearances were halted during the Second World War and only started again in the mid-1950s when the economy had recovered from the catastrophic consequences of the war. In the five years between 1955 and 1959 213,000 houses were demolished or closed affecting nearly 670,000 people. The clearance programme reached its post-war peak in the second half of the 1960s when between 1964 and 1969 339,000 house were demolished. (*Annual Housing Statistics* and *Housing and Construction Statistics* HMSO.) The rate of clearance fell, in the mid-1970s, to about 50,000 per annum and declined sharply thereafter; by 1989 it was down to only 6,000 and has stayed below that level subsequently.

The new era of improvement grants

State aided renovation grants were made available to assist property owners – both landlords and owner occupiers – in the Housing Act 1949 but it was after the major re-focusing of housing policy away from investment in new building and towards rehabilitation of the existing stock at the end of the

1960s that renovation grants of various types became widely used as a mainstream instrument of housing policy.

Grants were introduced by the post-war Labour government as a complement to the public sector dominated construction programme. The aim, as Bevan, the Minister responsible for housing, argued was ' ...not to rescue slums ...or permit landlords to make good arrears of repairs' but to improve basically sound property as a means of increasing and sustaining the housing stock following the neglect of the war years (cited in Gibson and Langstaff, 1982). These improvement grants were therefore for the specific purposes of providing indoor toilets and hot water and to assist the conversion of single houses into flats. The grant was at the discretion of authorities and only covered 50% of the cost. The basic condition was that the dwellings would be improved to provide a minimum of 30 years life expectancy. In fact because of these very stringent conditions only 6,000 grants were approved between 1949 and 1953 (Gibson and Langstaff, 1982, p 54).

The Housing Repairs and Rents Act 1954 eased restrictions by reducing the approved life span of improved dwellings to only 15 years. The Conservative Government was keen to see a wider take up of improvement grants as a complement to slum clearance. The aim was to stop marginal housing in 'grey' areas from deteriorating into slums. The strategy was to allow rent increases in the PRS to help fund improvements while at the same time increasing grant levels. The campaign had a considerable impact and during the second half of the 1950s grants were running at or above 30,000 per annum, even though some authorities persisted in refusing to give grants.

One of the reasons for the partial decontrol of the PRS in the 1957 Rent Act was to provide a financial incentive for landlords to invest in the maintenance and refurbishment of their property and so strengthen the sector. In fact the long awaited 'revival' did not happen and, as we saw in Chapter One, the 1957 Act if anything hastened the demise of the PRS. The priority given to expanding home ownership was a major factor in the problems faced by the PRS. The House Purchase and Housing Act 1959 encouraged low income households into home ownership by assisting building socieities to enhance their loans to purchasers of low cost, mainly pre-1919 housing. In addition the 1959 Act introduced a second level of improvement grant, the 'standard' grant. These were mandatory grants, available by right if certain conditions were satisfied. Owners – both landlords and owner occupiers – had to ensure the installation of the five standard amenities in return for a fixed grant and on condition that the dwelling was given a minimum life expectancy of 15 years. This shorter term and lower level of 'standard' grant operated in parallel with the discretionary improvement grants which continued to support property improvement to a higher standard and 30 year life expectancy.

Take up of the standard grant accelerated rapidly and after only one year two thirds of new grants were of this type. Between 1959 and 1964, 600,000 grants in total were approved but it is important to note that 80% of these were taken up by owner occupiers, taking advantage of the mandatory standard grant. As we argued in Chapter One this tenure distribution represented a massive injection of public investment into home ownership at the expense of the PRS which continued to decline both absolutely and relatively.

Area improvement

Towards the end of their third continuous term of office the Conservative Government of 1959-64 began to reassess the problems still very much apparent in the inner cities. The scale of urban renewal, despite the increase in grants and the slum clearance programme, was still inadequate for the task. Under pressure from the gathering tide of 'twilight' decay and facing a general election the Housing Act 1964 made, for the first time, a specific pledge to increase grant aid, to 200,000 grants per annum, and as a corollary included the idea of specifically targeted areas where it was hoped all the houses would be improved to a minimum standard. Accordingly private landlords (not owner occupiers) could be forced to take up improvement grants and so the introduction of Improvement Areas also brought an element of compulsion into the hitherto voluntary system of grants. Authorities were also given powers to compel owners of houses of multiple occupation (HMOs) to improve their property to a specified standard. The 1964 Act is significant because it signalled a drift towards a more comprehensive approach to urban renewal.

By the end of the 1960s national housing policy was on the verge of breaking from the strategy of large scale construction of new dwellings to a programme based on renewal of existing stock. The underlying reason for this was that the era of absolute housing shortages was at last coming to an end. In the short term economic crisis was looming, coming to a head with the devaluation crisis of 1967, and there was considerable opposition to the slum clearance programme from community action groups.

Having won the 1964 election the incoming Labour Government (1964-70) initially opted to run a parallel policy of clearance and improvement. A number of area based feasibility studies were influential at this time in promoting the idea of area rehabilitation. The Deeplish Study (an area in Rochdale) was particularly important because it showed how an area of old terraced property, most of which was owner occupied, could be improved. A major problem was the reluctance of some landlords and elderly owner occupiers to undertake or to afford their share of the improvement work even with grant aid. It was concluded that the adoption of a cheaper, lower standard of improvement together with state aided *environmental* improvement was an effective mechanism for overcoming resistance to area improvement. It was thought that environmental improvement could enhance property values and so stimulate owners to invest.

Pressure on public spending following the devaluation crisis forced Labour to abandon its National Housing Plan target to build 500,000 homes and the peak year of building in the public sector was reached in 1968. Resources were increasingly committed to the renewal strategy. This took legislative form in the Housing Act 1969 which, following the Deeplish study, established the idea of General Improvement Areas (GIAs) to replace Improvement Areas. GIAs were small areas designated by authorites into which they would focus their urban renewal and housing improvement effort supported by a new subsidy to invest in environmental improvements. Within GIAs the conditions of the old improvement grants were altered (by reducing the minimum life expectancy and minimum periods before the resale of the property) and the level of financial support for eligible expenses was increased. An additional grant, Special Grant, was also introduced in the 1969 Act to assist with the provision of improved facilities in HMOs.

The effect of the 1969 legislation was to generate a huge increase in the level of housing improvement and was one of the few positive developments in housing policy at the time. Nevertheless, based on an essentially voluntary approach and in the context of limited resources, the GIA approach itself made a very limited impact. The number of GIAs declared was relatively small and the number of grants targeted at GIAs was small – only 5% of all grants. As Leather and Mackintosh observe, 'By 1974, declared GIAs contained only 273,000 dwellings and improvement work had been completed in only 14% of these dwellings' (Leather, P and Mackintosh, S 'Housing Renewal in an Era of Mass Home Ownership' in *Implementing Housing Policy* Malpass, P and Means, R (eds) Open University Press, 1993, p 114). Moreover, it is clear that large numbers of grants were not being taken up by the poorest households in the worst housing because they were unable to afford their share of the grant aid which remained at 50% of the cost. By the same token many landlords especially in London used grants to improve their properties prior to selling them at profit to owner occupiers and a large number of grants went to more affluent home owners living outside the inner cities. Criticisms were also made that the standard of repair work was sometimes not high due to the inability of authorities to monitor or supervise the work.

The response to this catalogue of problems came in the new Labour Government's Housing Act 1974. In recognition of the difficulties faced by low income households the rate of grant aid was increased to 75% in newly designated Housing Action Areas (HAAs) and authorities had discretion to increase this level of funding to 90%. Grants in GIAs were increased to a ceiling of 60% of eligible costs. This repair grant, as it was known, was designed to stop affluent home owners from exploiting the grant system by focusing much more generous grant aid into HAAs and GIAs and authorities were encouraged to buy out private landlords in HAAs if they failed to take up improvement grants voluntarily.

As with the GIAs the declaration by authorities of the new HAAs was slow and in practice a very small proportion of total grant expenditure was dispersed in these specially designated areas, only 14% by 1978. Problems for poor households in meeting their share of costs persisted even with grants at 90%. The results of the 1981 House Condition Survey confirmed that the grant system was failing to tackle the worst housing. The survey found virtually no change in the number of unfit dwellings from the previous survey in 1976 (DoE, HMSO, 1982 and 1983). Between 1974 and 1979 slum clearance had slowed dramatically and by 1979 was down to 33,000 the lowest figure since clearance resumed after the war in 1955. More significantly, given the emerging emphasis on renovation of old property, improvement and standard grants had fallen by 1979 by over 60% from their peak in 1973. The switch from clearance to renovation had done little to stimulate progress in urban renewal and the policy was running hard to stand still. A great deal of effort was expended by some authorities to stimulate a more refined and consumer friendly approach to area renewal but it is difficult to avoid the conclusion that this slowing down and so called 'gradual' approach was one of economic expediency.

From 'old' to 'new' systems

The improvement grant system began by assisting owner occupiers and landlords to install *basic amenities* but this gradually evolved to include 'home improvements' such as new kitchen units and bathroom extensions and structural repairs and more recently some authorities have used so called 'enveloping' schemes whereby the external shell of groups of dwellings in

Figure Four Renovations using public funding by tenure, Great Britain, 1973-1992

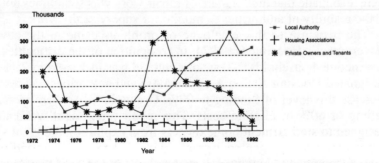

HAAs and sometimes whole streets are renovated. The argument in favour of this sort of project was that it did achieve a concentration of resources – using a variety of funding sources such as Urban Programme funds – and by using one builder the work could be done fairly rapidly. The aim was to induce owners to invest their own resources in internal improvements together with grant aid and also tackled the problem of large numbers of 'cowboy' builders who were able to operate freely in a system dominated by individual grants. But as with so many aspects of public policy the victory of the Conservatives in the 1979 General Election heralded a radical departure from the story of urban renewal and the drive for improved housing standards thus far.

Urban renewal in the 1980s

As is well known the new Conservative Government initiated a vigorous campaign of support for home ownership not least of which was the right to buy policy in the Housing Act 1980. A few changes were made in renewal policy in the 1980 Act, the most important of which was the extension of the repair grant available only in GIAs and HAAs to *all* pre-1919 houses, and in 1983 the level of grant aid was increased to 90% for all repair and intermediate grants. This led to a boom in applications, particularly for repair grants, and for several years funding was provided to meet all these grants reaching a peak of over 300,000 awards in 1984 at a cost of over £1 billion. After 1984 expenditure on private sector grants was incorporated into the HIP system which meant that they were in effect in competition with public sector renovation and, until the introduction of the completely new grant system in the early 1990s, grants to private sector applicants levelled out to about half the 1984 level. This was a considerably higher level overall than in previous decades but the policy of area renewal was in effect abandoned because the surge of applicants created so called 'pepper-potting' of grants.

The level of resources devoted to the authorities' own housing stock grew rapidly during this period. Public sector renovation reached a peak of expenditure of nearly £2 billion in 1988/89. This surge in public sector renovation was partly due to a 'creative' definition of capital work – receipts from the sale of council houses could not be used routinely to build new houses but were channelled instead into renovation – and partly because authorities were anxious to retain the support and confidence of tenants under an alleged threat of takeover by predatory landlords through the 'Tenants' Choice' legislation. Thus although the evidence showed a much greater scale of problems in the private sector, the majority of investment in the mid and late 1980s was made in public sector renovation. Grant aid continued to miss the target of the growing number of low income households who were or had become owner occupiers – often through lack of alternatives – in dwellings that were unfit or, at the very least, were in a poor state of repair.

A response to this issue was, however, on the drawing board at a fairly early stage and arose specifically from the disappointing findings of the English House Condition Survey 1981 to which reference was made above. A period of consultation led to the publication in 1985 of a Green Paper *Home improvement – a new approach* (Cmnd 9513) which laid the foundations for a fundamental change to the 'traditional', post-1949 renovation system. In common with the political philosophy of the government there was to be a shift of responsibility away from state aid and towards greater individual responsibility. It was argued that too high rates of grant had induced complacency and an expanding commitment of public funds. Indeed 10% of dwellings had received more than one grant and the enveloping schemes had signalled to many people that the state would undertake any necessary external repair work. Accordingly the old system was to be withdrawn and replaced with a new grant regime targetted at the very poorest households through means-testing. The standard of improvement was to be significantly reduced to achieve a merely habitable standard rather than a 15 or 30 year life expectancy. Moreover, it was proposed to compel private owners to take out loans secured against the value of the property for improvement work above the basic fitness standard – although in the subsequent legislation this proposal was dropped. There was a considerable emphasis in the Green Paper on the establishment of a variety of agencies to help owners understand the system and assist in getting work done. It followed from the emphasis on targeted assistance that renewal areas were to be very much a secondary consideration in the 'new' system.

Initially there was a vociferous critical response, notably from authority officers, on the lines that the proposals reduced standards and in effect would privatise the grant system. But the evidence suggests that something had to be done to target resources at those in greatest need. The existing system was very complicated with many levels and standards of grants available. It was clear that area renewal had been of very limited success in tackling the worst problems because for various reasons authorities did not focus their grant aid into GIAs or HAAs. Neither did the HIP system of housing finance target authorities with the greatest problems and, most fundamentally, as Leather and Mackintosh argue,

> '...grant aid since 1969 had been widely available for all older properties meeting broad eligibility criteria, (but) it had rarely been sufficiently generous to enable the poorest households living in the worst condition properties to benefit.'

(Leather and Mackintosh, 1993, p 116)

In fact due to delays and the response of the government to criticisms of the original Green Paper a new round of consulation took place and the 'new' system was finally introduced through the Local Government and Housing Act, 1989.

The 'new' system

The 1989 Act completely overhauls the grant system more or less in line with the Green Paper. There are now four main types of grant: Renovation, Common Parts, HMOs and Disabled Facilities. Provision is also made for minor works assistance which is a discretionary award of up to £1,080 (three awards are allowed in a three year period) and is aimed particularly at elderly owner occupiers for such works as thermal insulation and adaptations. The 'staying put' scheme for elderly home owners is built around the availability of these small grants which can also be used for minor repairs and maintenance.

The new fitness standard is based on a series of individual criteria rather than a 'package' and is designed to provide for immediate habitation with much less emphasis on giving the property a long life expectancy. Fitness is, however, determined by a broader range of factors than previously, including minimum heating levels in habitable rooms, availability of hot and cold water at the sink where food is prepared, and so on. Authorities must under this legislation take action on unfit dwellings.

The main grant is the renovation grant which takes the place of the old improvement and repair grants. These grants are mandatory for unfit dwellings and grant aid is determined by the applicant's income and, if needs be, covers 100% of the cost of the work. Grants to renovate or repair the building above the unfitness standard are also available but these are discretionary and the evidence of the first few years of the new system shows that very few resources have been targeted at discretionary work; in northern authorities less than 10% of grant aid was discretionary (excluding minor works grants). At the time of writing the common parts and HMO grants appear to have been very little utilised; only 127 HMO grants were paid in the first full year of the new regime and even fewer common parts grants (Leather and Mackintosh, 1993, p 120).

Disabled facilities grants have been very useful in enabling disabled people to remain at home and for the preparation of accommodation for people moving into a new home through the community care policy. The grant is to make the house more suitable for the needs of disabled people and for adapting buildings containing flats for the disabled. These grants can be mandatory or discretionary depending on the condition of the building and how and for what purpose it needs to be adapted. 12,000 such grants were approved in the first year of the new system but there have been problems with its implementation due to the inter-agency nature of the scheme. Top up finance should theoretically be available from social service departments if individual applicants cannot afford their share of the costs but no provision appears to have been made in social service budgets for this funding.

Minor works grants have been very popular and widely used, some 20,000 were approved in the first year. But the overall assessment of the new system at the present time is somewhat pessimistic mainly because it is being pressured by cuts in public spending. After a slow start the new system is now fully operational but is awarding far fewer grants than under the old system. In 1993, excluding minor works assistance, less than 60,000 mandatory grants were made and only 6,000 discretionary awards (*Housing and Construction Statistics*, HMSO, 1993) much less than half the level of grants paid out in the latter years of the previous system.

There has been a considerable increase in the average size of grants which indicates that many of those in need due to low income are now being helped. The operation of the means test is, however, very complex and has been a stumbling block to the smooth running of the new system. Certain categories of people appear to be excluded from the grant sytem because of the way the means test is calculated, for example, young couples with heavy mortgage commitments find it hard to obtain an affordable level of grant aid because mortgage costs are excluded from the means test calculation.

The 1989 Act also changed the area renewal strategy in line with the proposal in the Green Paper to abolish GIAs and HAAs. In their place authorities may now identify and declare Renewal Areas (RAs). These areas incorporate anything from 300 to 3,000 dwellings many of which must be unfit. RAs are thus generally bigger in scale then their predecessors. They must contain at least 75% of households in the private sector and at least 30% of residents must be in receipt of welfare benefits as their main source of income. The thinking behind the RA concept is to treat the area as a wider economic and social unit of which housing is one part and into which both public and private finance can be concentrated. At the time of writing very few RAs had been declared.

Between 1969 and 1992 some £15 billion has been paid to private owners in the UK in the form of grants for the improvement of almost 3.5 million dwellings (*Housing Research Findings* No 104, Joseph Rowntree Foundation, January 1994). In addition there has been, of course, an extensive programme of renovation of council housing – over 2.5 million dwellings have been renovated since 1979. These are impressive figures and extremely costly to the public purse. But as the historical overview above has shown there is no room for complacency not least because, as the most recent house condition survey, in 1991, estimated there were 1,456,000 dwellings in *England* unfit according to the 1989 standard, one dwelling in every twelve, or 7.4% of all dwellings. Most unfit dwellings dated from before 1919, even so bad conditions were not confined to older housing and 143,000 unfit dwellings were of post-1964 construction. By housing type the worst conditions were found in terraced housing and houses converted into flats, while by tenure, of the total number of unfit occupied dwellings, the largest number, 726,000 were owner occupied; 284,000 were privately rented, 262,000 were rented from authorities and 39,000 from associations. By region the worst stock was concentrated in Inner London, followed by the North West, Outer London and the rest of the South East. By reason of unfitness the largest number of properties, 562,000, were those needing repair, with lack of food preparation facilities coming a close second at 560,000. By degree of severity of unfitness 54% of dwellings were unfit on only one of the statutory criteria, while houses unfit on four or more criteria counted for only 13% of the total (*English House Condition Survey: 1991, Preliminary Report on Unfit Dwellings* (DoE 1993)).

The current law

The rest of this chapter now describes the current law and unless where expressly stated the remedies referred to apply to both public and private sector tenancies. We begin by considering the common law remedies available to tenants and others injured by the substandard condition of rented property.

Historically neither contract nor tort gave protection to tenants. The attitude of the law was encapsulated in the maxim caveat emptor, or as Erle CJ said in *Robbins v Jones* (1863) 15 CBNS 221 at 239: '…fraud apart, there is no law against letting a tumbledown house: and the tenant's remedy is upon his contract, if any'. See *Gordon and Teixeira v Selico and Select Management Ltd* (1986) 18 HLR 219 for an application of this principle. There was no liability in tort whether the damage arose from the landlord's mere neglect or from the careless doing of works of maintenance or installation. In *Travers v Gloucester Corpn* [1947] KB 71, [1946] 2 All ER 506 a local authority let a house with the vent pipe of a gas geyser terminating under the eaves of the house. This dangerous installation led to a build-up of toxic exhaust fumes and as a consequence the tenant's lodger was gassed in the bathroom. The corporation was held not liable in tort.

A growing body of opinion viewed the exemption of lessors from liability in negligence with growing distaste and various attempts were made to end it. For example it was said in *Ball v LCC* [1949] 2 KB 159, [1949] 1 All ER 1056 that landlords could be liable in *contract* to tenants for negligent installation work carried out *after* the start of the lease, though non-contracting parties could not sue under this rule. Great changes have now, however, been made in the law.

Landlords' obligations in tort

At common law

Following the decisions in *Cunard v Antifyre Ltd* [1933] 1 KB 551 and *Taylor v Liverpool Corpn* [1939] 3 All ER 329 there is no difficulty in holding landlords liable in negligence for damage caused *by buildings retained in their occupation* to persons or to buildings let to a tenant. In *AC Billings & Sons Ltd v Riden* [1958] AC 240, [1957] 3 All ER 1 the House of Lords stated that, irrespective of the lack of a contractual relationship, persons who execute work on premises are under a general duty to use reasonable care for the safety of those whom they know, or ought reasonably to know, may be affected by or lawfully in the vicinity of the work. Thus landlords can be liable in tort for dangers created *after* the commencement of the tenancy.

In *Rimmer v Liverpool City Council* [1985] QB 1, [1984] 1 All ER 930, the plaintiff was the tenant of a flat owned, designed and built by the local authority. One internal passageway contained an unprotected thin glass panel. The tenant tripped in the passageway, put out his hand to save himself, and his hand went through the panel, as a result of which he suffered injury. The Court of Appeal repeated that *the 'bare' landlord of unfurnished premises, who has done no work on them, owes no duty of care to a tenant in respect of the state of the premises when they were let,* but held that a landlord may owe a duty of care in respect of being the *designer or builder* of premises. This duty is owed to all persons who may reasonably be expected to be affected by the design or construction of the premises, and is a duty to take reasonable care to ensure such persons do not suffer injury from design or construction defects (which *may* extend to defects in work of modernisation or conversion etc). The authority was in breach of that duty on this occasion. Liability here arose from the fact of negligent design and/or construction. Where, however, there is no evidence of negligent design or construction, the old rule survives, see *McNerney v Lambeth London Borough Council* (1988) 21 HLR 188. In *Targett v Torfaen Borough Council* [1992] 3 All ER 27 it was held that the fact that a plaintiff *knows* of the landlord's bad design or construction work will not automatically negative the landlord's duty of care. The question in such cases is whether the plaintiff can reasonably be expected to remove or avoid the danger. It is not normally reasonable to expect a tenant to avoid a danger by giving up the property, though knowledge of a defect may point to a need for a tenant to take greater heed for personal safety, and failure to do that may result in the tenant being contributorily negligent in respect of harm suffered. See also *Sharpe v Manchester Metropolitan District Council* (1977) 5 HLR 71 where the plaintiff took a tenancy of a flat in 1972 and found it infested with cockroaches. The authority tried to eliminate the insects for two years by using emulsified DDT, but failed in their attempts. They were found negligent in that they had failed to treat the service ducts and other spaces in the walls and floor and had used a discredited insecticide. However, contrast *Habinteg Housing Association v James* [1994] EGCS 166, where there was held to be *no* liability on a landlord where a *house* was infested and there was no part of the property in the landlord's possession from which an invasion of the tenant's home could proceed.

Under statute

Civil liability may arise under the Defective Premises Act 1972. Section 1 provides (inter alia):

'(1) A person taking on work for or in connection with the provision of a dwelling (whether the dwelling is provided by the erection or by the conversion or enlargement of a building) owes a duty:

  (a)   if the building is provided to the order of any person to that person; and

  (b)   without prejudice to paragraph (a) above to every person who acquires an interest (whether legal or equitable) in the dwelling; to see that the work which he takes on is done in a workmanlike or, as the case may be, professional manner, with proper materials and so that as regard that work the dwelling will be fit for habitation when completed ...

(4) A person who:

  (a)   in the course of a business which consists of or includes providing or arranging for the provision of dwellings or installation in dwellings; or

  (b)   in the exercise of a power of making such provision or arrangements conferred by or by virtue of any enactment; arranges for another to take on work for or in connection with the provision of a dwelling shall be treated for the purposes of this section as included among the persons who have taken on the work.'

This provision imposes liability on authorities and associations, their builders, sub-contractors and architects if they fail to build in a professional or workmanlike manner (as the case may be) with proper materials, or fail to ensure the dwelling is fit for human habitation, a phrase which may be capable of covering such matters as defective design or lay-out. It extends to work not done as well as that badly done so that a dwelling lacks after the work is done some essential attribute making it unfit, *Andrews v Schooling* [1991] 3 All ER 723, [1991] 1 WLR 783. The duty, *which is strict*, is owed to, inter alia, those persons having legal interests in the dwelling, for example tenants, but *not* their children or visitors. Moreover, the duty only arises in connection with the provision, whether by new construction, conversion or enlargement, of a *dwelling*. Mere enlargement of an existing dwelling would not be enough. The provision only applies to dwellings constructed after 1 January 1974, by virtue of section 7(2) of the Act. This provision seems to have been strangely ignored by public sector tenants affected by design or construction defects.

Section 3(1) of the Defective Premises Act 1972 provides:

'Where work of construction, repair, maintenance or demolition or any other work is done on or in relation to premises, any duty of care owed, because of the doing of the work, to persons who might reasonably be expected to be affected by the defects in the state of the premises created by the doing of the work shall not be abated by the subsequent disposal of the premises by the person who owed the duty'.

This statutory displacement of a landlord's immunity in negligence only applies, by virtue of section 3(2)(a), to those lettings of premises entered into after the commencement of the Act, 1 January 1974. Liability can only arise where there has been a defect created by a positive act classifiable as 'work of construction, repair, maintenance or demolition or any other work done on or in relation to premises'. It seems not *all* 'work' can give rise to liability but only that of specified kinds, or other 'work' which can be said to be 'done on or in relation to premises' such as, for example, installation of central heating. Nor does this section impose any liability for negligent omissions to do repairs.

Liability for an omission may arise under section 4 of the 1972 Act. Section 4(1) provides:

'Where premises are let under a tenancy which puts on the landlord an obligation to the tenant for the maintenance or repair of the premises, the landlord owes to all persons who might reasonably be expected to be affected by defects in the state of the premises a duty to take such care as is reasonable in all the circumstances to see that they are reasonably safe from personal injury or from damage to their property caused by a relevant defect.'

This imposes tortious liability on landlords towards tenants, their families and those other persons foreseeably likely to be in the premises, and, by section 6(3) of the Act landlords cannot exclude or restrict this duty.

This section also poses problems of interpretation. Liability can only arise in respect of a 'relevant defect'. Such is defined by sub-section (3) as

' ... a defect in the state of the premises existing at or after the material time and arising from, or continuing because of, an act or omission by the landlord which constitutes or would if he had notice of the defect, have constituted a failure by him to carry out his obligation to the tenant for the maintenance or repair of the premises ...'.

Such defects must arise 'at or after the material time', which is further defined by the sub-section as being, in general terms, for tenancies commencing before the Act, the commencement date of the Act (1 January 1974), and in other cases the earliest date on which the tenancy commenced or the tenancy agreement was entered into. Liability arises out of those defects which constitute a breach of the landlord's obligations to repair and maintain. These obligations will include any express covenant to repair given by the landlord and, by virtue of sub-section (5), those implied by statute, such as section 11 of the Landlord and Tenant Act 1985. An even more extended meaning is given to 'obligation' by sub-section (4) which deems for the purposes of the section any *power* a landlord has to repair actually to be an *obligation* to repair. Such powers can arise in many situations. A landlord may have power to enter and do repairs simply because the tenant has defaulted on the tenant's repairing covenants. In such circumstances the Act provides that the landlord, while remaining liable to third parties, shall not be liable to the tenant. The effect of dicta in *Mint v Good* [1951] 1 KB 517, [1950] 2 All ER 1159 should also be remembered. Somervell LJ said (at page 522): ' ... in the case of a weekly tenancy, business efficacy will not be effected if the house is allowed to fall into disrepair and no one keeps it in reasonable condition; and it seems to be, therefore, necessary…that the… landlord should at any rate have the power to keep the place in proper repair …'.

An implied power to enter and do repairs may arise in relation to any *weekly* tenancy of a dwelling-house and will be deemed to be an obligation to repair under sub-section (4).

In *Smith v Bradford Metropolitan Council* (1982) 44 P & CR 171, a tenancy agreement provided the tenant should give the authority and its officers and workmen reasonable facilities for inspecting *the premises let*, their state of repair, and to carry out repairs, and the 'premises' in question were defined as the dwelling, and, where the context required, its garage, outbuildings, yards and gardens. The tenant of the dwelling was injured by the defective condition of a rear concrete patio constructed between the house and its garden by a previous tenant. The Court of Appeal found the power to enter the premises fell within section 4(4) of the 1972 Act, and was a deemed obligation to repair. The context required that the patio be regarded as part of the premises in relation to which the power, and deemed obligation, to repair existed. In *McAuley v Bristol City Council* (1991) 23 HLR 586, however, there was merely a clause that the tenant should give the authority 'all reasonable facilities for entering upon the premises ... for any purpose which may from time to time be required by the council'. It was, nevertheless, held that this clause gave the council power to enter the premises, and that the tenancy agreement contemplated that the council would keep the premises in a reasonable and habitable condition. To give business efficacy to that understanding there had to be implied a term that the council would carry out repairs wherever there were defects in *the premises* – in this case including the garden – which would expose a tenant or visitor to a serious risk of injury. Thus because the council had the right to enter the premises they could be liable under section 4.

There are a number of subsidiary points to note about section 4. Sub-section (2) provides:

> 'The said duty is owed if the landlord knows (whether as the result of being notified by the tenant or otherwise) or if he ought in all the circumstances to have known of the relevant defect'.

There is no need to give notice of defects provided they would be patent on reasonable inspection.

In *Clarke v Taff Ely Borough Council* (1980) 10 HLR 44, Mrs Clarke visited her sister's council house and was injured when the rotten floorboards gave way beneath a table on which she was standing. The house was one of a number of pre-war council houses known to have a potentially dangerous floor construction. The authority's chief housing surveyor agreed that in view of the age of the house, its type and the presence of damp it was foreseeable that rot would occur. Damages of £5,100 were awarded.

A very extended meaning is given to 'tenancy' by section 6 of the 1972 Act. The term includes leases and underleases, tenancies at will and sufferance and statutory tenancies, and rights of occupation given by contract, see also section 4(6).

Liability under the Occupiers' Liability Act 1957

The common law imposes liability on landlords for defects on their premises, eg the common parts of blocks of flats, which cause injury to their tenants. The Occupiers' Liability Act 1957, section 2, also imposes liability in such circumstances, and the 1957 Act adds to the landlord's obligation by stating in section 3(1):

> 'Where an occupier of premises is bound by contract to permit persons who are strangers to the contract to enter or use the premises, the duty of care which he owes to them as his visitors cannot be restricted or excluded by that contract, but (subject to any provision of the contract to the contrary) shall include the duty to perform his obligations under the contract, whether undertaken for their protection or not, in so far as those obligations go beyond the obligations otherwise involved in that duty.'

The effect is that landlords cannot by virtue of their contracts with tenants reduce obligations to tenants' visitors below the standard required by the Act, the 'common duty of care'. Furthermore tenants' visitors are enabled to claim the benefit of any more onerous obligations inserted in the lease, unless the lease itself specifically excludes this.

Landlords' obligations in contract

At common law

Contractual remedies only apply as between contracting parties. Any third party injured by the defective state of a dwelling-house must find a remedy in tort. That said, landlords may be liable to tenants for a breach of express covenants to repair and maintain a dwelling-house. In such a case the extent of the liability will depend upon the wording of the covenant. Such express covenants are rare, particularly as many leases of ordinary dwelling-houses in the past have been created orally on a weekly basis under section 54(2) of the Law of Property Act 1925. Where authorities and associations use express terms in their tenancy agreement these frequently do no more than replicate the statutorily implied terms considered below. However, such terms may go further and relate not just to the dwelling-house but to the whole of the premises let. They may also impose specific burdens such as promises that particular items of repair will be carried out within particular periods of time. Express covenants are construed taking into account the state of the dwelling at the time it was let, its age and locality, see *Anstruther-Gough-Calthorpe v McOscar* [1924] 1 KB 716, thus a covenant to repair is not to be interpreted to require a landlord to renew a decayed hovel by turning it into an up to date home. However, a covenant to keep a building in 'good and tenantable' condition may require a landlord to put it into that state even where it has not previously attained it, *Credit Suisse v Beegas Nominees Ltd* [1994] 4 All ER 803.

The common law has also been unwilling to imply terms into leases. In *Smith v Marrable* (1843) 11 M & W 5, Parke B implied a term into a letting of *furnished* premises that, at the start of the lease, they would be in a habitable condition. According to *Sarson v Roberts* [1895] 2 QB 395, the obligation will not arise if the premises become uninhabitable during the course of the lease. What is likely to make a house unfit for habitation in this context are matters likely to affect the health of incoming tenants such as infestation by bugs, or defects in drains, or recent occupation by a person suffering from an easily communicable disease. The meaning given by the common law to 'unfit for human habitation' is therefore different from the meaning the phrase has under the unfitness provisions of the Housing Act 1985. If furnished premises are 'unfit' at common law the tenant is entitled to quit them by repudiating the tenancy, and may also sue for any loss suffered, see *Wilson v Finch Hatton* (1877) 2 Ex D 336, and *Charsley v Jones* (1889) 53 JP 280. This implied condition is limited to lettings of furnished dwellings. In *Sleafer v Lambeth Borough Council* [1960] 1 QB 43, [1959] 3 All ER 378 it was said that where a landlord lets unfurnished dwellings there will generally be no implied term that they are free of defects.

However, in *Liverpool City Council v Irwin* [1977] AC 239, [1976] 2 All ER 39 the House of Lords implied a term into a letting of a flat in a high rise block. The authority owned a tower block of flats, access to which was provided by a common staircase and electrically operated lifts. The tenants also had the use of internal chutes into which to discharge rubbish. The condition of the block deteriorated, partly as a result of vandalism, and defects included: failed lifts; a lack of lighting on the staircases, and blocked rubbish chutes. The tenants refused to pay rent and the landlord applied for possession orders on the flats, to which the tenants replied with a counter-claim that (inter alia) the landlord was in breach of covenant of quiet enjoyment. The House of Lords said this was a contract in which the parties had not themselves fully expressed the terms and the court could imply certain terms solely to prevent the contract of letting from becoming inefficacious and absurdly futile. The House of Lords then went on to state:

1)   the tenants had in their leases an implied right or easement to use the stairs, lifts and rubbish chutes as these were necessarily incidental to their occupation of high-rise flats;

2)   the landlord was therefore under an implied obligation to take reasonable care to maintain those common areas and facilities;

3)   such an obligation is not, however, absolute because tenants of high-rise blocks must themselves resist vandalism and co-operate in maintaining the common areas in reasonable condition, and

4)   the courts have no power to imply such terms in tenancy agreements as they think 'reasonable'. They may only supply such terms as are truly necessary for the functioning of the contract.

Thus in *King v South Northamptonshire District Council* [1992] 1 EGLR 53 where a wheelchair bound tenant was forced to use a rear access path, over which she had only a right of way, as the way into her home, and it was clear the dwelling could not be enjoyed without that access way, an obligation on the part of the landlord was upheld to keep the path in repair.

Under statute

Parliament has on a number of occasions attempted to remedy the omission of the common law, but, sadly, the courts have adopted a somewhat restrictive interpretation of the legislation, while Parliament itself has been remiss in not keeping some of the remedies up to date. This is particularly true of the provision which began life as section 12 of the Housing of the Working Classes Act 1885, and which is now section 8 of the Landlord and Tenant Act 1985. This states that in a letting to which it applies there is an implied term of fitness for human habitation at the commencement of the tenancy and that the landlord will keep it so fit throughout its currency.

The problem is that section 8(3) limits its applicability to contracts of letting where the rent was not originally, on or after 1 April 1965, more than £80 in relating to Inner London Boroughs or £52 elsewhere in the country, and thus hardly any properties are now covered. The courts have 'discovered' other difficulties in the wording of the provision, and these have hardened into rules of interpretation which apply not only to section 8 but also to section 11 of the Landlord and Tenant Act 1985. Thus *Middleton v Hall* (1913) 108 LT 804 and *Ryall v Kidwell & Son* [1914] 3 KB 135 state that only the tenant can sue. While these decisions have been effectively overruled in tort by section 4 of the Defective Premises Act 1972 (see above) the technical rule remains that privity of contract limits the possibility of suing on the implied covenant only to the contracting parties. Next it should be noted that landlords cannot be liable under the implied covenant unless tenants have previously given notice of the defect. This was decided, in the case of patent defects, by *McCarrick v Liverpool Corpn* [1947] AC 219, [1946] 2 All ER 646, and was applied to latent defects by *O'Brien v Robinson* [1973] AC 912, [1973] 1 All ER 583: again remember the tortious remedy under section 4 of the Defective Premises Act 1972 is not made so dependent upon the giving of actual notice. In the case of authority dwellings, it was held in *Sheldon v West Bromwich Corpn* (1973) 25 P & CR 360 that where an appropriately qualified authority employee knows that premises are defective that knowledge will be treated as giving the authority notice, and notice does not have to be given personally by the tenant, see also *Griffin v Pillet* [1926] 1 KB 17.

In *McGreal v Wake* (1984) 269 Estates Gazette 1254 though it was stressed that tenants should inform landlords of works necessary to meet breaches of repairing obligations, it can be enough to 'trigger' a landlord's responsibilities if the tenant complains to the local authority and they then serve notice requiring works under their Housing Act 1985 powers. Similarly in *Dinefwr Borough Council v Jones* (1987) 19 HLR 445 a district valuer's 'right to buy' report to an authority which specified defects was held to constitute notice, even though it was not submitted as a disrepair complaint, see also *Hall v Howard* (1988) 20 HLR 566.

The most serious limitation on section 8 was imposed by the Court of Appeal in *Buswell v Goodwin* [1971] 1 All ER 418, [1971] 1 WLR 92. Here a cottage was statutorily unfit and, as the local authority had made a closing order on it, the landlord had commenced possession proceedings against the tenant. He argued the house was only unfit because the landlord was in breach of implied contractual obligations under section 8. The Court of Appeal, however, restricted the ambit of operation of the implied covenant to cases where houses are capable of being made fit at reasonable expense. The obligation is not absolute. Where a house has fallen into an extreme state of disrepair the tenant can no longer rely on the implied covenant. The paradox thus emerges of tenants of the worst housing receiving the lowest level of legal protection. Furthermore where statutorily unfit houses are retained by authorities under their Housing Act 1985 powers, section 8 will not apply to letting such houses, see section 302(c) of the Housing Act 1985.

A similar process of judicial reasoning has emptied much of the meaning from the other statutorily implied covenant: section 11 of the Landlord and Tenant Act 1985. This applies, under section 13 of the Act, to leases of dwelling-houses granted on or after 24 October 1961 for terms of less than seven years, so a lease for a term of seven years is not caught, see *Brikom Investments Ltd v Seaford* [1981] 2 All ER 783, [1981] 1 WLR 863. The obligation is to keep in repair the structure and exterior of the dwelling, including its drains, gutters and external pipes, *and* to keep in repair *and* proper working order the mains services installations, including basins, sinks, baths and sanitary conveniences, but excluding appliances etc, for making use of a mains service, eg a refrigerator, *and* to keep in repair and working order space and water heating installations. The standard of repair required is determined by having regard to the age, character, prospective life and locality of the dwelling. It is not possible to contract out of this obligation, see section 12 of the Act, save with the consent of the county court.

The provision now requires, with regard to tenancies granted on or after 15 January 1989, that a landlord is to keep in repair the structure and exterior of *any* part of a building he/she owns of which the tenant's dwelling forms part, see section 11(1A) of the 1985 Act. A similar extension of the original section 11 covers mains services installations which serve a dwelling-house directly or indirectly *and* which either form part of any part of the building in which the landlord has an interest or are owned by the landlord or are under the landlord's control. However, the landlord's obligations can only be relied on where the disrepair, etc, is such as to affect the tenant's enjoyment of the dwelling or of the common parts of the property in which it is, see section 11(1B). Nevertheless this provision may be relied upon by, for example, tenants of flats adversely affected by disrepair of stairways and access paths.

The policy of Parliament in creating the implied covenant was to prevent unscrupulous landlords from imposing unreasonable repairing obligations on tenants. It cannot be said, however, that the law has been successful in *preventing* disrepair and bad housing conditions. Tenants are generally ignorant of their rights, and often do not complain about disrepair until it becomes exceptional and intolerable. Alongside this there exists the same restrictive judicial attitude already seen in relation to the section 8 covenant.

This can be seen in decisions as to which matters fall within the scope of the implied covenant. In *Brown v Liverpool Corpn* [1969] 3 All ER 1345, paving flagstones and shallow steps leading to a house were held to be part of its 'exterior'. They were necessary for the purpose of gaining access to the house and fell within the scope of the implied covenant. In *Hopwood v Cannock Chase District Council* [1975] 1 All ER 796, [1975] 1 WLR 373 slabs in a back yard were held not to fall within the scope of the covenant as the back yard was not the essential means of access to the house. In *Irvine v Moran* [1991] 1 EGLR 261 it was considered ' structure' is that which gives a property its 'essential stability and shape', not the ways and means in which a house is fitted out, eg garages, gates, wall plaster, door locks, internal decoration, though external doors, windows, window glass and painting are part of the 'exterior'. So far as flats are concerned, dicta in *Campden Hill Towers v Gardner* [1977] QB 823, [1977] 1 All ER 739 are most important. Where the structure is concerned the landlord's obligation extends to anything which can ordinarily be regarded as part of the structure or exterior of the dwelling in question. Thus section 11(1)(a) applies, irrespective of the words of the lease, to the outside walls of a flat (even though they may have been excluded from the lease), the outer sides of horizontal divisions between flats, the outside of the inner party walls of the flat and the structural framework and beams directly supporting the floors, ceilings and walls of a flat. The test to be used in determining the scope of the implied covenant is whether the particular item of disrepair affects the stability or usability of the particular flat in question.

In *Douglas-Scott v Scorgie* [1984] 1 All ER 1086, [1984] 1 WLR 716 the Court of Appeal held that the roof of a building above a top floor flat may be part of the structure and exterior of that flat, irrespective of whether or not it forms part of the demised premises. Note also the extension of the implied obligations by section 11(1A) of the 1985 Act outlined above. The content of the obligations of public and private sector landlords are the same under this implied covenant, see *Wainwright v Leeds City Council* (1984) 270 Estates Gazette 1289.

The covenant is one to repair, so what is the meaning of the word 'repair'? In *Ravenseft Properties Ltd v Davstone (Holdings) Ltd* [1980] QB 12, [1979] 1 All ER 929 a distinction was made between the process of repair and a completely different process which is replacement. Replacement is a process of reconstruction so drastic that at the end of the lease the landlord receives back a wholly different property from that which he/she demised. 'Repair' on the other hand, according to the decision in *Greg v Planque* [1936] 1 KB 669, simply means making good defects, including renewal where necessary. In other words, simply keeping the property in a condition suitable for the purpose for which it was let. The distinction between these two processes is the scale and degree of the work involved. The fact that work, because of modern statutory requirements or building practices, has to be done to a higher standard than that of the original does not necessarily mean that it cannot be classed as 'repair'. Work will not be classifiable as 'repair' if it results in a reconstruction of the whole, or substantially the whole, of a building.

In *McDougall v Easington District Council* (1989) 21 HLR 310 Mustill LJ put forward three tests which may be applied 'separately or concurrently' to decide whether a matter is one of repair or renewal/replacement:

1) do any alterations go to the whole, or substantially the whole of the structure;
2) is the effect of the work to produce a building of a wholly different character from that which was let;
3) what is the cost of works in relation to the building's previous value, and what is their effect on its value and life expectancy?

Thus if the landlord can show that the work required on any given house is so drastic that it would amount to his/her getting back, at the end of the term, a substantially different house from that which was let, then that work is outside the obligation to repair. In *Pembery v Lamdin* [1940] 2 All ER 434 a landlord let certain old premises not constructed with a damp-course or with waterproofing for the external walls, and covenanted to keep the external part of the let premises in good repair and condition. The tenant claimed this put the landlord under an obligation to waterproof the outside walls and render the premises dry. It was held the obligation was only to keep the premises in repair in the condition in which they were let. In this case the landlord would be required only to point the external brickwork. However, contrast *Elmcroft Developments Ltd v Tankersley-Sawyer* (1984) 270 Estates Gazette 140. The court found that replacing an incorrectly laid *and existing* damp proof course in a block of flats was an act of 'repair'. Similarly, contrast *Mullaney v Maybourne Grange (Croydon) Management Co Ltd* (1986) 277 Estates Gazette 1350 and *Reston Ltd v Hudson* [1990] 37 EG 86. In the former the replacement of wooden framed windows with double glazed ones was considered an improvement, in the latter the comprehensive replacement of all windows at one time when only some were rotted was considered a 'repair'.

The burden of proving a particular repair is needed is, moreover, on the person alleging its need, *Murray v Birmingham City Council* (1987) 20 HLR 39.

It is also necessary to show disrepair as opposed to a lack of amenity or inefficiency, see *Quick v Taff-Ely Borough Council* [1986] QB 809, [1985] 3 All ER 321. Here a council house built in the early 1970s was thermally inefficient with uninsulated concrete window lintels giving rise to condensation that produced intolerable living conditions. The Court of Appeal accepted that the eradication of a design defect, such as affected the dwelling, may fall within the ambit of the implied covenant, provided the work required does not amount to substantial reconstruction or improvement, *and* provided the work is necessary to remedy disrepair. To repair is to make good some damage: eradicating a design defect that simply makes a dwelling inefficient or ineffective as a habitation is not automatically therefore repair. In *Quick* the Court found the condensation simply made the house function badly or inefficiently, there was no damage or deterioration as such to any components of the structure of the dwelling. The obligation to repair only arises where there is damage or deterioration, though where this can be shown to exist, discharging the obligation may require eradicating a design defect giving rise to the damage so that to some extent the dwelling is 'improved'. Note also *Stent v Monmouth District Council* (1987) 19 HLR 269 where there was actual deterioration damage of a badly designed and installed entrance door which could be characterised as 'disrepair'.

The content of the obligation to repair has also been the subject of judicial atention. In *Newham London Borough v Patel* [1979] JPL 303 the Court of Appeal considered the forerunners of section 11(3) of the Landlord and Tenant Act 1985. This states that the standard of repair is to be determined by having regard to the 'age, character and prospective life of the dwelling-house and the locality in which it is situated'. Mr Patel's house was a poor, old dwelling in bad condition shortly destined for redevelopment. The court concluded the prospective life of the dwelling affected the content of the section 11 duty. The authority could not be required to carry out repairs which the court categorised as 'wholly useless'.

Courts are unwilling to impose over heavy burdens to repair on landlords who are trying to do the best they can with old property, and may be more ready to require them only to 'patch up' a house than to carry out more extensive repairs, see *Trustees of the Dame Margaret Hungerford Charity v Beazley* (1993) Times, 17 May. On the other hand a landlord cannot always justify a poor standard of repair simply on the basis of a low rent being charged for an old house, see *McClean v Liverpool City Council* (1987) 283 Estates Gazette 1395 and *Sturolson & Co v Mauroux* (1988) 20 HLR 332. To succeed on this basis a landlord would need to show that the rent is truly 'nominal' or very low, while any repairs needed would be wholly useless, or that the dwelling has no prospective life.

Once the landlord has notice of disrepair the work should be carried out within a reasonable time – this will depend upon the nature of the work needed, any problems associated with obtaining the necessary materials, the landlord's work load, etc, see *Morris v Liverpool City Council* [1988] 14 EG 59.

Tenants are not, however, entitled to treat their homes in a cavalier fashion. It was made clear in *Warren v Keen* [1954] 1 QB 15, [1953] 2 All ER 1118 that tenants are always under some sort of obligation to look after their homes. In the case of a long lease, say 99 years, the tenant is usually made subject to full repairing covenants.

On the other hand weekly tenants are usually bound to use the premises in a tenant-like manner. This means taking proper care of the premises, for example cleaning chimneys and windows, replacing electric light bulbs, mending fuses, and unstopping blocked sinks. In *Wycombe Health Authority v Barnett* (1982) 264 Estates Gazette 619 it was stated that in very cold climatic conditions a tenant *may* have to lag water pipes, or use additional heat, or turn off the water supply according to the circumstances, such as the severity of the cold, the duration of contemplated absence from home and the internal condition of the house, in order to behave in a tenant-like manner. See also *Mickel v M'Coard* 1913 SC 896 where a tenant left a house for a month, without telling the landlord, in very cold weather and was held liable for burst pipes. The landlord is under no duty under section 11 of the 1985 Act to lag domestic water pipes, but may be held liable in tort for a failure to protect a tenant against a flood caused by the bursting of communal water pipes where they have been warned of a problem, *Stockley v Knowsley Metropolitan Borough Council* (1986) 279 Estates Gazette 677.

Remedies for breaches of covenant

Specific performance

Though there appear to be few reported cases on the issue, section 17 of the Landlord and Tenant Act 1985 permits orders of specific performance to be made in cases where tenants' alleged breach of landlords' repairing covenants occur. The remedy is available whether or not the breach relates to a part of the premises let to the tenant, and notwithstanding any equitable rule which would otherwise restrict the scope of the remedy, eg that the tenant does not have 'clean hands' because of arrears of rent. Specific performance is, however, a discretionary remedy and the court will not order a landlord to do unnecessary or extravagant work. Though the remedy is available as a final or an interim, or 'interlocutory', order it is arguable an interim order would only be made before a decision on liability for repairs where the situation was extreme and some immediate danger needs to be removed.

Appointing a receiver

Where a landlord is neglectful of repairing obligations, so that serious deterioration of the dwelling(s) in question is likely, and it can be shown that the landlord is taking no real interest in the property, either to collect rent or to perform obligations, it may be possible to apply to the High Court under section 37(1) of the Supreme Court Act 1981 for the appointment of a receiver if it appears just and convenient. The receiver will then manage the property in accordance with the lease until further order, see *Hart v Emelkirk Ltd* [1983] 3 All ER 15, [1983] 1 WLR 1289. However, this remedy may not be sought by *local authority* tenants, see *Parker v Camden London Borough Council* [1986] Ch 162, [1985] 2 All ER 141.

Where the premises consist of two or more flats in a block, section 21 of the Landlord and Tenant Act 1987 permits a tenant to apply to the county court for the appointment of a manager of the premises, though a preliminary warning notice has to be given to the landlord under section 22 specifying the grounds on which the court will be asked to appoint a manager. A manager may be appointed where the landlord is in breach of obligation, where that breach is likely to continue and where it is just and convenient to make the appointment. This power, does *not*, however, apply to any premises where the landlord is 'exempt' (eg a district or London borough council, an urban development corporation, a housing action trust, the Housing Corporation, a housing trust or a registered housing association) or where the premises are on the functional land of any charity.

Self help

In *Lee-Parker v Izzet* [1971] 3 All ER 1099, [1971] 1 WLR 1688 it was held that, irrespective of the common law rules as to set off, occupiers of property had a right to recoup themselves out of *future* rent for the cost of repairs to the property, in so far as the repairs fell within the landlord's express or implied covenants, provided the landlord was in fact in breach, and only after due notice had been given. Tenants have no rights to *withhold* payment of rent to compel landlords to carry out repairs, and if they do they will be in breach of their own obligations under the lease. The rule only authorises the deducting of the *proper* costs of repairs from future rent: a tenant is not entitled to expend vast sums and then present the landlord with the bill. The following steps should be taken before reliance is placed on the rule:

1) the tenant *must* notify the landlord of the disrepair which itself must arise from a breach of the landlord's covenants;
2) the tenant should obtain at least two builders' estimates as to the likely costs of the repairs and send them to the landlord, warning that if repairs are not affected the tenant will carry out the work and will deduct the cost from future rent;
3) to be absolutely safe, a county court declaration should be obtained authorising this course of action, and
4) having given his landlord time to execute the repairs, the tenant may then proceed to do them.

Some authorities phrase their tenancy agreements in such a way as to attempt to exclude the operation of the *Lee-Parker* principle. Such a clause, provided it specifically denies the right to 'set-off' and is not merely a clause denying a right to make deductions from rent may be sufficient to exclude the *Lee-Parker* principle, see *Electricity Supply Nominees Ltd v IAF Group plc* [1993] 3 All ER 372, [1993] 1 WLR 1059.

In *Asco Developments Ltd v Lowes* (1978) 248 Estates Gazette 683 a landlord sought summary judgment for arrears of rent under RSC Ord 14 alleging that there was no defence to the action. The tenants sought to defend on the grounds that the landlord was in breach of repairing obligations. Megarry V-C held that in certain special circumstances the *Lee-Parker* principle could be applied to monies accrued in rent arrears, and the tenants could defend the action. However, the court stated that nothing in the decision should be taken to encourage rent strikes as a means of forcing action on the part of a landlord. It was made clear in *Camden Nominees v Forcey* [1940] Ch 352, [1940] 2 All ER 1 that it is no answer to a claim for rent by a landlord for the tenant to say that the landlord has failed to perform his obligations. If tenants are to use the *Lee-Parker* principle in respect of rent arrears, they must specify to the court the sums and costs in question, and must particularise the issues. A judge faced with such issues should act with considerable discretion before allowing the tenant to defend the claim for rent.

In *British Anzani (Felixstowe) Ltd v International Marine Management (UK) Ltd* [1980] QB 137, [1979] 2 All ER 1063, Forbes J indicated that *in equity*, as a set-off raised by way of defence, unliquidated damages, for example claims for inconvenience and loss of enjoyment, might be recoverable against rent under a tenancy agreement. The tenant must be able to show it would be inequitable in view of the condition of the dwelling to allow the landlord to recover the whole amount of rent claimed. The tenant's contention should be raised as a defence to the landlord's action, and the tenant should make a counter-claim which particularises the nature of the landlord's breach of obligation and the consequent damage. Though it is not *absolutely* necessary that a claim and counter-claim should arise from the same contract, both must stem from very closely connected transactions so that equity can recognise that the tenant's counter-claim goes to the very root of the landlord's claim.

A set-off of unliquidated damages is a defence to as much of the plaintiff's claim as is represented by the eventual amount of the award made. If defendants limit damages to a sum less than that claimed from them then they must pay the balance over and above the counter-claim. But where the defendants' damages are claimed at large, finally to be decided by the court, and where it is bona fide claimed they top the plaintiff's claim, even though they are not yet quantified, then the defendant's set-off amounts to a complete defence to the whole of the plaintiff's claim.

However, this equitable relief is discretionary, and as 'he who comes to equity must come with clean hands', it is unlikely to be available to a tenant who has been guilty of wrongdoing in relation to the transaction in question.

Damages

What damages can be recovered for breach of a covenant to repair? The law was exensively reviewed in *Calabar Properties Ltd v Stitcher* [1983] 3 All ER 759, [1984] 1 WLR 287. The object of damages is to restore the tenant to the position he/she would have been in had there been no breach. In relation to periodic lettings the measure of damages will, in general, be as stated in *Hewitt v Rowlands* (1924) 93 LJKB 1080, ie the difference in value to the tenant of the premises, from the date of notice of want of repair down to the time of the assessment of damages, between the house in the condition in which it currently is and the condition in which it would be had the landlord, on receipt of notice, fulfilled the obligation; in other words the difference in value to the tenant of the premises in their current condition and the condition in which they should be, bearing in mind age, character and locality. This sum is likely to be what the tenant would have to spend in performing the landlord's obligations for him, though it may be a sum computed by reference to a proportion of the periodic rent, plus a sum in respect of inconvenience and discomfort.

Where the dwelling is occupied under a 'long' lease the appropriate measure of damages will be *either*, where the tenant wishes to sell the dwelling, the difference in the price he/she received for the dwelling as damaged and the price it would have fetched on the open market had it been repaired, or, where the tenant wishes to remain in the dwelling, the cost of taking reasonable alternative accommodation, the cost of redecorating plus some compensation for inconvenience in addition to the cost of repairs.

It is not enough simply to claim 'damages', the issues must be particularised. 'Special damage' ie the precise amount of pecuniary loss suffered by the tenant flowing from the facts must be specifically pleaded. This means that claims for, inter alia, damaged personal property, money spent discharging a landlord's obligations, or remedying damage consequent on a landlord's failure to act, costs of redecorating, the cost of taking alternative accommodation, should this be reasonable, have to be specified. Some general damage, compensation for which will be computed by the court according to the nature of the tenant's interest in the property, must also be generally pleaded, and this includes matters such as inconvenience and discomfort, as mentioned above.

Awards of damages vary in such cases, contrast *Taylor v Knowsley Borough Council* (1985) 17 HLR 376 with *Downie v Lambeth London Borough Council* [1986] Lag Bulletin 95, but the trend is for awards to be increasing. It will be of no avail to a landlord to plead a low rent has been paid where a tenant has had to endure extremely poor living conditions for a long period of time, and where a tenant is clearly a victim of a landlord's default a substantial award of damages is acceptable, see *Chiodi's Personal Representatives v De Marney* [1988] 41 EG 80, and *Davies v Peterson* (1988) 21 HLR 63.

It should be remembered that the onus of proof in relation to these matters is on the tenant, see *Foster v Day* (1968) 208 Estates Gazette 495, and tenants should act in good time and ensure relevant defects are brought to their landlord's attention, otherwise general damages may be reduced, *Minchburn Ltd v Peck* [1988] 15 EG 97.

The right to repair

Section 96 of the Housing Act 1985 and SI 1985/1493 established a 'right to repair' under which *secure* tenants were entitled to carry out certain repairs for which their landlords were responsible and to recover the costs from their landlords. In practice this right was little used.

A new section 96 is now substituted by section 121 of the Leasehold Reform, Housing and Urban Development Act 1993. This empowers the Secretary of State to make regulations to allow local authority secure tenants to have certain repairs carried out at their landlord's expense. (Housing association tenants were excluded from the scope of the statutory scheme, but a scheme appropriate to associations is to be drawn up by the Housing Corporation.) The basic notion of the scheme is that landlords should inform tenants of the existence of the right to repair and should maintain lists of approved contractors (which may include the landlord's own workforce) prepared to carry out qualifying repairs.

The matters as specified in SI 1994/133 (Schedule) *include*: electrical power/lighting faults; faults in or loss of gas supply; faults in or loss of water supply; loss of heating (November to April); burst pipes, blocked or leaking foul drains and WCs, leaking central heating pipes and cisterns; water penetration of roofs; non-flushing WC; loss of heating (May-October); loose handrails; weeping pipes; seized stopcocks; defective WCs and unusable or insanitary sanitary ware; blocked flues; solid fuel heating defects; entryphone defects; non-securable doors and windows; rotten timber flooring; failed extractor fans. Most such defects should be repaired in one working day, though some may take three and others up to seven. For a repair to qualify, a financial limit of £250 is also imposed, while a landlord must also have at least 100 houses let on secure tenancies to fall within the scheme.

Tenants may apply for qualifying repairs to be carried out. Landlords must then inspect, if this is felt necessary, and if satisfied the disrepair in question is 'qualifying' must issue a notice specifying the nature of the repair, the listed contractor by whom it is to be carried out and the target time by which any work is to be done. Where such a notice is issued the tenant must be provided with a copy. If the initially specified contractor fails to carry out the work in the prescribed time, the landlord must (if the tenant states he/she requires another contractor to do the work) issue a further notice specifying a new target time for the work. The landlord may be liable to pay some compensation to reflect the inconvenience of delay to the tenant determined in accordance with the regulations if a repair remains incomplete after the second target time has passed. See DoE Circular 2/94 for further details.

The right to information

Section 104 of the Housing Act 1985 requires landlords who grant secure tenancies to publish within two years of the commencement of the Act (and thereafter to revise and republish) information, in simple terms, about their secure tenancies. This information must explain, inter alia, the effect of the implied covenant to repair under section 11 et seq of the Landlord and Tenant Act 1985. All secure tenants must be supplied with a copy of this information.

Public law remedies for dealing with sub-standard housing

Grudging Parliamentary interference with the contractual relations of landlords and tenants has never been enough by itself to deal with bad housing conditions. In many – maybe most – cases tenants have lacked the financial and other resources to enable them to vindicate their rights via breach of covenant actions, while, historically, some dwellings have been in such poor conditions as to be beyond the help of 'repair' within the meaning outlined above. The existence of *areas* of substandard housing also made it unrealistic to expect action to depend solely on individual initiative. As we pointed out in the historical introduction to the chapter, the Artizans' and Labourers' Dwellings (or Torrens) Act 1868 first made provision for clearance, while the subsequent Artizans' and Labourers' Dwellings Improvement (or Cross) Act 1875 coupled clearance with area redevelopment procedures. However, little use was made of this or subsequent legislation until after the First World War when the Acquisition of Land (Assessment of Compensation) Act 1919 – coupled with Exchequer subsidies for new council house building – helped to lay an effective legal basis for authorities to acquire sub-standard dwellings and rehouse their occupants. Even so many of the acquisition procedures remained cumbersome until the Housing Act 1930 was passed which streamlined the process and led to a demolition rate of some 90,000 houses per annum by 1939.

Area action was then interrupted by the Second World War and it was not until 1955 that area clearance of poor housing recommenced and continued, as we described in the introduction to the chapter, into the 1970s. Housing *improvement* was not a new policy in the 1970s. The Moyne (1933), Ridley (1945) and Hobhouse (1947) Reports had all drawn attention to the need to prevent housing decline and to take action on improveable property. Some limited powers in this connection were given by the Housing Act 1935, but it was the Housing Act 1949 which introduced grant aid for housing improvement. As we described above, at first take up of grant was very slow due to the restrictive conditions but reforms in the grant aid system under the Housing Repairs and Rents Act 1954 led to a greater take up of improvement aid.

Powers to bring about *area* improvement were introduced by the Housing Act 1964, and an area based rehabilitation policy to deal with sub-standard housing was promoted by the Housing Acts of 1969 and 1974. With modifications this policy remains the basis of dealing with poor quality housing conditions although, as we have seen, it has been of limited success in reaching the poorest households in the very worst housing. Legislative changes introduced in the Local Government and Housing Act 1989 were an attempt to deal with this and put into formal order policy changes heralded in 1983 by the Green Paper *Home Improvements: A New Approach*, Cmnd 9153 which promised the introduction of means testing for grant aid to target grants at those in most financial hardship while at the same time reducing public expenditure.

The 1989 legislation also provided an opportunity for revision of the definition of unfit housing which had by then become hopelessly outmoded, the version on the statute book being traceable back to 1909.

The 1989 fitness requirements

Section 605 of the Housing Act 1985, inserted in 1989, imposes a *yearly* obligation on district and London borough councils to inspect their areas to consider action in relation to:

1) repair notices;
2) slum clearance;
3) houses in multiple occupation;
4) housing renewal areas;
5) grant aid for housing.

DoE Circular 6/90 indicates this means there should be a yearly planning exercise to:
a) identify types and numbers of unfit housing, and the best ways of dealing with problems;
b) monitor action in progress;
c) initiate regular physical surveys;
d) develop comprehensive renewal strategies to direct funding more effectively;
e) consider data available from other sources.

These powers apply to dwellings generally, ie houses, houses in multiple occupation, flats, 'bedsitters' and indeed any property used as a dwelling, see *Ashbridge Investments Ltd v Minister of Housing and Local Government* [1965] 3 All ER 371, [1965] 1 WLR 1320.

Sub-standard housing may also be brought to the attention of authorities by individuals. Authorities must take account of reports of unfit housing made by their 'proper officers' while local magistrates may also complain in writing to such an officer that a dwelling is 'unfit', and that imposes a duty on the officer to inspect and report on the dwelling, see section 606 of the 1985 Act. The consideration of information received activates the specific duties to take action.

Authorities must in the discharge of functions pay attention to the new unfitness standard of section 604 of the 1985 Act (as substituted). This is stricter and more up to date than previous law, and lists criteria which must be positively met if a dwelling is to be classed as 'fit'.

The criteria for houses (including HMOs) are is the house:
1) structurally stable;
2) free from serious disrepair;
3) free from dampness prejudicial to health of occupants;
4) adequately provided with lighting, heating, and ventilation;
5) adequately provided with wholesome water;
6) adequately provided with facilities for cooking/preparing food, including a sink with hot and cold water;
7) provided with a suitably located water closet for occupants' exclusive use;
8) provided with a suitably located bath/shower and basin with hot and cold water for occupants' exclusive use;
9) provided with a system for water drainage?

Thus:

(a)   a house is unfit if, in the opinion of the authority, it fails to meet one or more of the above criteria, *and*

(b)   by reason of that failure it is not reasonably suitable for occupation.

The criteria for *flats* are as for houses, but a flat may also be unfit if the building of which it is part is affected by structural instability/disrepair/ dampness/inadequate ventilation/an ineffective drainage system, and by reason of that the flat is not reasonably suitable for occupation.

Though there is considerable room for subjective evaluation in a decision as to whether a property is/is not 'fit', the 1989 standard encourages a 'check list' approach to decision making which prevents authorities considering the effect of an accumulation of minor defects, which was the position under the previous law, and some authorities now consider a property which might previously have been considered unfit because of its cumulative defects may now evade control, it does not fail to meet any one of the stated criteria, see further DoE, *Monitoring the New Housing Fitness Standard*, HMSO, 1993, pp 45-47. See also further below on the relationship between sections 189 and 190.

Further guidance on the criteria is given in DoE 6/90 Annex A. 'Unfitness' is primarily to be determined in terms of health and safety, having regard to the severity, location, persistence, duration and extent of any defects in the property, though discomfort, inconvenience and inefficiency may also be considered. The standard should be applied by considering the dwelling rather than its occupants, though a house should be suitable for all types of occupants who might reasonably be expected to occupy it, including, as appropriate, the elderly and children. Each of the statutory criteria must be considered, individually and in relation to each other, and thorough internal and external inspection of each relevant dwelling is counselled. Authorities must not only consider failure to meet the criteria, but whether by virtue of that failure the dwelling is not reasonably suitable for occupation. A mere minor failure to meet a criterion does not doom a property otherwise perfectly sound. However, if a defect is persistent it may lead to action being necessary. Decorative condition is generally not to be considered, though its exterior lack may have led to an independent problem of disrepair. Dwellings should be assessed on their 'as now' condition.

DoE Circular 6/90 makes the following points about the various statutory criteria. The structural stablility criterion is concerned with the overall integrity of a building, while 'serious disrepair' arises usually from deterioration. Disrepair can arise from a single item or a combination of individual smaller items. Disrepair should be considered against a background of whether it prejudices safety, or prevents a property from being normally used, or prevents surfaces from being cleaned, or gives rise to risk of fire/explosion, toxic fumes or electrocution, or to a risk of water penetration or other structural risks. The criterion is concerned with seeing that houses function as intended, and are wind and weather tight, and do not give rise to long term deterioration so as to prejudice the integrity of the dwelling. However, the Courts have also held that the test of 'serious disrepair' is whether by ordinary use of the property personal injury or injury to health by damage may naturally be caused to the occupier, *Morgan v Liverpool Corpn* [1927] 2 KB 131, and *Summers v Salford Corpn* [1943] AC 283, [1943] 1 All ER 68 irrespective of whether an individual item of disrepair is one that can be quickly and easily repaired. In coming to a decision on such matters authorities must act in a judicial spirit, *Hall v Manchester Corpn* (1915) 84 LJ Ch 732.

Dampness *which is prejudicial to health* may either be rising or penetrating damp or persistent condensation damp arising primarily from design/ construction defects. The ventilation, lighting and heating criterion allows authorities to consider, inter alia, whether a dwelling's main living room has fixed heating provision which can maintain a room temperature of 18°C(+) when the external temperature is -1°C. Wholesome water supplies are those which are adequate and continuous with piping that does not contaminate the water and adequate taps at sinks, while the food preparation criteria enable authorities to consider matters such as the adequacy of work surfaces, cookers and the size and layout of kitchens, the porosity of kitchen surfaces and their ability to be cleaned. Foul water systems must also be considered with regard to any propensity to be blocked, their ability to cope with rainfall and their siting so as to prevent flooding or the spread of ice.

Certain matters are not criteria for fitness, for example infestation by bugs or vermin, a lack of gas or electricity or modern wiring or insulation, though such matters may be considered, *provided* a dwelling also falls in some way to satisfy the statutory criteria, see *Steele v Minister of Housing and Local Government* (1956) 168 Estates Gazette 37.

Once an unfit dwelling is discovered a duty to take action arises, and under the 1989 amendments action is primarily to take place according to an integrated area based policy. Section 604A of the 1985 Act provides that authorities must consider with regard to sub-standard housing the most satisfactory course of action, whether it be repair, closing, demolition, etc. This is to ensure a flexible area based response to the eradication of bad housing, which allows for an approach that is appropriate to the problems and needs of the area ranging from renovation to demolition and rebuilding, *in conjunction with the private sector* according to central policy.

But what is the most satisfactory course of action? Using powers under section 604A the Secretary of State has issued a code of guidance which forms Annex F to DoE Circular 6/90.

The Code

This is a 'factor to be taken into account' (compare the Code under Part III of the 1985 Act), but it is so detailed that it will be hard for authorities to adopt alternative modes of proceeding. It lays down the following principles.

First, identify the need for action either by means of survey, or complaints from tenants or applications for grant aid. Where a survey is required, the *recommended* means is the Neighbourhood Renewal Assessment (NRA) which has the following components: (a) stated purposes, (b) defined aims and objectives, (c) a defined area, (d) a physical survey, (e) a survey of residents' socio-economic characteristics, and their views and preferences, (f) a survey of the non-residential characteristics of the area, (g) a socio-environmental assessment, (h) consideration of scope for private investment, (i) creation of a broad range of options for dwelling(s) in the area and (j) development of options into workable categories for option appraisal on economic and socio-environmental bases, and (k) reporting the *reasoned* preferred option for the dwelling(s).

Socio-environmental factors should have equal weight with economic issues, though costs are also to be considered over a period of years using a formula which is to include *all* action costs, including administrative costs, not just those attributable to publicly aided/required works. This enables authorities to consider the overall economics of various forms of action over a 30 year period. It may be necessary to work the formula more than once in relation to any given property to consider both its individual fate and that of a group of dwellings in which it is situated. While the formula is expressed in the circular in algebraic form, there is considerable room for subjectivity in its application. Though the NRA formula was developed as a means of determining whether or not to take action by way of declaring a renewal area (see further below), DoE Circular 6/90 Annex F para 8 points out it can be adopted as a basis for other forms of housing action, while Annex G argues its applicability to individual premises. In all circumstances the object is effectively to allow authorities to take decisions following a series of sequential steps designed to enable the costs and socio-environmental implications of decisions to be explored, with a systematic appraisal of alternative courses of action, so as to identify the option likely to produce the greatest community benefit on a long term basis.

Second, consider most satisfactory course of action by taking into account a wide range of issues such as: (a) costs, (b) social implications of any action taken, (c) alternative courses and their implications, (d) impact of the various forms of action on other nearby dwellings, (e) area strategy factors, (f) the local character and life of the community, (g) the views of those affected by the work/action, (h) the effect of any action in relation to the total needs of an area, and (i) the size of the area against which the effect of the work is measured.

The courses of action available

After the evaluation process described above authorities should be in a position to make a choice as to which course of action to take in relation to the area/property in question.

Individual houses (including flats)

A number of choices are available, the 'most satisfactory' should be chosen from: serving notice under section 189(1) or 189(1A) of the 1985 Act (repairs procedure), or under section 264 (1) or 264(2) (closure of whole premises or parts), or under section 265 (1) or 265(2) (demolition). (For action under section 289 clearance procedure for areas, or group repair action, see further below.) Section 604A(2) provides that the Secretary of State may issue guidance in relation to the choice of action. That guidance is contained in Annex F of DoE Circular 6/90. This provides that general considerations in relation to *all* choices include: considering premises in their setting, and the effect of action on neighbouring dwellings and on the area; the size and nature of the area in question; the costs of action and their long term social implications; the views of those likely to be affected by any decision.

With particular regard to action under section 189 authorities should consider the physical condition of dwelling; its life expectancy as repaired; comparison of repair costs as against other courses of action; other proposals for the area; condition of neighbouring properties; group repair proposals (see below); the need (long and short term) locally for the type of accommodation provided by the dwelling; owners'/occupants' wishes and ability to carry them out; local environment.

With regard to section 264 the following are relevant: comparison of cost of closure versus other options; whether the building is listed or in a conservation area; position of dwelling with regard to neighbouring buildings; the need locally for accommodation as provided by the dwelling; wishes of owners/occupants, and alternative uses for the building; effect of closure on the cohesion etc of area; availability of accommodation for displaced residents.

With regard to section 265 the following are relevant: relationship of the dwelling to neighbouring buildings; comparison of costs of alternative action; the need for the type of accommodation provided; future proposals for area – eg conservation area status; availability of accommodation for the displaced; wishes of owners/ocupants etc; prospective use of the cleared site; the local area, its future residentially, and the impact of the cleared site on it.

Where the building in question contains flats some of which are unfit the authority should additionally consider the condition of the common parts, and the proportion of fit to unfit flats – a 75% level of unfit flats points to demolition of the building, as also where defects threaten stability.

The object of these provisions as modified is to ensure flexibility of action in respect of unfit dwellings. It appears judicial review of an authority's decision is available should irrelevant factors be taken into account, for example a general desire to protect the environment when it was alleged a cottage was unfit because it discharged sewage directly into a stream, see *R v Forest of Dean District Council, ex p Trigg* (1989) 22 HLR 167, and this remedy is available to tenants as well as landlords.

The legal procedures

Action under section 189 etc (repair notices)

Where an authority is satisfied this is the most satisfactory course of action in respect of a dwelling house or house in multiple occupation (HMO) they must serve a repair notice on the person having control, or, in the case of a HMO, on its manager. With regard to unfit flats, whether or not in multiple occupation, where the cause of unfitness is the condition of another part of the overall building notice is served on the person having control of the relevant part. 'The person having control' is defined by section 207 of the 1985 Act as the person who receives the rack rent of the premises, ie a rent of not less than two thirds of their full net annual (or 'rateable') value.

A repair notice requires the execution of specified works of *repair or improvement* which are to be begun by a reasonable date, not earlier than 28 days after the notice is served, and are to be completed within a specified reasonable time. The notice must state that in the authority's opinion the works will make the property fit for human habitation. Copies of the notice must also be served on the freeholder, mortgagee or lessee of the property. The notice becomes operative if there is no appeal at the expiry of 21 days from its date of service, and is then a local land charge.

An authority is not, however, under a duty to serve a repair notice if, though satisfied the property in question is unfit, they determine that the premises form part of a building which would be a 'qualifying building' in a group repair scheme, and that they expect to prepare such a scheme for the building within a period of 12 months, see section 190A of the 1985 Act. See further below on group repair schemes.

Action under section 190

A repair notice may also be served under section 190 where an authority is satisfied a dwelling house or HMO is in such a state of disrepair that though it is *not* unfit either *substantial repairs* are necessary to bring it to a reasonable standard considering its age, character and locality, *or* though not unfit that the state of disrepair is such as to interfere materially with the personal comfort of the occupying tenant, or persons occupying the HMO as the case may be. These powers extend to buildings containing a flat under section 190(1A), whether singly or multiply occupied, where though the flat is not fit, *either* substantial repairs are required to parts of the building outside the flat to bring it to a reasonable standard in view of its age, character and locality, *or* where the condition of part of the building is such as to interfere with the personal comfort of occupying tenants. But under section 190(1B) such a notice may *not* be served, unless there is an occupying tenant of the dwelling house or flat in question, *or* the property is within a renewal area within Part VII of the Local Government and Housing Act 1989 (see further below). An 'occupying tenant' is a person *other than* an owner occupier, who occupies the dwelling as a lessee, while an 'owner occupier' is a freeholder or 'long' leaseholder, ie one for more than 21 years. The person served with the notice will normally be the 'person having control', ie generally the landlord or owner of the premises, see section 207 of the 1985 Act as amended, but in the case of a HMO notice may be served on the manager, see section 190 (1C). Copies must also be served on any other person having an interest in the property as freeholder, mortgagee or tenant, see section 190(3).

The notice may *not* require the doing of works of internal decorative repair, section 190(2), and must be clear on its face as to what works are required, see *Our Lady of Hal Church v Camden London Borough Council* (1980) 255 Estates Gazette 991. Once a repair notice has become operative it is a local land charge, see section 190(5), and a deliberate failure to comply with a notice is a criminal offence under section 198A.

Section 190 contemplates action against two kinds of property, houses in need of substantial repair and fit houses in disrepair where conditions interfere with the personal comfort of occupying tenants, and though there is evidence to suggest authorities make less use of these powers than they could, the powers have been recognised as permitting action to prevent properties becoming unfit, and as allowing the consideration of wider policy issues in the taking of decisions on houses falling into disrepair, see *Kenny v Kingston upon Thames Royal London Borough Council* (1985) 17 HLR 344. However, what is this provision's relationship with section 189? Section 189 deals with properties that are *unfit*, section 190 with those that are *fit*. Yet a property may be unfit and *also* affected by other defects which fall only within section 190. It appears *practice* is to serve notices under both sections each requiring specific works to commence on the same date, yet it would be preferable if section 189 was amended to allow the requiring of works to make a dwelling fit *and* to bring it up to a reasonable standard considering its age, character and locality, see *Monitoring the New Housing Fitness Standard*, p 78.

Appeals

A person aggrieved (a phrase undefined by the statutes, though here it may extend to include tenants) by the service of a repair notice may, under section 191, within 21 days of service appeal to the county court. There are particular grounds of appeal, without prejudice to the general right to appeal, allowing the appellant to argue that some other person who is an owner of the property ought to execute required works or pay their cost in whole or full, see section 190(1A), and, *in the case of a notice under section 189*, that some other action, such as closure or demolition would have been the most satisfactory course of action, see section 190(1B). On an appeal the court has discretion to confirm, quash or vary the repair notice, and all relevant factors can be taken into account such as the expense of the works required, the value of the property, the financial position of the owner, see *Hillbank Properties Ltd v Hackney London Borough Council* [1978] QB 998, [1978] 3 All ER 343, though where an appeal is brought under section 190(1B), see above, the court *must* have regard to the guidance issued under section 604A. Where an appeal against a section 189 notice is allowed and the reason is that making a closing or demolition order would be the most satisfactory answer the judge shall, if requested by the appellant or the authority, include a finding to that effect in his judgment.

Enforcement of repair notices

Authorities have power under section 191A to execute required works by agreement with the person having control of the property, at that person's expense. Otherwise, if a repair notice is not complied with authorities have power under section 193 to do required work, and may recover their costs under Schedule 10 of the 1985 Act. 'Compliance' in this context means that the works specified in the notice must be begun and completed within the due time allowed, see section 193(2), while section 193(2A) also allows authorities to do required works where it appears that reasonable progress is not being made towards compliance before the end of the appropriate period for doing the works. Written notice of intention to exercise the section 193 powers *must* be given to the person having control of the property, and may be given to any owner of them, see section 194, while section 195, inter alia, empowers a magistrates' court to order a person who has received notice of intended action (and who prevents the officers, servants or agents of an authority from carrying into effect any of the relevant statutory provisions) to permit all things requisite to be done, on pain of committing an offence. Powers of entry for survey and examination purposes before or after a repair notice has been served are given by section 197 which enables authorities to authorise their officers in writing to enter premises for a specified purpose(s), and thereafter such an officer may enter the premises by giving seven days notice to the occupier and owner, and it is an offence under section 198 to obstruct such an authorised officer. It is a further offence under section 198A for a person having control of premises subject to a repair notice to fail intentionally to comply with that notice *either* by not starting the works by their due commencement date *or* by not completing works on time, and the obligation to complete required works continues notwithstanding that the period for their completion has expired.

It should be noted that under section 203(3) no action taken under, inter alia, section 189 and 190 etc, prejudices or affects any remedy available at common law or under statute to the tenant of any premises against the landlord.

Action under section 264 etc (closure/demolition)

Section 264 provides that where an authority is satisfied, having considered the Secretary of State's guidance, that a dwelling house or HMO or one or more of the flats in a building is unfit and that the most satisfactory course of action is closure of the relevant premises it shall make a closing order. This is an order under section 267(2) which prohibits the use of the premises in question for any purpose not approved by the authority, though such approval is not to be unreasonably withheld, and a person aggrieved by its withholding may appeal to the county court.

Section 263(1) provides that where an authority is satisfied that a dwelling house (but not a flat) or an HMO (but not a flat multiply occupied) is unfit and that demolition is the most satisfactory course of action it must make a demolition order. Where a building contains one or more flats and some or all are unfit and the authority considers demolition is the most satisfactory course of action it must make a demolition order under section 265(2). Such an order requires premises to be vacated within a specified period (of at least 28 days) from the time it becomes operative and to be demolished within six weeks after the end of that period, or if not vacated before the end of that period to be demolished within six weeks of when it is vacated, though the authority may specify such longer period as they consider reasonable, see section 267(1). The provision that the premises are to be required to be vacated is mandatory, even where they are vacant when the order is made, see *Pocklington v Melksham UDC* [1964] 2 QB 673, [1964] 2 All ER 862 and *R v Epsom and Ewell Corpn, ex p RB Property Investment (Eastern) Ltd* [1964] 2 All ER 832, [1964] 1 WLR 1060. It should further be noted that where a closing order has been made the authority may at any time revoke it save where the building in question is listed, or the dwelling is a flat – and substitute a demolition order, see section 279.

Where a demolition or closing order is made copies must, under section 268, be served on any person who is an owner of the premises and on any reasonably ascertainable mortgagee. Where the premises in question is a building containing flats notice must in addition be served on those who are the owners of the flats, see section 268(1A). An order against which no appeal is brought becomes operative at the end of 21 days from its date of service, see section 268(2). A person aggrieved by such an order thus has 21 days under section 269 to appeal to the county court, though this right does not extend to any person who is in occupation under a lease with an unexpired term of three years or less. The grounds of appeal include, under section 269

(2A) that another course of action, eg a repair notice, was the most satisfactory course of action rather than demolition/closure as the case may be, and in such cases the court must consider the Secretary of State's guidance in coming to a decision. Otherwise the court has considerable discretion in deciding appeals.

Once a demolition order has become operative in respect of any premises the authority must serve on any occupier of them, or any part of them, a notice which states the order's effect, the date by which the premises are to be vacated and requiring the surrender of possession before the vacation date. Possession may thereafter be obtained by order in the county court, irrespective of any security of tenure existing under the Rent Act 1977 or the Housing Act 1988, see section 270. But a property owner may not recover damages for loss as a result of an authority's failure to serve a section 270 notice on a sitting tenant, *R v Lambeth London Borough Council, ex p Sarkbrook Ltd* (1994) Times, 14 December. It is an offence under section 270(5) to enter into occupation of premises, or to permit someone to enter into occupation, after the date by which an order requires it to be vacated, provided it is known that the order has become operative and applies to the premises. Similar provisions apply in respect of closing orders under sections 276 and 277.

Section 271 and 272 grant powers to authorities to demolish relevant premises in default of action by their owners and to recover their expenses. They may also secure, under section 273, the cleansing of premises subject to demolition orders of vermin.

Once a demolition order has become operative the owner of the premises, or any other person in a position in the opinion of the authority to put his/her proposals into effect, may propose the reconstruction of the premises, including their enlargement or improvement. If satisfied this work will lead to the creation of one or more fit dwelling houses or houses in multiple occupation, as the case may be, they may afford the person an opportunity to do the work by extending the period within which demolition is required, and further extensions of this time may be granted provided satisfactory progress with no unreasonable delays is being made on the work. If this is then completed to the authority's satisfaction they may revoke the demolition order, see section 274. (A similar power to determine a closing order on relevant premises being rendered fit exists under section 278.) Section 275 permits the substitution by an authority of a closing order for a demolition order where proposals are submitted by the owner of relevant premises, or by any other person interested in them, for their use other than as housing accommodation.

Where either a closing or a demolition order is made under sections 264 or 265, compensation must be paid to affected owners under section 584A. The basis of compensation is the diminution in the compulsory purchase value of the property determined in accordance with the Land Compensation Act 1961. But where such an order is brought to an end, any compensation received must be repaid, see section 584B.

A building which is 'obstructive', ie dangerous or injurious to health simply because of its contact with or proximity to other buildings, may be made subject to an obstructive building notice which gives the owner notice of a time and place when the building's demolition will be considered by the local authority, see sections 283 and 284 of the 1985 Act. After giving the owner a hearing on this matter the authority may determine, by an obstructive buildings order, to demolish the building or part of it, and to require its vacation. If no appeal is then made the order will then become operative on the expiration of 21 days from the date of service of the order on the building's owner(s). A person aggrieved by such an order may, however, within that time appeal to the county court under section 285, though this right does not extend to occupiers who hold the building under leases or agreements whose unexpired term is three years or less. The court has wide discretion to confirm, quash or vary the order on an appeal, the making of which suspends the order until the final determination of the appeal. Once such an order has become effective the authority may serve notice on the occupier stating the effect of the order and requiring vacation of the premises; thereafter possession may be obtained by court order, irrespective of any security of tenure under the Rent Act 1977 or the Housing Act 1988, see section 286. The prime responsibility for executing an order lies on the relevant building owner(s), under section 287(2) but such owners may, before the end of the period within which an obstructive building is required to be vacated, sell their interests to the authority for the compulsory purchase value of the premises, and the authority is then under a duty to carry out demolition, see section 287(1). Where there is a failure by owners to carry out demolition the authority is under a duty under section 287(3) to do the necessary work and they may recover their expenses from owners under section 288.

Note that buildings other than houses can be dealt with under these provisions, see *Jackson v Knutsford Urban Council* [1914] 2 Ch 686, while they are specifically excluded from applying to buildings owned by local authorities, and statutory undertakers unless in this case they are used as dwellings, showrooms or offices, see section 283(2).

Where an authority would otherwise be required under sections 264 or 265 to make a demolition or closing order in respect of a dwelling house, HMO or the whole of a building, they may, under section 300, where it appears to them that the premises can be made to provide accommodation of a standard 'adequate for the time being' purchase the property instead. Notice of determination to purchase the property must be served on those persons who would otherwise have been served with copies of a demolition/closing order. Thereafter the property may be acquired by agreement or compulsorily. This provision only allows authorities to acquire property on a temporary basis, it may not be used to add to an authority's permanent housing stock, see *Victoria Square Property Co Ltd v London Borough of Southwark* [1978] 2 All ER 281, [1978] 1 WLR 463.

Clearance area procedure under section 289 et seq

Clearance area procedure remains available where, after survey procedures (see above) an authority is satisfied this is the most satisfactory way of dealing with the condition in the area. Authorities must therefore consider alternative options, the views of residents, rehousing provision, after use of the area, and the ability to attract private sector investment. They must then be satisfied that the residential buildings in the area (ie houses, HMOs or buildings containing flats) are unfit, or are by reason of their poor arrangement, or by virtue of the narrowness and poor arrangement of streets, dangerous or injurious to the health of inhabitants, and that other buildings in the area are similarly dangerous or injurious to health, see section 289(2)(a) and (b). 'Houses' has been interpreted as covering a wide range of premises eg shops and garages with living rooms over them , see *Re Bainbridge, South Shields (D'Arcy Street) Compulsory Purchase Order 1937* [1939] 1 KB 500, and *Re Butler, Camberwell (Wingfield Mews) No 2 Clearance Order 1936* [1939] 1 KB 570, and also tenement houses, *Quiltotex Co Ltd v Minister of Housing and Local Government* [1966] 1 QB 704, [1965] 2 All ER 913.

Clearance area procedure was modified in 1989 so that section 289 (2B)-(2F) of the 1985 Act now provide that consultation with those persons directly affected (ie freeholders, lessees and mortgagees of affected buildings) must be undertaken before a clearance area is declared, with notice served on every person having an interest in any building in the area, while other occupants of residential property should be informed of the authority's proposals. Local press advertisement must take place and representations invited and considered. As a matter of good practice consideration should be given to ensuring the provision of the above information in languages other than English where appropriate. At least 28 days shall be allowed for the making of representations. The consideration of representations procedure necessitates that those who are asked for their views should be given full information as to the proposals so that they may make a properly informed response. Before deciding to declare a clearance area an authority should also consider the relative proportions of fit and unfit dwellings in the proposed area.

As a result of considering representations the authority may decide to declare/not declare a clearance area, or declare it subject to the exemption of certain unfit residential buildings, see section 289 (2F)(a), (b) and (c). Where they decide to declare a clearance area, the authority must pass a resolution to that effect and have the area defined by a map, but *excluding* any residential building which is not unfit, or dangerous/injurious to health, any residential buildings which though unfit have been exempted, and any other buildings which are not dangerous or injurious to health. A clearance area should, generally, be a contiguous area of land, with no outlying separated parcels of land, see section 289(5B), though the authority may also include land in a clearance area which belongs to them, provided they could have included it had it not belonged to them, see section 293(1). Furthermore before the resolution is passed the authority must be satisfied that, in so far as suitable accommodation does not exist for those who will be displaced by clearance, they will be able to secure such accommodation as it becomes necessary and that they have the necessary resources to carry their resolution into effect, section 289(4). 'Suitable accommodation' in this context means suitable *dwelling* accommodation, see *Re Gateshead County Borough (Barn Close) Clearance Order 1931* [1933] 1 KB 429, while the need for an authority to be satisfied as to its resources does not require the placing before the authority of specific figures, see *Goddard v Minister of Housing and Local Government* [1958] 3 All ER 482, [1958] 1 WLR 1151. Upon making the resolution the authority must 'forthwith' send a copy to the Secretary of State together with a statement of the number of occupants of buildings in the clearance area on a specified day.

Where a residential building which is unfit is *not* included in a clearance area, for example because of exemption under section 289(2F)(b), the authority is under a duty to take action in respect of it under whichever of sections 189, 264 or 265 it considers the most appropriate course of action.

As soon as the authority have declared land to be a clearance area they must, under section 290, proceed to secure its clearance by purchasing the land and undertaking clearance themselves, or by otherwise securing demolition of buildings. The power to acquire the land (which may be exercised by agreement, or under compulsory powers if authorised by the Secretary of State) extends to land surrounded by the clearance area acquisition of which is reasonably necessary for securing a cleared area of convenient shape and dimensions, and adjoining land whose acquisition is reasonably necessary for the satisfactory development or use of the cleared area. Such adjoining land must be shown by the authority, should they wish to acquire it compulsorily, to be reasonably necessary as a question of fact, see *Coleen Properties Ltd v Minister of Housing and Local Government* [1971] 1 All ER 1049, [1971] 1 WLR 433 and *Gosling v Secretary of State for the Environment* [1975] JPL 406. The land must also be partly contiguous with land in the clearance area, see *Bass Charrington (North) Ltd v Minister of Housing and Local Government* (1970) 22 P & CR 31.

Detailed treatment of compulsory purchase procedure is beyond the scope of this work, but it should be noted that since 1 April 1990 under sections 578 and 578A of the 1985 Act, the appropriate procedure is generally that under the Acquisition of Land Act 1981, Part II, under which the authority makes a compulsory purchase order on the land in prescribed form, which is then given publicity in local newspapers, while notice of the effect of the order is also served on all owners, lessees and occupiers of relevant land, except tenants for a month or less. The order is then submitted for ministerial confirmation which may not be given until after any objections to the order have been heard and considered. Once the order is confirmed the acquiring authority must publicise that fact locally, and serve notice of that fact on the affected landholders. Compensation for compulsorily acquired unfit property is paid on the same basis as acquisitions of fit property assessed under the Land Compensation Acts 1961 and 1973, which is, effectively, market valuation. Where a person is displaced from a dwelling in consequence, inter alia, of its compulsory acquisition, and he/she occupied that dwelling as an only or main residence for a period of one year ending with the displacement, by virtue of an interest in it or as a statutory tenant under the Rent Act 1977, etc; a *home loss payment* may be claimed under section 29 of the Land Compensation Act 1973, and the position is similar where a *tenant* is displaced by the acquisition of the *landlord's* interest in a property *by agreement* by an authority possessing compulsory purchase powers, see section 29(6). Where the conditions relating to entitlement to claim a home loss payment are *not* met a discretionary payment may still be made to a displaced occupier, see section 29(2) of the 1973 Act as amended. Note that a person is not 'displaced' if he/she gives up occupation before the date on which the acquiring authority was authorised to acquire under section 29(3). Claims must be made in writing, with particulars as required by the authority, within six years of displacement, section 32. The amount of a home loss payment for a periodic tenant is fixed at £1,500 by section 30 of the 1973 Act. A *disturbance payment* may additionally be payable to a tenant displaced by compulsory acquisition under section 32 of the 1973 Act and this will cover, inter alia, reasonable removal expenses, see section 38. To qualify for a disturbance payment a person must be in lawful possession of the land in question, and must have no entitlement to compensation under another statute. See also SI 1990/613.

It is clear policy that clearance and compulsory purchase procedure should only be used where there is a compelling case for their use on grounds of public interest, with the burden of justification falling on the acquiring authority. An authority must be satisfied that clearance is the most satisfactory way of dealing with the area, and must have considered alternative uses for the area, the views of residents, arrangements for rehousing and after use of the land. More than one survey may be needed to satisfy an authority on these issues. Compulsory purchase orders will be confirmed where the Secretary of State is satisfied that the economic and other interests of an area are best served by clearance. Authorities must argue their case for being granted compulsory purchase powers in a written document. This will include statements of the reasons for concluding relevant buildings are unfit, the proposals for rehousing residents and relocating any commercial or industrial uses, evidence as to the proposed after use of the site, evidence that the economic aspect of clearance has been considered, see DoE Circular 6/90 para 68. Circular 5/93 adds to this, para 11, that compulsory purchase is *generally* justified as a 'last resort' where a clear housing gain can be achieved and where other means of bringing about housing improvement have failed, and normally the Secretary of State does not expect an owner occupied house to be included in a compulsory purchase order unless it has defects adversely affecting other housing. Paragraph 63 of Circular 6/90 concludes by stating that 'Where authorities acquire any property or land they will wish to consider disposing of it to the private sector,' a clear indication that it is policy that slum clearance powers should be used to facilitate action by the private sector rather than to build up public sector land banks.

Once an authority has acquired land under section 290, section 291 requires them to ensure that buildings on the land are vacated and are then demolished, though they may, under section 301 postpone the demolition of residential buildings on land they acquire if they consider those buildings are capable of providing accommodation of a standard 'adequate for the time being'. Such property will almost certainly be of a standard lower than that of 'fitness', but it must not be of such a poor quality that it is prejudicial to health or a nuisance, otherwise its occupants will be in a position to take statutory nuisance proceedings against the authority, see further below *Nottingham Corpn v Newton* [1974] 1 WLR 923 and *Salford City Council v McNally* [1976] AC 379, [1975] 2 All ER 860. The period of postponement of demolition can be quite long – 24 years was considered not unreasonable on the facts in *R v Birmingham City Council, ex p Sale* (1983) 9 HLR 33. However, in that case Forbes J argued that exercise of the power to postpone requires more than that the housing is 'capable of providing accommodation adequate for the time being'. There must be some exceptional reason why demolition is postponed over and above 'need' for houses and the fact that the houses in question can be maintained to the standard of adequacy. The scheme of the Act is that once demolition is decided on, demolition should proceed unless proper and exceptional reasons justify postponement of demolition. Section 583 of the 1985 Act further permits authorities to permit continuation of tenancies of houses compulsorily acquired and to continue in use as housing accommodation. In such cases they may serve notice on the occupants authorising continued occupation on specified terms.

Those who are displaced from residential accommodation as a result of compulsory purchase action, and who have no suitable alternative accommodation available to them on reasonable terms, are entitled to look to the acquiring authority for housing, see further below on section 39 of the Land Compensation Act 1973.

An assessment of the use of unfitness powers

In 1993 the Department of the Environment published research undertaken by the Legal Research Institute of the University of Warwick, *Monitoring the New Housing Fitness Standard,* following local authority concern at possible variation in interpreting the 1989 fitness standard.

With regard to the ways in which unfit dwellings may come to authorities' attention, it was found that 65% of inspections arose following grant inquiries, 19% were responses to occupiers' complaints, while there was generally wide variation between authorities in the reasons for undertaking an inspection. Fewer than half the authorities surveyed had conducted a house condition survey representative of all dwellings in their areas within the previous five years while some authorities had insufficient staff and financial resources to respond to unfitness, and most authorities considered their resources before inspection. Of the 1,369 dwellings which fell within the survey, 68% were held to fail the fitness test, but once again there was a wide variation between authorities in the proportion of dwellings which failed, while dwellings inspected after a grant inquiry were more likely to be found unfit than those inspected following complaint by an occupier. The pattern of fitness was in any case found to be affected by local conditions such as underlying geology, mining subsidence and construction technique. Local officials were found to determine more dwellings to be unfit than a central group of re-surveyors of the properties, but in only 16% of instances was there complete disagreement between members of the two groups. Local officials reported that most failures of the fitness standard were due to disrepair and dampness, while a dwelling failing on one requirement of the standard was also likely to fail on more. However, when attention was concentrated on HMOs the most common reasons for officers determining property to be *unfit for multiple occupation* were in connection with failures under section 352 of the 1985 Act in respect of means of escape from fire and other fire precautions, see further Chapter Eight below.

It was found that the phrase 'not reasonably suitable for occupation' allowed divergent findings as to fitness because of the element of subjective evaluation, and officials indicated they would welcome clarification on a number of issues, for example the requirements as to stability, heating, cooking facilities and locations of water closets. Similarly there is often local confusion as to what is meant by a 'building' for the purposes of the legislation. When it comes to taking action in respect of properties found to be unfit, in 54% of instances local officials were likely to recommend action by way of renovation grant (see further below) with repair notices being served in 23% of instances, and clearance, demolition or closure is an option in 3% of cases. Some authorities, however, have an informal 'do-nothing' option where an occupier is unwilling to undergo disruption consequent on works needed to make a dwelling fit.

The research concluded that overall the new fitness standard can be uniformly applied by authorities and their officers, but clarification of particular issues was recommended ie structural stability, dampness, lighting, heating and ventilation, water supply, food preparation facilities, water closets and drainage. It was also suggested that certain other indicators of fitness should be included in an amended section 604, ie internal arrangements and dangerous design features, thermal and sound insulation, hazards outside a dwelling, eg problems of gaining safe access, fire precautions and precautions to guard against radon penetration., It was further concluded there is still too much room for subjective variation in the application of the section 604 standard and that the phrase 'and, by reason of that failure, is not reasonably suitable for occupation' should be repealed.

The research also pointed to the plethora of guidance available on the fitness standard – Circular 6/90 is not a 'stand alone' document. What is needed is guidance advising on *attainment standards* ie the standard a dwelling should reach on the completion of any works, while any guidance should clearly state the purpose for which it has been issued. Guidance on model approaches to housing surveys, specifications to make houses fit and on setting pricing guidelines for common repair items would also be welcome.

Authorities would also like wider powers simply to close parts of dwellings unsuitable for habitation, and to require the doing of certain works only so as to avoid the disruption to certain occupiers consequent on the determination than an extensive package of works is needed to make a dwelling fit. This would make legal the 'do-nothing' approach identified above.

Many of the shortcomings of the operation of the law were found to relate to lack of resources – an issue to be returned to in relation to grant aid after consideration of the more modern forms of housing action now found in the law following amendments made in 1989. One issue, however, can be dealt with at this point – energy efficiency as a requirement of fitness. Cm 2453 *Energy Efficiency in Buildings*, the response of the government to a report from the House of Commons Select Committee on the Environment in 1994 indicated official unwillingness to make energy efficiency a criterion for assessing the fitness of dwellings. It was accepted that creating such a criterion would increase the number of dwellings classified as unfit and the cost of making dwellings fit. There remains also doubt about the numbers of sub-standard dwellings. The 1994 report *Papering Over the Cracks* (National Housing forum) argued for an immediate £7 billion programme to bring privately owned housing up to fitness standards, and stated more than one owner occupied dwelling in 20 does not meet the fitness standard, while one home in every thirteen overall is unfit.

Renewal areas

Improvement of poor housing conditions on an area basis has been a policy option available to authorities for some 25 years. The Housing Act 1969 introduced the notion of the General Improvement Area (GIA). Housing Action Areas (HAA), as already noted, were introduced under the Housing Act 1974 to deal with more run-down areas. These types of action continued to be available under the Housing Act 1985, but the law was subject to criticism in that it did not provide one single, comprehensive mode of dealing with poor housing and also because it tended to separate consideration of housing conditions from other important issues such as employment, education facilities etc. Though changes have been made to the law it is by no means certain that these have come about as a result of desires to answer the foregoing criticisms as opposed to wishes to foster individual effort to target resources and to reduce overall public expenditure. Under the changes made by the Local Goverment and Housing Act 1989, HAAs and GIAs can no longer be declared, see section 98 of the 1989 Act. The GIA programme was due to be wound up by 1 April 1991. Existing HAAs were to come to end, in the case of those declared up to 31 March 1987, at the end of their period of designation, those declared after that date were to come to an end on 1 April 1991. Existing HAAs could be extended in duration under powers in the 1985 Act at the discretion of the Secretary of State but this was to be exceptional, eg to allow completion of works.

In place of GIAs and HAAs the 1989 Act introduced the concept of the Renewal Area (RA) and Annex C of DoE Circular 6/90 made it clear that land within a GIA or HAA could be instead designated as, or as part of, a RA.

The new law is part of the overall 'flexible approach' to a renewal and improvement strategy introduced by the 1989 Act. Renewal action is to be undertaken after careful appraisal of the options available for an area. Where declared, RAs will be larger than GIAs and HAAs were, and will normally last for ten years, during which time comprehensive action is to be undertaken to renew housing and tackle social and environmental problems. The basis is akin to partnership between the authority, residents, associations, and the private sector, including financial institutions for the object of using local authority powers is to give others 'market confidence' in the area, so helping to reverse processes of decline and to encourage spin offs for the local economy in the form of employment and training opportunities.

Authorities are required by section 605 of the Housing Act 1985 to consider declaring RAs. This will involve selecting appropriate areas for action. DoE 6/90 makes it clear the worst will not necessarily be the first; in some cases preventive action in respect of areas in danger of decline may be more appropriate. RAs will be declared against a policy background of choosing the 'most satisfactory course of action' which runs as a skein throughout repair and renewal legislation. Within a RA there may also be a need for pockets of clearance and/or group repair schemes etc (see further below).

Note, however, that a RA may *not* include any land designated as a housing action trust (HAT) area, nor any parcel of land not contiguous with another parcel of land in the area, see section 89(2) of the 1989 Act.

The statutory basis for declaring a RA is a report prepared under section 89 of the 1989 Act which must include particulars of the living conditions in the area in question, the ways in which they could be improved, powers available to the authority, the authority's detailed proposals for using those powers, costs of the proposals and the financial resources actually, or likely to be, available for implementing proposals. The report must also contain a reasoned recommendation as to whether a RA should be declared. In considering whether to make a declaration an authority must have regard to guidance issued by the Secretary of State, and must comply with any directions given as to publicising their proposals and receiving representations. DoE Circular 6/90 Annex E requires authorities to publicise proposals in local newspapers, and also to post site notices indicating their intentions. The publicity must identify the area and name a place where a map defining it may be inspected, and the place to which representations should be sent. Similar information must be posted to each address in the area along with a summary of the section 89 report. Any representations received must be considered before declaration takes place. Authorities must also be satisfied that the living conditions in the area, which must consist *primarily* of 'housing accommodation', are unsatisfactory and that this problem can be most effectively dealt with by declaring an RA. Housing accommodation, see section 100, means dwellings (buildings occupied or intended to be occupied as separate dwellings), HMOs and hostels.

The report referred to above should, on the basis of DoE Circular 6/90 para 26, be based on use of NRA principles, see earlier notes, and should also draw on a wide range of relevant expertise, eg in planning, valuation, accountancy, environmental health, highway planning and the social services, together with the views of private sector agencies.

Certain conditions also have to be met before a RA can be declared, see section 90 of the 1989 Act. The actual conditions are laid down in DoE Circular 6/90, Annex E, part 3. Thus an RA *must* have at least 300 dwellings in it, though as a guideline the normal minimum should be 500 dwellings: a maximum guideline size would be 3,000 dwellings. 75% of the dwellings in the area must be privately owned; RAs are not designed to deal with the needs of run down public sector estates, these are the subject of other programmes.

The most important of these were the Priority Estates Project (PEP) and Estate Action (EA). The PEP was set up in March 1979 by the DoE as a response to the problem of so called 'difficult to let' estates. The idea was to develop locally based housing management with much more direct involvement of residents. Initially three pilot projects at Hackney, Bolton and Lambeth were set up but the initiative quickly spread across the country. Critics of PEP pointed out that the focus on management limited the scope of the benefits at a time when council housing was subject to many other pressures and the financial framework of PEPs has never been very secure. EA was launched in June 1985 when 69 authorities were targetted for support and a special unit, the Urban Housing Renewal Unit (UHRU) was set up in the

DoE to co-ordinate the programme. The nature of the funding of EA projects involved the 'top-slicing' of existing housing budgets and there was much criticism of this and the fact that few new resources were being made available. This led many authorities and commentators to believe that EA was in effect priming estates for sales and privatisation. However, by 1992 340 EA schemes were in progress and 120 new projects started during that year involving the expenditure of £320 million drawn from the authorities' Housing Investment Programmes. EA projects are diverse in nature and include not only refurbishment and renovation work but include environmental improvement, anti-condensation work, heating installation, insulation and security measures.

Thus action on run down authority estates is possible, but this takes place largely within an administrative structure. Elsewhere it is the law which lays down the parameters within which action takes place, as the following paragraphs make clear with regard to RAs.

The physical condition of dwellings in a RA must be such that 75% are 'unfit' or would qualify for works under sections 112, 113 or 115 of the 1989 Act (see further below), and the financial circumstances of those living in the area must be such that at least 30% of them appear dependent to a significant extent upon certain state benefits, eg housing benefit, income support, etc.

If the above conditions are met an authority may proceed to declare a RA, and section 91 requires them to publicise this fact, and take steps to inform those who reside, or who own property, in the area, particularly as to the name and address of the person to whom inquiries and representations concerning action to be taken should be addressed. Information and advice should also be provided for those wishing to carry out works on housing accommodation. Certain specified information also has to be sent to the Secretary of State, see DoE Circular 6/90, Annex E, para 4. The duty to publish information on action taken or to be taken, and assistance available in respect of carrying out works in a RA is a continuing one once the area is declared, see section 92, and once again the Secretary of State may issue directions as to fulfilling this duty, see DoE Circular 6/90 Annex, para 5.

Under section 93 of the 1989 Act extensive powers are conferred on authorities to implement RA strategy. They may, under section 93(2), acquire land by agreement or compulsorily, and provide housing thereon. Such activity must serve one or more of the following objectives, ie the improvement or repair of relevant premises, the proper and effective management of housing accommodation, or the well being of residents. Land may also be similarly acquired for the purposes of effecting or assisting the improvement of the amenities of the area, section 93(4). Authorities may carry out works on land they own and may assist in respect of works on other land by making grants, loans and providing guarantees and materials, etc. However, assistance may not be given where grant assistance under Part VIII of the 1989 Act is otherwise being given (see further below, and section 93(5)).

The compulsory purchase procedure to be used is that under Part XVIII of the 1985 Act and the Acquisition of Land Act 1981 (see above), but the wording of the statute and guidance given in DoE Circular 6/90, Annex D, indicate compulsory acquisition is to be used to secure improvements only where this cannot otherwise be achieved, and where necessary to achieve the objects of the RA. DoE Circular 3/93 reinforces this guidance and indicates that an authority must indicate the relationship of a proposed compulsory acquisition to their overall strategy where they are seeking central approval. Where land is acquired the necessary works on it should be done quickly so as not to undermine public confidence in renewal, and it is the clear implication of law and policy that acquisition powers should be used as a component in partnership exercises between authorities and other bodies such as associations or commercial developers. Indeed section 93(6) provides that authorities may agree with such bodies for them to carry out works within a RA. Further stress is laid on the need to maintain the commitment and impetus of a renewal strategy and to retain the involvement of the private sector by DoE Circular 6/90 paras 50 and 51.

Section 96 of the 1989 Act empowers the Secretary of State to grant subsidies to authorities in respect of RAs, though this is effectively entirely at the discretion of central government. Circular 6/90 Annex E, section 8, details the expenditure towards which contributions will be paid, these *include* street works, traffic management schemes, landscaping, improving the exteriors of buildings, converting buildings to provide community facilities and other environmental works, but *exclude*, inter alia, works on the interior of houses, works on commercial or industrial premises and works of routine maintenance. The rate of contribution is 50% of costs per annum up to a limit of 'aggregate eligible expenditure' of £1,000 multiplied by the number of dwellings in the area. For the rest of the expenditure within a RA authorities are expected to maximise private sector contributions though clearly some public sector input is needed and this should be determined as a priority in drawing up HIPs, see further DoE 6/90 paras 46 and 47.

Though the general expectation is that RAs will last for ten years, they should be kept under constant review, though re-surveys may be needed no more than once or twice, DoE 6/90 para 53. Section 95 gives power by resolution, however, to exclude land from a RA or bring designation to an end. Before doing this there must be compliance with the Secretary of State's requirements under DoE 6/90 Annex E para 6 which requires local publicity for the proposal, delivery of statements about the proposal to each address in the area, consideration of any representations received, delivery to the Secretary of State of specified information. Thereafter the resolution may be made and its making and effect must be publicised.

Once a RA comes to an end, it is recommended that the authority should retain a presence in the area, for example, to encourage householders to maintain their improved properties.

Group repair

Part VIII of the 1989 Act introduces 'Group Repair Schemes' (GRS). These replace enveloping schemes which could previously be declared in HAAs. 'Enveloping' was developed as a way of bringing about the *external* rehabilitation of groups of properties to prevent their deterioration, and the use of standardised works reduced repair costs by achieving economies of scale. A GRS may be utilised within a RA, but an authority can utilise their powers wherever a block or terrace needs attention on an area basis.

Section 127 of the 1989 Act permits authorities, with the approval of the Secretary of State, to enter into agreements to secure the carrying out of external works to 'qualifying buildings' to ensure their exteriors are put into reasonable repair. Persons who have 'owner's interests' (ie the freehold or certain leaseholds, see section 104(2)) in a dwelling or other premises in a building subject to a GRS may be 'assisted participants' provided certain conditions are fulfilled. These conditions are that: (i) the person is able to give possession of any part of the building to which works are to be carried out, *and* (ii), save in the case of a charity, the person must give a 'certificate of future occupation' (ie that the person intends to live in the property or to let it, see further on section 106 of the 1989 Act below), *and* (iii), save in the case of a charity, where the 'owner's interest' is in a HMO, the person must give a certificate that the building will be subject to residential licenses. Certain legal 'persons' are excluded from participating in a GRS as 'assisted' persons but they may take part as 'unassisted' participants. These bodies include local housing authorities, HATs and registered housing associations. Outside a RA one third of participating households must be significantly dependent on state benefits, see DoE Circular 7/93 para 42, and Annex C para 4.

The Secretary of State has given block approval to certain types of GRS, ie where all the properties were originally constructed as houses; at least one third of the relevant households are dependent to a significant extent on state benefits, eg housing benefit; the average total cost per house is less than £13,000 (£16,000 in London); fees are less than 15% of the total cost of the scheme; the net present value of the relevant properties as calculated according to a prescribed formula is lower than that for renovating the properties individually or demolishing and replacing them, DoE Circular 7/93 Annex C, and see also Annex D. Where a proposed GRS does not meet these criteria it must be submitted for central approval according to its merits, see DoE 12/90 para 160.

Every GRS, under section 128, must relate to at least one 'qualifying building', known as 'the primary building', which was constructed to comprise not less than four separate houses. For this purpose a terrace of houses is generally to be treated as one building, and a 'house' means a dwelling which is not a flat and does *not* include a house *constructed* as a HMO. This primary building must not be in reasonable repair and that condition must affect at least 75% of the houses contained in the building. Once a 'primary building' exists other 'qualifying buildings' may be added to it provided they are contiguous with or adjacent to the primary building and each was constructed so as to include at least *one* house, and provided their exteriors are not in reasonable repair *and* carrying out works to the additional building(s) and the primary building at the same time is the most effective way of dealing with them. It is specifically provided that unless a building's exterior is substantially free of rising or penetrating damp it may not be regarded as in reasonable repair. Otherwise authorities should take note of the exterior of the dwellings, and the standard of repair throughout the whole block and generally in the area. 'Exterior' in this context means any part exposed to the elements, especially roofs, chimneys, walls, exterior pipework etc, see section 128(6) of the 1989 Act. Authorities are, however, warned in general against expending money on buildings which are structurally unsound save where this is necessary to secure the success of other work, see DoE 12/90 para 145.

A GRS should be designed to secure the reasonable repair of a group of properties which are primarily residential, though some commercial or other buildings may be included, eg shops, offices and garages, but parts of buildings containing *two or more purpose built* flats are excluded. Houses *converted* into flats or HMOs or corner shops may be included, see section 128(4)(b). The life expectancy of the properties after repair should normally be 30 years, and public investment in external refurbishment should be designed to lead to private investment in individual dwellings and in their wider locale. Such a scheme is therefore appropriate for an area whose inhabitants have lower income levels that have inhibited their investment in their homes in the past. Properties should also not normally have received significant amounts of grant aid, and the Secretary of State is unwilling to subsidise any scheme previously included in an enveloping scheme. Moreover, authorities should carefully appraise a proposed scheme to ensure that it is the most appropriate solution to the housing problem in question and offers good value for money, DoE 12/ 90, paras 148 and 149, and see further economic appraisal analyses in annexes B and H. Authorities should also consider any other proposals for the properties and their likely impacts, their overall condition, layout and density, the need for such properties, likelihood of improvement without a GRS, potential alternative site uses, life expectancies of properties following repair, views of owners and occupants and their social and demographic characteristics, visual impact of the group upon the street scene.

No GRS may proceed until all participants have signified their agreement to go ahead – and this *should* be in writing. There is, therefore, a need to involve them during scheme preparation. Only when they consent may implementation of the scheme begin, and then they become liable to pay their apportioned contributions due in respect of their properties, see section 129(1). 'Unassisted participants' are liable to meet 100% of their costs. Assisted participants outside RAs are liable to pay 50% of the cost of works, while those inside RAs are liable to meet 25% of costs, see section 129(4). But where an assisted participant has an owner's interest in a house, including a HMO, or flat they *may*, under section 129(6) be eligible for a reduction in contributions, maybe a 100% reduction. In exercising this discretion authorities are to apply the resources test provided for by sections 109 and 110 (see further below page 347-8). Because of the liability to meet costs, authorities must calculate the costs of a GRS with great care and agree them with participants before works are commenced, for the figures are the basis of their consent. Costs should in general be apportioned to each house according to the value of work to be done there. Once costs have been agreed authorities are liable to meet any additional expenses. Section 129(7) forbids any work to be done on a building in respect of which no eligible participant has given consent, but there are exceptions where no one with an appropriate interest can be traced, *or* where works have to be carried out to the property in order to complete satisfactorily works required on the remainder of the building, *and* the owner has indicated agreement to those works on his property, see section 129(8).

Once the decision to proceed is taken the authority sets up the necessary arrangements for all concerned and lets and manages the contract. Once works are completed section 130(1) requires that each assisted participant is sent a certificate stating the date of the completion of works. Section 130(2) further requires authorities to 'claw back' part of the costs should such a participant dispose of the property within three years of the certified completion of the scheme, *save* where the disposal is 'exempt' under section 124 (see further below page 351) *or* where the disposal is made for no consideration, or for a consideration *less* than an amount specified in regulations made under section 130(6) of the 1989 Act. The amount of the 'claw back' is the 'outstanding balance', ie the difference between the notified cost of works and the contribution made, though authorities may reduce the sum reclaimed by up to two thirds on taking into account the circumstances of the disposal, see section 130(2) and (3) and DoE 12/90 para 162.

Grant aid

In this portion of the chapter statutory references are to the Local Government and Housing Act 1989 unless otherwise indicated.

In one form or another grant aid to repair and improve private sector housing has been available for almost 50 years. The current system of grants was introduced in 1969 but was transformed radically under the Housing and Local Government Act 1989, since when grant aided work has declined so that by 1993 it was, in real terms, less than 30% of its 1983 level in England and 75% of that level in Wales. This has come about because of reductions in authorities' capital budgets so they have less to spend on renovation, reduced treasury subsidies under section 132 for grants, ceilings placed on maximum grants, reducing the categories of grants that are mandatory and means testing grant aid strictly so that only the poorest are grant aided. These reductions must be set against the persisting continuance of houses in poor condition: 1.5 million dwellings (7.6% of the stock) in England in 1991 were unfit, and up to 15% of dwellings in England (16% in Wales) lack some basic amenities. Likewise the condition of the housing stock has hardly improved over the last five years: it is certainly ageing more rapidly as fewer new houses are built and the rate of demolition declines. It has thus been calculated that: 'At the current rate of renovation not including future deterioration, it will take two generations to bring all private housing up to standard. Further cuts in public funding will lengthen that time'. *(Making a Difference: Rescuing Renovation Grants*, National Housing and Town Planning Council, 1993, p 5).

The official view, as declared in DoE Circular 12/90 is that the grant system is now an integrated part of a 'package of measures ... designed to encourage the development of renewal strategies which incorporate a more balanced mix of clearance and renovation'. The scheme of grants is that in some cases aid is mandatory because of the nature of the work required, while outside the 'core' of mandatory grants discretionary aid may be given to applicants *or* in respect of work over and above that to be funded by a mandatory grant. Thus applications for renovation grants trigger a duty on authorities to consider whether relevant dwellings are 'fit', and, if not, whether renovation is the most satisfactory course of action using those criteria established by the Secretary of State already considered above. A further feature of the 1989 system is that where relevant works are grant aided the dwelling *must* achieve the revised standard of fitness, though authorities have discretion in respect of works that go beyond achieving that standard, and they may consider both local circumstances and the needs of individuals when determining levels of grant aid, and also the expected life of a property. DoE Circular 8/94, which points to the need to concentrate scarce resources on the cases of greatest need, however, urges authorities to remember the fitness standard is *not* an optimum standard, and work required should only be that which is appropriate on a case by case basis.

The grants

Section 101 lists the various grants: renovation grants (RG) are payable in respect of the improvement or repair of a dwelling, or where a dwelling is being provided by the conversion of a house *or* other building; common parts grants (CPG) are payable in respect of the improvement *or* repair of the common parts of a building (which includes, under section 138, the structure and exterior of a building and common facilities provided for persons who include the occupiers of one or more flats in the building); a disabled facilities grant (DFG) is payable to provide facilities for a disabled person in a dwelling or in the common parts of a building containing flats, and a HMO grant (HMOG) is payable for the improvement or repair of a house in multiple occupation, or the provision of a HMO by conversion. Certain bodies may not receive grant aid, see section 101(3), in particular a local authority, and a housing action trust, otherwise the system of applying for grants and the preconditions for aid are as follows.

Applications for, and restrictions on, grants and who may apply

Applications for aid must, under section 102, be made to the local housing authority in writing *and* in prescribed form (see SI 1994/565) stating the works in respect of which a grant is sought ('relevant works') and accompanied by two contractors' estimates of the cost. An application may not be entertained (save for a DFG) unless the property was built or converted not less than ten years previously (the age restriction) see section 103. Nor, under section 104(1)(a) (personal restrictions), may an application be, in general, entertained (save for a CPG) unless the authority is satisfied that the applicant has, or proposes to acquire, an 'owner's interest' (ie the fee simple or a term of years with at least five years unexpired) in the relevant land. This is known as an 'Owner's Application'. Section 104(4) empowers the Secretary of State to relax this requirement within limits to enable applications to be entertained in respect of works *part of which* take place outside the curtilage of the relevant building, see Housing Renovation etc Grants (Owner's Interest) Directions 1994, DoE Circular 8/94 Annex 1 which relates to works needed to provide utility services for the applicant's dwelling or to facilitate access for a disabled person.

However, tenants may apply for RG or DFG, provided they are not acquiring an 'owner's interest' in the dwelling, and also provided that, in the case of a RG, the work is improvement or repair only. Furthermore a 'Tenant's Application' (other than for a DFG) may not be entertained unless the tenant is under a tenancy obligation to carry out relevant works, or the tenancy is of a description specified by order of the Secretary of State.

The nature of these conditions was examined in *R v Bristol City Council, ex p Naqvi* (1994) Times, 9 May, a decision which indicates decisions on grant aid are open to judicial review.

Here the applicant owned premises which comprised a basement, a shop (*which was subject to a closing order*) and a first floor flat. There was planning permission to change the use of the shop to residential use and to combine it with the flat as one dwelling. The application for RG was refused initially on the basis that it could not be entertained for mandatory grant aid under section 103 of the 1989 Act on the basis that the basement, shop and flat were built or converted less than ten years before the application. There was an internal appeal and the application was then refused on the basis the works were not *alterations* to the flat, but its *replacement* with a house.

Harrison J pointed out that it is necessary to determine the true nature of an application for a grant under section 101(1) for RG. It must be asked whether it is for the improvement or repair of a dwelling *or* for the provision of a dwelling by conversion of a house or *other building.* The restriction in section 103 applies, in the latter case, to the age of the building. In the present instance the RG application was for conversion of a building over ten years old into a house.

The next issue was whether the application for RG was bad in that it was 'hybrid' relating to both improvement and conversion works which could attract both mandatory and discretionary aid. Again Harrison J pointed out the need to determine the true nature of the application. Where the application is for a *conversion*, approval is a matter of discretion under section 115, see below. Where it is for *improvement or repair*, then approval is mandatory for works required to make a dwelling fit, see section 112 below, while additional works *may* be considered for aid under section 112(4). In the instant case the application was for a conversion, and so the matter was one of discretion.

Further preliminary conditions under section 105 apply to CPG. An application for such a grant may not be entertained until the authority are satisfied that at the application date at least a 'required proportion' (75%) of flats in the building concerned are occupied by 'occupying tenants', ie those who occupy the flats as their only or main residences and who have unexpired terms of five years, or whose tenancies fall within section 1 of the Landlord and Tenant Act 1954, or whose tenancy is assured/protected/secure/statutory, or a protected occupancy and that the application is either a landlord's application or a tenant's application. The former is one from a person who has an 'owner's interest' (see above), while the latter is one made by at least 75% of 'occupying tenants' who have a duty to carry out or make a contribution towards the relevant works. (Joint tenants for these purposes count as one person, while to be an occupying tenant for the purpose of a tenant's application, a person has to be a member of a class specified for that purpose by the Secretary of State.)

Applications for RG or DFG may not under section 106 be entertained unless accompanied by a certificate of future occupation. This may be an 'owner occupation certificate' stating the applicant has or proposes to acquire an owner's interest in the building, and that he/she or a member of his/her family intends to live in the dwelling or a flat in the building, as their only or main residence for a period of not less than 12 months running from the 'certified date' (ie the date under section 138 certified by the authority as the date of satisfactory completion of eligible works). Or the applicant may submit a 'tenant's certificate' certifying that he/she is tenant required to do the works by the terms of the tenancy, or that he/she is a tenant of a description specified by the Secretary of State, or that the application is for DFG, and that he/she or a member of his/her family intends to live in the dwelling as their only or main residence. A tenant's application may not be entertained unless accompanied by a certificate of intended letting (see below) from the landlord, save where the authority consider it unreasonable to seek such a certificate. Or an applicant may submit a 'certificate of intended letting' where it is certified the applicant has or proposes to obtain an owner's interest and intends to let the dwelling, or flats in the building, to persons other than family members and for a period of not less than five years from the certified date on a tenancy which is not a long tenancy (ie 21 years or more). An application may be accompanied by a 'special certificate' where the applicant has or proposes to acquire an owner's interest and is a person of a prescribed class.

In the case of an application for a HMOG, under section 106(7) the application may not be entertained unless accompanied by a certificate that the applicant has or proposes to acquire an owner's interest and intends to license the residential use of part of it by persons other than family members for a period of five years, or to let part of it as a residence.

An application for a CPG must be accompanied by a certificate signed by the applicant, or applicants, which states the interest of the applicant(s) in the building, and also certifies that the required proportion under section 105 (supra) of flats in the building is occupied by 'occupying tenants'.

These various certificates only state the applicant's *intention* at the time of the application. Where, however, a fraudulent application is made the matter could be criminally investigated or made the subject of an action for deceit.

The scheme of the restrictions is to produce the following consequences:
1) some applications are excluded from aid because they cannot be entertained;
2) some which can be entertained are subject to restrictions on approval;
3) owner occupiers are in general eligible for grant aid, the aid will be either mandatory or discretionary according to the works required (see further below);
4) landlords in the private sector normally receive grants only at the discretion of an authority, but a mandatory grant will be payable towards costs of bringing dwellings up to the standard of fitness where works are also required by virtue of a statutory notice;
5) tenants subject to repairing obligations may apply for RG;
6) any tenant may apply for DFG;
7) a non local authority landlord who applies on behalf of a disabled tenant for DFG may receive either a mandatory or discretionary grant;
8) both landlords and tenants can apply for CPG;
9) only landlords may apply for HMOG;
10) both RG and DFG can be applied for, where appropriate, in respect of a dwelling.

What may a grant cover?

Certain works and dwellings are excluded from grant aid by section 107. Unless a grant is mandatory under section 112 (duty to approve applications to render a dwelling fit) *and* completion of works is necessary to comply with a notice under section 189 of the 1985 Act (repair notice) *or* a grant is mandatory under section 113 (applications arising from certain statutory notices), a grant may *not* be *approved* where:

(a)   in the case of a dwelling which is not fit the authority consider that carrying out 'relevant works' will be insufficient to make it fit;

(b)   'relevant works' have been completed before the date of service of notice of refusal under section 116(1), see below;

(c)   the authority intend to make a closing or demolition notice within three months of service of notice of refusal;

(d)   the authority intend to declare a clearance area to include the dwelling within 12 months of service of notice of refusal;

(e)   the dwelling falls within the ambit of the defective buildings provisions, Part XVI of the 1985 Act (see below);

(f)   where the application is for a CPG and the authority consider the works insufficient to meet the requirements of section 604(2)(a) to (e) of the 1985 Act (see above).

Section 107(2) provides that where there is an approved GRS, an application for a grant may not be approved save in so far as it relates to work to be carried out under the aegis of the scheme, similarly certain works are excluded from grant aid by directions made under section 107(4). Likewise excluded from the possibility of *approval* are applications for HMOG relating to works concerned with means of escape from fire or other fire precautions, which are required under or by virtue of *any* Act, *unless* the application falls within section 113, ie following certain statutory notices, see section 107(5).

Section 126 provides that no application for RG may be made in respect of more than one dwelling, save where it is made to help towards the cost of works needed to provide two or more dwellings by conversion of a house or other building.

Section 108 provides that, generally, applications may not be approved if 'relevant works' have begun before approval is given, save where:

(a)   the application is required to be approved under section 112 if completion of works is necessary to comply with a repair notice under section 189 of the 1985 Act, or

(b)   the application falls within section 113, or

(c)   the relevant works have not been completed and the authority conclude that there were good reasons for the premature start.

The amount of grant aid

Once an application is received, a process of means testing begins, but this takes different forms according to whether the applicant is an owner occupier, a landlord or a tenant.

Where an application is made with an owner occupier's certificate, a tenant's certificate or a 'special certificate' (see above) and the applicant's resources exceed the 'applicable amount', (see below) the amount of any grant paid must be reduced in accordance with regulations made by the Treasury, see section 109. The *basic* scheme is that, under Housing Renovation etc Grants (Reduction of Grant) Regulations 1994, SI 1994/648 the financial resources, the needs and outgoings of the applicant (ie the 'applicable amount') where that person is applying for RG or DFG, are determined. Where financial resources exceed the applicable amount grant aid is reduced by amounts prescribed in regulations, the notion being to reduce aid by a sum equal to an 'affordable loan' (ie that which could be financed if taken from a bank or building society) thus taking into account the excess of financial resources over the 'applicable amount'. Similar provisions apply to tenant's applications for CPG under section 111 and to determining individual participant's contributions under a GRS scheme (see above). The detail of the scheme is beyond the scope of this work, and interested readers are referred to DoE Circulars 12/90 and 8/94. However, the system works in a similar way to that governing housing benefits and other income support benefits. Thus there is a basic personal allowance and 'additional premiums' to take account of circumstances such as age, family status, disabilities, etc. One major difference from housing benefit is that not only the resources of the applicant are taken into account, but also those of other 'relevant persons' associated with the applicant, eg a person who is not the applicant but is entitled to make the application and who lives or intends to live in the dwelling.

Where a landlord makes an application, ie where there is a certificate of intended letting or where there is application for a HMOG or CPG from a landlord, the general rule under section 110 is that the *amount* of any grant is at the discretion of the authority, subject to any limit fixed by the Secretary of State under section 116(5). In exercising their discretion the authority must consider the cost of relevant works, the amount of any rent payable or which might be reasonably obtained and any likely increases therein, and any other matters directed by the Secretary of State (see DoE Circular 7/93 Annex B, and paras 33-39, and Circular 5/91 paras 18-21) and in discharging this function the authority may seek and act on the advice of rent officers.

Approval, notification and payment of grants

Where an application for RG is received (*other* than one in respect of the provision of one or more dwellings by conversion – in which case the matter is one for a discretionary decision under section 115, see section 112(1) and *R v Bristol City Council, ex p Naqvi* (supra)) the first task of the authority is to determine whether the dwelling is 'fit'. Mandatory approval is required where the authority determine the dwelling is not fit, *but* they consider the relevant works will make the dwelling fit *and* they are satisfied completion of the works is the most satisfactory course of action taking into account central advice issued under section 604A of the 1985 Act. However, this particular duty to approve does n*ot* apply where an application is accompanied by a certificate of intended letting and is not a tenant's application, or where the dwelling in question is intended for inclusion in a GRS within 12 months. A further mandatory obligation to approve exists where an owner occupier's application is made and the works are necessary to comply with a repair notice under section 190 of the 1985 Act (see above) section 113(2). Where an authority has discretion to refuse a grant, and also allows internal appeals against refusals, the appellate body is not required to give reasons for its decision, *R v Bristol City Council, ex p Bailey* (1994) Times, 23 November.

Landlords' applications are thus generally not subject to mandatory approval, but such approval must, under section 113(1), be given where completion of relevant works is necessary to comply with a notice under sections 189 or 190 of the 1985 Act (ie repair notices, see above) or section 352 of that Act (ie works needed in a house in multiple occupation to render it fit for the number of its occupants, see Chapter Eight).

Where an application for DFG is made it cannot, under section 114, be approved unless the authority is satisfied the relevant works are necessary and appropriate to the needs of a disabled occupant, *and* it is reasonable and practicable to carry the works out having regard to the age and condition of the dwelling, taking into account the views of the local social services authority. Similarly a DFG application may not be approved in respect of works to the common parts of a flat block unless the applicant has a power or duty to the works. However, subject to other general restrictions, DFG applications must be approved where the purpose is: to facilitate access by disabled occupants to dwellings or within dwellings to principal family rooms or a bedroom or a bathroom; to provide a bedroom or bathroom for a disabled occupant; to facilitate preparation and cooking of food by a disabled occupant; to improve a heating system to meet a disabled occupant's needs, or to facilitate use of a source of power, light or heat by such a person; or to facilitate access and movement by a disabled person who is also a 'carer' for another resident. Discretionary approval *may* be given to applications for DFG falling outside the above classes and directed towards *making* a dwelling suitable for the accommodation or welfare of the disabled occupant.

Any application falling outside the mandatory classes *may* be approved under section 115. Thus where relevant works go beyond, or are other than, those which are needed to make a dwelling fit, they may be treated as 'additional' and may be approved where the authority consider they are needed:

to put the dwelling in reasonable repair taking into account its age, character and locality; to provide the dwelling(s) by way of conversion; to provide adequate thermal insulation; to provide adequate space heating facilities or satisfactory internal arrangements; to ensure compliance with the Secretary of State's requirements as to construction, physical condition, services and amenities.

Particular rules apply to applications for CPG. Here approval may be given where the authority consider a grant is needed for any of the purposes specified in the previous paragraph, *save* that of actually providing dwellings by conversion, *and* that the works will enable the building to meet the requirements of section 604(2)(a)-(c) of the 1985 Act, see above.

In considering whether to exercise their discretion an authority must have regard under section 115(5) to the expected life of the building in question.

It is generally possible for an authority to approve a landlord's application under section 115(6) where works are to be done to render a dwelling 'fit', or, where the application is for HMOG, where the purpose is to make the house meet the requirements of section 352(1A) of the 1985 Act, see Chapter Eight, provided in both cases the authority are satisfied the relevant works are necessary.

Authorities have, in relation to discretionary approval, powers under section 115(7) to vary, with the applicant's consent, grant applications so that relevant works are limited to, or include, those works the authority considers necessary for the purpose in hand.

Section 116 of the 1989 Act provides that decisions on applications shall be notified in writing, within a reasonable time, not being more than six months from the date of application.

Where a grant is approved the authority must, under section 116(2), determine which of the relevant works are 'eligible works', ie they qualify for assistance. They must then fix the 'estimated expenses', ie the amount of expenses properly to be incurred in executing those works, the amount of costs which have been or will be properly incurred with regard to preliminary or ancilliary service and charges ie services, etc, which related to an application and preparation for and carrying out of works, as specified by the Secretary of State under section 102(3) and the amount of grant they have decided to pay, subject to any maximum fixed centrally under section 116(5). (For the formula to fix this maximum see SI 1993/2711, and see below.) The various issues must be specified in the notification. Grants may be recalculated under section 116(4) where the determination of figures proves incorrect due to circumstances beyond the applicant's control, eg because additional unforeseen works have to be done.

The maximum amount of *mandatory* grant aid *awardable* under SI 1993/2711 is £20,000, and the amount thus *payable* is the cost of the works necessary, eg to make a dwelling fit, to comply with statutory notices, or to meet the needs of a disabled person *plus* any agreed, preliminary or ancillary costs *or* £20,000 *whichever is the less*. Where unforeseen costs occur they may only be aided, where they are needed to make a dwelling 'fit', up to the limit of £20,000, see further DoE Circular 8/94 para 11. It appears, however, that the cost of works needed to meet the minimum standard of fitness averages out, at 1991 levels, at £3,300, while the average level of DFG is some £4,000. Where RG *and* DFG are both applied for, each has a separate £20,000 limit.

An approved grant may, under section 177, be paid whole after completion of works or in instalments as they progress, but payment is conditional on the works being done to the authority's satisfaction, and provision to them of acceptable invoices and receipts etc.

Conditions may not *generally* be imposed on grants save with central consent under section 116(3)(a). Section 118, however, enables authorities to require that eligible works are carried out in accordance with their specification, and it is a further condition of *all* grants that the works are carried out within 12 months of the approval of the application, though this period may be extended, particularly where unforeseen circumstances have made necessary the doing of other works. Section 134 reinforces this provision by stating that where eligible works are not satisfactorily completed in due time, *or* where the authority ascertain the aggregate cost of the necessary works is likely to be lower than the estimated expense, *or* where they ascertain that, without their knowledge, eligible works were started before the application was approved and the case did not fall within the mandatory requirements of sections 112 and 113 (duties to approve certain applications to make dwellings fit or to comply with statutory notices), the authority may refuse to pay the grant or any outstanding instalment, or may reduce the grant, and may demand repayment of the grant in whole or part.

Particular grant conditions

Where an application for RG or DFG (other than one in respect of works to common parts of a flat block) has been approved, *and* there was a certificate of intended letting with the application, under section 119(2) it is a condition that the dwelling be let or available for letting, on a tenancy other than a holiday or 'long' tenancy to a person unconnected with the dwelling's owner, *or* that the dwelling will be occupied or available for occupation by an agricultural worker under a contract of service and not as a tenancy. This restriction applies for 'the initial period', ie a period of five years, under section 138, from the date the works were satisfactorily completed. A person is 'connected' with the owner if he/she is a member of the owner's family, or, where personal representatives or trustees are the owner, he/she is a person beneficially entitled to an interest in the dwelling under a will or an intestacy. Supplementary conditions under section 119(4) enable the authority to obtain proof from the owner that the above restrictions are being complied with.

The conditions under section 119(2) and (4) are local land charges, and are furthermore binding on those who acquire title under the original owner. Breach of these conditions entitles the authority to demand repayment of the grant.

Section 120 supplements the foregoing in a case where a RG (other than on a tenant's application) has been approved and the application was accompanied by a certificate of intended letting. It is a condition here that where a 'relevant disposal' with vacant possession is made within the 'initial period', on the authority's demand for repayment of the grant it must be made. Where a disposal takes place with vacant possession the grant may be demanded back subject to an abatement of one fifth for each complete year passed since the works were completed. Again such a condition is a local land charge and is binding on anyone who becomes an owner of the dwelling. A 'relevant disposal' for this purpose, is under section 124, a conveyance of the freehold or assignment of a lease, or the grant of a lease for a term of more than 21 years other than at a rack rent. However, certain 'exempt disposals' are free from the repayment conditions, and these are, inter alia, disposals of a whole dwelling *to* a 'qualifying person' (ie the person or one of them by whom the disposal is made, or the spouse or former spouse of such a person, or a member of that person's family, or, in the case of a company, it is an associated company of that by which disposal was made); *or* vesting of the whole building under a will or intestacy; *or* disposal under the matrimonial jurisdiction (see Chapter Five supra).

Where, under section 121, an application for RG, accompanied by a certificate of owner-ocupation, has been approved, and a 'relevant disposal' other than an 'exempt disposal' is made within a period of *three* years from completion of the works, on the authority's demand for repayment of the grant it must be made, though an abatement of one third must be made for each complete year passed since the works were finished. Authorities have under section 121(7) a discretion to relax the repayment requirements in the case of an elderly or infirm owner who is selling his/her only or main residence with a view to moving into sheltered housing or residential care.

Where a HMOG has been approved it is a condition, under section 122, that throughout the 'initial period' the house will be available for multiple occupation by persons unconnected with the owner. Furthermore the authority may require the owner to furnish them with a statement that this condition is being complied with. Where this condition is breached the authority have a discretion to demand repayment. Similarly if a 'relevant disposal' etc of the house is made, on the demand of the authority for repayment it must be made. In the case of an approved landlord's application for a CPG, a relevant disposal leads, under section 123, to liability to repay the grant on demand. As with the other conditions above the condition under section 123 is a local land charge and binds subsequent owners of the property throughout the initial period.

Where a grant condition is in force under sections 119(2) and (4), 120(2), 121(2) or 122(2),(4),(6), or 122(3) the condition may be discharged under section 125 by repayment of the grant.

Minor Works Aid (MWA)

Section 131 provides that authorities may assist, by grant aid or the provision of materials: the provision/improvement of thermal insulation in dwellings; carrying out of repairs to a dwelling in a clearance area; an elderly owner or tenant wishing to carry out works of repair, improvement or adaptation; the carrying out of works to enable an elderly person to be cared for in a dwelling, or for any purpose specified by the Secretary of State. But assistance is limited so that aid given on any one application must not exceed £1,080, nor may aid given over a three year period in respect of any one dwelling exceed £3,240, nor may assistance be given in respect of works included as 'eligible works' in an approved grant application. Assistance may only be given to persons in receipt of certain state benefits, see SI 1993/554 and DoE Circular 7/93 paras 27-28. Note also SI 1992/1837 and SI 1992/1845 which extend MWA to replacement and associated works on lead plumbing, see DoE Circular 7/93 paras 29-32.

Housing standards, renewal strategies and grants: an assessment of the practice

As the NHTPC's report, *Making a Difference: Rescuing Renovation Grants*, points out grant aid is reactive and demand led, and demand now exceeds the available resources which are likely to decline further over the two years from 1993. A declared object of the 1989 changes in the law was to target resources on those living in the worst housing on low incomes. (See also DoE 8/94, para 6.) With further public expenditure reductions even this objective is hardly likely to be met, and there have even been proposals to break the link between unfitness and mandatory grant aid. It is, however, difficult to see how, without grant aid, good housing standards can be maintained in a housing market where most homes are owner occupied, while many owner occupiers are so heavily committed to mortgage repayments that they cannot make adequate provision for maintenance and repair. This is especially so in relation to the 1.2 to 1.5 million homes affected by 'negative equity' ie mortgages higher than their current market value, and, on 1991 figures, those 50% of all outright home owners and 15% of mortgagors with incomes of less than £150 per week.

As we pointed out in the introduction to the chapter, currently mandatory grants consume 90% of grant resources available, and there is little left for, inter alia, discretionary aid or to fund improvements to HMOs, or to convert large old properties into small self-contained dwellings to increase the supply of accommodation, or to pay for minor works assistance. In many districts the statutory requirement that grant applications are dealt with in six months is of little effect and waiting lists for grants are mounting. Yet other authorities are avoiding serving statutory notices lest these lead to applications for mandatory grants. Yet at the same time clearance of poor quality housing has virtually ceased since many authorities no longer have the resources to afford it. The constant reduction since 1989 of central funding for grant aid has forced authorities to concentrate what resources they have there – and even so they cannot afford to promote grant aid policies, while some, it has been alleged, operate on the verges of legality in trying to prevent grants being paid.

Even where a grant is paid it is means tested, and 60% of grants now go to households on income related benefits. But the means test used is based on an applicant's weekly income with the applicant's contribution calculated according to a hypothetical loan, *irrespective* of prior financial commitments and the applicant's *actual* ability to raise a loan.

If grant aid is to make a real contribution to improving the state of the nation's ageing housing stock then the public need to be made more aware of the availability of assistance. That assistance needs to be centrally subsidised, and in real terms that subsidy should be the former 90% it was rather than the 60% of costs it currently is in England under section 132. Public investment in renewal strategies has fallen from £1.5 billion in 1983 to under £0.5 billion in 1992 while 1994-95 saw a further 23% reduction in funding. The result is that in 1992 only 94,928 RGs were awarded. Special allocations need to be made under local authority capital budgets to encourage authorities to spend on renewal schemes while they could be given a discretion to modify the means testing rules in particular circumstances, for example with regard to disabled applicants. Private investment in housing improvement could also be encouraged if central government created a low or no interest loan fund for, and reduced VAT on, housing repairs. Indeed there have been calls for a £21 billion programme of grants to meet urgent repair costs whereby 75% of costs would be met by public funding (see Leather, Mackintosh and Rolfe *Papering Over the Cracks*, National Housing Forum, 1994). This would cover major issues such as rewiring or damp proofing where costs per job are likely to be £1,000 or more.

Defective dwellings: a note

Part XVI of the 1985 Act was designed to deal with the consequences of certain types of defectively constructed public housing having passed into individual private ownership. Assistance for affected owners was made available according to a statutory scheme. This came to an end on 30 November 1994, which was the last day on which most owners of designated dwelling types could apply for assistance, though some few owners may qualify until 7 April 1997. Further details may be found in DoE Circular 3/94.

Remedies under the Environmental Protection Act 1990

So far as housing is concerned the general object of this Act is the protection of public health, the measures being derived from the Public Health Act 1936 which in turn followed on from the 'great' Public Health Act 1875. The law is therefore here not so much designed to lay down housing standards as to protect the health of individuals. The existence of separate housing and public health 'codes' of legislation has undoubtedly caused confusion over the years, though the ability of, for example, a tenant to initiate criminal sanctions against a neglectful landlord under public health law has undoubtedly enabled individuals to bring about improvements in their housing conditons. One thing is clear: compliance by a landlord with standards under housing legislation will not automatically mean there is compliance with public health standards under the 1990 Act, see *Salford City Council v McNally* [1976] AC 379, [1975] 2 All ER 860. Likewise the fact that a tenant is seeking a parallel civil remedy in respect of a housing defect is no reason for refusing a remedy under the 1990 Act, *R v Highbury Corner Magistrates' Court, ex p Edwards* (1994) 26 HLR 682.

It is the duty, under section 79 of the 1990 Act, of district councils and London boroughs to inspect their areas from time to time, and also to investigate complaints from the inhabitants of their areas, in respect of 'statutory nuisances'. These include: premises; accumulations or deposits; animals; noise; any other matter declared by statute to be a statutory nuisance, provided in each case the matter is prejudical to health, ie actually injurious, or likely to cause injury, to health, or a nuisance, see section 79(7). Health seems to mean physical as opposed to mental health, see *Coventry City Council v Cartwright* [1975] 2 All ER 99, [1975] 1 WLR 845. This case arose out of an alleged nuisance caused by dumping of rubbish, the Divisional Court gave some consideration to whether mental health could be within the protection of the law but reached no concluded opinion on this point. It can be argued that a breakdown in mental health can be caused as a result of a person having to live in a sub-standard house. However, judicial opinion seems to disagree, and to hold that conditions that are 'prejudicial to health' are those which are likely to cause physical illness or disease or to result in an infestation by vermin.

If premises are to be shown to be a statutory nuisance their condition *as a whole* must be so serious that in consequence they are a real risk to health or are a nuisance; a mere lack of internal decorative repair is not enough: see

Springett v Harold [1954] 1 All ER 568, [1954] 1 WLR 521. Nor is any matter which merely affects the *comfort* of the occupants, even if it amounts to an act of harrassment. However, it is unnecessary to prove that a dwelling is *both* prejudicial to health, *and* a nuisance. It may be enough for conditions to be 'prejudicial to health' if they are such as to cause a person who is already ill to become worse: see Kelly CB in *Malton Board of Health v Malton Manure Co* (1879) 4 Ex D 302 at 305.

In *Bennett v Preston District Council* (1983) Environmental Health (April) it was held that defective wiring in a dwelling may be prejudicial to health. Similarly in *Southwark London Borough Council v Ince and Williams* (1989) 21 HLR 504 it was held that traffic noise penetrating a dwelling made it prejudicial to health.

Furthermore condensation may amount to a statutory nuisance, even where the structure is unaffected, see *Dover District Council v Farrar* (1980) 2 HLR 32 and *Greater London Council v Tower Hamlets London Borough Council* (1983) 15 HLR 54, especially where it gives rise to extensive growths of mould and dampness, and results from a condition arising from the failure of the responsible person (in this case the landlord) to take remedial or preventative action, such as the installation of ventilation, insulation and heating systems. See further *Birmingham District Council v Kelly* (1985) 17 HLR 572. The cases appear to support the propositions that a landlord may be liable for a statutory nuisance arising from condensation caused by an unsuitable or defective heating system, lack of a reasonable system of heating and ventilation, design and construction defects and disrepair. Once, however, a proper system of heating, insulation and ventilation is provided it is for the tenant to use that system sensibly so as to avoid condensation. It remains a moot point as to whether questions of the expense of running a heating system can be considered in determining whether the system is reasonable and proper.

Premises may also come within the statutory definition if they are 'a nuisance'. Does this mean that any common law nuisance is also *ipso facto* a statutory nuisance? The answer is partly 'yes'. For a person to prove an allegation based on the 'or a nuisance' limb of the definition he/she must show that the act or default complained of is either a public or private nuisance, ie something causing deleterious affectation to a class of Her Majesty's subjects, *or* a substantial interference with land (or the use and enjoyment thereof) arising outside that land and then proceeding to affect it. So much is clear from *National Coal Board v Neath Borough Council* [1976] 2 All ER 478, [1976] 1 WLR 543. However, there is a judicial tradition stretching back to *Malton Board of Health v Malton Manure Co* (1879) 4 Ex D 302, *Great Western Rly Co v Bishop* (1872) LR 7 QB 550, and *Bishop Auckland Local Board v Bishop Auckland Iron and Steel Co* (1882) 10 QBD 138, that situations contemplated as falling within the 'or a nuisance' limb of the definition must have some relation to health.

Thus where it is alleged that premises are 'prejudicial to health' it will not matter that only the occupier is affected by the acts, defaults or state of affairs complained of. Where on the other hand it is alleged that the premises are 'a nuisance' the act or default, etc, *must affect persons other than the occupier of the premises*. Furthermore in this latter situation the person must, it appears, be able to prove that the nuisance is one that in some way affects, or has relevance, to health. It must also be remembered that *R v Newham Justices, ex p Hunt* and *R v Oxted Justices, ex p Franklin* [1976] 1 All ER 839, [1976] 1 WLR 420 established that proceedings brought in respect of a statutory nuisance are criminal in nature and thus the burden of proof on any informant will be correspondingly high. See also *Botross v Hammersmith and Fulham London Borough Council* (1994) Times, 7 November. In *Patel v Mehtab* (1980) 5 HLR 78 the court pointed out that the question whether premises are prejudicial to health will turn upon expert evidence, and that the magistrates must pay due heed to the expert testimonies given by one or both sides, and not advance their own lay assessments of the facts over those of expert witnesses.

The procedure for taking action in respect of a statutory nuisance

Local authorities and private citizens may take action in respect of statutory nuisances: it is convenient to consider authorities first.

Section 80 of the 1990 Act provides that where an authority is satisfied a statutory nuisance exists, *or* is likely to occur or recur, they must serve an abatement notice which will require the nuisance's abatement or prohibit or restrict its occurrence *or recurrence*, and may require the execution of works or taking of steps for such purposes, specifying the time within which compliance is required. See also *Bristol Corpn v Sinnott* [1918] 1 Ch 62. Where works are required they must be specified for notices must be clear and certain, see *R v Fenny Stratford Justices, ex p Watney Mann (Midlands) Ltd* [1976] 2 All ER 888, [1976] 1 WLR 1101 and *R v Wheatley, ex p Cowburn* (1885) 16 QBD 34. This notice is to be served on the person responsible for the nuisance, save in cases of nuisances arising from structural defects, or where the person responsible cannot be found, in which case the owner is to be served. This is apparently so in relation to structural defects even where the tenant is responsible, see *Warner v Lambeth London Borough Council* (1984) 15 HLR 42. Failure to comply with a notice without reasonable excuse is an offence. However, it should be noted that authorities are not statutorily bound to prosecute offences (see further below) even though they may have taken default action themselves under section 81(3), which enables them, under section 81(4) to recover their expenses. Section 81(5) further empowers authorities to commence High Court proceedings where they are of the opinion that statutory nuisance proceedings before the justices would provide an inadequate remedy. An abatement notice must specify works to be done, not merely ends to be achieved, though a builder's specification is unnecessary. It should not require its recipient to engage in a series of attempts to eradicate a problem, *Network Housing Association v Westminster City Council* (1994) Times, 8 November.

A person served with an abatement notice may, under section 80(3) of the 1990 Act, appeal to the justices within a period of 21 days beginning with the date of service of the notice. Schedule 3 to the Act enables regulations to be made concerning such appeals. The Statutory Nuisance (Appeals) Regulations 1990, SI 1990/2276, provide in reg 2 as grounds of appeal that: the abatement notice was not justified; there has been an informality, defect or error in, or in connection with the notice; the authority has unreasonably refused compliance with alternative requirements, or the notice's requirements are otherwise unreasonable in character or extent or unnecessary; a reasonable amount of time has not been specified for compliance; the notice should have been served on some other person or it might lawfully and equitably have been served on someone else, or on someone else in addition to the appellant.

Certain general requirements from decisions on the previous law relating to statutory nuisances would also seem to apply under the 1990 Act. Thus the legislation lays down a procedure which an authority has to follow in the abatement of statutory nuisances, and it would seem from *Cocker v Cardwell* (1869) LR 5 QB 15 that this procedure is mandatory once an authority decide to act. Where an authority are satisfied of the existence of a statutory nuisance the Act says they 'shall serve' an abatement notice on the person responsible requiring the abatement of the nuisance. However, it was said in *Nottingham Corpn v Newton* [1974] 2 All ER 760, [1974] 1 WLR 923, the first case where an authority was successfully prosecuted in respect of unfit property also constituting a statutory nuisance, by Lord Widgery CJ that 'shall' is not mandatory. Where *an authority has a choice of remedies* between the 1985 and 1990 Acts the courts may not order them to use the latter in preference to the former. The Encyclopaedia of Housing Law and Practice, however, argues the 'requirement to serve an abatement notice is mandatory ... the local authority have no discretion'. The point is not therefore entirely clear or decided.

It is a defence to a prosecution under section 79 to show that there was a 'reasonable excuse', see section 79(4). Where, however, a person (which includes a legal person such as an authority) is convicted of an offence, because of the criminal nature of the proceedings, in addition to other penalties, an order may be made under section 35 of the Powers of Criminal Courts Act 1973 for the payment of compensation by the accused, see *Herbert v Lambeth London Borough Council* (1991) 24 HLR 299, and *R v Crown Court at Inner London, ex p Bentham* [1989] 1 WLR 408. However, from statements in *Herbert* it appears inappropriate to use the compensation remedy as a way to award substantial sums of money in respect of personal injuries where a civil action could be brought to deal with such matters. See also *Botross v Hammersmith and Fulham London Borough Council* (1994) Times, 7 December.

Taking action in respect of statutory nuisances by private citizens

The majority of statutory nuisances are dealt with by authorities but an individual wishing to proceed may rely on section 82 of the 1990 Act. This provides that the magistrates may act on a complaint made by a 'person aggrieved', and where they are convinced the alleged nuisance exists, or is likely to recur, they must make an order to require the defendant to abate the nuisance, and execute any necessary works, and/or may prohibit a recurrence of the nuisance. They may also fine the defendant. In addition the magistrates have powers to direct the local authority to take abatement measures in respect of a nuisance where neither the person responsible or the owner/occupier of the premises can be found, and to prohibit the use of premises for human habitation where a nuisance renders them unfit for that purpose, see section 82(1) and (3). As with local authority proceedings it is the person responsible for the nuisance who is generally to be proceeded against, though where the nuisance is of a structural character, or where the 'person responsible' cannot be found, it is the owner of the premises who will be liable. Before complaining to the magistrates, however, the person aggrieved must give the potential defendant written notice of intention to commence proceedings, specifying the matter complained of. In the case of alleged noise nuisances three days' notice must be given, in all other cases not less than 21 days' notice is required, see section 82(6) and (7).

Who is a 'person aggrieved'?

It was held in *R v Epping (Waltham Abbey) Justices, ex p Burlinson* [1948] 1 KB 79, [1947] 2 All ER 537 that a private citizen can proceed against a defaulting local authority under this provision, and in *Salford City Council v McNally* (supra) it was further held that the fact that the nuisance arose as a result of an authority's exercise of Housing Act powers was no defence to an action taken by one of their tenants deleteriously affected in consequence. In order to use the provision an individual must be a 'person aggrieved'. In the present context this includes anyone whose health has actually been injured by the nuisance, or any occupant of the premises or indeed anyone with a legal interest in a house which is permanently affected by the nuisance. In *Gould v Times Square Estates Ltd*, Camberwell Magistrates Court, 1 April 1975, [1975] LAG Bulletin 147, even a squatter in an empty former shop and dwelling accommodation was held able to use this procedure, but the applicability of this provision to trespassers was expressly left undecided in

Coventry City Council v Cartwright (supra). Where, however, a person is a tenant in a block of flats and only some of the flats are in sub-standard order, it is not possible for that person to be 'aggrieved' in relation to the whole block, *Birmingham City Council v McMahon* (1987) 19 HLR 452.

The consequences of action taken

Once the court is satisfied under section 82(2) that a statutory nuisance exists, or though abated is likely to recur on the same premises, they *must* make an order as outlined above, see also *Coventry City Council v Doyle* [1981] 2 All ER 184, [1981] 1 WLR 1325. Similarly, evidence of the existence of a statutory nuisance will normally require the court to issue the necessary summons against the defendant, *R v Highbury Corner Magistrates' Court, ex p Edwards* (1994) 26 HLR 682.

In this context the *Newton* case states clearly that the justices *must* issue a nuisance order if the existence or future recurrence of the nuisance is proved. But they have a very considerable discretion as to the *terms* of the order. When deciding the terms of the order justices should consider all the circumstances of the case including the possible gravity of the danger to the health of the occupants and the imminence of demolition. They may properly require work to be done in phases, allowing for absolutely necessary jobs to be done first, while other tasks can be left till later, perhaps to be rendered unnecessary by demolition, thus saving expense.

A decision illustrates the ambit of the justices' discretion. In *Lambeth London Borough Council v Stubbs* (1980) 78 LGR 650, an authority owned an old house the tenants of which were Mr and Mrs Stubbs. The condition of the house constituted a statutory nuisance, which was admitted by the council before the justices in proceedings commenced by the tenants. The justices refused to adjourn the hearing so that the authority could obtain vacant possession, and instead made a nuisance order requiring the remedying of the most serious defects within 21 days of the vacation of the premises and of the others in 42 days. Shortly thereafter Mr and Mrs Stubbs were rehoused and the house was simply left vacant until it was demolished. The question for the court was whether the action of the council in securing vacant possession was sufficient abatement to comply with the nuisance order. It was held that it was not. Where a house is prejudicial to health simply to move the present occupiers out does not cure the problem, for if other occupiers should move in at a future date their health will then be imperilled. Where justices make a nuisance order requiring the doing of remedial work, that work must be done; moving the sitting tenant is not enough. See also *Coventry City Council v Doyle* (supra), where it was, however, pointed out that different considerations might apply in a case where the premises have been effectively rendered incapable of occupation. Of course where the authority intend to demolish the property within a very short time the court should take that into account when drawing up the order. In such circumstances the authority should ask the justices to exercise their discretion to order that the house shall not be used for human habitation. Such an order will remove the need for great expenditure. Any order made, however, must be clear and certain.

Where on the hearing of proceedings in respect of an alleged nuisance it is shown that the nuisance did exist when the initial complaint was made, then, irrespective of whether it still exists or is likely to recur at the date of the hearing, the court *must* order the defendant to compensate the complainant for expenses incurred in bringing the proceedings. The court may also direct the relevant local authority to perform any requirements of an order to abate a nuisance where the defendant is in default, see section 82(12) and (11).

The relationship between the Housing and Environmental Protection Acts

It cannot be sufficiently stressed that the requirements of the two 'codes' are separate and equal. Remedial action taken under one will not necessarily satisfy the requirements of the other. Of course action taken to eliminate unfitness in a house will nearly always ensure that it will not be prejudicial to health because in general the standards required by the 1985 Act are higher than those under the 1990 Act. This can be illustrated by a simple example: if a house is unfit through dampness caused by the lack of a damp-proof course then the 1985 Act would require the insertion of such a course to make the house fit and free from damp; if the same house is prejudicial to health because of damp, then the 1990 Act will only require it to be made reasonably free from damp on a periodic basis which may be achieved by lining the walls with damp-proof paper.

There are times when the two codes do appear to be in conflict: thus in the *Newton* case the court said local authorities have a discretion as to how best to deal with sub-standard housing; in *R v Kerrier District Council, ex p Guppy's (Bridport) Ltd* (1975) 30 P & CR 194 the unfitness provisions were said to be mandatory, while in the *Salford* case action taken under the Housing Act was said to be no defence to subsequent prosecution under the public health legislation. In fact there is no real conflict between the codes and the cases can be reconciled. The question always to bear in mind in these situations is: w*ho* is seeking to do *what to whom* by *which* procedures? This question can receive different answers in different circumstances as the following instances will show.

The individual sub-standard house in private or housing association ownership

This situation can be illustrated by the facts of the *Kerrier* case. The landlords owned two unfit dwelling-houses, both tenanted. The owners were prepared to make one good house of the two but could not do so without obtaining vacant possession, and had no accommodation for the displaced tenants. The local authority said it had no accommodation either and decided to commence proceedings against the landlords under the Public Health Act 1936 (predecessor of the 1990 Act) to require remedial action on the roofs of the houses. The landlords countered by alleging the houses were statutorily unfit and that the authority were in breach of mandatory duties under the unfitness provisions if they failed to proceed under them. The court accepted the landlords' contention. Thus where a *local authority* commence proceedings under the 1990 Act in respect of any house which is a statutory nuisance, the *owner* of the house may allege that they are in dereliction of duties under the Act of 1985 and may apply for mandamus to compel the performance of relevant duties. Even here it must be remembered that mandamus is a discretionary remedy and so landlords are not guaranteed success if they adopt the counter argument developed in the *Kerrier* case. Where the proceedings are between the *tenant* and the *landlord* the authority's duties have no relevance save insofar as the landlord, having begun separate proceedings against an authority to compel performances of their duties, might argue that the justices should consider the possible outcome of those proceedings when deciding the content of any order issued under section 82 of the 1990 Act.

The sub-standard house in local authority ownership

The unfitness provisions do not apply to a local authority's own houses *within its own area*, save in the cases where another person also has a relevant interest in the property, for an authority cannot serve a housing order on themselves, see *R v Cardiff City Council, ex p Cross* (1982) 6 HLR 1. However, in such circumstances provided the existence of a statutory nuisance can be proved, the 1990 Act can be used and any prior action taken under the 1985 Act will be no defence to the local authority.

This was the situation in the *Salford* case. In 1967 Salford Corporation declared certain areas to be clearance areas, and at the same time made compulsory purchase orders on the houses within the areas. However, the Corporation realising it could not rehouse all the residents quickly, deferred demolition of the houses for a *minimum* period of *seven* years. By 1974 Mrs McNally's house suffered from an accumulation of refuse, dampness, defective sanitary fittings, unsealed drains, rats, defective windows and/or doors, a leaking roof, defective drainage, and defective plaster work. She commenced proceedings in respect of the statutory nuisance comprised by her house and succeeded. The House of Lords held that the resolution to defer demolition was no defence to statutory nuisance proceedings. It must be remembered, however, that where an old sub-standard house is made the subject of a nuisance order the justice's discretion should be so used as to prevent expenditure of unnecessary sums. The best that can be hoped for is a 'make and mend' operation designed to make the house reasonably bearable as a dwelling, though following *Saddleworth UDC v Aggregate and Sand Ltd* (1970) 114 Sol Jo 931, a lack of finance does not seem to be a reasonable excuse for not complying with a nuisance order. Landlords cannot plead poverty in the hope of entirely escaping from the requirements of nuisance orders!

The sub-standard modern council-built house

Evidence is not lacking that bad construction, poor design, unproved building techniques and misguided planning policies have led to the erection of many council houses and flats whose inhabitants frequently have to endure extremely unpleasant living conditions. In some modern council properties there are severe problems of damp and condensation which can lead to ruined furniture and clothes and illness in the occupants.

The decision in *R v Cardiff City Council, ex p Cross* (supra) of course applies to council built as well as council acquired housing. But statutory nuisance proceedings can bring some relief to tenants. In *Birmingham District Council v Kelly* (1985) 17 HLR 572 the proceedings concerned council built dwellings comprising low rise flats. The dwellings had defective windows, and were also extensively affected by mould which was found to be prejudicial to health. The mould was found to be the result of the act, default or sufferance of the local authority because of, inter alia, the poor thermal quality of the flats, the absence of heating provision in the hallways, a gap under the front door of one flat, the poor quality of ventilation in bathrooms and kitchens. In some, but not all cases, mould could be attributable, in part to disrepair, though the court found that there was no breach of any obligation laid on the authority as a landlord qua landlord. But that was not enough to prevent inquiry into whether there was liability for the existence of a statutory nuisance. The court pointed out that three questions arise: is there a statutory nuisance, is it due to the act, default or sufferance of the local authority, and what steps are necessary to abate it? The court concluded that the answer to the first two questions was 'yes': the mould was a consequence of condensation attributable to design defects in the flats. But the court pointed out that magistrates should use discretion as to the terms of a nuisance order, and that statutory nuisance proceedings should not be used as a means of obtaining for tenants benefits which they were aware did not exist when they took their tenancies, and which would over generously favour them in relation to other tenants of the authority. An authority may be required to do works of improvement, but the need for such works must be justified by the evidence and the circumstances. Magistrates should behave reasonably in imposing orders on local authorities, bearing in mind the heavy duties already laid upon them. Even so it appears that use of the statutory nuisance provisions, while enabling individuals to secure improvements of their conditions, can also have the effect of disrupting planned maintenance and improvement programmes devised by authorities as they are forced to switch resources from the programme into reactive responses to individual problem premises whose existence and needs have been made inescapable following actual or threatened statutory nuisance proceedings.

Rehousing displaced residents

Section 39 of the Land Compensation Act 1973, as amended, provides:

'(1) Where a person is displaced from residential accommodation on any land in consequence of

(a) the acquisition of the land by an authority possessing compulsory purchase powers;

(b) the making...or acceptance of a housing order...or undertaking in respect of a house or building on the land;

(c) where the land has been previously acquired by an authority possessing compulsory purchase powers or appropriated by a local authority and is for the time being held by the authority for the purposes for which it was acquired or appropriated, the carrying out of any improvement to a house or building on the land or of redevelopment on the land;...

and suitable alternative accommodation is not otherwise available to that person, then, subject to the provisions of this section, it shall be the duty of the relevant authority to secure that he will be provided with such other accommodation'.

Within the context of action on unfit properties, this means that authorities have an obligation to rehouse persons displaced as a result of the making of demolition, closing or clearance orders or the accepting of undertakings under section 264 of the Housing Act 1985. Some authorities adopt a wider obligation as a matter of administrative practice, and the strictly limited nature of the section 39 obligation should be noted. It does not apply to squatters, nor to persons permitted to reside in a house pending its demolition or improvement. The duty only applies, in general terms, to persons resident in the dwelling on the date when the order, or undertaking, etc, was made or accepted or when notice of its making was published, as the case may be. Moreover, in the case of displacements arising out of the doing of works of improvement, the obligation is only owed to persons who are *permanently* displaced.

The greatest restriction on the obligation is that it confers no right on persons displaced to have priority over other persons on the housing waiting list. In *R v Bristol Corpn, ex p Hendy* [1974] 1 All ER 1047, [1974] 1 WLR 498 the applicant lived in a basement flat where he enjoyed Rent Act security of tenure but which was also statutorily unfit. Mr Hendy had a history of rent arrears with another local authority and Bristol Corporation offered him only temporary accommodation, pending an offer of suitable residential accommodation, on the terms usually offered to prospective municipal tenants. He applied for an order of mandamus to compel the authority to fulfil their rehousing duty, contending this was to provide him with permanent accommodation on terms that gave him a security of tenure equivalent to that which he had enjoyed under his former tenancy. The Court of Appeal refused the order. They concluded that the duty is only to act reasonably and to do the best practicable job in providing a displaced person with other accommodation. See also *R v East Hertfordshire District Council, ex p Smith* (1990) 23 HLR 26, and DoE Circular 73/73.

NB Where a dwelling is closed for human habitation by order of the justices under section 82(3) of the Environmental Protection Act 1990, there is no obligation to rehouse on the local authority under section 39 of the 1973 Act.

Further reading

Bourne, P 'Grants for renovation, improvements and facilities for disabled people' (1995) *Legal Action* (January) 20

Burridge, R, Ormandy, D, Battersby, S *Monitoring the New Housing Fitness Standard* (DoE/HMSO 1993)

Hadden, T B *Compulsory Repair and Improvement* (Centre for Socio Legal Studies, Wolfson College, Oxford, 1978)

Hadden, T B 'Public Health and Housing Legislation' (1976) 27 NILQ 245

Hawke, J N and Taylor, G A 'The Compulsory Repair of Individual Physically Substandard Housing: The Law in Practice' [1984] JSWL 129

Hughes, D 'Public Health Legislation and the Improvement of Housing Conditions' (1976) 27 NILQ 1

Hughes, D 'What is a Nuisance? The Public Health Act Revisited' (1976) 27 NILQ 131

Hughes, D 'Housing and Public Health – A Continuing Saga' (1977) 28 NILQ 233

Hughes, D 'Housing Repairs: A Suitable Case for Reform' [1984] JSWL 137

Leather, P and Mackintosh, S *Papering Over the Cracks* (National Housing Forum), 1994

Luba, J *Repairs: Tenants' Rights* (Legal Action Group, 2nd Edition, 1990)

NHTPC *Making a Difference: Rescuing Renovation Grants* (National Housing & Town Planning Council, 1993)

Reynolds, J I 'Statutory Covenants of Fitness and Repair' (1974) 37 MLR 377

Watkinson, D 'Legal Remedies for Condensation Damp in the Home' Legal Action November 1985, p 153 and April 1986, p 49

Chapter Eight

Multi-occupancy and overcrowding

Introduction

Multi-occupation and overcrowding may occur together to convey an impression that they are always associated evils. In fact the problem of overcrowding is not restricted to multi-occupied dwellings, nor even primarily associated with them. Nor should it be assumed that conditions in all multi-occupied houses are bad.

Multi-occupation and overcrowding arise for totally different reasons in areas of varying housing types. In the past a typically overcrowded house was 'two-up-and-two-down', situated in industrial towns and cities. They were overcrowded either because of the sexual composition of the families occupying them, or because they were simply too small to be able to accommodate large families. The law relating to overcrowding developed to deal with situations of the above kind.

In our day the problem is different. Anyone familiar with British urban geography will be aware that a great unanswered problem of housing policy is the use and management of larger older houses in inner suburban areas. Obviously ripe for conversion into multi-occupation, where that is sympathetically done the result is the provision of much useful accommodation. However, unthinking or unscrupulous owners indulge in unsatisfactory divisions, failing to provide proper cooking and sanitary facilities, and frequently resorting to overcrowding individual units of accommodation to extract the maximum financial return. The result is danger, particularly from a fire safety point of view, and squalor. In properties such as these multi-occupation and overcrowding occur together.

The current problem and the policy response to multiple occupation

The size of the problem

The 1985 Physical and Social Survey of Houses in Multiple Occupation in England and Wales (Thomas & Hedges) published in 1986 concluded there were at least 290,000 Houses in Multiple Occupation (HMOs) in England and Wales, providing accommodation for 2.6 million people. Four fifths of HMOs surveyed were unsatisfactory in relation to management, occupancy or provision of amenities. Half needed repairs costing more than £10,000, and only one quarter were assessed as of a 'good' standard. In most houses occupants had only a single small room each. Damp and condensation were frequently encountered physical problems, while four fifths of HMOs had defective, inadequate or non-existent means of escape from fire, a problem particularly associated with smaller HMOs and those owned by private landlords. The occupants of HMOs tend to be young, single and hard up; they rarely occupy such accommodation out of choice.

The policy response

Following the Thomas & Hedges survey certain changes were made in the law in 1989, but before these are detailed current central policy on HMOs must be examined. The principal documents here are The HMO Management Guide (The Guide) issued by the DoE in 1992, and DoE Circular 12/93.

These point to wide variation in local authority policy with regard to HMOs, and encourage adoption of best practice to harmonise standards throughout the country. The Guide is also both a strategic and a detailed advice document.

Policy: The first steps

Authorities are encouraged to produce formal policy documents on HMOs, providing for *aims* – eg to stimulate a thriving market in acceptable quality accommodation in HMOs, *objectives* – ie steps on the way to achieving *aims* – *targets*, ie administrative action to facilitate achieving aims and objectives, such as serving all requisite notices within present time periods – *performance indicators*, and *provision for review of aims, objectives, etc.* A realistic budget in respect of the foregoing is recommended.

A strategy is needed to meet the requirements of section 605 of the Housing Act 1985 to provide for a regular review of HMOs in an area, and also to ensure that authorities do not proceed in a fragmented and inefficient way in dealing with HMOs. Policy should bring together and harmonise the practices of planners, environmental health and housing officers who otherwise might apply different criteria and policies with regard to HMOs. The policy should also be debated *at corporate level* so that the entire authority is committed to it.

Drawing up the policy

Both The Guide and Circular 12/93 counsel authorities to gather accurate information on numbers, types and conditions of HMOs, which may require specially commissioned research. The local housing market should then be considered to determine what level of demand there is for housing at particular prices and the relative advantages/disadvantages of HMOs as opposed to non-HMO provision. Authorities should also consider information about residents' attitudes to existing HMOs, demographic and environmental issues and the spread and location of HMOs throughout their areas. Policy should address three key issues:
1)   maximising HMO contribution to safe, quality accommodation;
2)   minimising risks from unsafe accommodation;
3)   using planning controls to ensure that HMOs do not have an unacceptable environmental impact.

Central guidance urges authorities not to accord too low a priority to HMO work in the allocation of resources. However, the policy an authority develops should reflect its needs and problems – eg whether it has a real scarcity of accommodation.

Implementing policy

Guidance stresses the need for a multidisciplinary approach to the HMO issue: either the creation of a specific inter departmental team (costly in terms of resources); or setting up project teams of key staff from relevant departments who have regular meetings to inform colleagues of their work. The latter approach is recommended for small authorities with fewer HMO problems.

Both The Guide and Circular point to raising standards as a central element in any authority's HMO strategy, and suggest this can be done via formal enforcement action or, eg, by contractual requirements when an authority itself is a major customer of HMO landlords for Bed and Breakfast accommodation for the homeless. Authorities are encouraged to use whatever means are most conducive to achieving policies, and to link tactics in a concerted attempt to improve conditions.

Where, however, a sanctioning approach is adopted authorities are advised to ensure that what they require is formulated in the light of local housing conditions, bearing in mind the risks and discomforts of occupants relevant to the size and type of property in question, *enforceable, defensible* and *justifiable* in court. Neither should a sanctioning approach be inflexibly applied.

Where a sanctioning approach is adopted authorities should delegate legal authority to officers to ensure that powers are effectively and expeditiously used. Effective communication is needed so that relevant officers receive all necessary information and advice. In any case staff must receive proper written guidance in the form of a manual to ensure standardisation of approach and operational consistency in relation to all HMO powers and duties. Standards should be regularly reviewed and amended where necessary in the light of experience. In connection with prosecutions authorities were particularly counselled by The Guide to consider the implications of prosecution, eg, will it have a deterrent effect, or secure the doing of necessary works; what are the financial implications for the authority of either doing the works themselves or relying on a prosecution? Authorities were also advised to consider how well landlords have been made aware of legal obligations: moral and economic issues play a part in prosecution policy. It is the culpable rather than the deficient landlord who is likely to be prosecuted.

Supervision of multi-occupation by planning control

Under planning law 'development' may not generally be carried out without planning permission from the local planning authority. Can authorities use planning powers to prevent the inception of undesirable multi-occupation developments?

Section 55(1) of the Town and Country Planning Act 1990 defines development as:

> 'the carrying out of building, engineering, mining or other operations in, on, over or under land, or the making of any material change in the use of any buildings or other land'.

Section 55(2)(a) excludes from this definition:

> 'the carrying out for the maintenance, improvement or other alteration of any building of works which (i) affect only the interior of the building or (ii) do not materially affect the external appearance of the building...'

But Section 55(3)(a) goes on to provide:

> 'For the avoidance of doubt it is hereby declared for the purposes of this section – the use as two or more separate dwelling-houses of any building previously used as a single dwelling-house involves a material change in the use of the building and of each part thereof which is so used'.

Unfortunately doubt has not been avoided. It is uncertain whether any change from single residential to multi-occupied use inevitably constitutes an act of development by falling within section 55(3)(a) above, and so requiring planning permission. In *Ealing Corpn v Ryan* [1965] 2 QB 486, [1965] 1 All ER 137 a planning authority alleged unauthorised development had taken place in that the use of a house had changed from being a single dwelling to use as two or more separate dwellings. The house contained several families who all shared a common kitchen, and presumably the lavatory and bathroom also. It was held the house had not been divided into *separate* dwellings. A house may be occupied by two or more persons living separately under one roof, without their occupying 'separate dwellings', provided they are sharing certain common living accommodation, which, following *Goodrich v Paisner* [1957] AC 65, [1956] 2 All ER 176, includes kitchens. Multiple occupation by itself *may* be insufficient to bring section 55(3)(a) of the Town and Country Planning Act 1990 into operation. That is designed to deal with situations where new dwellings can be regarded as truly separate, self-contained and independent; here the existence of physical reconstruction will be a factor of great importance.

But multi-occupation may still constitute development where conversion amounts to a material change of use under section 55(1) of the 1990 Act. In *Birmingham Corpn v Minister of Housing and Local Government and Habib Ullah* [1964] 1 QB 178, [1963] 3 All ER 668 three former singly-occupied houses were let in parts to a number of occupants each paying a weekly rent. The Divisional Court pointed out there had been a change of use. The houses, which had previously been used as single family accommodation, were being used for gain by their owner letting them out as rooms. The material change of use is constituted by alteration from family/residential to commercial/residential use.

It has been argued, following *Duffy v Pilling* (1977) 33 P & CR 85 that where a single person owns or rents a house and lives there with lodgers, generally providing meals for them but sometimes allowing them to provide for themselves, there is no change of use unless there is some physical division between the parts each person occupies. This decision is most unsatisfactory. The better view of the law is that a material change of use occurs as soon as a predominantly single family use alters into a predominantly non-family use. Once the lodgers predominate then a change of use has taken place. In *Lipson v Secretary of State for the Environment* (1976) 33 P & CR 95 a change of use of premises from self-contained flats to individual bed-sitters was found to be a material change of use. The test is to ask a simple question of fact in each case: 'who has control over the property?' If control is in the hands of one person who has a small number of others living with him/her there is no material change of use, but if effective control has been 'parcelled out' amongst individuals, the best evidence of which is physical partitioning of the premises, then multi-occupancy will have arisen and a material change of use. See also *Panayi v Secretary of State for the Environment* [1985] JPL 783, where use of four self-contained flats as a hostel to house homeless families was held to constitute a material change of use.

Central guidance points out that housing and planning policies on HMOs should complement each other. But there can be conflicts between housing and planning functions in an authority – particularly where one department wishes to improve a property which another wishes to eradicate. Use of corporate strategy should help to minimise conflict, while placing policies on HMOs in development plans is another way of ensuring harmonious relationships.

It is questionable how far an authority may go in using planning powers to prevent the spread of undesirable multi-occupation. An outright policy of refusing any application for planning permission to convert premises to multi-occupation would be an illegal fetter on discretion. Nor would it appear generally proper for an authority to take into account the character of the person applying for planning permission. Past housing misdeeds are matters relevant to other areas of law and do not raise planning issues as such. Neither could an authority impose restrictive conditions designed to regulate future behaviour on a grant of permission; the whole thrust of the cases is that planning conditions must always relate fairly to physical development, and not subsequent use by developers of powers of letting and management.

On the basis of ministerial decisions on planning appeals the proper factors to be taken into account by a planning authority in deciding applications to convert houses to multiple use include: density of housing; possibility of overcrowding; amenities of the neighbourhood; any locally prevailing shortage of accommodation; suitability of premises for conversion; architectural considerations and, occasionally, problems that might arise from an increase in numbers of cars that incoming residents might wish to park. All these are proper land use considerations.

The Guide and Circular 12/93 remind authorities that, under section 171B of the Town and Country Planning Act 1990, any unauthorised change of use to multiple occupation acquires immunity from planning enforcement action, and becomes a lawful use of land, once ten years have elapsed from the time the change was made. They also point out that enforcement action does not have to be taken, and where *planning considerations* indicate that no action would be appropriate then an unauthorised change of use may be allowed to continue, though permission may be retrospectively granted and subjected to conditions. Where, however, it is desired to take enforcement action a number of considerations should be borne in mind before it is taken, eg, effects on residents and on any housing action that has been, or may be, taken to improve the state of the property.

One issue worthy of special mention is whether taking housing action may undermine subsequent planning action. The Guide made it clear that safeguarding the occupants of HMOs is the first and most important consideration. Where dangerous housing conditions exist they should not be left unremedied simply because planning enforcement action is pending. Where the situation is not one of danger it should be remembered the Housing and Planning Acts are separate codes. Use of one does not preclude use of the other provided what is required is reasonable, and provided one is not used as a covert way of achieving the objects of the other. In practical terms this means where an unauthorised HMO is discovered and planning enforcement is a possibility, housing action should be limited to requiring what is reasonable in the circumstances, bearing in mind the overriding duty to protect health and safety, and the need to minimise wasteful expenditure.

The supervision of multi-occupation under the Housing Acts

Section 345 of the Housing Act 1985, Part XI is the principal legislation, as amended in 1989.

The definition of multi-occupation

Section 345 of the Housing Act 1985 as amended, provides that multi-occupancy arises when a house 'is occupied by persons who do not form a single household'. 'House' is not defined by the legislation, though it *includes* any part of a building which would not, apart from the requirements of the statutory provision, be regarded as a house, and which was *originally constructed* or *subsequently adapted* for occupation by a single household. Similarly a unit of accommodation which is a flat can be in multiple occupation. DoE Circular 5/90 explains this change was introduced to ensure that Part XI powers could be used in relation to individual flats, such as large flats in mansion blocks, a circumstance not entirely clear before amendment.

A great deal of artful device has been employed by devious landlords trying to ensure their premises are not 'houses', so as to escape regulation. Property has been described as 'hostels' or 'hotels', and has been deconstructed and reconstructed. The judges have responded by giving an extended meaning to the word 'house'. Whether or not any given property is a 'house' is a question of mixed fact and law – 'fact' in that the first question is to determine all relevant facts about a building, and 'law' in that the application of the word 'house' is a matter for judicial interpretation of relevant statutory provisions. Essentially a house is a building used for ordinary dwelling purposes, see *Reed v Hastings Corpn* (1964) 62 LGR 588, or one constructed or adapted for use as a dwelling. A shop with living accommodation attached may be a house, as may premises consisting of a workshop with dwelling rooms over it. A building used partly for residential and non-residential purposes may be a house, even an unfinished house may be a house. Hostels and lodging houses may be houses, and properties subdivided into flats may remain houses – indeed a good 'rule of thumb' which has a degree of judicial approbation is 'once built as a house, always a house', see *Pollway Nominees v Croydon London Borough Council* [1987] AC 79, [1986] 2 All ER 849 at 852. A large holiday home may be a house, and only a totally drastic process of rebuilding would take a property built as a house outside that classification, see *R v Kerrier District Council, ex p Guppys (Bridport) Ltd* (1985) 17 HLR 426. The basic principle is that 'house' covers any place fitted and used and adapted for human habitation, see also *R v Southwark London Borough, ex p Lewis Levy Ltd* (1983) 8 HLR 1, and *R v Hackney London Borough, ex p Evenbray Ltd* (1987) 19 HLR 557. On the question of whether premises are a HMO or a house in which individuals merely board (in which case they will fall within *fire* controls under the Fire Precautions Act 1971 and SI 1972/238), see *R v Mabbott* [1988] RVR 131. There the Court of Appeal held the distinction is a matter of fact and degree; where persons are transient occupiers that is a factor to take into account. However, the court also considered it would be wrong to conclude that in *all* cases premises that are boarding houses cannot be HMOs. Premises can be both, and satisfying the requirements of the 1971 Act will not necessarily absolve those responsible for a property from compliance with the 1985 Act and vice versa. The important point is that the 'label' placed on a property by its owner is not conclusive of its status, see also *Thrasyvoulou v Hackney London Borough* (1986) 18 HLR 370.

'Household' is also undefined. In *Wolkind v Ali* [1975] 1 All ER 193, [1975] 1 WLR 170 Mr Ali occupied certain premises which he used as a lodging house. The local authority served on him notice prescribing the number of persons who could lawfully sleep in certain rooms. These restrictions were observed by Mr Ali until he was joined by his large family from abroad. Thereafter the premises were occupied solely by the family. The Divisional Court held multi-occupancy powers did not apply to this house as it was being used only by a single household.

In *Okereke v Brent London Borough Council* [1967] 1 QB 42, [1966] 1 All ER 150 it was held that once a property is divided between separate households it makes no difference whether multiple occupation arises from physical division of the building or not. Here a house built originally for occupation by one family had been converted into separate self-contained dwellings. The basement and ground floor were each occupied by one family and the first floor by two or more families, who shared a bathroom, water closet and kitchen. The second floor was unoccupied and unfit for occupation. It was held the house as a whole was multi-occupied.

Where there is a clear division of control over a house between two or more households the multi-occupancy powers apply. Likewise where a person lives in or occupies a house, and shares control with others living there, as a commercial enterprise, a multiple occupation arises.

But what about the situation where persons live together freely and communally in a house? In *Simmons v Pizzey* [1979] AC 37, [1977] 2 All ER 432 Mrs Pizzey occupied a property in a London suburb as a refuge for 'battered women'. The local authority fixed a maximum number of persons who might lawfully occupy the house. Mrs Pizzey was subsequently charged with a failure to comply with this. Her defence was that the house was not multi-occupied as all residents lived there communally as one household. The House of Lords rejected this and laid down tests to be applied in deciding whether a group of persons do/do not form a single household.

1) The number of persons occupying the property, and the place of its location must be considered. 30 or more persons occupying a suburban house can hardly be regarded as forming a single household.

2) The length of time for which each person occupies the property must be considered. A fluctuating and constantly altering population is a clear indication that the property is multi-occupied.

3) The intention of the owner of the property has to be taken into account.

This approach was applied in *Silbers v Southwark London Borough Council* (1977) 122 Sol Jo 128. Here a common lodging house was used for accommodating some 70 women; some were alcoholics, others were mentally disturbed. They stayed for varying periods or indefinitely. It was held such a fluctuating group could not be regarded as forming a single household. It is not necessary for persons to have exclusive possession of different parts of the property for them to form individual households. Indeed it seems from dicta in *Milford Properties v London Borough of Hammersmith* [1978] JPL 766 that a multi-occupancy can arise even where some occupiers are in the premises unlawfully, for example as unlawful sub-tenants. In *Hackney London Borough v Ezedinma* [1981] 3 All ER 438 the court stressed what constitutes a household is a question of fact and degree. Students each of whom has a separate tenancy of a room in a house may nevertheless group together to form a 'household'. On the other hand, homeless families may be so accommodated in a house as to occupy it not as a single household, see *Thrasyvoulou v Hackney London Borough* (1986) 18 HLR 370. Many so called 'hotels' are occupied on this basis. Circular 12/93 also counsels authorities to consider the way in which cooking and washing facilities are used, whether occupants eat and clean communally, whether each has a separate contract, and whether the landlord or the occupants fill any vacancy casually arising.

Local authority housing and fire precaution powers

Registration

Section 346 of the 1985 Act empowers authorities to make various registration schemes for HMOs for the whole or part of their area, subject to approval by the Secretary of State. Authorities are required to publicise the making of a scheme and its submission for approval, see section 349. Schemes may contain specified details of HMOs and may impose duties (enforceable by prosecution) to notify the authority of registrable properties and subsequent changes relevant to registration. Schemes are designed to provide authorities with information the better to discharge HMO functions. Model schemes are available from the DoE. Charges may be made in connection with registration, see further SI 1991/982 and DoE Circular 6/91.

A scheme – known as a *Notification Scheme* – empowers an authority to seek particulars for registration from any person with an estate or interest in a HMO or living in it. Section 350(2) of the Housing Act 1985, makes it an offence to fail to provide an authority with information in connection with registration enquiries. The 1985 Act allows the application of *regulatory* or control provisions in a *regulatory* scheme under section 347 where a house is occupied by *more* than two households, or, apart from one household (if any), by *more* than four individuals. Thus an authority may under section 348 refuse to register a house: (a) on grounds that it is unsuitable and incapable of being made suitable for such occupation as would be permitted by registration; (b) because the person having control, or intended as the manager is not 'fit and proper'. They may also require, inter alia, execution of works as a condition of registration. Written statements of reasons for refusing to register a house must be given, and there is a period of 21 days thereafter in which appeal can be made to the county court, which may confirm, reverse or vary the authority's decision. Under section 347(1) registration schemes may contain control provisions for *preventing* a house from being multi-occupied, *unless* the house is registered, *and* the number of households or persons occupying it does not exceed its registered number. Thus a desire to increase the number of registered persons/households has to be the subject of an application to the authority. Control provisions may also, under section 347(2), prohibit persons from *permitting* others to take up residence in a house, but may not prohibit a person from taking up or remaining in residence in the house. It is an offence not to comply with requirements imposed under a registration scheme, see sections 346(6) and 347(4). A *Notification and Regulatory Scheme* is similar to the foregoing but enables a more detailed register to be kept, see DoE Circular 12/93, paras 4.12.5-4.12.9 on this and other forms of register.

Management regulations

By virtue of section 369 of the Housing Act 1985 (as amended) the Secretary of State has power to make a code to ensure proper standards of management in HMOs, see the Housing (Management of Houses in Multiple Occupation) Regulations 1990 SI 1990/830. By virtue of Schedule 9 of the Local Government and Housing Act 1989 the code automatically applies to HMOs, and its breach may lead to immediate prosecution under section 369(5), and service of a notice under section 372 of the principal Act requiring rectification of specified relevant defects of management. Under section 369(5) it is an offence *knowingly* to contravene management regulations, and an offence of *strict* liability where there are relevant defects in premises to fail without reasonable excuse to comply with the regulations, see *City of Westminster v Mavroghenis* (1983) 11 HLR 56. Central guidance, however, counsels authorities to publicise their powers well before resorting to prosecution and always to ask how far any given landlord could have been reasonably expected to comply with the code.

The regulations generally require managers of HMOs to ensure that:

1) all means of water supply and drainage are maintained in repair, clean condition, good and proper working order, with water fittings (which includes baths and WCs) being protected against frost damage;

2) supplies of water, gas and electricity to any resident are not unreasonably interrupted;

3) common parts are maintained in repair, clean condition and good order, reasonably free from obstruction, with handrails and bannisters replaced, maintained and provided where necessary on grounds of safety;

4) specified installations in common use, or serving parts of premises in common use, are maintained in repair, clean condition and good working order, including installations for supplying gas and electricity for lighting and heat, sanitary provision, sinks, installations for cooking/ storing food;

5) internal structures of any part of a house occupied as living accommodation are in clean condition at the start of a period of residence, and are maintained in repair, with mains installations being kept in repair and working order, though managers are absolved from carrying out repairs needed in consequence of failures by residents to use accommodation in a tenant-like manner;

6) windows and means of ventilation are to be maintained in repair and proper working order;

7) means of escape from fire and associated fire precautions and apparatus are in good order and repair and are unobstructed, with suitably displayed signs indicating all means of escape from fire;

8) outbuildings, yards, areas, forecourts, gardens in common use are to be kept in repair, clean condition and good order, with boundary walls, fences and railings so maintained as not to be dangers to residents;

9) refuse and litter are not to accumulate;

10) reasonably requisite precautions are taken to ensure residents are protected against injury having regard to the design and structural conditions of any given HMO, including where needed, preventing access to any unsafe roof/balcony;

11) the name, address and telephone number of the manager is to be visibly and suitably displayed;

12)   information is given to the authority as to numbers of individuals and households accommodated in response to specific written requests by that authority.

Residents are required to assist managers in the effective discharge of the above duties. A 'manager' in the present context is (a) that person who as owner or lessee of premises receives directly, or via an agent or trustee, rent or other payments from residents, (b) an agent or trustee who receives rent etc on behalf of the owner/lessee, see section 398(6).

Powers to require the doing of further works

If in the opinion of a local authority a HMO is defective because of neglect in complying with the management regulations they may serve notice under section 372 of the 1985 Act on the manager specifying and requiring execution of works necessary to make good the defects. The notice must allow at least 21 days for doing the works, though this may be extended from time to time with the written permission of the authority. Information of service of the notice must also be served on all other persons known to the authority to be owners, lessees or mortgagees of the house. Following service the person served has, under section 373, a period of 21 days (or such longer period as the authority may allow) to appeal to the magistrates' courts. The grounds on which an appeal may be made are that:

1)   the condition of the house did not justify the authority in requiring execution of the specified works;
2)   there has been some material error, defect or informality in, or in connection with, the notice;
3)   the authority have refused unreasonably to approve execution of alternative works, or that works required are otherwise unreasonable in character or extent, or are unnecessary;
4)   the time allowed for doing the works is not reasonably sufficient, or the date specified for doing the works is unreasonable, or
5)   some person other than the appellant is wholly or partly responsible for the state of affairs, or will benefit from the doing of the works, and therefore ought to bear the whole or part of their costs.

The appeal powers can be productive of delay in implementing remedial action; delays of between 15 and 18 months have not been unknown.

Power to require execution of works to render premises fit for number of occupants

Section 352 of the 1985 Act, as amended in 1989, empowers authorities to require execution of works to render premises fit for the number of their inhabitants. An authority may, subject to section 365 which relates to means of escape from fire, serve a notice, on the person 'having control' ie the person receiving the rent, or on the person managing the house, where (a) it considers a HMO fails to meet one or more of a number of stated criteria, and (b), having regard to the number of persons accommodated in the premises, by reason of that failure the premises are not reasonably suitable for occupation by the individuals or households in question. The listed criteria are, under section 352(1A):

1)   are there satisfactory facilities for storage, preparation and cooking of food including adequate numbers of sinks with hot and cold water;
2)   is there an adequate number of suitably located WCs for exclusive use by occupants;
3)   similarly are there fixed baths/showers and wash hand basins with hot and cold water for occupants;
4)   subject to section 365 are there adequate means of escape from fire, and
5)   are there other adequate fire precautions.

This special standard of fitness for HMOs is in *addition* to the general fitness standard for houses existing under section 604 of the 1985 Act. Under section 189 notice may thus be served to ensure a HMO is provided with adequate lighting, ventilation and heating, while action may be taken under section 190 to deal with disrepair, see further Chapter Seven.

W   thy of special note are the provisions relating to means of escape from fire and other fire precautions. It is argued by DoE Circular 5/90 that the power relating to 'other adequate fire precautions' enables authorities to take steps to require fire detection and warning systems along with fire fighting equipment in addition to 'means of escape from fire' an expression in the past regarded by fire law experts as not extending to matters such as smoke detection systems – a distinction being made between a means of escape from fire and a means of warning people to make use of that means of escape.

Authorities have a general discretion under section 352(2) to serve notice requiring works to be done to make a property fit for the number of occupants, while subsection (2A) provides that where an authority have exercised or propose to exercise powers under section 368 to secure closure of part of a house, they may in their section 352 notice specify such work as is necessary to make the house fit bearing in mind that a part has been closed. Where a section 352 notice is served the authority is under a duty, under subsection (3), as amended, to inform the occupiers of the property, as well as the person having control and the house's manager, while notices once served become local land charges, thus warning future potential purchasers of the property, see section 352(5A). Notices served must be noted in a public register open to public inspection, free of charge at reasonable hours.

Where notice is served section 352(4) provides that the person served must begin required works not later than a specified reasonable date – which must not be earlier than 21 days after the date of service of the notice, and must further complete them within a specified reasonable period. This enables authorities to think about and fix a definite period within which work must be done.

Further guidance on implementing the fitness standard required under section 352 is contained in DoE Circular 12/92. This continues the recent trend of DoE housing standards guidance in being extremely detailed, thus tending to restrict local discretion, despite encouragement to use discretion in Circular 12/93 para 4.2.1. The more detailed the guidance the harder it is to depart from it, despite the somewhat platitudinous statement in Annex A para 1.3 'The Guidance is advisory. Authorities are reminded they must be flexible in forming their own opinions.' More restrictive is the warning against adoption of over strict standards a little later where: 'Authorities are reminded that excessively high standards of accommodation may deter landlords from making accommodation available at all'. Authorities are also effectively barred by Annex A para 1.5 from applying fitness requirements higher than those generally applying to new buildings 'and buildings may be expected to fall considerably short of current regulation standards and codes before they fail to meet the requirements of section 352'. General guidance touches upon matters such as the nature of premises, arguing, for example, it would be inappropriate to insist on provision of separate catering facilities for all residents in a HMO where the property is a hotel or hostel where meals are centrally provided. Similarly the nature of occupancy is always to be considered. The Circular argues it may be appropriate to set different standards for HMOs let for only a few days at a time or on an unfurnished basis as opposed to those occupied furnished and long term. General consideration should also be given to the Institution of Environmental Health Officers' guidance setting differing standards for different size categories of HMOs, though these, legally, may not be applied as rigid rules.

Turning to specific requirements under section 352 what does the 1992 Circular recommend? So far as satisfactory food preparation facilities are concerned it points to avoiding food having to be carried between floors, and the desirability of providing sufficient cooking facilities, which should be well laid out, and adequately screened. Reference is made to other standards which may be used as guidance, eg BS 5482 on domestic butane and propane gas burners. To come to a decision under this part of section 352 authorities are recommended to have regard to the type of provision and location of facilities, the scale of provision, the suitability of sinks, H & C supplies, cookers, work surfaces, food storage facilities, layout and lighting and ventilation issues. The aim is to provide *generally* adequate kitchen facilities in each unit of accommodation, or access for each unit to shared facilities on the same floor.

So far as WCs are concerned the Circular makes specific reference to using the Building Regulations BS 6465 and DoE Design Bulletin 24 as yardsticks for assessing the fitness of a HMO, though once again it adds:

'failure to meet these would not in itself, necessarily constitute grounds for unfitness'. The basic factors to consider are type, provision, scale, location, suitability, and layout of WCs and like facilities, their compartmentation, lighting and ventilation; the *ideal* is separate facilities for each unit of accommodation.

With regard to fire safety the Circular draws upon, and replaces, the earlier 'blue' guide on means of escape from fire and related issues jointly published by the Home and Welsh Offices with the DoE.

Only a brief overview can be given of the guidance which relates to hostels and houses divided into two or more units of accommodation, including 'bedsitters' and properties divided into flats. Authorities should seek *adequate* means of escape from fire and other fire precautions, with *basic provision* of means of escape always being necessary, the principal aim being to ensure all occupants of a HMO should be able to leave safely in the event of fire. This is to be achieved by combining measures to *prevent* the spread of fire with those to provide escape routes and means of warning of fire, bearing in mind: protection and fire resistance of escape routes against products of combustion; distances to be travelled to make a final exit from premises; nature of means of escape and their suitability to occupants, eg width of corridors, steepness of stairs; need for precautionary and warning systems. The Circular reminds authorities that HMO management must be conducive to maintenance of fire safety standards, with regular maintenance of alarms and extinguishers, etc. The adequacy of management to meet such standards must be considered: inadequacy could lead to service of closing orders, see further below. Authorities are urged to counsel managers to hold fire drills and advise residents of good fire safety practice, and are also recommended to distribute checklists of fire safety reminders to residents of non-hostel HMOs. With regard to hostels it is recommended that staff should be instructed in fire safety and drills.

Appeals against section 352 notices are available under section 353. It is a ground of appeal that, inter alia, the condition of the premises in respect of means of escape from fire and fire precautions did not justify requiring the specified works, and further that the date specified for beginning these works, is not reasonable. It may alternatively be argued that an authority has no power to serve the notice because the property is not an HMO. This may be done by way of appeal to the County Court rather than by judicial review, see *Nolan v Leeds City Council* (1990) 23 HLR 135.

Provisions supplemental to section 352

The power of authorities under section 354 to limit the number of occupants of a house so as to prevent the occurrence of, or to remedy, a state of affairs otherwise calling for service of notice under section 352 was modified in

1989. They may limit the number of occupants allowed for a HMO based on consideration, inter alia, of whether the property has adequate means of escape from fire and other adequate fire precautions in addition to consideration of whether it has adequate cooking and sanitary facilities. At least seven days before making a direction the authority must serve on the owner and every known lessee, notice of their intention, and also post a copy of this notice in the house in some place accessible to the occupants. A right to make representations is given to those on whom notice is served. The direction once given makes it the duty under section 355, of 'the occupier', which includes any person entitled or authorised to permit individuals to take up residence in the house, to keep the number of persons within the permitted number. In *Hackney London Borough v Ezedinma* [1981] 3 All ER 438 a managing estate agent was held to fall within this definition: he had been authorised to let out rooms. Copies of the direction must be served, within seven days of its making, on the owner and known lessees of the house, and also posted within the house in some place where the occupants can have access to it. It is an offence under section 355(2) knowingly to fail to comply with a direction.

A section 354 direction can only be issued when the house to which it applies is multi-occupied, and further multiple occupation of the premises at the time of an alleged offence is an essential requirement for liability. However, it seems from *Simmons v Pizzey* [1979] AC 37, [1977] 2 All ER 432 that once a direction is validly given temporary cessation of multiple occupation does not end the direction but merely suspends its operation; it will revive and be applicable as soon as the house is again multi-occupied. There is no right to appeal against a section 354 direction as such. However, authorities have power under section 357 to revoke or vary directions, following changes of circumstances affecting the house, or the execution of works there, on the application of anyone having an estate or interest in the house. An unreasonable refusal to exercise this power can form the subject of an appeal to the county court. A section 354 notice may be served in addition to, or instead of, one under section 352. The latter is designed to ensure that facilities in a HMO are adequate for the number of occupants, while the former is used to specify a maximum number who may occupy the house with existing facilities. If served together they may specify the maximum number of occupants for a HMO after works have been carried out.

Section 365 of the 1985 Act (as amended in 1989) gives authorities wide power of choice in cases where a HMO presents fire risks. Where an authority considers a HMO fails to meet the requirements of section 352, and one reason, or the reason, why they are of this opinion is because there are *no* adequate means of escape from fire, they may, as an alternative to requiring works, accept an undertaking *or* make a closing order under section 368. But this choice is only available where the HMO does not have adequate means of escape from fire; *not* where, for example, it lacks other adequate fire precautions. Where that is so the authority must rely on section 352 powers to require execution of works.

Section 365(2) (as amended) provides that where the foregoing powers are available, the authority's discretion is total; it is up to them to make whichever order seems appropriate. However, they are under a duty to make some appropriate order where the house is of such a description, or is occupied in such a way, as may be specified by the Secretary of State in an order, though the Secretary of State is also given power by section 365(2A) to specify houses of a particular description or occupied in a particular way in respect of which the range of powers is not to be exercised. Properties subject to the *duty* to take action remain those specified in SI 1981/1576, ie those at least three storeys high with floor space of 500m². According to Circular 5/90 there are no proposals to extend these categories. Apart from those cases specified by the Secretary of State, the 'fire powers' are discretionary: there is no general duty to take action in respect of HMOs save that under section 605 of the 1985 Act (as amended) whereunder authorities must at least once every year, consider housing conditions of their district to decide what action to take in pursuance of, inter alia, their HMO powers, though they are subject to direction by the Secretary of State in relation to this. Furthermore the fitness provision, the substituted section 604, though specifically declared in section 604(3) to apply to HMOs, contains no specific reference to means of escape from fire or adequate fire precautions as criteria for determining whether a house is fit.

It is accepted that there is an overlap between sections 352 and 604. Circular 12/93 counsels authorities to pursue the most satisfactory course of action on a house by house basis, bearing in mind the need to minimise risks on an interim basis.

However, before action can be taken under section 352 in respect of remedying want of adequate means of escape from fire, the housing authority must under section 365(3) consult the relevant fire authority. Circular 12/92 indicates HMOs constitute a significant fire hazard. Between 1978 and 1981 550 people died in HMO fires, while in 1986 alone in Bayswater there were 50 HMO fires. The risk of death or injury from fire in a HMO is ten times that in other houses. There is a need for consultation, not just to determine which legislative codes are applicable, but also to ensure which authority is to take the 'lead' concerning a property. It is desirable that housing authorities should normally heed fire safety recommendations from fire authorities, and joint inspection of relevant properties should occur.

Where it appears that means of escape from fire would be adequate if part of a house ceased to be used for human habitation, the authority may under section 368 secure that. They may also secure closure of part of a house while serving notice under section 365 specifying works necessary to supply the rest with adequate fire escapes. In the execution of these powers they may accept undertakings from owners or mortgagees that part or parts of houses will not be used for human habitation without the consent of the authority. It is an offence to use, or to permit use of, any part of a house subject to a closing undertaking. Where such an undertaking is not accepted, or if one accepted is found to be broken, the authority may make a closing order on the relevant part of the house. The provisions of Part IX of the 1985 Act apply to closing orders made under section 368, see Chapter Seven. Use of section 368, is, however, subject to section 365, and it appears authorities should use this in preference to more drastic closure powers.

The term 'means of escape from fire' was given a wide meaning in *Horgan v Birmingham Corpn* (1964) 108 Sol Jo 991 to include not just fire escapes as such but also ancillary matters such as screens operating to keep escape routes clear of smoke. In deciding what 'means' to require authorities should consider the personal circumstances of the occupants of any given HMO, eg their ages and whether they are supervised, see *Kingston-upon-Hull District Council v University of Hull* [1979] LAG Bulletin 191.

If a notice under section 352 or 372 is not complied with, or if persons on whom they are served inform the authority in writing that they are unable to do the works, section 375 of the 1985 Act allows the authority to do the work. They may recover reasonable expenses under Schedule 10 of the Act from the person on whom notice was served, or where an agent or trustee was served, in whole or part from the person on whose behalf the agent or trustee was acting. Recovery may be by action in the county court or the authority may sequestrate rents from the property. Authorities may even recover costs where the works have been belatedly done after they have started the work in default.

A *wilful failure* to comply with notices issued under sections 352 or 372 of the 1985 Act is, by virtue of section 376(1), an offence punishable by a fine. Under section 376(2), where a person initially convicted of the offence created by section 376(1) commits a further new offence if he/she then wilfully leaves the work undone. This meaning of 'wilful failure' to do works was stated in *Honig v Islington London Borough* [1972] Crim LR 126 to include voluntary omissions to act, irrespective of motive. It appears the only allowable reasons for not acting are force majeure, accident or impossibility.

Section 377 of the 1985 Act applies where any person, being an occupier, or owner of premises, and having received notice of intended action under sections 352 or 372 of the Act prevents the carrying into effect of proposals. A magistrates' court may order that person to allow doing what is necessary. Failure to comply with a court order is an offence.

Further powers to prevent overcrowding in multi-occupied houses

Section 358 of the Housing Act 1985 applies where it appears to an authority that an excessive number of persons, having regard to the number of rooms available, is being, or is likely to be, accommodated in a HMO. They may serve on the occupier, or on the person exercising management of the house, or on both, an 'overcrowding notice'. This must state, under section 359, in relation to every room what the authority consider to be the maximum number of persons who can suitably sleep therein, if any. Special maxima may be included where some or all of the persons occupying the room are below a specified age. An authority may require a number of courses of action from persons on whom such notice is served. The first, under section 360, is to refrain from:

1) knowingly permitting any room to be occupied as sleeping accommodation otherwise than in accordance with the notice, or

2) knowingly permitting persons to occupy the premises as sleeping accommodation in such numbers that it is not possible to avoid persons of opposite sexes, not living together as husband and wife, and over the age of 12, sleeping in the same room, it being assumed that persons who occupy the premises as sleeping accommodation sleep only in rooms for which the notice sets a maximum, and that the maximum for each room is not exceeded.

The alternative course of action, under section 361, is that the person on whom notice is served must refrain from:

1) knowingly permitting any *new* resident to occupy a room as sleeping accommodation otherwise than in accordance with the notice, or

2) knowingly permitting a new resident to occupy part of the premises for sleeping if that is not possible without persons of opposite sexes, and not living as man and wife, sleeping in the same room.

Not less than seven days before serving notice, under section 358(2), the authority must:

1) inform the occupier of the premises, and any person appearing to exercise management, in writing of their intention to serve the notice, and

2) ensure, so far as reasonably possible, that every other person living in the house is informed of their intention.

Those informed must be given an opportunity of making representations regarding this proposal. A person aggrieved by such an 'overcrowding notice' may, under section 362, appeal to the county court within 21 days of service. The court may confirm, quash or vary the order. Once an order is in force it is an offence to contravene it.

A notice may, under section 363, be revoked or varied at any time by the authority on the application of any person having an estate or interest in the house. If they refuse, or fail to notify the applicant of their decision, the applicant may appeal to the county court.

During the currency of overcrowding notices, under section 364, authorities may give notice requiring occupiers to furnish them with written particulars as to:

1) numbers of individuals on specified dates using the premises as sleeping accommodation;

2) numbers of families or households to whom the individuals belong;

3)   their names, and the names of heads of families and households;
4)   rooms used by those individuals and families or households respectively.
   It is an offence to fail to supply such particulars or to file a false return. Even so it appears hard to amass evidence to bring a successful prosecution for 'Part XI overcrowding'. Furthermore the provisions grant only powers, and there is an element of subjectivity in their application.

Supplementary powers

Authorities have a number of supplementary powers to assist in the exercise of multi-occupation functions. Under the Housing Act 1985, section 395(1) an authorised officer may enter any house, after giving 24 hours' notice in writing of his intention to both occupier and owner, if the latter is known, in order to determine whether multi-occupation powers should be exercised. By virtue of section 356 at any time after a section 354 direction is in force an authority may serve further notice on the occupier of the house requiring a written statement of:
1)   numbers of individuals living in the house (or part of it) on a specified date;
2)   numbers of families or households to which those individuals belong;
3)   names of individuals, and of heads of families or households, and
4)   rooms used by those individuals and families or households respectively.
   Failure to reply, or making a false reply, is an offence.
   The Housing Act 1985, section 395(2) empowers authorities to enter houses to ascertain whether there has been contravention of any regulation or direction made under sections 346, 355, 358, 368, 369, 376 of the Act, and in such a case notice need not be given in advance.

Control orders

To deal with HMOs in the worst condition authorities may make 'control orders' allowing them to take over management for up to five years and act as if they were the owners. It is a proper use of this power to make an order to ensure continuance in use and operation of a house, see *R v Southwark London Borough, ex p Lewis Levy Ltd* (1983) 267 Estates Gazette 1040. An order allows an authority to take the necessary steps (other than sale) to bring a property up to a satisfactory standard.
   Under section 379 of the 1985 Act an order can be made if:
1)   a notice has been served under sections 352 or 372 (execution of works) or if a direction has been given under section 354 (limits on numbers of occupants); *or*

2) it appears to the authority that the state or condition of the house is such as to call for taking any such action, *and*

3) it also appears that the state of the house is such that it is necessary to make a control order to protect the safety, welfare or health of persons living therein.

Control orders are designed to deal with the most squalid conditions and while there is no lengthy legal procedure as to their making much staff time and effort may be consumed. An order comes into force when made (section 379(2)) and as soon as practicable thereafter the authority must enter the premises and take such immediate steps as are necessary to protect residents' health, welfare and safety. A copy of the order has to be posted in the house where it is accessible to residents. Copies must also be served on every person who, before the order, was the manager of the house, or had control of it, or was an owner, lessee or mortgagee. These copies must be accompanied by a notice setting out rights of appeal under section 384 of the 1985 Act (see below).

The effect of a control order

A control order transfers full possession and control of the house to the authority (see generally section 381) and cancels orders, notices or directions already made under the management provisions, but without prejudice to criminal liabilities incurred. It is possible to exclude from control, under section 380 of the Act, any part of the house occupied by an owner or tenant of the whole house. Such a part will be subject under section 387(3) to the authority's right of entry for purposes of survey etc. The authority may grant, under section 381(2), weekly or monthly tenancies within the property, but rights and obligations of existing residents are protected by section 382.

Section 385 then lays a double duty on the authority:

1) to maintain proper standards of management and take any action necessary under the management provision of the Act, and

2) to keep the house insured against fire.

Thereafter section 386 requires them to prepare a scheme and to serve a copy on the dispossessed proprietor and on all other owners, lessees and mortgagees, not later than eight weeks from the making of the control order. The scheme must, under Schedule 13 Part I, provide for execution of, and payment for, works involving capital expenditure needed to satisfy statutory requirements. The scheme must state what the authority consider to be the highest number of individuals who should be allowed from time to time to reside in the house, and also an estimate of the balance of the moneys that will accrue to the authority in the form of rents, etc, from residents, after they have paid the dispossessed proprietor compensation (see below), and disbursed all other payments, other than those in respect of management powers under the Act, ie capital expenditure. Throughout the life of the control order the authority must also keep half yearly accounts under Schedule 13, para 4. They must balance capital expenditure against surplus balances (revenue) arising from the rents, etc, referred to above. The cost of expenditure constitutes a charge on the premises.

During the currency of a control order section 389 of the 1985 Act requires the authority to pay the dispossessed proprietor (ie the person otherwise entitled to rents from the property) compensation at an annual rate of one half of the rental value of the house, ie the amount the house might reasonably be expected to fetch if let, see Schedule 13 of the 1985 Act as amended by SI 1990/343.

Appeals

Any person having an estate or interest in the house, or otherwise prejudiced by a control order, may appeal to the county court under section 384. A similar right exists under Schedule 13 against the authority's scheme. The period for appeal runs out six weeks after a copy of the scheme has been served.

Control orders expire after five years, unless they are revoked earlier by the authority; Housing Act 1985, section 392. A person may apply, with reasons, for early revocation. If this application is rejected, or ignored for six weeks, he/she may apply to the county court for revocation of the order. An unsuccessful appeal precludes further applications for a period of six months.

An authority has power under section 17 and Schedule 13 Part IV of the 1985 Act to make a compulsory purchase (CPO) on a property subject to a control order. Where they make the CPO within 28 days of making the control order they need not prepare or serve a management scheme until after the decision of the Secretary of State to reject or confirm the CPO. Provision is made for satisfaction of the financial obligations of both authority and owner: the latter is to receive any surplus revenue balance in the hands of the authority; they may recover their capital expenditure on necessary works from revenue balances derived from rents received from the house or from the compulsory purchase compensation. A CPO is a last resort measure, generally only authorised where an authority proposes to transfer the property on or after improvement to an acceptable manager such as an association, see also DoE Circulars 6/85, 3/89 and 12/93. A CPO may not be used merely to punish a landlord, but is to be used where it is clearly improbable a landlord will be able to do required works, see *Bell v Secretary of State for the Environment* [1989] 13 EG 70 and *Riddle v Secretary of State for the Environment* [1988] 42 EG 120. A CPO may be made even after a lapse of time from obtaining a control order provided the authority can show that despite the landlord being given repeated opportunities to do remedial works these have been ignored, see *Orakpo v Wandsworth London Borough Council* (1990) 24 HLR 370.

Further general guidance on the use of control orders is given by both DoE Circular 12/93 and the 1992 Management Guide. Where possible preliminary studies should be undertaken to assess the effects of making an order, but where action is needed in a hurry, however, streamlined procedures and detailed coordination of steps within authorities are essential. Once an order is in place there must be an appropriate management structure for the house, and a properly thought through and costed strategy for its improvement in which the authority may wish to involve a local housing association as a manager. The need for procedural correctness was stressed by the Court of Appeal in *Webb v Ipswich Borough Council* [1989] EGCS 27 where, despite shortcomings, a landlord was able to upset a control order on appeal by showing that officers had not followed their authority's procedure before serving the order.

Common lodging houses

Common lodging houses (CLH) fall within the powers of authorities under Part XII of the Housing Act 1985 which lays down certain standards to ensure a basic level of cleanliness and repair within such premises. A CLH, under section 401 of the Act, is: 'a house (other than a public assistance institution) provided for the purpose of accommodating by night poor persons, not being members of the same family, who resort there and are allowed to occupy one common room for the purpose of sleeping or eating, and includes, where part only of a house is so used, the part so used'. The definition appears to *exclude* reception facilities provided by the Social Services Secretary, and also accommodation provided under the National Assistance Act 1948, such premises surely being 'public assistance' institutions. The section covers dwelling-houses, and purpose-built common lodging houses, *but not premises not built as houses* eg a purpose-built hotel. Once a house is found to be within the definition it is immaterial that it is called a 'hostel' or 'guest house', nor does it matter whether the accommodation is let for a week, for a night or some other period of less than a week, see *People's Hostels Ltd v Turley* [1939] 1 KB 149, [1938] 4 All ER 72. However, in order to constitute a CLH there must be common sleeping or eating accommodation – see *LCC v Hankins* [1914] 1 KB 490 – though the division of a large room into smaller cubicles by screens will not prevent it being common sleeping accommodation – see *Logsdon v Trotter* [1900] 1 QB 617. A CLH can be a charitable institution, *Logsdon v Booth* [1900] 1 QB 401. A CLH can also be a house in multiple occupation, and fall within statutory nuisance and fitness powers of authorities, see *R v Southwark London Borough, ex p Lewis Levy Ltd* (1983) 267 Estates Gazette 1040, and *R v Camden London Borough Council, ex p Rowton (Camden Town) Ltd* (1983) 10 HLR 28.

Under sections 402 and 408 of the 1985 Act it is an offence for a person to keep a CLH unless registered with the local authority. Authorities must, under section 404, register keepers unless satisfied that:

1) an applicant for registration is unfit; or
2) the premises are unsuitable for use as a CLH having regard to sanitation, water supply, means of escape from fire, etc; or
3) use of the premises as a CLH would cause inconvenience or annoyance to persons in the neighbourhood.

Refusal to register must be in writing, supported by reasons. A person aggrieved by a refusal may appeal to the justices, see section 405 of the 1985 Act. The period of registration may be for up to 13 months. Many common lodging houses are unregistered, however, because 'keepers' do not realise they should apply for registration.

The keeper's duties

By section 407 of the 1985 Act the keeper, or duly registered deputy, must be on duty between 9.00 pm and 6.00 am as well as maintaining general management over the house and its inmates. The keeper must supply to the authority, on their request, a list of persons who occupied the house during the day or night preceding the request. Keepers must also allow the authority's duly authorised officers free access to all parts of their houses.

Supervisory powers of local authorities

Under section 39 of the Public Health (Control of Disease) Act 1984 common lodging house keepers must notify the local authority of persons in their houses suffering from 'infectious diseases'. Where authority officers have reasonable grounds to believe a person in a common lodging house is suffering from a 'notifiable' disease they may be authorised by justices to enter and ascertain the facts, see section 40 of the 1984 Act. Under section 42 premises affected by 'notifiable' diseases may be closed.

Authorities have powers under Section 406 of the Act to make byelaws:

1) for fixing the maximum number of persons allowed to use a CLH and to provide for separation of the sexes;
2) for promoting cleanliness and ventilation;
3) to provide for precautions against the spread of infection in a CLH, and
4) generally to secure the well ordering of such premises

Model byelaws have been centrally issued.

Authorities do not always enforce statutory standards because some keepers, if proceeded against, would close down their houses, leading to increased numbers of homeless persons. Nevertheless by section 408 of the Act any person who:

1)   contravenes or fails to comply with any provision of Part XII, or
2)   fails to maintain premises in a fit state to be used as a CLH, or
3)   deliberately misleads the authority in relation to an application for registration,

commits an offence. Where a keeper is convicted the court may cancel registration and disqualify him/her from registration for such period as it thinks fit, see section 409.

Multi-occupation and the powers of fire authorities

Section 10(1) of the Fire Precautions Act 1971 (as substituted) applies, inter alia, to any premises which are being, or are proposed to be, put to use to provide sleeping accommodation other than single private dwellings. With regard to such premises where the fire authority consider use of the premises involves, or will involve, a risk to persons so serious that their use ought to be restricted or prohibited, they may serve on the occupier a prohibition notice stating and specifying the issues, and giving directions as to the use of the premises until remedial measures are taken. In the case of imminent risk of serious personal injury a prohibition may take immediate effect. It is an offence under section 10B of the 1971 Act to contravene a prohibition notice, though section 10A allows an appeal to the magistrates' court within 21 days of service of the notice. The court may cancel, affirm or modify the notice. This statutory mode of appeal, it appears, is a preclusive mode of challenge, even where it is alleged the premises do not fall within the fire authority's jurisdiction, see *R v Chesterfield Justices, ex p Kovacs* [1992] 2 All ER 325.

The powers of fire authorities with regard to multi-occupied premises are extensive. It should be a matter of good practice for housing and fire authorities to work together in an integrated and coordinated way to ensure premises are not made subject to conflicting sets of requirements. Over zealous use of fire control powers may result in premises being closed with their occupants, only some of whom may qualify as 'homeless', displaced to the streets. On the other hand protection of human life demands vigilance from fire authorities for it appears it is not negligent for a housing authority not to have a system of pre-inspection of multi-occupied properties to which *non-priority* homeless persons may be referred, see *Ephraim v London Borough of Newham* (1992) 136 Sol Jo LB 13. Much depends upon the attitude of individual fire prevention officers and the nature and quality of relationships between authorities and their officers. (Cross reference should also be made to the grant aiding powers of authorities concerning HMOs in Chapter Seven. Concern has been expressed that reductions in grant aid may especially prejudice implementation of fire precautions measures in HMOs.) For landlords' duties in respect of gas appliances see the Gas Safety (Installation and Use) Regulations 1994, SI 1994/1886.

Overcrowding

Local authority powers with regard to overcrowding are found in Part X of the 1985 Act. This is derived from older legislation, and standards are open to criticism as out of date. Under sections 324 and 343 of the Act overcrowding powers apply in relation to 'dwellings' ie premises used or suitable for use as a separate dwelling. This would seem apt to include caravans, see *DPP v Carrick District Council* (January 1985, unreported, Truro Magistrates Court, 'Housing Aid').

The definition of overcrowding

A dwelling is overcrowded when the number of persons sleeping in it contravenes *either* section 325 (room standard) or section 326 (space standard). Under the former, contravention occurs when the number of persons sleeping in a dwelling and the number of rooms available for sleeping is such that two persons of opposite sexes, not living together as man and wife, must sleep in the same room. Children under ten are left out of account in the calculation, and rooms are available for sleeping if they are locally used *either* as bedrooms or living rooms, see section 326(2)(b). Under the latter standard contravention occurs when numbers sleeping in a dwelling exceed the permitted number having regard to numbers and floor areas of rooms in the dwelling available for sleeping. The permitted number for a dwelling is whichever is the *lesser* of *either* the number specified in Table I below, or the aggregate for all rooms available for sleeping in the dwelling of numbers of persons specified in Table II in relation to each room of the floor area specified in that table.

Table I

Number of rooms	Number of persons
1	2.0
2	3.0
3	5.0
4	7.5
5 or more	2 for each room

Table II

Floor area of room	Number of persons
110 square feet or more	2.0
90 – 100 square feet	1.5
79 – 90 square feet	1.0
50 – 70 square feet	0.5
Under 50 square feet	NIL

A child under one and a half years is not reckoned in these calculations, and a child between one and a half and ten counts as half a unit.

All persons who use the house as their home should be counted when deciding whether there is overcrowding, not just those sleeping there at any given time, otherwise the law could be ignored by persons sleeping on a shift basis. In *Zaitzeff v Olmi* (1952) 102 L Jo 416 (county court) a daughter at a boarding school was held to be living at home for the purposes of the permitted number standard.

Section 330 of the Act permits authorities to license occupiers to exceed the permitted number standard, but only up to numbers specified and only for periods of up to 12 months. Within that period the licence may be revoked by the authority giving the occupier one month's notice. Licences may be granted to take account of seasonal increases of population in a district, for example to allow for the accommodation of migratory agricultural workers, or in other 'exceptional circumstances' – an otherwise undefined phrase.

Offences

These are principally defined by sections 327 and 331 of the 1985 Act and can be committed by the occupier of a dwelling-house and by the landlord where the property is let. The occupier who causes or permits overcrowding commits a summary offence save where acting under licence granted under section 330 (see above), or where the case falls within either section 328 or 329. Under the former where a dwelling becomes overcrowded solely by virtue of a child attaining the age of ten, then the occupier commits no offence *provided* he/she applies, or has so applied before the relevant birthday, to the housing authority for suitable alternative accommodation, *and provided that all persons* sleeping in the dwelling are those who were living there when the child reached the relevant age and who live there continuously afterwards, or are children of those persons. The exemption ceases to apply if either suitable alternative accommodation is offered to the occupier and he/she fails to accept it or otherwise fails to take reasonable steps to secure the removal of persons not members of the family from the house. A mere visit by a member of the occupier's family who normally lives elsewhere which causes temporary overcrowding is not an offence, see section 329.

Section 342 of the Act defines 'suitable alternative accommodation' as a dwelling-house where the following conditions are satisfied:

1) the house must be one where the occupier (and family) can live without causing it to be overcrowded;
2) the authority must certify the house to be suitable to the needs of the occupier (and family) as respects security of tenure, proximity to place of work and otherwise, and in relation to the occupier's means; and
3) where the dwelling is a local authority house, it is certified as suitable to the needs of the occupier and his family, with a two bedroom dwelling providing accommodation for four people, three bedrooms accommodating five people and four bedrooms seven people.

Landlords commit offences under section 331 and are deemed to have caused or permitted overcrowding if:

1) after receiving notice from the local authority that a house is overcrowded they fail to take reasonable steps to abate the overcrowding, or
2) the house was let with the landlord having reasonable cause to believe that it would become overcrowded.

To aid landlords section 101 of the Rent Act 1977 takes away security of tenure in a house which is so overcrowded that the occupier is guilty of an offence, while authorities themselves may take possession proceedings under section 338 of the 1985 Act. Note there is no equivalent provision to section 101 in respect of assured tenancies under the Housing Act 1988.

Landlords are under a duty, see section 333 of the Housing Act 1985, to inform authorities within seven days of overcrowding within any of their houses that has come to their knowledge.

In order to inform occupiers of their rights, section 332 of the 1985 Act requires that a summary of Part X of the Act shall be contained in any rent book or similar document given to the tenant, together with a statement of the permitted number of persons in relation to the house. Authorities are under an obligation to inform either occupiers or landlords if any apply, of permitted numbers of persons in relation to relevant houses.

Enforcement and remedial powers and duties of local authorities

The Housing Act 1985, section 339 makes it the duty of authorities to enforce the overcrowding provisions, and only they may prosecute. Where an authority is responsible for overcrowding they can be prosecuted only with the consent of the Attorney-General. An authority may serve notice on an occupier requiring, within 14 days, a written statement of the number, ages and sexes of the persons sleeping in the house. Failing to comply with this request or deliberately making a false return is an offence, see section 335 of the 1985 Act.

Authorities are also under a general duty under section 334 of the 1985 Act to investigate overcrowding of which they become aware, to make a report to the Secretary of State of findings, and the number of new houses needed to relieve overcrowding. The Secretary of State may direct an authority to make such an investigation and report.

Further reading

Blake, J 'Safe as Houses?' *Roof* Jaunary/February 1995, pp 34-35

Campbell, R 'Houses in multiple occupation – the new regulations' *Housing* December 1991/January 1992, pp 24-25

Department of the Environment *The HMO Management Guide* DoE (1992)

Grosskurth, A 'Lives on the line' *Roof* November/December 1984, pp 11-14

Kirby, K, and Sopp, L *Houses in Multiple Occupation in England and Wales* HMSO (1986)

National Consumer Council *Deathtrap Housing* NCC (1991)

Randall, G, Brown, S and Piper, J *Houses in Multiple Occupation, Policy and Practice in the 1990s* The Campaign for Bed Sit Rights, 1993

Summers, D 'Overcrowding: The Human Cost' *Roof* May/June 1981, pp 16-17/23

Thomas, A D and Hedges, A *The 1985 Physical and Social Survey of Houses in Multiple Occupation in England and Wales* HMSO (1986)

Wolmar, C 'Overcrowding in Southall', *Roof* July/August 1980, pp 117-118

Index